Harvard Historical Studies

Published under the direction
of the Department of History
from the income of the
Henry Warren Torrey Fund

Volume XCVII

Draft article "concerning the souls of them which be departed from this life," from the "king's book" (1538), with emendations by Henry VIII (P.R.O. SP 6/8, f. 95).

English Chantries

The Road to Dissolution

Alan Kreider

Harvard University Press
Cambridge, Massachusetts
and London, England
1979

Library of Congress Cataloging in Publication Data
Kreider, Alan, 1941-
  English chantries.

  (Harvard historical studies; v. 97)
  Bibliography: p.
  Includes index.
  1. Chantries. 2. Reformation—England.
3. England—Church history—16th century.
4. Purgatory—History of doctrines. 5. Purgatorial
societies—History. I. Title. II. Series.
BR377.K73   274.2   78-12453
ISBN 0-674-25560-7

For Eleanor

Acknowledgments

At every stage in the preparation of this book I have been aided by mentors, friends, and institutions, and I would like to give thanks to them here. To Professor W. K. Jordan my debt is enormous. He not only sensed the sort of topic that would challenge me; he has also assisted me by criticizing my early efforts, by encouraging me repeatedly, and by providing a wealth of information in his own writings. To Professor A. G. Dickens I also owe much. It was his treatment of the dissolution of the chantries in *The English Reformation* that initially persuaded me of the importance of the topic; and over the years he has shared numerous insights with me and shown me many kindnesses. An early formulation of my ideas concerning purgatory in the Reformation profited from exposure to criticism in his seminar in the Institute of Historical Research, London. Professor G. R. Elton came to my aid at a somewhat later stage, assisting me with incisiveness and generosity when I was having difficulty making sense of late medieval mortmain. Several portions of the text have benefited from his detailed criticisms. Mrs. Madeleine Rowse Gleason, the editor of the Harvard Historical Studies, has subjected every line of the text to close scrutiny, and at many points has helped me to express my ideas more clearly and succinctly. Mr. Peter Clark, Dr. L. P. Fairfield, Professor I. B. Horst, Dr. E. W. Ives, and Dr. Linda L. Peck have also made useful comments. My most informed friend and critic has been Dr. Christopher Kitching of the Public Record Office. A significant thesis and several articles have demonstrated that no one knows more about the actual dissolution of the chantries than he. As I proceeded with my study of the events leading up to the dissolution, he generously shared his expertise with me. And his careful reading of the almost completed manuscript saved me from numerous lapses in judgment and flaws in fact. But as I record my gratitude to him and to my other friends and mentors, I would like to absolve them of any responsibility for the defects which still remain.

I am also beholden to several institutions, without whose financial support it would have been impossible to complete this book. To the Danforth Foundation, which munificently supported my post-graduate study; to Harvard University, which granted me a Harvard Travelling Fellowship for thesis research in England; to Goshen College, whose Faculty Research Committee supplied me with funds for microfilming, for the purchase of books and calendars, and for two research trips to London; to the American Council of Learned Societies, which honored me with a fellowship that enabled me to spend the years in England necessary to expand the scope of my dissertation; and to the Mennonite Board of Missions, which has encouraged me to complete the manuscript while serving at the London Mennonite Centre — to all of these institutions I would like to express heart-felt thanks.

Finally, I owe an incalculable amount to my family. My Mennonite family of faith has provided sustaining grace; my parents and parents-in-law have instructed me by word and example; my father, Carl Kreider, has expertly assisted with the editing and proofreading of the book; and our son, Andrew, has given real joy. But most of all I owe to my wife, Eleanor. Throughout our married life she has been living amidst chantry priests, mortmain licenses, and purgatory. She has also done a major portion of the research upon which chapter 3 is based. That she has cheerfully put up with all this — and has spurred me on when the way became wearisome — says worlds about her abilities, her resilient love, and her sense of humor. In "thanks-giving" I dedicate this book to her.

Highgate, London

Contents

Tables

Figures

English Chantries

Introduction

On Christmas Eve 1547 the House of Lords, in the presence of King Edward VI, gave a third reading to a bill "for the dissolution of chantries" and voted to pass the controversial measure.[1] That very day the bill received the royal assent. Thus, almost anticlimactically, ended one of the most tumultuous sessions of Parliament in the first half of the sixteenth century. Thus also began — only a decade after the suppression of the monasteries — the second wave of the dissolutions and confiscations which swept across England during the Reformation. In the early months of 1548, commissioners of the crown began touring the realm to survey the lands, buildings, and possessions of the doomed institutions. And, according to the provisions of the act which Parliament had just passed, on Easter Day 1548 all the surveyed institutions — chantries and colleges, stipendiary priests and guilds, free chapels, obits and lights — became the possession of the crown.* The question of ownership was thus settled with remarkable dispatch (although haggling about details would clog the courts for generations); the dismantling of the legally dissolved institutions could now begin; and the people of England and Wales, whose parliamentary representatives had passed the act, were left to adjust as best they could to major changes in the supply of clergy, the endowment of education, and the provision of poor relief.

For many years, historians of Tudor England were accustomed to give the intercessory institutions only a fraction of the scrutiny which they have lavished upon the monasteries. This was possibly because the Edwardian dissolutions were accomplished with businesslike dispatch and comparative ease. No chantry priests presented themselves, as did the Franciscan Observants and Carthusians in the 1530s, as martyrs for the old religion. Even those chantry priests who had offered opposition to the measures of the Henrician reformers went along meekly enough with the Edwardian dissolutions, accepted their pensions, and vanished quietly from the pages of history. No major uprisings ensued.[2] Hence the political impact of the Edwardian dissolutions was

---

*The term "intercessory institutions" is a convenient collective designation for these foundations.

far less potent than the symbolically portentous suppressions of Henry VIII.

The architectural loss which the destruction of the chantries entailed was also vastly less grievous than that wrought by the defacing and dismantling of the monastic houses.[3] It was difficult for anyone but a high-flying churchman or a thoroughgoing romanticist to be outraged by the sight of an isolated chapel of ease which had been converted into a pigeon-house. Yet the majestic ruins of Fountains and of Glastonbury were there for all to see, awe-inspiring witnesses to a byegone era and way of life. Furthermore, the chantry priests lacked nineteenth- and twentieth-century successors who, like the monastic historians, could recount in detail the iniquities which had been visited upon their brethren in the Reformation era.

In recent years, however, some historians have treated the Edwardian dissolutions more adequately. In part, this is because we have learned much more about the intercessory institutions of the Middle Ages; the devoted labors of Miss K. L. Wood-Legh and of Professor A. Hamilton Thompson have borne rich fruit.[4] Professor Hamilton Thompson was especially early in calling for a reassessment of the importance of the dissolution of the chantries which, he believed, "effected a change in the religious life of England, even more widely spread than that effected by the suppression of the religious houses." More recently, Professors T. M. Parker, H. J. Hanham, and A. G. Dickens have echoed this judgment. And Professor W. K. Jordan, in the most detailed survey to date of the effects of the dissolution of the chantries, has asserted that "the most shattering and irreversible action of the Reformation in England was the proscription of prayers for the repose of the souls of the dead."[5] These scholars have not followed an earlier fashion in making enthusiastic claims concerning the contribution of the chantries to the educational system of pre-Reformation England. They have concentrated rather upon the parochial impact of the dissolution. Since the intercessory institutions were scattered throughout the realm in a vast number of parishes, they inevitably "bore a far closer relation to the daily life of the people than did the majority of the monasteries."[6]

Such a reassessment is significant. It will not, however, be fully persuasive until historians have subjected to rigorous examination the complex and voluminous source materials pertaining to this second wave of dissolutions. Using the chantry certificates, state papers, par-

ish records, diocesan archives, and the extensive documents of the
Court of Augmentations, we must reconstruct the narrative of the dissolution — assessing the contributions which the intercessory institutions were making to the parochial life of England, ascertaining the
extent to which the Edwardian government allowed them to remain
effective, and measuring the pain and exhilaration of doctrinal and
institutional change.

In this volume I shall attempt only a part of this task. I have, in the
first place, limited my scope geographically. Although I have drawn
examples from all parts of the realm, I have systematically studied only
four sample counties — in part because of their geographical distribution: Essex, a Home County; Warwickshire, a county in the Midlands;
Wiltshire, a southwestern county; and Yorkshire, a vast northern
county.[7] Of equal importance to their selection is the excellent quality
of their surviving records: not only several sets of chantry certificates,
but also pensions certificates and continuance warrants. The inherent
interest of the institutions in each of these counties was also a major
consideration in their selection. Essex was notable for the large number of schools which the commissioners claimed were being taught by
the intercessory priests. Few counties could have had a more remarkable concentration of large and active guilds than Warwickshire. Wiltshire's plains were dotted with an unusual number of free chapels. And
Yorkshire — that giant among English counties — evidenced a particular attachment to the foundation of chantries and other intercessory
institutions. In no other county were there so many chantry-supported
schools, so many important chapels of ease, or so many institutions —
with their curates, preachers, schoolmasters — which the Edwardian
commissioners ordered to be continued with governmental stipends.

In the second place, I have limited my scope chronologically. Rather
than attempting to write a complete history of the second wave of dissolutions of the English Reformation, I have confined myself to setting
the stage for the dissolutions — to placing them in their historical context. I have thus not studied the actual process of suppression, the pensioning of the priests, or the selling of chantry properties. Nor have I
systematically weighed the short and long-range effects of the dissolution upon the parish life of England. Much remains for other scholars
to do.[8]

Only when these topics have been studied, and when the entire narrative of the dissolution has been reconstructed, will we be able confi-

dently to assess the comparative significance of the suppression of the monasteries and the dissolution of the chantries. Until then, however, we can ponder the evidence supplied by this volume, which proves, beyond the shadow of a doubt, that the dissolution of the chantries was important—far more momentous indeed than has generally been acknowledged.

1 / The Intercessory Institutions and Their Priests

The Henrician and Edwardian Chantries Acts together threatened a web of institutions which was intricate and many-faceted. Yet each of the two acts was aimed at a different complex of intercessory foundations. The chantry act of Henry VIII's last Parliament (1545)—which was never carried out systematically—placed at the king's disposal all "colleges, free chapels, chantries, hospitals, fraternities, brotherhoods, guilds, and stipendiary priests having perpetuity for ever." To this list the act of Edward VI's first Parliament (1547)—which was most methodically put into effect—added priests for terms of years, obits, anniversaries, and lights, while exempting the hospitals. Binding these heterogeneous institutions together was their common task of intercession for the souls of the departed, for this was fundamental to all pious foundations of the Middle Ages, from the mightiest abbey to the smallest obit.[1]

In many ways the perpetual chantry was the most important of these intercessory institutions. It was, except for the ubiquitous obits and lights, the most common of them all. And it supported a larger share of the clerical population than any other. It was an ecclesiastical benefice which had been endowed with lands or rents by its founder, who hoped to be the beneficiary of the prayers and masses offered by an endless succession of chantry priests. A chantry priest, like the other beneficed clergy of England, was usually presented by a patron, instituted by the bishop of his diocese, and inducted by an appropriate local ecclesiastical official. His security of tenure in his benefice was considerable. But he differed from a rector or vicar inasmuch as his function was never primarily a pastoral one; his fundamental responsibility—his reason for being, in fact—was to maintain an incessant rhythm of intercession for the soul of the founder.[2] Upon a cantarist's death or resignation, another priest would succeed him in the chantry, thus forging (so the founders hoped) an unbroken chain of intercession across the centuries.

Less secure in tenure than the cantarists were the stipendiary priests, whose intercessory functions were similar if less elaborately defined than those of the chantry priests. They were hired, supervised, and dismissed at will by the trustees, in whom the founders had vested the annual stipends. Although these foundations were commonly perpetual, their informality, and the ease with which they could be founded, made them popular with those who wished to endow prayers for specified terms of years.[3]

In some instances a group of individuals, none of whom were sufficiently wealthy or concerned to endow perpetual prayers from their own resources alone, joined together to found a religious guild, brotherhood, or fraternity. These guilds, which became especially common in the fifteenth century, varied greatly in size. The more elaborate and pretentious ones, which were often located in the greater urban centers, provided their members with numerous benefits. They sponsored feasts, fostered fellowship, and ensured burials of suitable sumptuousness and solemnity. Frequently they also hired one or more guild chaplains, who presided at the worship services of the guild on festive occasions and who day by day maintained a regimen of prayers and masses for guild members both quick and dead. Many poorer parishes, both urban and rural, had guilds which confined their efforts to less ambitious tasks such as securing and maintaining a perpetually burning taper in the local church. But all guilds, both splendid and simple, were primarily devoted to carrying out the purpose which was fundamental to all intercessory institutions — the offering of ceaseless prayer in behalf of the souls in purgatory.[4]

The most imposing of all the foundations listed for suppression under the chantries acts were the colleges. Broadly speaking, they were of two constitutional types.[5] The "classical" colleges, such as the munificently endowed minsters of Beverley and Ripon, were composed in the first instance of a dean or provost and of numerous prebendaries. Since the latter were usually non-resident, their spiritual duties were performed by deputies called "vicars choral."[6] Bishops and other eminent clerics especially valued this form of collegiate organization, for the prebends provided them with a source of income for their officers and suppliants, thereby increasing the fund of patronage at their disposal. By the later Middle Ages a second type of college — the chantry college — was becoming increasingly common. The colleges of this type, such as those at Stratford-on-Avon or at Halstead (Essex), were generally smaller than the classical colleges, and their priests almost always bound to residence. Some of the colleges, such as those of Hemingbrough, Howden, and Lowthorpe in the East Riding of Yorkshire, had at some point been superimposed upon a preexistent parish church. This church was henceforth appropriated to the college, while the warden or provost of the college served it as rector. Other colleges, such as that at Knowle (Warwicks), were located in nonparochial chapels. Still others were founded within the environs of a great church without affecting its governance: St. Willi_m's College, for example, composed of the chantry priests of York Minster.

The colleges of late medieval England, of whatever type, commonly performed at least one of three characteristic functions. The college of the vicars choral of York (the Bedern), Rotherham College, and numerous other collegiate bodies had all been founded at least in part to bring a modicum of order and discipline to communities of chantry priests, vicars choral, and prebendaries who otherwise might have been "vagrant abroad in the . . . town."[7] Rotherham and Acaster Selby had founded to provide educational facilities for the youth of the surrounding territory. But the most general and indispensable function of the collegiate churches was liturgical and intercessory. Whatever else they might do, the colleges were expected to maintain in as beautiful a form as possible the worship of God and the ministry of intercession on behalf of their benefactors through the countless services which the resident priests performed daily.

Less conspicuous than the collegiate churches, but at times no less significant for the people living near them, were the free chapels. These were not exclusively chapels in castles or on manors belonging to the crown and exempt from ordinary jurisdiction.[8] A few such foundations do occur in the chantry certificates, but more frequently the chantry commissioners, whose duty it was to survey the institutions granted to the crown by the chantries acts, designated as "free chapels" those situated some distance from a parish church yet subordinate to it. Some were much-frequented houses of worship, such as the chapel of the Holy Trinity, Hull, in the parish of Hessle, or the chapel of Woodstock in the parish of Bladon. A few, such as the famous chapel on Wakefield Bridge, were buildings of considerable beauty and architectural merit.[9] More often, however, the free chapels were minute and mundane structures which in the Middle Ages had been scattered throughout the towns and countryside of England. By the sixteenth century they were often served — if they were not altogether derelict — either by chantry priests or by unbeneficed stipendiary chaplains.

Also important to the life of some sixteenth-century parishes were the hospitals,[10] consisting generally of a few buildings in which the staff provided sustenance and housing for a handful of resident almspeople. The premises of no hospital were complete without a chapel. For, as with virtually all institutions of pre-Reformation England, the foundation ordinances of the hospitals imposed upon the aged and infirm inmates the obligation to pray daily for the soul of their benefactor.[11] In their intercessions they were usually led by one or more resident chaplains.

Finally, there were the minuscule foundations which were marked for suppression by the Chantries Act of 1547—the endowments for obits, lights, and other parochial services. The popular and relatively inexpensive obits were annual exequies for the souls of the deceased founders.[12] Often taking place on two consecutive days, one of which if possible should be the anniversary of the founder's death, the obit involved the tolling of bells, the recitation of vespers, matins, and lauds for the dead on the evening of the first day,[13] and the celebration of a requiem mass on the following morning. The ceremonies were attended by a variety of persons—kinsfolk of the founder, as many clerics as possible, and the village poor—all of whom joined in common supplications for the departed soul. The obit frequently concluded with a dole to the poor. The lights, on the other hand, were wax tapers which were placed on various altars, before images or pictures of certain saints or the Virgin, in the rood loft, or in front of the reserved sacrament.[14] It was the hope of the founder that passers-by on earth and saints in heaven, being thus reminded of the departed soul, would pray for its repose. Other minor institutions were founded in support of such worthy causes as the "drinking in Rogation Monday" in Odell (Beds) and "the ringing of the curfew nightly within the parish church" of Croscombe (Soms). Although the income of the more substantial intercessory foundations derived almost invariably from real estate, the smaller institutions were frequently supported by sums of money or endowed with such commodities as "twenty bushels of rye," "one cow," or even "a stock of bees."[15]

These then were the varieties of the intercessory institutions affected by the two chantries acts. Historians have never worked out with precision the total number of institutions in any of these categories, but have relied rather on a set of traditional and ostensibly exact totals of the suppressed foundations: 2,374 chantries and free chapels, 110 hospitals, and 96 non-university colleges. Ultimately these figures seem to have derived from William Camden's *Britannia*.[16] But because he failed to indicate the sources of his information, the reliability of his statistics has been suspect. On the basis of a manuscript in the Cotton Collection in the British Library, however, it is now possible to indicate the source of Camden's totals. "A Brief Declaration of the number of all promotions ecclesiastical of what name or title soever at the taxation of the first fruits and tenths" is written in a secretary hand of the sort that was characteristic of the 1560s and 1570s. Its provenance is uncertain, but there can be no conjecture concerning its contents.[17] In its seventeen folios the "declaration" supplies data concerning the numbers of prebends, benefices, religious houses, hospitals, colleges, chantries, and free chapels for each of the twenty-six post-Reformation dioceses. It concludes with the totals for each of these categories for all of England and Wales. And, significantly, its total numbers of chantries and free chapels, hospitals, and colleges are precisely those cited by Camden — 2,374, 110, and 96 respectively.[18]

The information was drawn, with a fair degree of accuracy, from the records of the "taxation of the first fruits and tenths," or the *Valor Ecclesiasticus,* compiled under the supervision of Thomas Cromwell in 1535.[19] This was a remarkable survey, as complete and authoritative as was possible under early sixteenth-century conditions, of all "manner of dignity, monastery, priory, church collegiate, church conventual, parsonage, vicarage, chantry, free chapel, or other dignity, office, or promotion spiritual."[20] But the "substantial accuracy"[21] of this survey was by no means complete or uniform. The *Valor* tended to under-value (generally by more than 15 per cent) the worth of many ecclesiastical institutions and was substantially more precise and informative about the larger foundations than the smaller ones. Yet in the whole realm only five monasteries seem to have been omitted;[22] and in my four sample counties only one collegiate foundation and four hospitals were overlooked.[23]

The commissioners who compiled the chantry certificates in 1546 and 1548 soon discovered, however, that the *Valor*'s listing of the intercessory institutions was often incomplete. To assist these commissioners in their investigations, the officials of the Court of Augmentations had provided them with abstracts — compiled from the *Valor* — which listed the institutions in their region.[24] The discrepancies between these abstracts and parochial reality were manifold and must have appeared rapidly. The 1548 commissioners for Lincolnshire uncovered the existence of numerous chantries and free chapels which were "found and certified upon this survey and [had] not [been] charged in the book of tenths." In some counties, such as Essex and Nottinghamshire, the compilers of the *Valor* had been relatively well informed in their reporting of the intercessory institutions; in others, they had been exceedingly inaccurate. In Wiltshire, for example, they failed to report the existence of ten of forty-seven chantries and fifteen of twenty-eight free chapels which were noted in the chantry surveys. In the North and West Ridings of Yorkshire the chantry commissioners discovered forty-four unrecorded chantries.[25] Even more remiss were the compilers of the *Valor* in the dioceses of Exeter and Gloucester. In the former diocese the commissioners reported only forty-five chantries and free chapels, whereas the chantry commissioners in 1546-1548 located ninety-five.[26] In the diocese of Gloucester, where the compilers for the *Valor* omitted mention of all institutions—parochial and intercessory—in the cities of Bristol and Gloucester and were unreliable in their reporting elsewhere, the *Valor* listed only thirty-three chantries, as against sixty-one such institutions in the chantry certificates.[27] Documents from Thomas Cromwell's office show that he had been well aware of the inadequacies of the *Valor*'s treatment of the lesser institutions. One of these brought to light certain omissions (several of them chantries) from the *Valor*'s return for the diocese of York, while a "remembrance to Master Secretary" informed him "that few chantries perpetual and specially chantries of terms of years and of lives be not certified in the king's books whereby his grace loses both the decimas and the first fruits also."[28]

The shortcomings of the overview of the English intercessory institutions provided by the *Valor Ecclesiasticus* went beyond the incompleteness of that great survey's coverage of the chantries and free chapels. For there were still other categories, most notably the guilds and fraternities and the services of stipendiary priests, which the Act for First Fruits and Tenths had not singled out for taxation.[29] The compilers of the *Valor* had therefore apparently received no specific instruction to inquire into these foundations, despite the fact that their obvious similarities to the chantries were so great that their titles were often confused in popular parlance with that of "chantry." As a result, the compilers were evidently confronted with a dilemma. Should they, at the risk of seriously limiting the revenues of the government, attempt to carry out their instructions literally? Or, in order to maximize the ecclesiastical revenues of the government, should they report the existence of these chantry-like institutions which were technically exempt from taxation? Here too, the listings reveal marked differences of practice. The commissioners for Wiltshire, for example, punctilious in the execution of their instructions, reported no fraternities or stipendiary priests in their county, although the chantry certificates of 1546-1548 indicate the existence of a number of foundations of both types. Almost as strict were the commissioners for the diocese of Exeter, who reported only two of the sixty-five fraternities and stipendiaries in their area. On the other hand, the commissioners for Essex and for the West Riding of Yorkshire were rather less meticulous, listing some but far from all of the guild and stipendiary priests in their counties, often under the flexible rubric of *cantaria*.[30]

The importance of these inaccuracies is obvious. Since the *Valor Ecclesiasticus* failed to include large numbers of chantries and free chapels which were active in the mid-1530s, and since it was, furthermore, wholly unsystematic in its listing of other minor intercessory institutions not specifically mentioned in the instructions to the commissioners, the totals of chantry foundations which have been derived from it are bound to be markedly lower than the actual number of the institutions affected by the acts of 1545 and 1547. Camden's estimates, which have served the historical profession for so many years, must therefore be revised.

It is not simple to arrive at new figures, however. By far the most reliable and informative indicators of the number and state of the intercessory institutions on the eve of their dissolution are the chantry certificates. These documents, which were compiled in the springs of 1546 and 1548 by commissions appointed primarily from substantial gentry and officers of the Court of Augmentations,[31] have innumerable strengths. But they also have some serious shortcomings. In the first place, not all of them have survived intact. During the past four centuries, one or occasionally both of the sets of chantry certificates for many parts of the realm have simply vanished from the archives, leaving us almost entirely without evidence. In Cambridgeshire, for example, the only surviving materials are draft returns for three parishes (Wisbech, Shalford, and Haslingfield) and a listing of obits and miscellaneous other institutions in a Duchy of Lancaster document.[32] Duchy materials also provide the only—and very sketchy—information about the chantries of Huntingdonshire and Norfolk. For Devon,

Derbyshire, and Leicestershire only the 1546 certificates have survived, for Cumberland, Lincolnshire, and Somerset only those of 1548.[33] The survival rate of Yorkshire's chantry records varies from 1546 to 1548 and from riding to riding. The 1546 certificates give a relatively detailed picture of the intercessory institutions of the West Riding. But the 1548 returns — vitally important for this area, which was so densely populated with chantries and chapels — are far from complete, since the Duchy of Lancaster return for this territory (in which the Duchy's holdings were extensive) has disappeared.[34] And for most of the East Riding, neither the Henrician nor the Edwardian certificates are extant.

In addition, those documents which have survived vary considerably in quality. There is occasionally a considerable variation in the completeness and accuracy of the entries for various parishes within the same shire. This flaw may generally be attributed to the local priests, churchwardens, and parishioners who were required to supply evidence to the chantry commissioners. These men, though "straitly examined upon their oaths," nevertheless at times seem to have crossed the indistinct line separating reluctance to testify from dissimulation.[35] The institutions thus "concealed" could not be kept secret forever, and for the rest of the century informers and crown agents submitted a stream of reports concerning the foundations which the commissioners had overlooked at the time of the surveys.[36] More serious than these internal variations are the marked differences in quality between the various chantry certificates. Some teams of commissioners were obviously more meticulous, persistent, and honest than others. Furthermore, the judgments of some commissions were influenced by perceptible signs of Protestantism, while other commissions seem to have bent over backwards to overlook some institutions and to present others in the most favorable light possible.[37] Various chantry certificates may also reflect differing emphases between the Henrician and Edwardian Articles of Inquiry. Thus, whereas the earlier interrogatories placed great emphasis upon the value of the lands and the possessions of the intercessory institutions, the Edwardian articles of instruction were more interested in the current spiritual and charitable functions of the institutions and in the quality of their personnel.[38] Yet some of the best descriptions of the cantarists' contributions to the cure of souls are found in certain of the Henrician certificates; a number of the Edwardian certificates contain interminable lists of the lands and tenements of the dissolved foundations; and a few certificates, both Henrician and Edwardian, contain little useful information of any sort.[39]

Fortunately, other sources are available as supplements and correctives to the chantry certificates. The most important of these is a second series of chantry documents entitled the "Brief Declarations" or "Brief Particulars." Compiled later in 1548 by the particular surveyors of the Court of Augmentations to assist Sir Walter Mildmay and Robert Keilway (who had been appointed on 20 June to determine which institutions should be allowed to continue and to assign pensions to the dispossessed priests), these brief declarations have survived for a large number of shires.[40] Although in general most of the information which they supply is a mere digest of the data contained in the 1548 chantry certificates, some of the declarations do provide illuminating insights. Especially useful are the supplementary details concerning the ages and abilities of the priests, the values of their livings, and their contributions to the life of their parishes. For certain areas, furthermore, the brief declarations provide the sole source of reliable information about the functioning of the intercessory institutions.[41] In those instances where both the chantry certificates *and* the brief declarations are lacking, the last resort is to collate the ministers' accounts of the Courts of Augmentations and the Duchy of Lancaster, warrants from Mildmay and Keilway ordering the pensioning of erstwhile incumbents and the continuance of certain institutions, and the records of the sale of the lands of the dissolved institutions. From these sources it is then possible to reconstruct the general outlines of an area's chantry system.[42]

Even using all of these sources, it still remains difficult to arrive at a plausibly accurate estimate of the total number of intercessory institutions on the eve of the dissolution. In the four counties under study here, I have uncovered the traces of 861 foundations, each of which had resources sufficient to support at least one priest (Table 1.1). But even this figure is approximate, for it is impossible to know how many institutions were successfully concealed from the attention of the commissioners. How much more difficult to reach precise numbers in those parts of the realm whose chantry certificates have survived less well than in my four shires! It is clear, therefore, that any attempt to revise Camden's traditional estimate of the total number of institutions affected by the chantries acts will likewise result in an estimate—more reliable, to be sure, but still necessarily approximate. This revised estimate will inevitably be higher than Camden's, probably higher even

Table 1.1.   Institutional totals, 1546-1548.

County	Chantries	Stipendi- aries	Free chapels	Guilds	Colleges	Hospitals
Essex	45	10	19	18	1	2
Warwicks	34	7	3	11	4	5
Wilts	44	7	28	7	1	8
Yorks	406	117	33	20	10	21
(East Riding)	(82)	(11)	(7)	(4)	(5)	(7)
(North Riding & City of York)	(156)	(22)	(10)	(7)	(2)	(9)
(West Riding)	(168)	(84)	(16)	(9)	(3)	(5)
Total	529	141	83	56	16	36

Sources: Essex: E 301/19, 20, 30, 83; E 101/75/12; DL 38/4; E 315/30, f. 44; *L.P.*, XXI, i, 1538 (p. 777).

Warwicks: E 301/31, 53, 57; E 101/76/4; E 319/6.

Wilts: E 301/56, 58, 59, 101; E 101/76/6; E 319/1.

Yorks: *Y.C.C.*; E 301/102, 103, 119; E 101/76/8-10; E 319/22; DL 28/27/18; DL 29/564/8945; DL 42/135; LR 6/121/6; *Valor*, V, 134, 141, 113, 110; *C.P.R.*, *Edward VI*, I, 170; Y.M.L., MS. M. 2(4)a, f. 62. These totals do not include "concealed" institutions such as those discovered in Richmond (L. P. Wenham, "The Chantries, Guilds, Obits, and Lights of Richmond, Yorkshire," *Y.A.J.*, 38 [1952-1955], 96-111, 185-214, 310-332) or possibly in Boynton (C. V. Collier, "A Sixteenth Century Note-Book," *Y.A.J.*, 20 [1909], 257-258). They do, however, include institutions which the chantry certificates record as having recently been dissolved by private action.

Note: The chantry commissioners seem to have used the terms "chantry," "service," and "stipendiary" loosely, at times interchangeably (e.g., for Rotherham: *Valor*, V, 61; E 101/76/9, m. lv; *Y.C.C.*, I, 208). This terminological confusion, along with the large number of "concealed" and incorrectly reported institutions, makes precise categorization and exact totals impossible. I have divided the foundations into categories, not according to the commissioners' precise labeling, but rather according to their foundation and functioning, which I have interpreted in light of the criteria of Miss Wood-Legh (*Perpetual Chantries*, 30-64). In the case of institutions whose foundations and workings the commissioners failed to describe, I have followed their labeling uncritically.

than the more generous totals of Professors Jordan and Dickens.[43] In a cursory totaling of the intercessory institutions of twenty representative counties, comprising just over half of the parishes of England and Wales (Table 1.2), I have identified 2,182 intercessory institutions capable of supporting at least one priest. If this figure is at all accurate (in all probability it will be low rather than high), it is evident that there were substantially more intercessory foundations prior to the dissolution than scholars have realized.

These institutions were distributed throughout the realm in a fascinating and significant geographical pattern. The greatest density of chantry foundations was in London, where 314 institutions capable of supporting priests were crowded into all but eight of the city's ninety-nine parishes. But London was a special case. In part, this was a result of the concentration of wealth in the city; in part, it was due to the immunity that founders of ecclesiastical institutions in the city apparently enjoyed from the mortmain laws.[44] Nowhere else in the southeast of England was the incidence of substantial intercessory institutions remotely as high as this. In fact, the Englishmen of the southern, southeastern, and Midland counties seem to have been reluctant to make the financial sacrifice necessary to found chantries. Thus, in Kent there was on average an intercessory institution large enough to support a priest in only one out of five parishes; in Buckinghamshire, in only every sixth parish; and in Suffolk it took as many as eight parishes to produce such an institution. The southwest of England showed appreciably more enthusiasm for chantry foundations, with an average of just under three parishes per sizable intercessory institution in Cornwall, Somerset, and Wiltshire, and an institution for almost every one-and-a-half (1.61) parishes in Gloucestershire. It was, however, the people of the northwest and north of England who evidenced the greatest devotion to endowed prayers. These northern folk were admittedly not as able as their southern countrymen to endow their intercessory institutions munificently. But the sheer number of their institutions is impressive. In Cheshire and Northumberland there was on average almost one institution per parish. But the densest of all concentrations of chantry foundations outside of London was located in Yorkshire. In the West Riding, in fact, the average of almost one-and-a-half (1.48) intercessory institutions per parish was almost ten times the figure for Suffolk. In comparison with the intensity of the Yorkshiremen's trust in the efficacy of endowed masses for the dead, the piety of the inhabitants of Suffolk appears to have been cooler, more anti-institutional, more modern.[45]

Because some parishes had several intercessory institutions, the ratio of institutions to parishes is obviously higher than the ratio of the number of parishes which actually contained these institutions to the total number of parishes. In twenty shires, there were intercessory foundations capable of maintaining a priest in 1,047 parishes, or 22.7 percent of the parishes in these counties. This percentage, in much the same manner as the ratio of institutions to parishes, varies from one part of

Table 1.2. Geographical distribution of intercessory institutions, 1546-1548.

County	Parishes[a]	Total greater institutions[b]	Average number of greater institutions per parish
Bucks	175	29	.17
Cheshire	65	53	.82
Cornwall	161	55	.34
Essex	387	95	.25
Glos	232	144	.62
Hants	240	53	.22
Herts	120	20	.17
Kent	371	73	.20
London & Middx[c]	167	336	2.01
London	(99)	(314)	(3.17)
Middx	(68)	(22)	(.32)
Northants	267	43	.16
Northumb	56	48	.86
Notts	176	96	.55
Oxon	166	28	.17
Salop	161	76	.47
Soms	384	131	.34
Suffolk	424	63	.15
Warwicks	158	64	.40
Wilts	267	95	.36
Worcs	153	50	.33
Yorks[c]	490	637	1.30
East Riding	(147)	(134)	(.91)
North Riding, & City of York	(144)	(209)	(1.45)
West Riding	(199)	(294)	(1.48)
Total	4620	2189	.47

Sources: Bucks: E 301/4, 5, 77.

Cheshire: E 301/8.

Cornwall: Snell, *Chantry Certificates for Cornwall.*

Essex: see Table 1.1, sources.

Glos: E 301/21; Maclean, "Chantry Certificates, Gloucestershire."

Hants: E 301/51, 52.

Herts: J. E. Brown, ed., *Chantry Certificates for Hertfordshire* (Hertford, n.d.).

Kent: Arthur Hussey, ed., *Kent Chantries,* Kent Records 12 (1936), and *Kent Obit and Lamp Rents,* Kent Records 14 (1936).

London and Middx: E 301/34; SP 10/4, ff. 11-12; B.L. Harleian MS. 601.

Northants: Thompson, "Chantry Certificates for Northamptonshire," 87-178.

Northumb: J. Raine, ed., "The Certificates of all the Chauntryes, &c., within the Countye of Northumberland," Surtees Soc., 22 (1850), lxxvii-xc.

Notts: Thompson, "Certificates of Southwell," 63-158, and "The Chantry Certifi-

(Cont.)

Total parishes with greater institutions		Total parishes with lesser institutions only b	Total parishes with greater and lesser intercessory institutions	
Total	Percent		Total	Percent
24	13.7	72	96	54.9
32	49.2	11	43	66.2
36	22.4	15	51	31.7
67	17.3	129	196	50.6
75	32.3	71	146	62.9
34	14.2	25	59	24.6
18	15.0	63	81	67.5
56	15.1	156	212	57.1
107	64.1			
(91)	(91.9)			
(16)	(23.5)			
33	12.4	95	118	44.2
18	32.1	7	25	44.6
39	22.2	43	82	46.6
19	11.4	72	91	54.8
40	24.9	41	81	50.3
66	17.2	130	196	51.0
47	11.1	204	251	59.2
27	17.1	44	71	44.9
53	19.9	37	90	33.7
33	21.6	31	64	41.8
223	45.5	54	100	68.0
(46)	(31.3)			
(60)	(41.7)			
(117)	(58.8)			
1047	22.7			50.0[c]

cate Rolls for the County of Nottingham," *Trans. Thoroton Soc.*, 16 (1912), 91-133; 17 (1913), 59-119; 18 (1914), 83-184.

Oxon: Rose Graham, ed., *The Chantry Certificates and the Edwardian Inventories of Church Goods,* Oxfordshire Rec. Soc., 1 (1919).

Salop: A. Hamilton Thompson, ed., "Certificates of the Shropshire Chantries," *Trans. Shropshire Archaeol. and Nat. Hist. Soc.*, 3rd ser. 10 (1910), 269-392.

Soms: Green, *Survey of Somerset.*

Suffolk: V. B. Redstone, ed., "Chapels, Chantries, and Gilds in Suffolk," *Proc. Suffolk Inst. of Archaeol. and Nat. Hist.*, 12 (1906), 1-87.

Warwicks: see Table 1.1, sources.

Wilts: see Table 1.1, sources.

Worcs: E 301/60, 61.

Yorks: see Table 1.1, sources; Kitching, "Chantries of the East Riding," 178-194.

a. Authorities differ markedly on the precise number of parishes in the various

(*Cont.*)

English counties. For Yorkshire, Professor Hamilton Thompson counted 622 parishes in the pre-Reformation period (*English Clergy*, 115); the Jacobean antiquary Nicholas Wanton believed that there were "vij^c benefices" in the shire (Bodleian MS., Rawlinson B. 450, f. 293v); the "Burghley Atlas" of the 1570s listed 484 parishes (B.L. Royal MS. 18 D iii, f. 3); Father Philip Hughes (*The Reformation in England*, 5th ed., 3 vols. [London, 1963], I, 35) and I, who have made independent counts of the parishes mentioned in the *Valor,* have noted 450 and 490 respectively. In Essex the situation is also confusing. My count totaled 385 parishes; the "Burghley Atlas" found 387; an anonymous Elizabethan observer reported 396 churches (B.L. Lansdowne MS. 171, f. 240v); and Bishop Grindal in 1563 reported as many as 404 (B.L. Harleian MS. 595, f. 66). In light of this and similar conflicting testimony, I have decided generally to rely upon the evidence supplied by the "Burghley Atlas," which bases its figures upon "the Queen's Majesty's records of the first fruits and tenths remaining in the Exchequer." The exceptions to this are Kent (B.L. Lansdowne MS. 171, f. 240v), London and Middlesex (ibid.), and Northumberland (my count based on *Valor,* V, 327-330), because the "Burghley Atlas" provides no statistics for these shires; also Yorkshire (my count, based on *Valor,* V, 1-146), since the "Burghley Atlas" does not give separate totals for each riding.

 b. The "greater institutions" (chantries, guilds, free chapels, colleges, stipendiary services, hospitals) were usually great only in a comparative sense—i.e., unlike the "lesser institutions" (obits, lamps, lights, tiny guilds, etc.), they were large enough to provide full support for at least one priest.

 c. Because of the imperfect quality and survival of evidence for London and Middlesex and for the North and West Ridings of Yorkshire, I have excluded the 510 parishes in these areas from my calculations of the percent of parishes with intercessory institutions of all sizes.

---

the realm to another, with London and Suffolk at the two extremes. Oxfordshire was almost as lightly institutionalized as Suffolk. In fact, in none of the counties of the Midlands or the southeast save Middlesex did more than one-fifth of the parishes contain intercessory institutions. This percentage rose significantly in the west, and to an even greater extent in the north and northwest. In Cheshire and the West Riding of Yorkshire, where half of the parishes (49.2 percent and 58.8 percent respectively) contained institutions capable of supporting priests, the effects of the dissolution of the chantries would be widespread indeed.

When we add the humbler intercessory institutions to these more substantial foundations, the number of parishes affected by the chantries acts increases still further, and with a great deal of regional variation. The southeastern counties, which appear to have been comparatively uninterested in chantries, to some extent compensated for this by endowing a plethora of cheaper, but still presumably efficacious, obits and lights. Thus 57.1 percent of the Kentish parishes contained an intercessory institution of some sort, while in Suffolk and Hertfordshire, where the incidence of lesser institutions was even more impressive, the proportion of parishes containing intercessory institutions rose still higher (59.2 and 67.5 percent of parishes respectively). In the north, northwest, and west of England the concentration of all institutions—large and small—was at times as dense as in the southeast, but rarely more so. Only in the East Riding of Yorkshire and in Cheshire, where 68 percent and 66.2 percent respectively of the parishes contained intercessory institutions, did a greater proportion of parishes contain intercessory institutions than did Hertfordshire. In some counties of the west and southwest, there appears on the other hand to have been little confidence in the utility of obits and lights: in Cornwall and Wiltshire scarcely one parish in three possessed an intercessory institution of any sort. Although these figures are admittedly approximate—and probably far too low, because of the ease of concealing the minor institutions—it remains striking that exactly half of all the parishes in these twenty sample counties contained intercessory institutions. Furthermore, since the supporting endowments were scattered throughout numerous additional parishes, far *more* than half of the parishes of these shires would in some way be affected by the dissolution. Its impact, while varying in severity from parish to parish, must inevitably have been heightened because of the impressive geographical spread of these institutions.

To the student of the ecclesiastical history of the later Middle Ages, the priests serving the intercessory institutions have to a large extent remained faceless men. In spite of the detailed researches of Miss Wood-Legh, their obscurity has persisted in many areas.[46] What sort of men were these priests? The information in the *Valor Ecclesiasticus,* diocesan records, and the chantry certificates provides us with some interesting clues.

In the first place, the "mass priests" were, by clerical standards, generally not affluent. If, as some historians have suggested, the English clergy could be divided into two groups—the wealthy clerics who enjoyed education and connections, and the poorer clergy who tended to have neither—the chantry priests would generally have been found in the second group.[47] But this was not invariably the case. It would be a mistake cavalierly to dismiss the intercessory priests as "clerical helots."[48] To do so would be to ignore the fact that they, like the rectors and vicars, were not a uniform class. The lowliest among them were the unbeneficed clerics, who congregated in many parish churches waiting for steady employment.[49] They pieced together a living as best they could by celebrating trentals of masses, presiding at obits, and assisting at funerals and anniversary masses in the hope of profiting from the money which was doled out to those in attendance.[50] With reasonably good fortune such a priest might be chosen to serve one of the chantries which pre-Reformation founders frequently established for limited spans of years. In most parts of the realm, these priests-for-terms-of-years appear to have been paid relatively well. In Essex, for example, their median income in the early sixteenth century was ten marks (£6 13s. 4d.).[51] Although this was less than the median income of the chantry priests at the time of the dissolution (Table 1.3), it was a respectable and satisfactory remuneration — more, indeed, than that of the stipendiary priests, some of whom received less than £3 per year

Table 1.3.   Number of stipendiary and chantry priests, 1546-1548, by range of (net) annual income.

County	Less than £3	£3 to £4 19s. 11d.	£5 to £6 13s. 3d.	£6 13s. 4d. and above	Median
Essex					
Chantry priests	—	3	8	30	£7 17s. 10d.
Stipendiaries	5	2	—	3	3 0s. 0d.
Warwicks					
Chantry priests	3	4	13	14	6 13s. 4d.
Stipendiaries	1	1	4	1	4 16s. 0d.
Wilts					
Chantry priests	2	7	11	24	6 13s. 4d.
Stipendiaries	1	1	2	3	5 15s. 0d.
Yorks					
East Riding					
Chantry priests	5	27	26	20	5 5s. 0d.
Stipendiaries	1	6	4	1	4 13s. 4d.
North Riding					
Chantry priests	6	34	23	8	4 13s. 4d.
Stipendiaries	8	5	4	1	4 4s. 0d.
West Riding					
Chantry priests	13	78	52	26	4 16s. 8d.
Stipendiaries	28	24	16	3	4 0s. 0d.
City of York					
Chantry priests	14	8	12	6	4 13s. 0d.
Stipendiaries	2	—	—	—	—
York Minster					
Chantry priests	5	25	14	7	4 3s. 8d.

Sources: see above, Table 1.1, sources.

and were thus compelled to rely upon "the devotion of the . . . parishioners" for supplementary income. At least one parish (Ellesmere, Salop) organized a system for raising the priest's annual income to the comfortable level of £6 by requiring every married man and every "servant taking 5s. wages or above" to contribute 4d. and 2d. per year respectively.[52] Though most stipendiary priests received less than this, the substantial majority of them were paid well over £3 per annum, and thus were above the line of absolutely minimal existence.[53] Furthermore, they had steady work and the prospect of reasonable security of employment, at least until their powers began to fail.

The chantry priests proper, as incumbents of full-fledged ecclesiastical benefices, enjoyed a security of tenure unknown to the unbeneficed stipendiaries and were generally better off. In addition, since much of the chantry income came from endowments of land, the rents of which were rising in the 1530s and 1540s, and since many priests were able to supplement their food supplies by farming their own lands, the chantry priests were not as immediately affected by inflationary pressures as were the stipendiary priests.[54] Many chantries also possessed a "mansion house," the cantarist's equivalent of the parsonage, which enabled the incumbent to live in respectability and reasonable physical comfort.[55] But most significant was the fact that the chantry priests generally earned more than the stipendiaries (Table 1.3). There were, of course, exceptionally impoverished chantries and unusually comfortably situated stipendiary priests.[56] Nevertheless most chantry priests were also better off than the parochial curates, the craftsmen, and the agricultural laborers with whom they associated in the course of their daily activities, and a few were as comfortably situated as were some reasonably affluent farmers.[57] Furthermore, the priests had no families to support.

Though they were usually able to live more comfortably than many of their clerical and lay acquaintances, the chantry priests were still in general less well-to-do than the rectors and vicars (Table 1.4). In the mid-sixteenth century there was considerable discussion concerning the level of income which was necessary to support a beneficed cleric with cure of souls. Bishop John Longland suggested that eight marks (£5 6s. 8d.) was not sufficient for the maintenance of a vicar's "house and household, which by the law he is bound to keep." Archbishop Edward Lee bewailed the low value of the livings in Yorkshire which, often worth less than £8, "be so small, that no learned man will take

Table 1.4. Number of rectors, vicars, and chantry and guild priests, 1535, by range of (net) annual income.

County	Less than £5	£5 to £6 13s. 3d.	£6 13s. 4d. to £9 19s. 11d.	£10 and above	Median
Essex					
Rectors	6	4	44	196	£13 0s. 0
Vicars	1	2	33	98	12 3s. 4
Chantry & guild priests	8	11	42	6	7 0s. 0
Kent (Canterbury archdioc.)					
Rectors	16	13	33	57	9 11s. 8
Vicars	2	20	44	44	9 1s. 4
Chantry & guild priests	5	6	16	7	7 17s. 8
Kent (Rochester dioc.)					
Rectors	7	10	13	39	11 15s. 0
Vicars	2	6	16	30	10 0s. 0
Chantry & guild priests	1	5	8	2	7 0s. 0
Warwicks					
Rectors	8	9	12	41	11 10s. 7
Vicars	—	29	33	22	7 17s. 9
Chantry & guild priests	6	28	3	3	5 9s. 0
Wilts					
Rectors	11	11	27	93	12 6s. 8
Vicars	3	7	38	56	10 18s. 9
Chantry & guild priests	9	12	14	4	6 6s. 0
Yorks					
East Riding					
Rectors	5	2	9	36	14 7s. 7
Vicars	14	22	30	29	7 8s. 0
Chantry & guild priests	49	26	8	3	4 13s. 4
North Riding					
Rectors	2	7	10	44	13 2s. 6
Vicars	12	13	11	19	8 10s. 0
Chantry & guild priests	37	12	3	1	4 13s. 4
West Riding					
Rectors	4	6	11	57	14 6s. 10
Vicars	20	26	27	48	9 8s. 10
Chantry & guild priests	172	55	11	1	4 7s. 10
City of York					
Rectors	11	3	2	—	4 7s. 8
Vicars	7	1	1	1	4 0s. 0
Chantry & guild priests	30	11	1	—	3 13s.
York Minster (1548)					
Chantry priests	30	14	6	1	4 2s.

Sources: *Valor,* I, 435-450; II, 86-151; III, 52-98; V, 2-258; *Y.C.C.,* II, 431-449.

them."[58] This amount, in fact, appears to have been the ecclesiastical "poverty line" beneath which the Faculty Office in the 1530s adjudged parochial incumbents to be legitimately eligible for the supplementary income provided by pluralism.[59] By 1549, after some serious inflation had taken place, Hugh Latimer was able to claim that no priest whose benefice was worth less than twelve to fourteen marks (£8 to £9 6s. 8d.) would be able to "buy him books, nor give his neighbor drink."[60] In the 1530s and 1540s, then, a rector or vicar would have needed a net income of nearly £10 per annum from his benefice (to say nothing of the supplementary income which he might receive from baptismal and mortuary fees) in order adequately to carry out the duties associated with his living.[61]

It was fortunate for the sixteenth-century Church that (according to the *Valor Ecclesiasticus*) a substantial majority of the rectors in all of our four counties had annual incomes of over £10. It was a serious matter, however, that in Warwickshire and the North and West Ridings of Yorkshire, where there were significantly more vicarages than rectories, the median income of a vicar was markedly less than £10. And scattered across the land there were numerous rectors and vicars whose incomes were so small that a neighboring chantry priest might be earning more (Table 1.4). In all there were in 1535 a total of twenty-seven chantry priests in our four counties whose livings were worth at least £10. A few chantry priests were even sufficiently well-to-do habitually to absent themselves from their chantries and to send deputies to perform their spiritual duties.[62]

With these facts in mind, it is not hard to understand the numerous letters which came to Wolsey and Cromwell begging them to bestow certain chantries in the crown's gift upon particular clerics. Bishop Longland, for example, wrote to Cromwell concerning the chantry of Chalgrave (Beds), which was worth "better than £20 yearly. And [if] it were not for the love I bear unto you, I would bestow the same upon a good master of art, a preacher."[63] The candidate for this chantry was clearly no "clerical helot." Nor was William Copland, the Latin tutor of Gregory Cromwell, for whose maintenance Gregory's powerful father in 1533 obtained a chantry in All-Hallows-by-the-Tower, London.[64] These men were hardly representative of the vast majority of the chantry priests. But their cases are a reminder that the priests who served the intercessory institutions, far from being a uniform class of ecclesiastical proletarians, included many men whose well-endowed benefices must have been the envy of numerous rectors and vicars.

The priests who served these institutions at the time of the dissolution appear to have been a group of rather elderly men.[65] According to the chantry certificates their average age, in six shires, ranged from forty-seven to fifty-five years, with 7.6 percent of their number more than seventy years old (Table 1.5). Three of these cantarists claimed to be eighty-six, eighty-seven, and ninety years of age respectively—a remarkable longevity in any era.[66] And astonishingly few of the cantarists were younger than thirty at the time of the dissolution.

If the average life expectancy of Tudor-Stuart males of generally sedentary modes of life was approximately sixty years,[67] it is understandable that historians have speculated that the cantarists, most of whom had no obligation for cure of souls, "may have regarded their posts as equivalent to retirement pensions."[68] There is some evidence in support of this hypothesis, including a famous passage in Chaucer's Prologue.[69] In the early sixteenth century, however, it was unusual for chantries to serve as livings for superannuated parish priests (Table 1.6). Especially during the years following 1536, the English ecclesiastical job market was being glutted by the former religious, considerable numbers of whom became chantry priests (as many as one out of eight in some areas) after their houses were suppressed.[70] A fortunate few were promoted to chantries almost as soon as they were expelled from their houses.[71] These ex-monks were often on the elder side of middle-age when they were thrust out into the world, and their advent appreciably raised the average age of the chantry priests. It also in-

Table 1.5.   Number of chantry priests, etc., at date of chantry surveys (1548), by age group.

County	Under 30	30-39	40-49	50-59	60-69	Over 69	Average	Median
Essex	0	7	6	18	8	5	55	54
Kent	0	4	15	4	7	0	47.4	44
Lincs	2	18	33	35	29	9	50.9	52
Warwicks	2	8	23	21	9	7	50.5	50
Wilts	0	4	10	21	17	7	54.2	54
Yorks	5	39	120	97	70	24	50.8	50

Sources: Essex: E 301/19; DL 38/4; Kent: Hussey, *Kent Chantries;* Lincs: Foster and Thompson, "Chantry Certificates for Lincolnshire"; Warwicks: E 301/57; Wilts: E 301/58; Yorks: *Y.C.C.*; E 301/119.

creased the number of priests who were competing for a limited number of available livings. Many bishops therefore attempted to reduce the over-supply of clergy by restricting the number of ordinations in the years after 1536.[72] This policy, appropriate though it was in response to a difficult situation, had the effect of further raising the

Table 1.6. Number of chantry priests, etc., by age group at date of institution.

	Under 30	30-39	40-49	50-59	60-69	Over 69	Average	Median
By County								
Essex	0	2	2	0	1	0	44.5	42
Kent	2	7	2	4	0	0	40.4	37
Lincs	8	15	11	5	1	0	38.8	37
Warwicks	2	3	4	0	0	0	35.9	37
Wilts	0	9	6	1	1	0	41.6	39
Yorks	22	26	27	9	3	0	38.2	38
By Decade								
1500-1509	2	0	1	0	0	0	32.3	
1510-1519	5	1	3	0	0	0	32.3	29
1520-1529	8	11	6	2	0	0	35.9	36
1530-1539	10	28	19	10	0	0	38.3	38
1540-1548	9	22	23	7	6	0	41.8	40

Sources: Essex: E 301/19; DL 38/4; Reg. Stokesley; Reg. Bonner.

Kent: Hussey, *Kent Chantries* (provides both the chantry certificates and information concerning the dates of institution).

Lincs: Foster and Thompson, "Chantry Certificates for Lincolnshire" (provides both the 1548 survey and excerpts from episcopal registers giving the dates of the institutions of the chantry priests).

Warwicks: E 301/57; Reg. Silvestro de' Gigli; Reg. Ghinucci; Reg. Latimer; Reg. Blythe; Reg. Rowland Lee; Reg. Sampson.

Wilts: E 301/58; Reg. Campeggio; Reg. Shaxton; Reg. Salcot; Sir Thomas Phillipps, "Institutiones Clericorum in Comitatu Wiltoniae," 2 vols. (B.L., MS. list, 1825).

Yorks: *Y.C.C.*; E 301/119; Reg. Holgate; Y.M.L., Torre MSS. L 1(7), L 1(8), L 1(9); L 1(10).

Note: The chantry certificates of 1548 frequently provide the ages of the cantarists; by ascertaining, through episcopal registers, the dates of their institutions to their chantries, I have then calculated their ages at that time. This evidence is limited by the fact that the calculations are based on the ages of the priests who were living in 1548. Therefore the average ages under the county heading are certainly somewhat low, since most of the older priests who had been promoted to chantries in the early decades of the century had died by the time of the dissolution. To some extent the decade listing compensates for this distortion. Thus, although the evidence for the years prior to 1530 is somewhat misleading, the data for the 1530s and especially for the period 1540-1548 is relatively reliable. Furthermore, fully 77 percent of the priests whose ages and records of institutions are known (133 out of 173) were instituted during this eighteen-year period.

average age of the cantarists by reducing the likelihood that youthful priests would be presented to chantries. It is probable, therefore, that the average age of institution of the chantry priests was somewhat higher in the 1530s and 1540s than it had been in the earlier years of the century.

Nevertheless, from this evidence, studied in conjunction with other sources, it is possible to construct a hypothetical pattern for recruiting chantry priests in the half-century prior to the dissolution. During this period some priests were instituted to chantries in their late twenties and early thirties—shortly after they became canonically eligible. Roughly the same number of priests were instituted to chantries late in life, and a few may have viewed their chantries as comfortable, sheltered places of retirement. The preponderant majority of the chantry priests, however, were men "in middle life,"[73] men who came to their chantries—often as their first living—in their late thirties or in their forties.

The factor of age was of importance to the founders and patrons, who were primarily concerned to obtain faithful and effective service from the priests whom they promoted. The essential function of every chantry was intercession; and a youngish, vigorous priest was more likely to be able to devote himself to this with regularity than was a priest in his fifties or sixties. The chantry priests were sometimes required to perform additional tasks as well—to teach local children the rudiments of grammar, or to assist the curate in the cure of souls. These too were tasks which could be better performed by men in their middle years than by candidates for retirement. Therefore, rarely did patrons promote elderly priests to the chantries at their disposal.

Priests in the youngest age bracket were also generally excluded, because of "pressure for benefices."[74] The fundamental cause of pressure was no doubt population growth; but widespread pluralism and the debilitating inefficiency of the Church's patronage system also contributed. In the early sixteenth century all of these causes combined to produce the stark reality which confronted every newly ordained priest: there was a superfluity of clerics competing for a limited number of livings. For this reason, all but the well-connected priests were forced to wait for years following their ordinations before they could be presented to a benefice. During these years, which were often lean indeed, they attempted to eke out a living by the ecclesiastical equivalent of piece-work—by serving as private chaplains, as attendant priests at obits, or as priests celebrating month's minds and trentals. In his will of 1530, Sir Walter Griffith of Burton Agnes (E.R., Yorks) showed a sensitive awareness of this situation. In the realization that his private chaplain was about to face years of insecurity and enforced austerity while hunting for a benefice, Griffith bequeathed him an annual stipend of 40s. to pray for his soul "unto such time as he shall be promoted to a chantry or benefice."[75] No doubt there were some priests who never managed to obtain livings of any sort. Eventually, however, many priests were promoted to chantries.

Outlines of the careers of three priests will indicate what seems to have been a general pattern. Roger Frikley was ordained priest in 1509. Five years later, by which time he had still not obtained steady employment, he was appointed to sing for the soul of Sir Thomas Wortley in the church of Hemsworth (W.R., Yorks) for the term of seven years. By 1526, Frikley had moved to nearby Pontefract to serve as an unbeneficed chaplain. In the mid-1530s the commissioners for the *Valor Ecclesiasticus* recorded that he had been promoted to the chantry of St. Mary in the Chapel of St. Giles in the same parish, a living which he continued to hold until 1548.[76] It took even longer for another West Riding priest, Richard Langfello, to secure ecclesiastical promotion. Although ordained priest as early as 1523, by 1540 he still had only temporary employment — an engagement for one year to pray for the soul of a kinsman in the parish churches of Leathley and Calverley. In 1546 the chantry commissioners found him serving as chaplain of a slenderly endowed chantry in Aldborough.[77] Rather less typical was the successful and particularly well-documented career of William Pynder. In 1520, nine years after he had been ordained priest and while he was apparently an unbeneficed chaplain, Pynder was granted certain lands in the East Riding for the term of his life in return for praying for the soul of Thomas Boynton of Rousby. These lands seem not to have provided sufficient income, for by 1526 he had moved to York to become incumbent of the Russell and Thirsk chantry in the parish of Holy Cross, Fossegate. Three years later he managed to acquire yet another chantry in the city in the parish of St. John, Hungate; and at the time of the chantry surveys he was still incumbent of both chantries.[78] All of these men had been compelled to wait for some years after their ordinations before being presented to their chantries: only the well-connected obtained benefices immediately upon ordination, and such men did not usually become chantry priests. Therefore it is hardly surprising that the average cantarist was almost forty before he was instituted to his living. Though hardly a luscious ecclesiastical plum, his chantry must have seemed deliciously welcome to him after years of hand-to-mouth existence.

It is doubtful that very many chantry priests used their livings as stepping-stones to more prestigious and lucrative positions in the ecclesiastical hierarchy.[79] Some of them, however, did move from chantry to chantry, thereby improving their financial situation.[80] Such mobility, however, seems to have been exceptional, and the majority of the chantry priests probably viewed their chantries as lifetime callings. Mrs. Bowker has recently demonstrated that there was a remarkable amount of stability among the lower clergy in the diocese of Lincoln.[81] The same could be said of the chantry priests. In Lincolnshire, for example, almost one-third (21 of 64) of those listed in the chantry surveys (whose date of presentation is known or who were mentioned in the ecclesiastical subsidy of 1526) had been promoted to their livings over twenty years previously.[82] Similarly, in Yorkshire five cantarists had been serving their chantries for over forty years; and two of these—William Sheffeld of the chantry of St. Katharine, Leeds, and William Colte of a chantry in St. Mary's, Castlegate, York—had been instituted in 1500, forty-eight years prior to their forcible dispossession by the Edwardian Chantries Act.[83] Having been promoted to chantries which provided security and an acceptable degree of physical comfort, these men chose to hold on to a good thing.

The chantry priests were in general not a highly educated group of men, though the level of their education seems to have varied from one area of England to another (Table 1.7). In London—and, to a lesser extent, in the adjoining county of Essex—even the unbeneficed priests were frequently well educated.[84] In those parts of England far removed from London, however, one is struck by the relatively low level of the educational attainments of most priests. It is seldom clear what criteria the chantry commissioners used to judge the learning of the cantarists whom they met for such a short time. The 1548 commissioners for the West Riding of Yorkshire, however, were explicit in describing a Wakefield chantry priest as "indifferently learned and studious in Scripture"; the Kentish commissioners characterized a Reculver cantarist as "indifferently learned to serve a cure"; and the Edwardian commissioners for Lincolnshire described one of the priests of the chantry in Burton-upon-Stather as "sufficiently learned to preach the

Table 1.7.   Educational attainments of intercessory priests, 1548.

County	Well learned	Indifferently learned	Somewhat learned	Meanly learned	Not learned	Able to serve a cure	Unable to serve a cure
Beds	3	0	0	19	3	0	0
Essex	24	0	1	0	9	0	0
Lincs	0	0	0	0	0	53	127
Northumb	7	0	2	33	0	0	0
Wilts	0	0	0	0	0	13	31
Yorks							
East Riding	25	6	0	0	0	0	0
North Riding	25	17	0	23	6	0	0
West Riding	9	13	22	0	23	0	0
City of York	1	4	0	20	8	0	0
York Minster	7	20	0	18	0	0	0

Sources: Beds: E 301/2; Essex: E 301/19; DL 38/4; Lincs: Foster and Thompson, "Chantry Certificates for Lincolnshire," *A.A.S.R.P.*, 36 (1921-1922), 195; Northumb. E 301/62; Wilts: E 301/58; Yorks: *Y.C.C.*, II.

Word of God."[85] Biblical knowledge, pastoral learning, the ability to preach — all of these were flexible standards against which to measure the chantry priests. No doubt the commissioners in general were imprecise and impressionistic in their evaluations of the cantarists' learning; probably their standards also varied from commission to commission. It would therefore be unwise to read too much into the elastic categories and cold statistics which they recorded.

Nevertheless, it is sad to note the frequency with which the commissioners were forced to classify the incumbents of the chantries as "unlearned," "of mean learning," or "indifferently learned." It is also significant that of those clerics who warranted the commissioners' accolade of "well learned," very few possessed university degrees.[86] Furthermore, in those shires where the commissioners divided the cantarists into categories of those who were able or unable to serve cures,[87] fewer than half of the priests were adjudged to have had sufficient learning to be effective in the cure of souls.[88]

Alongside these "typical" priests, however, we must place those exceptional individuals of undoubted literary attainments who served as cantarists. One of these, John Rouse, who was one of the two priests in Guy's Cliff Chantry just outside Warwick, was an accomplished antiquarian who around 1490 penned a *Historia Regum Anglie* and compiled a list of deserted villages. A candidate for a chantry in Lord Lisle's patronage was described as being "well seen in physic, astronomy, and surgery, and can sing his plainsong well and is well appareled." William Gage, a cantarist in the diocese of Norwich, possessed books by Aristotle and Averroës as well as three astrolabes; Edmund Kyngestone, one of the chantry priests in Southwell Minster, was the owner not only of weighty grammatical and legal tomes but also of a "book of merry conceits"; and a number of other chantry priests possessed books of a more conventional sort.[89] A man of particularly remarkable attainments was William Corvehill, stipendiary priest in Much Wenlock (Salop). The parish register of his church describes him as having been

excellently and singularly expert in divers of the seven liberal sciences, and especially in geometry, not greatly by speculation but by experience; and few or none of handy craft but that he had a very good insight in them, as the making of organs, of a clock and chimes, and in carving, in masonry, and weaving of silk, and in painting.[90]

More representative of the generality of the chantry priests was Thomas Wyrall, incumbent of the chantry of St. Mary in the church of St. Michael, Spurriergate, York. Wyrall's learning, according to the commissioners, was "indifferent." Yet over and above his intercessory duties he found a number of ways to use his scribal and managerial talents for the benefit of the parish. From 1523 until the dissolution Wyrall supervised the repairs to the church fabric; he kept the parish accounts; and on frequent occasions he was mentioned in the churchwardens' records, which it was his duty to copy. None of these tasks required a great deal of learning, but the churchwardens indicated their gratitude for Wyrall's humble efforts by permitting him to occupy his chamber rent free.[91]

At a distance of more than four centuries, it is difficult to gauge the convictions and feelings of the chantry priests. One may assume that the vast majority of them were deeply if unthinkingly devoted to the intercessory doctrines and religious customs upon which their day-to-day activities were based. Their feelings may well have been symbolized by the outraged reactions of two of the Rotherham chantry priests to the local song school chaplain's rude denial of the existence of purgatory.[92] Other chantry priests also showed their opposition to the trends of the 1530s and 1540s. Some spread breathless rumors and uttered seditious words. Others, less articulate, silently expressed their unwillingness to collaborate with the Reformation by failing to expunge the prayers for the pope from their service books. Still others gave vent to their hostility more concretely by participating in the Pilgrimage of Grace or in the abortive Yorkshire rising of 1541.[93] One among the many cantarists opposed to the Reformation was Thomas Marshall, chantry priest of Holmpton in the East Riding, who was convicted in 1538 for misprision of treason for failing to inform the authorities of the activities of a woman whom he had recently confessed —she had been performing a "black fast" against the king and the duke of Norfolk.[94] In the early 1540s John Mores, the chaplain of the Eastbridge Hospital, Canterbury, was widely known for his antagonism to the reformers and their new-fangled heresies. He had reported one man for providing hospitality for such notorious Protestants as Richard Turner and John Bland; another local man had incurred his wrath for being a "reader of the Bible in corners"; and for good measure he had compiled a list "of certain that were thought to be the fautors of evil opinions and common readers of the Bible in service time."[95] Finally, the best that Sir Thomas Wentworth could say of one Ipswich chantry priest was that he had been "ever an enemy to the Word of God and never the lover or favorer therof."[96]

If this seemingly widespread attachment of the chantry priests to the old order was readily foreseeable, the fact that a number of cantarists were active in the Protestant cause may come as a minor surprise. Already in the second decade of the sixteenth century, Thomas Tykill, a London morrow-mass priest, was an industrious distributor of the vernacular Scriptures. In 1535 the curate of Winchcomb (Glos) gave glowing testimony concerning a local chantry priest who had been "to me a great helper in the Gospel." Ten years later two cantarists in Halifax and Pontefract were calmly serving as witnesses to vociferously Protestant wills. And in 1548 the chantry commissioners for Cornwall praised the cantarist-schoolmaster of Week St. Mary as "a great setter forth of God's Word." Also a nonconformist, though not necessarily in doctrine, was the Salisbury chantry priest John Fishepole, who in 1538 left his chantry to get married.[97] In the flux and confusion of these turbulent years, it is apparent that the incumbents of the intercessory institutions—conservative though they were, in general—were not fully united in the effort to stem the tides of change.

The chantry certificates seem to indicate that during this period the cantarists were rather more uniform in the excellence of their comportment. As a group these priests had never been noted for their tractable behavior, a fact which had led a number of founders to endow colleges in which the priests might be disciplined into a more seemly pattern of life.[98] But according to the certificates the behavior of the chantry priests was beyond reproach. The commissioners in fact reported only one cantarist in the four sample counties as being "of mean qualities and conditions."[99] And in the certificates for other shires which I have scanned, I have found only one other priest who was guilty of "ill behavior" and one who was "lunatic."[100] All the other priests—even those who had been active participants in the Northern Rebellion—are routinely commended as men of "good" or "honest qualities and conditions." Evidence from other sources suggests, however, that the behavior of the cantarists was often less exemplary than the chantry certificates indicate. Some were slackers of duty; some were sowers of discord. One was presented for enclosing land; another was hanged, drawn, and quartered "for clipping of gold." Some, such as Robert Downe, the wayward soul priest of Linsted (Kent), were individualists: Downe scandalized his parish by his activities as "a dicer, a carder, and a tennis player, [who] giveth ill example to many." And some, inevitably, succumbed to the temptations of the flesh. Indeed, Archbishop Cranmer, who had encountered one especially pathetic instance in Croydon, was moved to claim that it was common for the "poor purgatory priests [to] be taken in open adultery."[101] Cranmer was undoubtedly exaggerating—for polemical purposes. But the chantry certificates seem to have gone to the opposite extreme, glossing over (or failing to explore) the seamier side of sixteenth-century reality. The uniform approbation of the chantry commissioners is therefore no more credible than the overly condemnatory *comperta* of the monastic visitors of the previous decade.

The chantry certificates are also less than fully convincing in dealing with the pluralism and nonresidence of the chantry priests. Despite the strongly expressed will of most founders that the priests of their chantries have no other living which might deflect them from their primary calling of intercession,[102] for some time prior to the Reformation a number of cantarists were pluralists. It is hard to say how many. Papal dispensations for pluralism and nonresidence were granted until the establishment of the Faculty Office in November 1533; afterwards such dispensations were granted in England by and for Englishmen.[103]

They were granted in appreciable quantities: between 1535 and 1548 the Faculty Office issued letters relieving twenty-five cantarists from their foundations' requirements of residence and absolving them of pluralism.[104] It is noteworthy that these grants were primarily to the educated, well-connected priests—over half of them incumbents of chantries in cathedrals.

The evidence contained in the chantry certificates suggests that pluralism and nonresidence were vices which appealed likewise to many indifferently educated, poorly connected cantarists. In Essex, Warwickshire, and Wiltshire the commissioners discovered scattered cases of pluralism and nonresidence; in Yorkshire they uncovered these evils in considerable numbers. But the chantry certificates contain internal contradictions. In the parish of Topcliffe (N.R., Yorks), for example, the commissioners twice stated that the incumbents of two chantries had "no other promotions," whereupon they proceeded to list other livings which the same priests held in that very parish.[105] It appears, then, that the chantry commissioners often wrote "no other promotions" after the names of the cantarists in a routine fashion, without careful investigation, and that pluralism and nonresidence were far more widespread than the certificates indicate.[106]

Pluralism was more of an urban than a rural phenomenon. Well over half (twenty-four of forty-three) of the pluralist chantry priests of Yorkshire, for example, were active in the city of York, and in Wiltshire two of the four chantry pluralists were residents of Salisbury. The practice may be attributed in part to sheer clerical covetousness. Urban priests, especially cathedral cantarists, seem to have possessed to a greater degree than their rural counterparts the desire and the ability to accumulate lucrative benefices. Also, in an attempt to cope with the drastic decline in urban rents, numerous patrons and incumbents of urban livings had allowed, and even encouraged, chantry pluralism.[107] The decline of rental values for those livings, both parochial and chantry, whose endowments were based primarily upon urban lands were often disastrous. The fact that half of the rectories in the city of York were worth less than £4 7s. 8d. is ample proof of this dismal reality.[108] Patrons and incumbents had to adjust to this unfortunate state of affairs. In Coventry, for example, in the chantries with multiple priests' they first reduced the number of chantry priests. If the chantry's revenues could no longer adequately support even one priest, the patrons then diverted its remaining incomes to the augmentation of the living of some neighboring parish priest, on condition that he continue to pray for the soul of the chantry's founder.[109] In York, on the other hand, the patrons and incumbents of the urban chantries were more willing to fight diminishing incomes with pluralism. In the city and cathedral, eleven priests acquired additional chantries in order to enable them to subsist on a tolerable level (that is, to have an annual income of more than £3).[110] In addition, there were at least five priests who used the income of urban chantries to enable them to serve the cures of poverty-stricken parishes in the city.[111]

That both of these factors—clerical covetousness and the inadequate size of livings—were likewise present in the countryside explains why the amount of pluralism and nonresidence revealed by the Yorkshire chantry certificates and the "Tudor Crockford" is so considerable. In this one shire alone there were certainly forty-three, perhaps as many as fifty, chantry priests who were pluralists. Another ten chantry priests were not resident at their chantries. Furthermore, when we recall that the additional benefices held by the chantry priests were often other chantries, the number of chantry foundations affected by pluralism and nonresidence looms all the larger. There were thus at least sixty-nine, possibly as many as seventy-six Yorkshire chantries whose incumbents were pluralists or nonresident. By the eve of the dissolution, then, these twin evils had come to affect a substantial minority (between one-seventh and one-eighth) of the 523 Yorkshire chantries and stipendiary services. A careful examination of the episcopal registers, diocesan court records, episcopal visitations, and probate records in other dioceses would no doubt indicate that pluralism was more widespread than the chantry commissioners were able to detect.[112]

Finally, we must say a word about the collegiate churches. Several regional studies in recent years have reinforced the general impression that these institutions—if not usually in a disgraceful state—were not as a rule flourishing on the eve of the Reformation.[113] The collegiate churches of Essex, Warwickshire, Wiltshire, and Yorkshire were beset by many of the same maladies which afflicted their counterparts elsewhere. Some of them, such as the colleges of Halstead (Essex) and St. Edmund's, Salisbury, had originally been far more grandly conceived than their endowments would warrant, and they had been compelled to reduce the number of their personnel accordingly. The buildings of Beverley and Stratford-on-Avon were in such disrepair that they gave rise to adverse comment.[114] Fewer than one-half of the colleges in these four shires were providing educational facilities of any sort for the people of their localities.[115] And at least one collegiate priest was reported to have had traffic with a prostitute.[116]

Two colleges were in especially serious trouble in the 1530s because of perverse personalities among their leading clerics. At Warwick College, as Bishop Latimer bewailed, "the world doth wag" with rumors of intramural contentions. At the center of these was one of the canons, John Wattwood, whose colleagues in 1538 sent a deputation to Latimer to complain of the "wrongs and injuries" which Wattwood had been inflicting upon the college. On investigating their charges, Latimer found that Wattwood had gained sole possession of the three keys to the college's treasure house. Wattwood was also squandering the college's resources on extended trips to London while ostensibly transacting collegiate business. Meanwhile the college was facing a financial crisis, and the vicars choral and curate were forced to go about their duties without pay. Latimer, at his wit's end after several interviews with the recalcitrant canon, begged Cromwell for some disciplinary assistance.[117]

Cromwell was apparently reluctant to intervene, for in October Latimer was again appealing to him with renewed urgency. Could he not do something to bridle this canon who was purportedly a "lecher, a fighter, and a disquieter of his company"? Cromwell consented to an interview, in the course of which Wattwood turned belligerent, hurling accusations at Latimer, among others. But during the winter, as Cromwell continued to see Wattwood, the obstreperous fellow gradually mellowed. By the end of March 1539 the ardently Protestant William Benet could write to Latimer, rejoicing that Wattwood was "an honest new man" who was setting forth the royal and episcopal injunctions with diligence — even more so than were his fellow canons. Latimer, delighted by this "good change of renovation" in Wattwood, gave credit for the conversion to Cromwell, whom he praised for his efforts "to renew old bottles, and to . . . make them apt to receive new wine." We are unaccustomed to think of Thomas Cromwell as a pastoral figure; but perhaps his bluff touch was just what Wattwood needed. At any rate, by September 1539 Wattwood had become president of Warwick College. And in chorus with the canons, with whom he had previously had such a discordant relationship, he was doing all he could to dissuade his confessor Cromwell from forcing the college into a particularly disadvantageous exchange of lands.[118]

In an even worse state was the architecturally glorious collegiate church at Ripon. In this college almost all (five of seven) of the prebendaries were nonresident — as in most of the venerable colleges of the "classical" type. The burdens of leadership therefore weighed heavily upon the two canons who were on the scene.[119] And in Ripon, as in Warwick, it took only one strategically situated cleric to make a shambles of collegiate life. The culprit in this case was Christopher Dragley, canon residentiary and treasurer of the college. As a visitation of the minster by William Clyff, commissary to Archbishop Lee, revealed in 1533, Dragley had an objectionably casual attitude to the celebration of divine services.[120] As he mumbled his offices, he ambled to and fro in front of the high altar, wearing his hat. Administratively the incompetent and heavy-handed Dragley also left much to be desired. Refusing to seek the counsel of the rest of the chapter, or even of the other resident canon, he made appointments to chantries even before they became vacant and admitted vicars choral of obvious unsuitability. The college's common seal he kept in his personal custody. He even went so far as to keep the chapterhouse under lock and key, thus preventing the other members from consulting the collegiate statutes. Despite Clyff's injunctions, Dragley persisted in his ways. Tension was mounting within the college, and by 1537 Dragley seems to have been disintegrating morally. When Archbishop Lee himself visited the college he discovered that Dragley had wilfully been using the collegiate fabric funds to further his private business interests. Lee also detected a profusion of behavioral lapses on the part of both Dragley and the vicars choral. The following year Dragley was persuaded to surrender the office of treasurer, which he had mismanaged so badly, and for the good of the college to limit his residence to six weeks per year.[121] Despite Dragley's departure, the church was still in bad shape on the eve of the dissolution of the collegiate foundation. Several parts of its fabric were in a ruinous state, and the low corporate morale was reflected in a negligent performance of divine services. It would have been cold comfort to the people of Ripon to realize that conditions could deteriorate still further during the ensuing century.[122]

These weaknesses and abuses are disturbing. To some extent, however, they are offset by the fact that many collegiate churches were functioning normally and providing useful services. Although the prebends in certain colleges (such as Astley in Warwickshire and Hemingburgh in the East Riding of Yorkshire) were shriveled, those in Ripon, Beverley, and Howden were remunerative enough to be eminently use-

ful within the pre-Reformation network of patronage.[123] In Coventry
and Pontefract the colleges were making notable contributions to the
relief of paupers in their areas.[124] And in certain well-ordered instances such as Rotherham, the collegiate contribution to education,
which involved only certain of the colleges and was paltry enough in
relation to their total resources, was considerable.[125] Furthermore, it
could be argued that all the colleges—even those whose "enormities"
were particularly flagrant—were worth reforming. Such, at any rate,
was the opinion of the ambitious young Matthew Parker. Within three
years of his promotion to the mastership of Stoke-by-Clare (Suffolk),
Parker had given to the abuse-ridden college such strong leadership
and such well-considered statutes that it had become a model for
others.[126] With its provision for preaching, the teaching of grammar,
and the continual study of Scripture, it was symbolic of what the colleges might yet become.[127] But Henry VIII and his son had other ideas,
and by Easter of 1548 the colleges (including Stoke-by-Clare) had gone
the way of all intercessory institutions.

These then were the foundations and the men towards which Henry
VIII and the advisors of his son turned their attention in the mid-
1540s. The institutions were a varied lot. Some were flourishing, with
burgeoning rent rolls and able incumbents. Others, whose endowments were decaying and whose priests were nonresident or incapable,
had deteriorated to the point at which even the essential function of
each foundation—the intercession for the souls of its founders—was no
longer being performed. The men in whose hands lay the fate of these
institutions knew this—intuitively before the chantry surveys, and
thereafter from acres of data-filled parchment. They also were aware
that these intercessory institutions were performing, with varying
degrees of efficacy, a multitude of tasks which, though incidental to
their basic purpose, were often of real importance to the life of their
parishes. To these additional good deeds, incidental but important,
we must now turn.

2 / The Intercessory Priests' Practical Contributions

For more than four centuries the institutions which were threatened or swept away by the Henrician and Edwardian Chantries Acts have been the subject of a contentiously argued debate. Had these intercessory institutions contributed something essential and irreplaceable to the spiritual, educational, and social life of the realm? Was their dissolution therefore a disaster of major proportions for England?

From the outset there have been some who have answered these questions in resounding affirmatives. Many sixteenth-century Englishmen, from the eminent Sir Thomas More to obscure clergymen and innumerable common people, were deeply aggrieved by the threatened and actual loss of the prayers which had been provided by the intercessory institutions. Some contemporaries also noted angrily the baleful social effects of the dissolution. Bishop Edmund Bonner, preaching in 1555, bewailed the loss of the abbeys, colleges, and chantries, without whose openhanded charity "the hungry and needful people famish and cry out." Robert Crowley, a man who had little in common theologically with Bonner, with similar outrage lamented the heartrending condition of the poor, whose plight he blamed upon the dissolution of the hospitals. "Lord God!" he cried, ". . . in Turkey have I been, yet among those heathen none such cruelty have I seen." And another Protestant, Thomas Lever, fulminated against the damage which the chantries acts, which had ostensibly been designed to foster education, appeared to be doing to England's universities and grammar schools.[1]

These contemporary indictments have been echoed and amplified by more recent historians. A. F. Leach, for example, in a number of influential works criticized the chantries acts on the basis of his enthusiastic assessment of the educational contributions of some of the chantry priests. An even more severe critic was Father Philip Hughes, who was convinced that the chantry priests, in addition to carrying out their intercessory duties, were "generally" required to keep a grammar school. Cardinal Gasquet's estimation of the contribution of the intercessory institutions to the spiritual and social life of the realm was equally indulgent. The chantry priests, he contended vigorously, were the late medieval equivalents of the modern parish curates; their raison d'être was "to look after the poor of the parish, to visit the sick, and to assist in the functions of the parish church." In light of this roseate estimate of the contributions of the intercessory institutions to the life of pre-Reformation England, it is not surprising that some historians have, to say the least, thoroughly lost their tempers when contemplating the dissolution. As Augustus Jessopp put it, "It makes one sick to read the hateful story!"[2]

At no point, however, has this positive assessment of the intercessory institutions (with a correspondingly negative reaction to the dissolution) gone unchallenged. Erasmus with characteristic asperity declared that "debauched priests who do nothing but mumble masses are generally hated." Many of his English contemporaries were of like mind. The reforming preacher Robert Singleton denounced the chantry priests as "an idle sort of priests which be supported under the pretense of holiness." Archbishop Cranmer was convinced that they had been an unruly and adulterous lot. And the Protestant publicist Jean Veron was certain that the primary reason for the founding of chantries had been to enable the "holy shavelings" to "have a fat living by it."[3]

Many historians have been similarly unsympathetic in their view of the intercessory institutions. Far from claiming that the chantries were bountiful providers of curates and schoolmasters for the realm, Professor J. T. Rosenthal has asserted that "it serves no useful purpose to view them in terms of social utility." Canon H. Maynard Smith was convinced that the cantarists were frequently "pests in the parishes," while J. H. Blunt reported that they "clustered round the high altar and over-shadowed it; they crept along the aisles of the churches and elbowed out the congregations." Professor Norman Sykes saw the cantarists as "caterpillars of the Commonwealth," whose misdeeds contributed much to the coming of the Reformation, while R. S. Arrowsmith described them as a "class of clergy who brought little honour to the clerical order." This melancholy view has tended to prevent many historians from viewing the suppression of the intercessory institutions as in any sense cataclysmic. With Dr. A. L. Rowse, who has complacently regarded the dissolution as "a great saving" and "the extinction of a non-productive interest," we have come full circle from the indignant Dr. Jessopp.[4]

What in fact were the contributions of the intercessory institutions
to the fabric of life in pre-Reformation England? Were they performing vitally important functions, or were they "hives of drones (not of
bees, industriously advancing learning and religion)"?[5] This chapter
will contend that there are no easy answers to these questions. It will
note that some of the institutions were dormant and decayed on the
eve of the expropriation. It will also observe that other institutions —
perhaps the majority — were performing in a reasonably faithful manner the strictly intercessory services which their founders had intended.
But it will further demonstrate, on the other hand, that there was an
appreciable minority of institutions which was instrumental in meeting
the vital needs — spiritual, educational, and social — of the people who
lived nearby. As we proceed it will thus become clear that many com-
mentators have either optimistically overvalued or summarily dis-
counted the contributions of the intercessory institutions to the fabric
of English life.

Throughout the later Middle Ages, the primary motive behind the
founding of the chantries and their related institutions had been mani-
festly clear: by means of prayers, to secure relief for the souls of the
founder and others whom he might name, who were suffering in purgatory. There were, of course, other considerations which may have
motivated some founders. One of these was no doubt ostentation, for
to some extent the foundation of a chantry was the late medieval equivalent of the lavish modern funeral.[6] Rather more commendable were
the motives of those founders who specified that their foundations
should support such vital tasks as serving as assistants in the cure of
souls, teaching children, or presiding at the charitable doles to the
poor. One founder seems even to have been motivated by political concern, for he stipulated that his cantarist should pray daily for peace
between England and France. A final motive, which the antiquary
Leland may have construed in a moment of sardonic humor, was the
desire of an outraged parent to prevent his wealth from descending to
his "unthrifty children." To avoid this calamitous eventuality, he bequeathed his resources to the founding of eight chantries![7]

Real though these motives may have been at times, they were distinctly secondary to the overriding intent of securing prayers for the
souls of those who were suffering in purgatory. Of course, the Catholic
Church had not definitively formulated its teaching on purgatory prior
to the Council of Trent. And there were on the Continent writers, such

as St. Catherine of Genoa, who described purgatory as a place in which the happiness of the suffering souls steadily increased as the blot of their sins was gradually eradicated.[8] In England the view of purgatory, both popular and esoteric, was infinitely more forbidding. Most Englishmen, instructed by the graphically imaginative preaching which was prevalent in the late Middle Ages, had a lurid mental picture of the tortures which lay in store for the ordinary Christian after death. The souls in purgatory, according to a sermon of St. John Fisher, "be the prisoners of Almighty God, and lie there in prison for their debts. Great is the pains that they there endure." After recounting the excruciating pains—headache, toothache, gout, stone—which were a part of the ordinary experience of his hearers, Fisher warned that the "pains of purgatory be many times more grievous than any of these that I have rehearsed, or that ever were felt or thought in this world tofore." These pains, in fact, were fully as unbearable as those of hell. The only difference between the two, according to *A Lytell Boke, That Speketh of Purgatorye* (1534), was "that one shall have an end and that other none, for the pains of hell should never cease."[9] Mitigating this harrowing outlook somewhat was the promise that the quick could come to the aid of the dead by "procuring of masses to be said for them, or prayers of devout persons, or fastings and willful pains, sufferings of our own bodies, or doing of alms and charitable deeds." By these means it might be possible to moderate the intensity of the flames tormenting individual souls and to shorten the time of their "wonderful great" tribulation. Some founders went so far as to speak of this process rather incongruously as the "purchasing of grace."[10]

In light of the terrifying prospect of life after death and of the inviting possibility of its amelioration, it is easy to understand the readiness of late-medieval Englishmen to multiply the number of masses and suffrages through the endowing of chantries. They were fearful—fearful of "the manifold displeasure of our Redeemer and Judge," fearful of the purgatory to which He would inevitably condemn them, and fearful of a breakdown in the intercessory arrangements, which might prolong their posthumous suffering. If the monasteries were to be dissolved some social services would no doubt be discontinued; but more disruptive would be the impact of the cessation of masses and prayers upon the souls in purgatory.[11] Purgatory—that was the initial impetus underlying the foundation of the chantries as well as of most other medieval institutions. On this point contemporary observers, of otherwise incompatible attitudes toward Catholic institutions and dogma, could agree. "All they [the churchmen] have," William Tyndale asserted, "they have received in the name of purgatory . . . and on that foundation be all their bishoprics, abbeys, colleges, and cathedral churches built." Cardinal William Allen concurred. "This doctrine [of prayer for souls in purgatory]," he contended, "founded all bishoprics, builded all churches, raised all oratories, instituted all colleges, endued all schools, maintained all hospitals, set forward all works of charity and religion, of what sort soever they be. Take away the prayers and practice for the dead, either all these monuments must fall, or else they must stand against the first founders' will and meaning."[12] In comparison to purgatory, all other motives for chantry foundation, however real, were secondary.

The priests of the intercessory institutions were not, however, "mere living prayer-wheels to extract the well-to-do departed from the purgatory they had no doubt amply earned."[13] Many cantarists carried out certain more practical chores as well: assisting in the cure of souls, teaching local children, and relieving the poor. At times some founders had stipulated such supplementary duties as administering "the sacraments in urgent cases in absence of the vicar" to the inhabitants of the parish. Other founders were especially interested in providing educational facilities or poor relief for needy parishes. In some parishes the parishioners themselves took concerted action to provide endowments or stipends for the priests or schoolmasters whom they urgently desired.[14] Many intercessory priests, however, performed good works even when the foundation deeds of their institutions did not specifically require it. Some of them may have done so to ward off boredom — because their intercessory duties simply did not take up enough of their time.[15] Others did so in response to particularly pressing needs in their parishes.

The nonintercessory task which most occupied the time of the chantry priests was assistance with the cure of souls. It was not, of course, that they were generally (as Cardinal Gasquet claimed) the "assistant priests" or "curates" of their parishes.[16] Limited by their prior commitment to a regimen of intercession for the dead and by the parochial incumbents' jealous protection of their own fees,[17] the cantarists could not have spent all their waking hours in ministering to the spiritual needs of the parishioners. Though there must have been many who, loyal to their chief calling, contributed little to the religious life of their parishes, there is evidence that some cantarists were hearing confessions, saying "mass in my stead at the high altar" and officiating at "matins or evensong for me."[18] Furthermore, the chantry certificates of 1546 and 1548 make it abundantly clear that numerous chantry priests, above and beyond the routine of services laid out in their foundation ordinances, were giving assistance in the cure of souls which was extremely useful to parochial clergy and parishioners alike.

Because only imperfect and incomplete series of chantry certificates have survived — and even these are uneven in quality — it is impossible to be precise in defining the parochial contributions of the intercessory priests. Which commissioners, for example, should one believe: those of 1546, who reported that the chantry of St. James, Catterick (N.R., Yorks) was necessary "to pray for all Christian souls and to help in the choir," or those of 1548, who asserted that the "necessity thereof is to minister sacraments" (i.e., to assist in the cure of souls)?[19] And what of the testimony of the parish priests, cantarists, and respected parishioners, some or all of whom provided the information for the commissioners' reports? It is probable that the reliability of some of the certificates was marred by bias of these local witnesses, who hoped that their local chantry endowments might be selected for continuance as essential services, even if the real contribution of these institutions was in fact only marginal. Such a pious perversion of evidence may in its turn have been abetted by the haste, ignorance, and occasional collusion of the chantry commissioners themselves, thus further diminishing the credibility of their certificates. In parishes where there were few communicants and a generous supply of resident priests, the commissioners' claims that the "necessity of the chantry is to minister sacraments" do seem exaggerated.[20] In other parishes the statements of the chantry commissioners were rejected by Sir Walter Mildmay and Robert Keilway, whose assignment it was to scrutinize and supervise the continuance of essential parochial, educational, and social services of the newly dissolved institutions. They swept aside the plea of the chapelry of South Cowton in the parish of Gilling (N.R., Yorks) by stating, in flat contradiction to the chantry commissioners, that "there is ministered no sacraments &c. and they have in the same parish ministers enough." With the parish of Malmesbury (Wilts) they were equally brusque. When the inhabitants pleaded that their town numbered 860 communicants and had "no priest to help the vicars in administration of the sacraments saving the said stipendiary priests," Mildmay scrawled laconically in the margins of the brief certificate, "the vicars may do it well enough."[21]

In the opinion of some historians, the very possibility that some chantry commissioners were either perfunctory or amiably unseeing in their researches, thereby enabling local men to garb their neighboring cantarists in the cloak of pastoral indispensability, is sufficient reason to disqualify the chantry certificates as a source of insight into the parochial activities of the chantry priests.[22] Yet these documents by their very nature — and with their acknowledged limitations — provide valid and illuminating evidence for the close study of the parochial life of pre-Reformation England. In the first place, the composition of the commissions charged to survey the intercessory institutions guarded against an overly indulgent treatment. The commissions of all shires were made up of locally prominent gentlemen, who may occasionally have exerted their influence to shield particularly favored local institutions.[23] But it is likewise probable that those same gentry were quite as interested in locating the most desirable chantry properties for private purchase as they were in shielding them from confiscation. In addition, on the commissions there was invariably a liberal sprinkling of sharp-eyed Augmentations men. It was usually these men, rather than the more ornamental gentlemen and bishops, who did the actual work in compiling the chantry certificates. On occasion, in fact, the linguistic formality of the documents disappeared as their recorders, often the particular surveyors of the Court of Augmentations for the various shires, reverted into the first person singular.[24]

In the second place, in the course of compiling the surveys the chantry commissioners came into contact with each individual parish. They did not, of course, undertake the impossible task of visiting each of the over nine thousand English parishes in person. Instead, they established themselves for several days at a time in each of a number of the larger towns within their areas of purview. In Essex, for example, their itineraries included Braintree, Chelmsford, and Halstead, while in Somerset — Bruton and Taunton. In such towns they received the parish priests, cantarists, masters of colleges and hospitals, churchwardens, and substantial parishioners who comprised the deputations of the surrounding parishes. The commissioners perused the draft certificates which the deputations had written in answer to the questions contained in the visitation injunctions;[25] they examined the foundation deeds and other documents of the intercessory institutions in the respective parishes; and they compared their findings with the Henrician chantry certificates and the digests of the *Valor Ecclesiasticus* which they carried with them.[26] If doubtful points arose, they subjected the deputations to a "strait examination" upon their "corporal oaths."[27] On occasions when parish delegations sought to inconvenience or mislead the commissioners through failing to respond to their summons or through presenting false witness, the chantry commissioners could be persistent and determined in their efforts to counter these ploys. The 1548 commissioners for Gloucestershire, for example, incredulous of the initial report of the deputation from Arlingham, ordered eight "of the best and most substantial men" of that parish "to come and appear before us in three or four sundry places in the shire before we would receive their answer."[28] Such exertions to secure accuracy and completeness were probably exceptional. Nevertheless, the commissioners generally appear to have made every reasonable effort to benefit, albeit critically, from the expertise of both priests and laymen about the state of the intercessory institutions in their parishes.

The usefulness of the chantry certificates is further indicated by the manifest quality of the documents themselves. The quantity of information which they contain is almost always impressive; occasionally it is astonishing. It was the assigned task of the commissioners to compile, after the model of the *Valor Ecclesiasticus,* endless listings of the intercessory institutions along with the essential data concerning their endowments and incumbents. The amassing of this routine information would of itself have been a substantial administrative achievement. The letters of commission[29] do not, however, reveal that the Edwardian government (and possibly the Henrician government as well) issued detailed instructions to the commissioners urging them to probe even more deeply into the state of these institutions. In Surrey and Sussex, for example, they were to inquire "what number of housling people be within the said towns or parishes and how many other priests besides the parson and vicar been founded there for the assistance in serving the cure and what necessity there is of more priests to remain there and the causes of the necessities."[30] Many of the commissioners seem to have complied with alacrity. Indeed, their investigative zeal frequently prompted them gratuitously to write elaborate and illuminating memoranda on the function of the chantries in their parishes, the geographical distribution of the parishioners, and the location of such chapels of ease as might be scattered throughout the parish. In addition to supplying the required information about the ages, abilities, and other promotions of the cantarists, the certificates frequently indicate the identity of the parish priest, the value of his living, whether he was resident, and the number (as well as the names) of the chaplains whom he had hired for assistance in serving the cure.[31] The certificates occasionally report the hours of divine service, the category of persons for whom the service was provided, and the number of priests who were available to minister sacraments. Frequently they provide graphic descriptions of the physical impediments (swollen streams, mountainous terrain, and long distances), with which the parochial clergy had to contend in their cure of souls. In short, they contain information which illuminates as brightly as possible some of the darker recesses of pre-Reformation religious life on the parish level.

However fallible the chantry commissioners may occasionally have been in their reporting, the evidence available four centuries after the fact indicates that their records were usually as accurate, and their generalizations as conscientious, as possible. In the case of numerous parishes the chantry commissioners made no claims of any assistance by the intercessory clergy in the cure of souls. In Wiltshire, where the chantry certificates listed sixty-five chantry, stipendiary, and guild priests, the commissioners mentioned only twelve as having assisted in the cure of souls. Similarly, the Essex commissioners presented only twenty-seven of fifty-seven intercessory priests as having participated in pastoral activities. On occasion, the commissioners stated baldly that a given intercessory institution was "of no great necessity."[32] And even in those parishes where it seems unlikely, on the basis of other information which the commissioners supplied, that the cantarists were assisting in the parochial chores, we must not be too quick in discounting the assertions of the commissioners that they were helping "the curates in ministering of sacraments."[33] There may, in fact, have been real needs in the parishes (such as the advanced age or indisposition of the incumbent) which the commissioners failed to mention. In short, the commissioners' reports in general have the unmistakable ring of truth.

There are, in addition, a number of surviving sources which enable us to check the reliability of the information provided by the chantry certificates. One of these, a 1548 episcopal visitation of the Archdeaconry of Richmond, lists the clerical inhabitants of each parish and entirely corroborates statements by the chantry commissioners about priests whom the parochial incumbents had hired to assist with the cure of souls. In the parish of Burneston, for example, where the commissioners had noted the vicar, the cantarist of Leeming Chapel, and "one other priest at the finding of the vicar there, called Henry Metcalfe," the episcopal visitors concurred, likewise naming Metcalfe.[34] If those who presented evidence to the chantry commissioners had hoped to present as bleak a picture of local conditions as possible, it is curious that they should have supplied so detailed and accurate an account of these parochial chaplains.[35] The *Valor Ecclesiasticus,* although compiled from ten to twelve years before the chantry certificates, also bears witness to their reliability. This great survey, though less inclusive than the chantry certificates in its listing of the smaller institutions, provides a test of the reliability of the commissioners' information about parochial livings. In instance after instance it vindicates the accuracy of the chantry certificates.[36]

The testimony of the commissioners responsible for the continuance of useful functions of the dissolved institutions—Sir Walter Mildmay and Robert Keilway—provides a significant and reliable supplement to the certificates. Although Mildmay and Keilway rejected the hardship appeals of some parishes, they gave tacit recognition to the parochial contributions of numerous chantry priests. In our four shires, for example, they ordered that seventy-eight curates, who had apparently been supported in the past by the intercessory institutions, continue to function as assistants in the cure of souls in their parishes, and that they be supported by governmental stipends (Table 2.1).[37] At first glance this proportion—8½ percent of the 913 intercessory priests in these counties—may seem insignificant. However, it is important to recall that in mid-1548 the English government found itself in desperate financial straits and was therefore in no position to subsidize any priests who might have been useful though not essential in the cure of souls in their parishes. Nor could it justify supporting ex-cantarist curates when particularly well-heeled parishes or munificently endowed rectories might themselves foot the bill.[38] This governmental parsimony forced Mildmay and Keilway to be so circumspect in ordering the continuance of priests as to create some cases of real hardship, which had to be rectified in later years.[39] Furthermore, the curates whom the commissioners were now appointing were to assist with the services of an unashamedly Protestant Church of England. Under this

Table 2.1. Priests of intercessory institutions and the cure of souls.

A. Providing essential assistance in parish churches / chapels of ease

County	Chantry priests	Stipendi- aries	Guild priests	Collegiate priests	Total
Essex	8 / 3	1 / 4	2 / 1	0 / 0	11 / 8
Warwicks	5 / 1	0 / 1	8 / 5	2 / 2	15 / 9
Wilts	10 / 0	3 / 2	3 / 0	0 / 0	16 / 2
Yorks					
East Riding	6 / 6	0 / 1	0 / 1	12 / 1	18 / 9
North Riding and					
York City	13 / 9	1 / 8	0 / 0	0 / 0	14 / 17
West Riding	28 / 23	14 / 21	2 / 0	7 / 0	51 / 44
Total	112	56	22	24	214

B. Selected for continuance and to receive stipends to assist in parish churches / chapels of ease

County	Chantry priests	Stipendi- aries	Guild priests	Collegiate priests	Total
Essex	1 / 1	0 / 0	1 / 0	0 / 0	2 / 1
Warwicks	0 / 0	0 / 0	1 / 2	2 / 2	3 / 4
Wilts	1 / 0	1 / 2	0 / 0	0 / 0	2 / 2
Yorks	13 / 23	1 / 9	1 / 1	14 / 2	29 / 35
Total	39	13	6	20	78

Sources: Essex: E 301/19/5, 8, 9, 10, 18, 21, 24, 25, 26, 34, 36a, 40; E 301/20/7, 11, 13, 15, 23, 24, 31, 34, 37, 41, 44, 50, 54; E 301/83, mm. 3, 5; E 315/30, f. 44; E 315/67, ii, ff. 453-454; DL 38/4; E.R.O. D/ACV 1, ff. 12v, 23; D/AEV 2, f. 59v; Morant, *History*, I, ii, 198, 233, and II, 522; Richard Newcourt, *Repertorium Ecclesiasticum Parochiale Londonense,* 2 vols. (London, 1708-1710), II, 464; Elizabeth Ogbourne, *The History of Essex* (London, 1814), 215.

Warwicks: E 301/31/19, 23, 25, 28, 29, 31, 38, 41, 42, 44, 45, 47; E 301/53/4b, 20, 21, 23, 54, 55, 56, 57; E 301/57/23; E 319/2, 6; SP 1/219, f. 141 (*L.P.,* XXI, 966); B.L. Harleian MS. 594, f. 166v; ibid., MS. 595, ff. 212, 212v; *C.P.R., Edward VI,* II, 342-343; Sir William Dugdale, *The Antiquities of Warwickshire,* 2nd ed., 2 vols. (London, 1730), II, 882; *V.C.H., Warwickshire,* IV, 91.

Wilts: E 301/58/11-13, 14-18, 20, 28, 29, 34, 38, 39, 43, 44, 45, 54, 56, 71, 131; E 301/101, mm. 2, 2v-3, 3v, 4, 4v, 5, 5v, 8v-9; E 319/1; E 321/45/29; *Valor,* II, 138; Diocesan Record Office, Salisbury, Bishops' Act Book, 1550-1558, ff. 55, 110; J.J. Daniell, *The History of Warminster* (London, 1879), 206-212, 216.

Yorks: DL 1/58, f. 65; DL 42/135, ff. 124, 125; E 36/258, f. 16; E 117/14/106; E 159/338, m. 109; E 178/2552, mm. 10, 15, 17, 18-20; E 178/4752, f. 2; E 301/102, mm. 4, 4v, 5v, 6; E 301/103/4, 6, 9, 10, 12, 13, 14, 37, 39, 46, 47, 54, 58, 60, 64, 70,

83, 91, 105-106; E 301/119, mm. 1, 2-3, 4, 4v, 5, 6v, 7, 7v, 8, 8v; E 315/105, ff. 175v, 177v-178, 192v-193; E 315/123, f. 239; E 315/520, f. 24; E 319/22; E 321/19/61; E 321/35/35; E 321/36/22; LR 6/122/1, m. 39v; LR 6/122/2, mm. 29-29v; Borthwick Institute, MS. R VI A 5, ff. 11v, 17, 23v, 37v, 39v, 47, 49, 59v, 89, 90, 91v; MS. R VI A 6, f. 8v; B.L. Harleian MS. 594, ff. 103, 104, 105, 107; Y.M.L., Reg. Heath, f. 120v; Torre MS. L1(9), 1019-1020, 1056; ibid., L1(10), 861-863; *Y.C.C.*, I, 62-63, 71, 83, 88-89, 90-92, 96, 97-98, 105, 106, 115, 127, 128, 138, 140, 143-144, 151-153, 164, 165, 169-170, 174, 175-181, 188-189, 192, 193, 205-208, 209; ibid., II, 213, 216-217, 219-220, 221, 222, 227, 228, 230-231, 232-233, 235-236, ᴢ37, 240-241, 243-246, 247, 248, 250, 251-252, 253, 258-259, 260, 261, 264, 265-266, 266-268, 269-270, 272-277, 280, 282-283, 285-288, 293-299, 303, 307-314, 320-321, 341-342, 352-353, 355, 365, 375, 378-380, 385-386, 389, 391-393, 394, 395-396, 397, 398, 399-400, 401, 402-403, 404, 405, 406, 407, 408-409, 411, 413, 414-418, 420, 421-424, 454-455, 463, 469-470, 471-472, 475, 477, 479, 481-482, 487, 492, 495, 497, 499-500, 501, 506-507, 508, 512, 513-514, 515, 517, 520-521, 528-536; *C.P.R., Edward VI,* II, 36, 268; ibid., III, 261, 331; ibid., *Mary,* I, 171-172; ibid., *Elizabeth I,* III, 475; ibid., V, 130, 206, 332; *Y.A.J.,* 14 (1898), 394, 396, 404, 409, 414, 417, 419, 420, 430; *Y.A.J.,* 38 (1952-1955), 204, 232; Y.A.S.R.S., 71 (1928), 39, 49, 197-198, 213-214; ibid., 72 (1929), 70, 129; ibid., 75 (1929), 91, 152; W. P. Baildon, *Baildon and the Baildons* (St. Catherine's Press, n.d.), 170-173; John Ecton, *Thesaurus Rerum Ecclesiasticarum,* ed. Browne Willis (London, 1754), 523, 529, 531, 535; George Fox, *History of Pontefract* (Pontefract, 1827), 278-279; Joseph Hunter, *Hallamshire,* ed. Alfred Gatty (London, 1869), 239-242, and *South Yorkshire,* 2 vols. (London, 1828-1831), II, 125, 294, 452-456, 459; George Lawton, *Collectio Rerum Ecclesiasticarum de Dioecesi Eboracensi* (London, 1842), 53, 57, 66, 79, 95, 96, 100, 141, 157-159, 175, 182, 189, 229, 230, 265-266, 287, 290, 291, 306, 417, 456, 459, 461-462, 470, 519, 528, 556, 562, 563, 572, 582; A. F. Leach, ed., *Early Yorkshire Schools,* 2 vols., Y.A.S.R.S., 27 (1899), 33 (1903), II, 32, 33, 39; A.D.H. Leadman, "Hazelwood Chapel," *Y.A.J.,* 13 (1895), 537-539, 541; John Lister, "The Old Free Chapels in the Parish of Halifax," *Halifax Antiquarian Soc. Papers and Reports,* 1909, 43-45; Harry Speight, *Romantic Richmondshire* (London, 1897), 449; W. Thompson, *Sedbergh, Garsdale and Dent* (Leeds, 1892), 228; Walker, *Wakefield,* I, 223-225, 327-328, 339-340; Thomas D. Whitaker, *The History and Antiquities of the Deanery of Craven,* 3rd ed. (Leeds and London, 1878), 419-420, and *Loides and Elmete* (Leeds and Wakefield, 1816), 97.

---

new dispensation the sermon — not the sacraments — was emerging as the center of worship.[40] Mildmay and Keilway must therefore have calculated that fewer clergymen would be necessary than had been essential to the proper functioning of the old system. And whereas the cantarists, who were bound by their foundation ordinances to a regimen of intercession, had been able to devote only a portion of their time to parochial chores, as assistant curates these same priests would be able to direct their full attention to the spiritual welfare of their flocks. As a result, a smaller number of ministers would be needed than had been the case under the Catholic system. To a large extent, the decisions of Mildmay and Keilway authenticate the testimony of the chantry certificates as to the parochial role of the chantry priests. To take one random example, in Devizes (Wilts) there were three cantarists who according to the chantry certificates were helping the parson "in administration of the Word of God and sacraments" to the nine hundred communicants in the parish. The commissioners for continuance were sufficiently impressed by their contribution to the life of this parish to appoint one of them to be an assistant "to help to serve the cure."[41] We do the chantry priests a disservice if we take their contribution to the cure of souls less seriously than Mildmay and Keilway obviously did.

The evidence of the chantry certificates, then, establishes incontrovertibly the fact that many intercessory priests were active in the cure of souls, but it offers no tidy summations for calculating the approximate proportion of the total number of priests who were useful in this manner. Such an estimate can perhaps be arrived at by a "parish reconstitution," which attempts to visualize the actual situations in which the intercessory priests were working. It is based not only on the fundamentals of the chantry certificates but also on the random data which they contain (number of communicants, physical dimensions of the parish, geographical conditions within the parish, number of priests to serve the cure), as well as the visitation and other episcopal records and the evidence of the commissioners for continuance. In evaluating these sources, a primary criterion must be that the chantry or continuance certificates state specifically that a priest aided the parochial incumbent or that he assisted in the administration of the sacraments. This criterion will give a conservative coloration to our numerical estimates, inasmuch as many chantry certificates (especially those of 1546) were only slightly interested in the parochial contributions of the cantarists. The fact that for several shires the chantry certificates are incomplete will also tend to lower our figures. Nevertheless, without contemporary testimony it is unjustifiable to assume that a chantry priest was active in the cure of souls simply because he lived in a populous parish where there was obvious need. Many factors may have worked to prevent his involvement: the stipulations of his chantry's foundation deeds; his own age or ill health; or the eagerness of the parson to maintain his monopoly of parish fees.

A second, and arbitrary, criterion for designating a particular cantarist as essential to the cure of souls in his parish is a ratio of four hundred communicants to each available priest. Where the ratio was lower than this it is unlikely that an intercessory priest was performing an *essential* parochial function. The parochial documents seem to imply that such a ratio would impose a reasonably demanding but not impossibly burdensome load upon a parish priest with cure of souls. The commissioners for continuance seem to have been convinced that this was a viable ratio, for it was the lowest communicant:priest ratio which they used at least twice in the four sample shires. Elsewhere in the realm, the commissioners opted for a similar ratio. For example, in Edlesborough (Bucks) the commissioners declared the cantarist to be "of no great necessity for they [the 300 communicants] have a vicar to serve them." In Kempsey (Worcs), on the other hand, the commissioners decided that one priest was not sufficient because it was "a great parish" and had four hundred housling people.[42] Although the commissioners did occasionally establish ratios of less than 400:1,[43] their general tendency was to establish somewhat higher ratios. In Rotherham, as also in Scarborough, they ordered the continuance of three priests, thus establishing a ratio of 667:1, and in Tewkesbury they continued a single intercessory priest, for a ratio of 800:1.[44] Such a ratio, however, was getting dangerously high. In Sheffield a ratio of 1,000:1 caused such "great discomfort . . . by reason of the great decay of . . . godly service" that the crown was forced to restore two stipendiary priests to the parish, thus creating a more tolerable communicant: priest ratio of 500:1.[45]

For purposes of my analysis, I have adhered to the slightly lower ratio of 400:1, and have allowed exceptions only in cases in which a special geographical condition was present. If, for example, a chapel of ease was farther than one-half mile from the parish church, I have allowed for the utility of a chantry priest who was by himself ministering sacraments for the benefit of fewer than four hundred communicants. My only departure from this half-mile rule has been in the case of a few chapels in larger towns or cities which could claim to be serving those who were suffering from plague or pestilence.

From the reconstitution along these lines of the structure of clerical services in the parishes of the four sample shires, an interesting picture of the involvement of the intercessory priests in the cure of souls has emerged. In brief, of the 913 priests who were being supported by the intercessory foundations in the 1540s, at least 214 (slightly less than one-quarter) were making important contributions to the cure of souls in their parishes (Table 2.1). For most of these priests, of course, the responsibility for the cure of souls was distinctly secondary to their intercessory duties and completely voluntary in nature. It is therefore not appropriate to refer to even this fraction of the intercessory priests as the "curates" of pre-Reformation England. Nevertheless, this parish-by-parish analysis of sixteenth-century materials has demonstrated that many cantarists were actively involved in the cure of souls.[46] The following pages will provide examples of the types of situations in which the cantarists were most useful.

In many parishes, to be sure, the intercessory institutions contributed nothing to the cure of souls. In some, where there were already enough well-remunerated resident clergy, there was no need. Because the English parochial "system" was a most unsystematic accretion over the centuries, the number of available parochial clergy, like the level of clerical income and the geographic and demographic size of the parish, fluctuated from parish to parish. In some the parochial incumbent had hired a number of curates to assist him in his pastoral duties. In Helmsley (N.R., Yorks), for example, the vicar had hired three curates to assist in serving the cure, while in Plymouth, a much larger parish of twenty-five hundred communicants, the vicar could afford to hire only two priests to help him. In still other parishes, such as Todwick (W.R., Yorks) and Hampton Lovett (Worcs), there were so few housling people (fifty-six and eighty respectively) that the incumbent might well serve the parish by himself with no additional assistance.[47] And for such parishes as these, it is notable that the chantry certificates make no claim for the necessity of the chantry priests to help with the cure of souls. Their function was obviously purely intercessory.

In other parishes the clerical shortage could become acute. In some parishes this was the result of a dense concentration of population. Elsewhere, especially in the moorland and mountainous sections of the West and North Ridings, the parishes tended to be geographically expansive and full of topographical impediments to the ongoing work of the Church. In still other parishes the poverty of the incumbent prevented him from hiring adequate clerical assistance. In all of these situations there was considerable likelihood that the intercessory priests might find themselves devoting their spare hours to the cure of souls.

The densely populated parishes, many of which included the newer and more rapidly growing urban centers such as Birmingham and Halifax, presented special problems. The incumbents were required, for example, to ensure the availability of divine service to all their parishioners despite the fact that their parish churches were sometimes not large enough to accommodate the entire parish. They also had to make allowances for a variety of schedules according to which the inhabitants lived and worked. In parishes of this type, the incumbents therefore turned time and again to the intercessory priests for assistance. In Doncaster it was the chantry priests who provided "mass at five o'clock in the morning, six o'clock, seven o'clock, eight o'clock, nine o'clock, ten o'clock, as well for the inhabitants of the said town as other strangers passing through the same." In towns such as Chelmsford, Derby, Halifax, Newark, and Pontefract similar arrangements were made for chantry masses to be said at special hours for the convenience of the townsfolk. And in the parish of St. Denys, York, "the advice of the parishioners" as well as concern "for their commodity as traveling people" persuaded a chantry priest to say his daily mass between four and five o'clock in the morning rather than just before noon as had been his custom.[48]

It was uncommon for laymen to receive communion at these services. In fact, most lay folk communicated only once in the year, at Easter. Since all those who communicated were required recently to have been shriven by a priest, a tremendous amount of priestly effort — both hearing confession and administering the sacrament — tended to be compressed into the Lenten season.[49] When thus overtaxed, the parochial incumbent and his assistants frequently turned to the intercessory priests for help. As a result, in Doncaster the vicar, his curate, and the seven chantry priests with some difficulty were able to hear the confessions of the two thousand communicants "from the beginning of Lent unto Palm Sunday, and to minister the blessed sacrament all the said week." In the parish of St. Michael Bassishaw, London, the incumbent and the priests from the Guildhall College similarly had their hands full coping with "the number of the parishioners and daily accidents among us," to say nothing of the press of communicants at Easter. In Birmingham the three chaplains of the Guild of the Holy Cross were accustomed to aid the parochial clergy in ministering sacraments and sacramentals to the two thousand householders and their families at Easter time; even the commissioners conceded that all of the priests working in concert "be not sufficient."[50]

In densely populated parishes the intercessory priests could be helpful in still other ways. In Bury St. Edmunds a cantarist regularly said mass "in the chapel of the jail Sundays and festival days," while in Worcester a cantarist was always standing ready "to ride and go late and early when need shall require in visitation."[51] In several towns the

chantries provided the services of a preacher, while in York their income supplemented the meager earnings of poorly endowed parish
clergy.[52] One parsonage there was in fact "so little worth no man will
take it," and the cantarist was serving the cure by himself.[53] Also significant were the urban chapels, which provided a refuge for either the
healthy or the diseased in time of the plague, and which were frequently manned by intercessory priests. In Doncaster, Wakefield, and
Stratford-on-Avon these chapels served "to do divine service . . . in the
times of the plague for the sick people thither to resort, that the rest of
the parishioners may come to their parish church without danger of
infection." In Coventry and Birmingham, on the other hand, it was
those who wished "to avoid ill airs and the press" who frequented these
chapels.[54]

The contribution of the chantry, stipendiary, and guild priests to
the parochial life of the heavily populated parish was significant. Not
all of the intercessory priests in an urban parish would surely assist with
the cure of souls. In Wakefield, for example, which in many ways was
a typical large parish, six of the fourteen intercessory priests seem
never to have turned aside from their primary duties on behalf of their
benefactors. But the reliance of the vicar of Wakefield and his two
hired *capellani* upon the assistance of the eight priests who did participate was obvious, and the commissioners for continuance responded
by appointing two ex-cantarists to continue in the parish as assistants
to the cure.[55]

In the parishes which presented special geographical difficulties to
the incumbent clergy, the intercessory institutions could be quite as
useful as they were in the densely populated parishes. In an age when
roads were bad and most people traveled by foot, certain topographical realities—substantial distances, swollen streams, flooded areas,
and mountainous terrain—could present formidable obstacles to the
cure of souls. There were crucial moments in the cycle of life, according to late medieval Catholic belief, when the presence of a priest was
imperative. The spiritual and physical consequences of his absence, no
matter how cogent the extenuating circumstances, were staggering.
The inhabitants of Henley-in-Arden (Warwicks), whose chapelry was
separated by one mile and one brook from the parish church of Woot-
ton Wawen, expressed their fears eloquently in a petition to Henry
VIII. In the winter, they asserted, the abundance of rain frequently
caused the brook to overflow to such an extent that the "marvelous

foul way" to the parish church became totally impassable. "What great danger and peril it would be . . . both in body and soul . . . ," they went on, "if it should chance any child to be born into this world or any other person to be sore vexed with sickness (the said water then being overflowed) [so that] they should perish before they should have the sacraments and sacramentals of the holy Church be ministered unto them."[56]

At times the geographical difficulty might simply be one of size, especially in the north of England, where many of the parishes were massive. Elsewhere too, as in Tanworth (Warwicks), where 104 families were spread out within a circumference of no less than twenty miles, the vicar found himself hard pressed to minister to the parishioners. In "time of plague or other sickness," the two chantry priests of the parish came to his aid, without which "many of them [the parishioners] should perish without ministration." And in the substantial mining parish of Newland (Glos), the stipendiary priest assisted the parish priest by going "from one smith to another and from one mining pit to another within the same parish twice every week to say them gospels."[57]

In some parishes the problem of size was compounded by such impediments as substantial rivers which separated one part of the parish from the parish church and made it difficult for the priest to reach a segment of his flock. In the parishes of Ilkley and Ripley (each situated on a river in the West Riding of Yorkshire), the intercessory priests were the ones who said divine service and ministered sacraments in the parish church while the curate was bringing spiritual comfort to some of his more distant parishioners. In Ripley, a parish of 164 households, this was especially necessary "for so much as the parish is of great circuit, and one great river, called Nidd, running and passing through the same, so that many times the curate, being forth of visitation in some part of the said parish, cannot come home to the said church by the space of two days, by reason of the let of the said river at such times when as there be great flood."[58]

Many large parishes with formidable geographical obstructions to the cure of souls could boast one or more chapels of ease, founded perhaps by a harried priest, or a pious lay benefactor, or even by the parishioners themselves. In the chapels founded by parish priests, which often constituted a part of the parochial living, the chaplains were hired by and responsible to the incumbent. In chapels founded by lay benefactors or local parishioners, on the other hand, the incumbents were usually either chantry chaplains or stipendiary priests, who would not be directly under the supervision of the parish priest. Before founding a new chapel of ease, a founder was therefore required to obtain the consent of the parish incumbent, who, to save for himself useful sources of revenue, often stipulated that no burials (which brought him a goodly fee) might take place in the chapelry.[59] Taken together, these chapels of ease, strategically located throughout numerous large parishes, made a significant contribution to the cure of souls in particularly isolated regions of the country.

The geographical conditions which necessitated their services were many and various. Early sixteenth-century Englishmen had given little thought to problems of drainage, and as a result large areas of the countryside lay inundated in the winter. This flooding, which affected many thoroughfares and made access to the parish churches difficult, led to the founding of some chapels with intercessory priests as chaplains. In the early fifteenth century a pious founder endowed a new collegiate chapel in Knowle (Warwicks), whose priests were to serve those who "shall not be able in winter to come to their parish church" of Hampton-in-Arden because of "a great and dangerous water which in winter at every rain so rageth and overfloweth all the country thereabout that neither man nor beast can pass without imminent danger of perishing." "Mire and water" were similarly responsible for the hiring by local men of a stipendiary priest to serve the chapel of Stainforth in the low-lying parish of Hatfield (W.R., Yorks).[60]

Swollen streams could be quite as persuasive as inundated paths in motivating the inhabitants of an out-of-the-way hamlet to found a chapel. The parishioners of Henley-in-Arden (Warwicks), spurred to action by the fact that between their village and the parish church "runneth a brook so that divers times in the year no man can escape without great jeopardy," erected at their own costs a chapel which was later converted into an impressively endowed guild. In the hamlet of Tinsley in Rotherham (W.R., Yorks), it was a pious benefactor who took the initiative to found a chapel so that even when the waters of the Rother and the Don became "so urgent, that the curate of Rotherham cannot to them repair . . . neither on horseback or boat" the villagers might receive the ministrations of religion from a resident priest.[61] In the rugged dales of the North Country it was the dangers of a "great snow" with the inevitably ensuing "flood" and raging streams which often inspired the founding of chapels. In Sedbergh (W.R., Yorks), for example, a chapel was deemed necessary in the remote village of Garsdale, which "being in the mountains . . . in winter many times there can nothing pass betwixt the same and the parish church."[62] And in County Durham, the inhabitants of the chapelry of St. John in the parish of Stanhope claimed that often in the beastly Hexhamshire winter "no man dwelling thereabout may come to the parish church neither to christen a child nor to bury the dead." Thus, whether the local problem happened to be floods or blizzards or "wild and moorish country," the combined inflictions of climate and topography worked together to bring about the spread of free chapels manned by intercessory priests.[63]

There were, of course, many free chapels dotting the English landscape which, like the majority of the chantries, had been founded solely for intercessory purposes and did not contribute to the cure of souls. By the 1540s some of these chapels had become inactive; others, having been deprived of their worshipers by the agricultural and demographic changes of the late Middle Ages, had been abandoned altogether.[64] Many were held by nonresident pluralists or even by laymen. In Wiltshire, to take a somewhat extreme example, on the eve of the dissolution there was an unusual concentration of twenty-eight free chapels. Of these, however, only six seem to have been playing a useful role in the cure of souls. Of the twenty-two remaining chapels, nine were held by nonresident priests, three by laymen, and one by a child aged seven. Only the chapel of Hindon in the parish of Knoyle appeared sufficiently important for Mildmay and Keilway to perpetuate it by a governmental stipend following the dissolution.[65] But the Wiltshire free chapels were not representative of trends in our four sample counties, where a total of eighty priests (only two of them in Wiltshire) were ministering in chapels of ease. Without these priests' faithful labors in their obscure chapelries, the cure of souls in pre-Reformation England would have been gravely impaired.

The intercessory institutions also provided vital assistance in numerous parishes in which the parochial clergy were impoverished. Appropriation to monastic houses, nonresidence, pluralism, the decay of rents—these factors worked either individually or together to render the parochial incumbents too poverty-stricken to hire the priestly assistance that they needed to serve their cures adequately.[66] The effects of this clerical indigence may be seen in Corsham (Wilts), where lands were given to hire a stipendiary priest "to help in administration of the sacraments . . . because the vicarage is so small a living that he is not able to hire a priest to help him."[67] In the parish of St. Martin, Leicester, the vicar, whose living had been reduced to £6 per annum by the decay of urban rents, relied on two chantry priests to serve a cure of over five hundred communicants. The harmful effects might have been even more acute in Otley (W.R., Yorks), where the twin rectors, William Holgill, the master of the Savoy, and Thomas Magnus, the prince of northern pluralists, had sent only one curate to minister to the seventeen hundred parishioners in territory that was "foul to travel in winter." What would the poor curate have done had it not been for the parish's four intercessory priests, two of whom had been appointed expressly "for assistance in serving the cure"?[68] By helping in this way to compensate for the manifest inequalities in the endowment and supply of parish clergy, the intercessory priests of many parishes did much to ensure that the more perverse quirks of the medieval clerical system deprived as few Englishmen as possible of spiritual ministrations.[69]

In many instances, the collegiate churches too — varied as they were in their discipline and in the quality of their observance — made contributions of immense value to the cure of souls. Such venerable foundations as Ripon and Beverley had always exercised parochial functions. Many of the more recent ones — Howden, Hemingbrough, and Stratford-on-Avon — had simply been established within already functioning parish churches. The cures which these collegiate bodies served were often large.[70] The number of priests (vicars choral and occasionally cantarists) available for parochial chores was correspondingly substantial. In Beverley the cure was served by nine vicars choral, in Lowthorpe (E.R., Yorks) by a master and three chantry priests, and in Stratford-on-Avon by a sub-warden, two curates, and two *capellani*. The quality of the collegiate pastoral care must have varied considerably. But it is notable that the commissioners for continuance, although they dissolved the collegiate foundations and allowed them to revert into mere parish churches, gave tacit recognition to their importance by appointing relatively large staffs of ex-collegiate priests to continue to serve the cures of their parishes.[71]

An even more common — indeed, almost universal — contribution of the intercessory priests to the life of their parishes was their responsibility for maintaining, and assisting at, divine service. The chantry certificates provide little information on this fascinating topic. But Miss

Wood-Legh has shown that most chantry priests were required by their foundation ordinances daily to celebrate a special mass and say the office of the dead in behalf of their founders. These "private masses" were not to distract from or coincide with the high mass, at which, just as at the major offices of matins and vespers, the cantarists were expected to be present in the choir.[72] There, clad in their surplices, the cantarists would participate, reading the gospel and epistle at mass, and helping to "maintain divine service in the choir."[73] Indeed, one of the major contributions of the intercessory priests was to the music of the church. Time and again the chantry certificates acknowledge the contribution of their vocal and organ-playing talents to the greater glory of God.[74]

In certain respects the contribution of the cantarists was of even greater significance for the services of the great collegiate and cathedral churches of the realm, where the chantry priests were concentrated in large numbers.[75] In the four sample counties alone there were 129 cantarists in collegiate and cathedral establishments: twelve in Salisbury Cathedral, fifteen in Beverley Minster, with the largest numbers of nearly fifty each in York Minster and St. Paul's Cathedral, London; at the other extreme, a paltry two, in addition to the warden, at Knowle (Warwicks).[76] The importance of these priests to the liturgical activities of these great churches was considerable. The officials relied heavily on the cantarists to swell the choir, to participate in the processions, and to maintain the constant succession of services which was the mark of a great house of God.[77] The full extent of their contribution to the maintenance of the "beauty of holiness" was to become clear only after the Edwardian dissolutions.

In the area of education the contribution of the intercessory priests was likewise significant, even though relatively few of the chantry priests were also schoolmasters. In fact, A. F. Leach, who tended to overstress the part played by the chantry schools in the medieval educational system,[78] was able to find in all of England and Wales only 193 grammar schools, 23 song schools, and 22 elementary schools which on the eve of the dissolution were being taught by priests from the intercessory institutions. Leach conceded that the "great majority" of the cantarists were not schoolmasters.[79] Indeed, it would have been quite impossible for a number of them to have taught anyone anything. For although the chantry priests, like the rest of the secular clergy, may have been somewhat more highly educated in the early sixteenth century than their predecessors of previous centuries had been,[80] many of them were still untutored and ignorant. It is therefore not surprising that so few cantarists seem to have responded to the episcopal injunctions of the 1530s and 1540s ordering all chantry priests to teach school.[81]

According to the chantry certificates and other surviving evidence, sixty-four cantarists—approximately 8 percent of all intercessory priests in the four sample counties—were engaging in some form of teaching on the eve of the dissolution. Forty-four of these priests were teaching in schools that might loosely be labeled "grammar schools," four were teaching in song schools, and sixteen were providing some sort of elementary education (Table 2.2). The majority of these cantarist-schoolmasters were involved in education for various reasons—to supplement their incomes, to avert boredom, to meet the needs of local children, or to respond to the injunctions of their bishops. But only eighteen (28 percent) of sixty-four seem actually to have been required to teach by the foundation ordinances of their institutions.[82] Thus in Bedale (N.R., Yorks) it was reported that the stipendiary priest "of late hath been used to teach a grammar school." Similarly, in Trowbridge (Wilts), the incumbent of Terumber's Chantry was reported to have "occupied himself in teaching a school there ever since he came first thither." On the other hand, there were priests, such as the incumbent of Horton's Chantry in Bradford-on-Avon (Wilts) who was "bound by the foundation to keep a free school at Bradford and to give to the clerk there yearly 20s. to teach children to sing,"[83] who were serving institutions which had definitely been founded for educational as well as intercessory purposes.

Not only were most of the "chantry schools" casual and uninstitutionalized; many of them also existed on what Professor Jordan has rightly termed "hazardously small and restricted endowments."[84] A few educational foundations, such as Rotherham College and the Guild of Stratford-on-Avon, were well provided for and possessed substantial endowments in land. Some of the cantarist-schoolmasters, such as the incumbent of Bishop Alcock's Chantry in Hull or the priest of Mountney's Chantry in Chelmsford, in like manner enjoyed incomes ample enough to enable them to live in modest prosperity.[85] Furthermore, some schools were supported by independent endowments, which the chantry incomes merely supplemented.[86] But the more typical financial situation in the chantry schools is indicated by a comparison of median incomes, which shows that the earnings of the school-masters were only slightly higher than those of the chantry priests in general (Table 2.2).[87] The remuneration at the median level was ad-mittedly sufficient to keep one celibate alive and reasonably comforta-ble, but since half of the schoolmasters had to subsist on less than that amount, many were indeed poor by any definition.[88]

Some of the endowments were as precarious as they were small. In parishes whose schoolmasters were supported, not by lands and rents, but by stocks of animals, a season of dearth or disease could threaten the very existence of the school. In Enford (Wilts) John Westley had endowed his chantry, which supported the village schoolmaster, with 1,000 sheep. Shortly thereafter some unnamed catastrophe decimated the flock, killing 692 of the sheep. Fortunately for the cantarist and his schoolchildren, "one parson Burde" intervened in timely fashion, gen-erously augmenting the diminished flock with 578 additional sheep, without which the chantry could scarcely have continued to function.[89] More predictable but no less precarious than endowments in livestock were donations of sums of money, from which at regular intervals the stipends of the priests could be paid. In Giggleswick (W.R., Yorks) two men bequeathed £24 13s. 4d. in 1545 for the maintenance of a song-schoolmaster. Since this man's salary was to be £4 per year, the life expectancy of the school was short. Even if the general dissolution of the intercessory institutions had not taken place, this song-school would necessarily have been abandoned by the mid-1550s.[90]

The chantry schools were also limited in scale and in quality of in-struction.[91] Most of the intercessory schools met under the supervision of a single cantarist — in his quarters, in an aisle of the parish church, or occasionally in a special "school house chamber."[92] Only nine schools in my four sample shires seem to have had more than one teacher. A fortunate rarity was Rotherham College, a highly devel-oped educational institution, in which three schoolmasters taught numerous children according to lengthy and carefully considered stat-utes. In my sample counties there were several well-educated school-masters, including two with university degrees,[93] but the majority of the cantarist-teachers seem to have been men of modest abilities. In Yorkshire, for example, the chantry commissioners classified as many schoolmasters "indifferently learned" (including the schoolmaster in the college of Acaster Selby) as "learned."

The chantry schools had one final and quite serious drawback. This

Table 2.2. Number of intercessory priests teaching school, 1546-1548.

	Essex[a]	Warwicks[b]	Wilts[c]	Yorks[d]
In grammar schools	12	6	2	24
In song schools	—	1	1	2
In elementary schools	11	—	2	3
(including				
a. priests teaching according to foundation ordinances	(4)	(2)	(1)	(11)
b. schoolmasters continued by commissioners of continuance, 1548)	(3)	(3)	(2)	(22)
Median income of cantarist/schoolmasters	£8 8s. 10d.	£6	£7 14s. 6d.	£5

Sources: Essex: E 301/19/1, 2, 4, 5, 8, 10, 13, 17, 19, 22, 26, 31, 36, 36b, 40, 41, 48; DL 38/4.

Warwicks: E 301/31/1, 25, 37, 42, 43, 47; *V.C.H., Warwickshire,* II, 299; ibid., III, 19; *C.P.R., Edward VI,* III, 334.

Wilts: E 301/58/16, 26, 36, 45; *V.C.H., Wiltshire,* III, 337-338.

Yorks: *Y.C.C.,* I, 88-89, 92-93, 196, 200-204; ibid., II, 262, 378, 380-382, 403, 407, 408, 409, 410, 412, 414, 416, 419, 486-487, 495, 496, 520; E 301/102, mm. 4v, 5, 6; E 301/119, mm. 3, 6; DL 42/135, f. 124; DL 29/564/8945, mm. 69-69v; LR 2/65, f. 117; Leach, *Early Yorkshire Schools,* II, 32, 39; Jordan, *Charities of Rural England,* 301-314.

a. The chantry commissioners' report of twenty-one intercessory priests schoolmasters for the county of Essex (i.e., more than one-fifth of the Essex cantarists allegedly teaching in schools of some sort) has prompted some incredulity (Jordan, *Edward VI,* II, 188). I share this disbelief, as did the commissioners of continuance. Mildmay was himself an Essex man, intimately informed concerning the institutions of his native county and deeply concerned for their well-being (see his efforts to secure the refoundation of the Chelmsford Grammar School [E 319/7]). Yet he and Keilway notably refused to grant stipends of continuance to any but three (Chelmsford, Rayleigh, and Saffron Walden) of the county's twenty-one purported schools (E 315/30, f. 44; Leach, *Early Yorkshire Schools,* II, 32, 38). It seems possible that as many as seven of the "schools" (two in Great Baddow, one each in Bocking, Harlow, Hornchurch, Prittlewell, and Writtle) may have been providing casual instruction at most. That the other fourteen institutions supported actively functioning schools seems to be borne out by the evidence. Some continued to exist in the years after the dissolution, sending students to various Cambridge colleges; and some are described in the chantry certificates with such data as the number of scholars. See the excellent article on the Essex schools by Miss C. Fell-Smith in *V.C.H., Essex,* II, 501-564.

b. My totals assume that the Chantry of Our Lady, Alcester, and Warwick College were maintaining actively functioning schools in the 1540s (*V.C.H., Warwickshire,* II, 303-304, and III, 19; Leach, *History of Warwick School,* 87, 94).

c. My totals have not included the school which was to have been kept by St. John's Hospital, Heytesbury (Bodleian MSS., Rawlinson D. 812, ff. 8v-9). Although the chantry certificate of 1548 asserts that "there hath been no schoolmaster by the space of five or six years" (E 301/58/88), it is likely that the school had been dormant for considerably longer than that (*V.C.H., Wiltshire*, III, 337-338). It was, however, shortly thereafter restored to full activity (Sir Richard Colt Hoare, *History of Modern Wiltshire*, 5 vols. [London, 1822-1844], I, ii, 125).

d. Two Yorkshire schools required by the foundation deeds of their chantries appear to have fallen into desuetude (Chantry of Our Lady and St. Anne, Long Preston; and Service of Our Lady, Thirsk [*Y.C.C.*, I, 92-93, and II, 250, 408, 482]). The teaching function of both of these erstwhile chantry schools was mentioned by the 1546 certificates, which probably means that it had been specified in the foundation deeds; it was, however, notably overlooked by the 1548 chantry certificates. Neither institution was granted a perpetual stipend for educational purposes by the commissioners of continuance. On the other hand, there seem to have been active chantry schools in Crofton, Darfield, and Tadcaster, which were not mentioned in either of the chantry surveys (Leach, *Early Yorkshire Schools*, II, 34, 39, 45, 46-47; DL 42/135, f. 124; LR 2/65, f. 117; *C.P.R., Edward VI*, V, 263).

---

was the fact that the cantarist-schoolmasters had far more to do than teach school. Their foundation ordinances almost invariably required them to say daily masses and offices for the souls of their benefactors. These ordinances also generally stipulated that they participate regularly in divine services in the choir, and occasionally that they assist in the pastoral duties within their parishes. When teaching was added to these responsibilities, the chantry priests' cumulative work load was onerous indeed. One wonders how Edmund Talbote, the 78-year-old incumbent of Hotoft's Chantry in Orsett (Essex), could have managed to say his masses and also teach a school and serve the cure. Or how Nicholas Clevelande, a cantarist from Gargrave (W.R., Yorks), who was "indifferently learned," found time to "pray for the soul of the founder and all Christian souls, and to help to maintain divine service in the choir every holiday, and also to aid the curate in the ministration of sacraments and sacramentals to the parishioners," nine hundred in number. To this already formidable list of duties the Edwardian commissioners dauntingly added "as well to teach their children."[94] Notwithstanding the shortcomings of the generality of the intercessory schools, the contributions which many of these institutions made to education in pre-Reformation England are impressive. A few of them were well endowed and governed by intelligently conceived statutes.[95] But the more typical "schools" taught by the cantarists had their own utility as well. Numerous parishes emphasized this by appealing for the continuance of their local chantry priests in the secular guise of schoolmaster.[96] In many instances Mildmay and Keilway concurred with the parishioners. In my four sample counties alone they ordered the continuance of the educational efforts of thirty of sixty-four schoolmasters (Table 2.2).[97] It is probable that even some of the schools which the commissioners failed to continue were of some use in their immediate parishes. For they provided, at an early date, the type of teaching in the parishes to which many clerics increasingly devoted themselves in the latter half of the sixteenth century.[98]

The intercessory institutions of pre-Reformation England also made limited if useful contributions to the relief of the poor, the aged, and the impotent. On the institutionalized level, relief was given to specified paupers under conditions which were clearly defined; and on the less formal, casual level, food and money were dispensed as an act of almsgiving to paupers (or others masquerading as such) attending the distribution. The agencies which were typically in charge of providing the more formal relief were the hospitals. These had often been founded with the intention of combining a disciplined program of intercession with the relief of the poor.[99] Throughout much of the medieval period the hospitals had been broadly effective in realizing the intentions of their founders. By the fifteenth century, however, many of these institutions had fallen on evil days. Endowments disappeared and revenues declined as a result of the embezzlement and peculation of acquisitive incumbents and patrons. At the same time, the religious and eleemosynary functions of many hospitals withered away. A parliamentary effort to rectify the situation in the second decade of the fifteenth century was unavailing. As a result, by the eve of the Reformation numerous hospitals had simply disappeared.[100] Others were extant in name only, having degenerated into sinecures compatible with other benefices for well-connected clerics. Simon Fish's caustic aspersion, that in the English hospitals "the fat of the whole foundation hangeth on the priests' beards," was uncomfortably close to the truth—yet, for all that, a half-truth. For there were other hospitals, many of them of recent foundation, which were still functioning usefully and at times with considerable fidelity to their founders' intentions.[101]

Of the thirty-three hospitals recorded by the Henrician chantry survey in the four sample counties, at least ten seem to have been performing no charitable function whatsoever (Table 2.3). In his perambulations of 1538, Leland had made note of the buildings of several hospitals which were "sore decayed." The small endowment of the Hospital of St. John at Calne (Wilts) was used to support a student at

Table 2.3. Hospitals, 1546.

	Essex	Warwicks	Wilts	Yorks
Total hospital foundations	3	4	8	18
Hospitals supporting only their incumbents	2	1	4	5
Priests resident in hospitals	2	1	6	27
Aged, poor or infirm persons supported by hospitals	2	22	29	110

Sources: Chantry certificates, supplemented by the *Valor* and *C.P.R.* for those areas (e.g., East Riding, Yorks) whose certificates have not survived.

one of the universities rather than poor people. The more sizable resources of the Hospital of St. Mary, Bootham, just outside York, were expended upon the maintenance of five healthy clerics, to the neglect of the "six lame priests" whom the hospital had been founded to support. In the town of Warwick, the chantry commissioners found that neither of the two hospitals was "used nor the possessions thereof employed according to the intent of their foundation."[102] Perhaps most indicative of the condition of many hospitals, and possibly also of the changing needs and aspirations of the time, was the plight of the Hospital of St. John in Marlborough (Wilts). The highest hope which the mayor and common council could entertain for this derelict institution in 1548 was, not that it might be more faithful to its founder's intentions, but that it might be converted "into a free school for the inducement of youth within the same town and in the country near thereabout."[103]

For every hospital which had ceased to provide relief for the poor, however, there were at least two that were still providing some useful service. The effectiveness of some of these hospitals in meeting the problems of indigence and illness was admittedly minimal. Neither the hospital of Ilford (Essex), which was able to maintain only "one priest and two poor men" from its endowments of over £16, or the hospital of Richmond (N.R., Yorks), which supported only "a poor body" in addition to its resident chaplain, was notably faithful in the stewardship of it resources. On the other hand, other hospitals, though not always able to realize their founders' intentions to the full, were making important contributions to the relief of the poor in their parishes. The Hospital of St. Michael in Hull, for example, was not able to support the twenty-six poor persons that its foundation ordinances required; but it could provide shelter for twelve paupers. St. Nicholas's Hospital, Salisbury, whose resources were similarly depleted, chose to save money by discontinuing the customary resident priests rather than by reducing its quota of twelve poor persons. There were also a few hospitals, such as Knolles' Almshouse in Pontefract or Sir William Bulmer's Hospital in Kirkleatham (N.R., Yorks) which seem to have been remarkably faithful in living up to the letter of their foundation ordinances.[104] All in all, the twenty-three hospitals in our four counties that were in 1546 still functioning to some extent as charitable institutions were supporting as many as 163 inmates — an indication that even in their depleted and decayed state the hospitals were playing a useful role in the relief of the English poor.

The hospitals were occasionally joined in the task of providing relief to the poor on a formal and institutionalized plane by a chantry, guild, or college (Table 2.4). The Guild of the Holy Cross of Birmingham, for example, "found, aided, and succored" twelve poor people "in money, bread, drink, coals" and burial expenses, as well as in rent-free housing. The incumbent of the Earl of Wiltshire's Chantry in Pleshy (Essex) annually set aside £4 to support two poor men, while the cantarist in Great Baddow (Essex) provided £2 0s. 8d. each year to supply "shirts, smocks, and herring" for local paupers. Far more general, however, among intercessory institutions was another pattern of almsgiving which was informal and casual. This type of relief conformed to the pattern of the bulk of medieval charitable giving, which was "quite indiscriminately given, quite sentimentally disposed, without much reference either to the present need of the recipient or his future fate."[105] The medieval founders who required their institutions to bestow alms upon the poor were not consciously attempting to eradicate poverty from their parishes, for they assumed that it was an ineradicable part of the human condition. Their charity might temporarily ameliorate the condition of certain paupers; it might provide occasions of satiety or inebriated jollity; it might provide a penny or two which the parsimonious poor might even choose to save. But its purpose was more intensely personal than this. The givers of alms, like the founders of chantries, were self-consciously performing an activity which, in the words of a Yorkshire testator, was "most pleasant to God and most ex-

Table 2.4   Other intercessory institutions providing poor relief, 1546-1548.

	Essex	Warwicks	Wilts	Yorks
Greater institutions (chantries, colleges, guilds, etc.)	£12 2s. 8d.	£25 2s. 1d.	£11 6s. 3d.	£61 3s. 3d.
Lesser institutions (obits, lights, etc.)	£60 15s. 1d.	£21 9s. 3d.	£ 0	£ 8 5s. 11d.

Sources: Chantry certificates and "brief particulars," supplemented by the *Valor* and *C.P.R.* (as in Table 2.3).

pedient for the health of my soul."[106] Almsgiving would thus reap extraterrestrial rewards, both by virtue of its own merits and through inspiring the recipients to reciprocate by praying for the soul of their benefactor.

Alms were dispensed in a wide variety of ways. Some of the intercessory institutions distributed a fixed sum each Sunday to the poor folk of their parishes;[107] others made their distributions on their patronal festivals or on the great feasts of the church year. Many endowments of casual poor relief were minuscule, quite unconnected with any intercessory institution and therefore administered by the local parson or by churchwardens. Often labeled simply "for the poor," these gifts were sometimes rigidly defined, as in Earls Colne (Essex), where "one cottage and a little yard" had been left, for "one poor man to go throughout the town to warn obits and to warn the whole town to pray for men and women when they chance to die."[108]

Some doubt remains concerning the amount of almsgiving performed in connection with the celebration of obits. These services, though often celebrated by chantry, collegiate, or guild priests on the anniversaries of their founders' deaths, were also held in countless parish churches throughout the realm as a result of small, independent endowments for the purpose. The expectation was that the poor would flock to these observances, join in the intercessions for the repose of the founder, and receive a dole of money or food at the end of the ceremony. Information in the chantry certificates indicates that at the time of the dissolution some of the institutions were faithfully distributing the stipulated alms: in the Rotherham College thirteen poor persons who attended the annual obit were fed a dinner and given a penny each; and in Thrybergh (W.R., Yorks), after each of the participating priests had been paid 4d., the remainder of the sum of 6s. 8d. was annually distributed among the paupers who had attended the obit.[109]

How generally were these distributions made at obits? Cardinal Gasquet, citing as evidence an example from the Edwardian chantry certificate for Hampshire, asserted that the obits were intended quite as much to be the "pittance of the poor" as the succor of the departed. Certainly the 1548 certificate for Essex, in which 213 of 264 obits were stated to be providing poor relief, would seem to offer substantial confirmation of his view. But other certificates tell a different story. Alms were given at only half of the Gloucestershire obits in 1548, and at only seven of fifty-one obits in Bedfordshire. In Wiltshire and Durham the 1548 commissioners failed to report any charitable activity at all from the endowments of local obits.[110] How can one explain this marked variation from county to county? Although the available evidence is sparse, three tendencies seem identifiable. First of all, within the realm there seems to have been considerable regional variation in devotion to obits and in insistence that they provide alms for the poor. Secondly, in counties which differed to an astonishing degree from their neighbors in patterns of obit-connected poor relief, it is likely that some of the chantry commissioners were inaccurate in their reporting. Occasionally, as perhaps in Essex, they may have exaggerated the charitable functions of the obits.[111] Elsewhere, as in Wiltshire or County Durham, they almost certainly either failed to investigate or refused to report the alms which must on occasion have been distributed at some of the local obits.[112] Finally, it is probable that in most counties alms were distributed at some of the obits and not at others. Only a minority of the pre-Reformation wills that I have read which established obits made specific provision for alms.[113] And while it is possible that many of the testators may have assumed that almsgiving was an integral part of the obit, one occasionally encounters wills which state explicitly that the obit money was "to be disposed equally to priests and clerks as far as it will last."[114] In the light of these statistical uncertainties, the amounts adduced as poor relief from "lesser institutions" (Table 2.4) must be viewed with considerable caution.

This is not, however, to diminish the role of obit-connected almsgiving in humanizing the lot of the poor. In the long run, as the Protestant Henry Brinklow observed, keeping an annual "drinking for the poor" or distributing a penny to each pauper attending a mass "helpeth little or nothing."[115] But the poor also needed to live in the short run. And it is certain that these activities helped to reduce, if only for brief periods, the sting of indigence, even if the alms did not permanently raise the living standards of the poor or succeed in lessening their numbers. For the founders' intent behind these institutions was theological and symbolic, and had no similarity whatsoever to post-Reformation schemes of social engineering. It would take other generations, driven by other assumptions about the meanings of life and death, to produce wars on poverty.

A wide variety of miscellaneous public services also accrued to the parishes from their intercessory institutions. Some chantries assisted in maintaining the local water banks, sea walls, highways and bridges.[116] A chantry in Houghton Regis (Beds) provided funds for needy parishioners "when the King's Majesty shall chance to have any fifteenths granted which they are not able of themselves to pay readily." In Ashburton (Devon) the Guild of St. Lawrence maintained the lead pipes which supplied water for the town; it also controlled the local market. In London a foundation by John Donne, mercer, maintained a light on the rood beam of St. Mary-le-Bow and subvented the "ringing of Bow Bell." A reprise out of a well-endowed obit was regularly spent "for the finding of a lantern at Fleet jakes, a common house," in the parish of St. Bride's, Fleet Street. And in Birmingham the Guild of the Holy Cross even managed to support the common midwife.[117] These contributions are pleasant to contemplate; they were also frequently useful to contemporaries. But they had no integral connection to the intercessory institutions. Shortly following the dissolution many of them were taken over by the secular authorities.

Taken as a whole, then, the intercessory institutions were making significant contributions to English life on the eve of their dissolution. This was so, not only in the cure of souls and in education, but also in poor relief through the disbursement of alms, however unsystematic. It is incontestible that many of these foundations—perhaps the majority—alleviated personal suffering primarily in a "ghostly" way through their masses and intercessions. But to the people of the late Middle Ages even this function may have been quite as important, indeed as charitable, as the more tangible services which later ages have come to value. The tradition was totally undermined during the revolution of the 1530s and 1540s. During these two decades increasing numbers of influential Englishmen espoused a new "paradigm," a new set of theological and social assumptions, according to which the intercessory institutions were expendable.[118] Their dissolution followed as a matter of course and was completed in 1548. It was only to be expected that the intercessory functions, now deemed to be "superstitious," would vanish. And vanish they did, almost completely, at no demonstrable loss to anyone save perhaps those tortured souls who stubbornly clung to outmoded doctrines. The institutions which provided pastoral, educational, and socio-economic assistance fared better, for if applied in new ways and given a new rationale they could be useful in a Protestant realm. To be sure, some of these services also disappeared with the dissolution. But a considerable number were continued by means of governmental pensions and re-endowments; and many others were soon being funded by private benevolence.

It is impossible to agree wholeheartedly either with those who view the dissolution of the chantries as an unmitigated disaster or with those who complacently view it as a "good thing." The dissolution, like other momentous events in history, was a fascinating mixture of profit and loss, of progress and calamity. But I cannot help empathizing with the people of the generation 1530-1560, who were forced to live, often to suffer, amidst the turmoil and uncertainties of the English Reformation. Many of these people were bewildered by the revolutionary flux which was swirling about them. Others of them suffered in more tangible ways as well. They were caught in the agonizing interval between the dismantling of the amenities of the Middle Ages and the implementation of the social services of Protestantism. If any generation suffered acutely from the disappearance of the intercessory priests' practical contributions, it was this one.

3 / The Founding of the Chantries:
Chronological Contours

On the eve of the Reformation did the English people still cherish an active belief in the existence of purgatory? And if so, were they confident that the chantries were appropriate and effective means for alleviating the pains of the faithful dead who were presumably suffering there? These questions are far from easy to answer. Nevertheless it is necessary to address ourselves to them, for our answers will be of critical importance in assessing the disruptive impact both of the antipurgatorial declamations of the English reformers in the 1530s and of the expropriation of the chantries in the following decade. In this chapter I shall examine one indicator of the devotion of the English people to purgatory: the chronological pattern of the foundation of intercessory institutions in the later Middle Ages. On the basis of this I shall then contend that as late as the early decades of the sixteenth century the doctrine of purgatory was still intensely important to a large number of Englishmen.

The obvious sources with which to begin an examination of the chronological contours of the impulse to found chantries are the mortmain licenses. These were first granted shortly after the passage in 1279 of the Statute of Mortmain (*de viris religiosis*), with which Edward I and his councillors forbade the alienation of lands and rents into the "dead hand" of the Church.[1] Any attempt illegally to circumvent this prohibition was to be punishable by forfeiture of the alienated property to the lord of whom it had been held. Had the crown strictly enforced the act, the Church's landholdings, which were already immense, would have ceased to grow, and the foundation of new ecclesiastical institutions would have been arrested.

Beginning in the late spring of 1280, however, Edward I and his councillors provided a legal loophole to allow certain alienations into mortmain under the careful supervision of the crown; they issued "mortmain licenses" suspending the operation of the new statute in carefully specified cases. Before they would grant such a license, they required that the escheators in the respective shires conduct an inquisition *ad quod damnum*: they should survey the lands to be alienated,

71

assess their annual value, and estimate the extent to which the king's feudal revenues would be diminished if the lands came into the hands of the undying Church. Furthermore, they often imposed a fine upon the prospective founder and would then issue letters patent stating the terms of the license and officially conferring the king's permission to alienate certain lands "notwithstanding the Statute in Mortmain." Generally speaking, the founders were eager to have these licenses formally recorded on the patent rolls.

The crown was soon granting numerous such letters patent, and before long the patent rolls were recording hundreds of licenses which granted permission for the conveyance of lands and rents into mortmain for the express purpose of founding chantries.[2] Since the time span of the mortmain licenses coincides almost exactly with the late-medieval era of chantry foundations, one might reasonably expect that a careful study of the mortmain licenses should elucidate the patterns of devotion of the English people both to the intercessory institutions and to purgatory.

Superficially at least, this expectation is fulfilled. The patent rolls contain records of 2,182 licenses issued between 1281 and 1534 for the alienation of lands into mortmain for founding chantries and related institutions (Table 3.1 and Figure 1). Although there were numerous regional variations, certain general trends are clear. In the late thirteenth century there was a slow increase in chantry foundations, followed in the first half of the fourteenth century by an overwhelming surge of enthusiasm which reached a peak in the 1330s. Thereafter the impulse to found chantries ebbed, at first gradually and then, in the 1370s and 1380s, more precipitately. After a brief recovery in the 1390s, in the wake of the second Mortmain Statute (1391),[3] the issuing of such licenses continued to dwindle throughout the fifteenth century until it eventually ceased altogether in the 1530s. On the evidence of the patent rolls, then, it seems that by the eve of the Reformation the English people may have lost their former urgent concern for chantry founding, possibly also their faith in the concept of praying for the dead (Table 3.2).

The evidence of the patent rolls, however, is by itself neither sufficient nor trustworthy. For one thing, the granting of a mortmain license was not an infallible indication of the founding of a chantry: it was an indication solely of the patentee's intent. But he (or his executors) might not have the sustained interest necessary to propel him (or them) actually to establish the institution; they might also find themselves short of money, in which case they might either settle for intercessions for a short term of years or even attempt to found the chantry upon inadequate endowments.[4] Many of the chantries for which the crown had granted mortmain licenses were either never actually founded or else were so poorly endowed or dishonestly administered that they had simply disappeared by the 1540s.[5] Of the 554 licenses which were issued for chantry foundations in our four sample counties, only 253 (45.7 percent) give evidence of any relationship to institutions recorded in the chantry certificates (Tables 3.3, 3.4). Furthermore, there is ample evidence that in the later Middle Ages large numbers of chantries sank into decay, or were combined with other more flourishing institutions, or simply vanished altogether.[6]

In the second place, there were countless perpetual chantries for which no crown grant exists, even among those 2,182 mortmain licenses. By the 1540s, however, there were surely more than 2,182 intercessory foundations in England. In a number of the remoter shires (for example, Cornwall, Cheshire, and Westmorland) the founders seem as a rule to have endowed their institutions oblivious of the mortmain laws. But most persuasive is the evidence that fewer than one out of three of the intercessory institutions in our four shires was founded in the officially sanctioned manner — by letters patent granting license to alienate into mortmain.[7] It is therefore abundantly clear that statistics derived solely from the mortmain licenses are highly misleading with respect to chantry foundations. It is only when we combine the evidence from the patent rolls with material from other sources that we are able to come to a satisfactory understanding of the chronology of chantry endowment in late-medieval England.

If the majority of these institutions were not founded by mortmain licenses, how were they founded? It is possible that on occasion — though certainly very rarely — a mortmain license was granted to a prospective founder who neglected to have the letters patent enrolled.[8] Far more widely used and significant were three devices which enabled founders to evade the requirements of the mortmain statutes.

The first and most elementary method was the quiet foundation and endowment of an institution by various informal deeds and conveyances, as if the mortmain laws simply did not exist. It is difficult to be specific about this method, for by its nature it was hazy, ill-defined, and surreptitious. In the chantry certificates mention of institutions

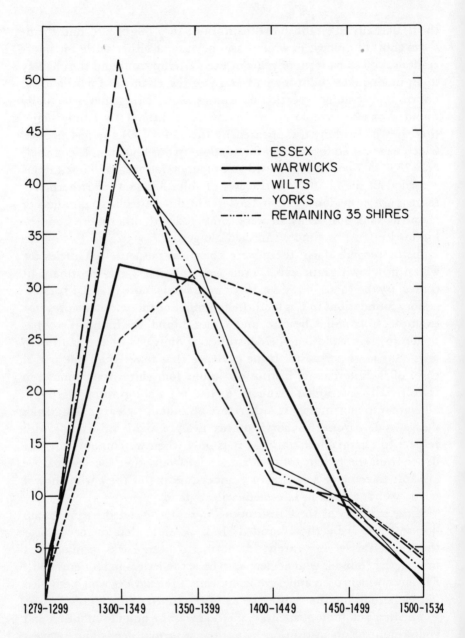

Figure 1. Proportion of mortmain licenses granted for the foundation of intercessory institutions, by periods, 1279-1534.

Table 3.1.   Mortmain licenses for the foundation of intercessory institutions, by periods, 1279-1534.

County	1279-1299	1300-1349	1350-1399	1400-1449	1450-1499	1500-1534	Total
Beds	0	10	7	2	6	3	28
Berks	1	19	17	7	4	2	50
Bucks	1	15	3	3	4	0	26
Cambs	1	14	13	2	5	1	36
Cheshire	0	1	3	0	0	0	4
Cornwall	1	2	0	1	1	2	7
Cumbld	1	5	4	0	0	0	10
Derbys	1	11	23	6	2	2	45
Devon	1	33	13	3	4	1	53
Dorset	0	23	14	8	4	0	50
Durham	0	0	5	3	0	0	8
Essex	1	18	23	21	7	3	73
Glos	0	38	27	12	12	0	89
Hants	2	20	5	3	5	1	36
Heref	2	22	20	10	2	3	59
Herts	1	11	6	1	6	1	26
Hunts	0	9	3	0	0	1	13
Kent	1	31	35	9	3	6	85
Lancs	0	9	3	2	4	0	16
Leics	3	19	15	3	2	3	45
Lincs	3	81	78	22	12	4	200
London & Middx	1	65	40	34	20	9	169
Norfolk	1	43	21	12	1	1	79
Northants	4	22	14	0	6	2	48
Northumb	0	31	11	4	1	0	47
Notts	3	30	17	8	6	0	64
Oxon	0	18	19	7	3	0	47
Rutland	0	3	6	0	0	0	9
Salop	1	20	10	4	6	1	42
Soms	0	36	14	12	4	2	66
Staffs	1	13	14	8	2	4	42
Suffolk	0	13	17	4	2	4	40
Surrey	0	7	4	4	7	0	22
Sussex	0	14	3	5	6	0	28
Warwicks	2	20	19	14	5	1	62
Westmld	0	3	0	0	0	0	3
Wilts	0	42	19	9	8	3	81
Worcs	0	19	9	3	2	0	33
Yorks	3	145	113	43	31	4	339
Total	36	934	666	289	193	64	2,182

Sources: *C.P.R.; L.P.,* I-VII.

Table 3.2. Proportion of mortmain licenses granted for the foundation of intercessory institutions, by periods, 1279-1534.

County	1279-1299	1300-1349	1350-1399	1400-1449	1450-1499	1500-1534
All England	1.6%	42.8%	30.5%	13.2%	8.8%	2.9%
Essex	1.4%	24.7%	31.5%	28.8%	9.6%	4.1%
Warwicks	3.2%	32.3%	30.6%	22.6%	8.1%	1.6%
Wilts	0	51.9%	23.5%	11.1%	9.9%	3.7%
Yorks	1.0%	42.8%	33.3%	12.7%	9.1%	1.2%
Remaining 35 shires	1.8%	43.7%	30.3%	12.3%	8.7%	3.0%

Sources: Table 3.1.

founded in this elusive fashion recurs time and again, and the authors of the Henrician Chantries Act were well aware that some of the intercessory foundations had their origins in what they termed "other devises, conveyance, & assurance."[9] That founders could resort to this informal illegality with considerable frequency (especially in the relatively remote shires) is indicated by the particularly well-documented case of Yorkshire, in which they appear to have used it in approximately one-quarter of the datable chantry and stipendiary foundations

Table 3.3. Rate of attrition of chantries, stipendiary services, free chapels, and fraternities for which mortmain licenses were granted.

Date of Foundation	Essex	Warwicks	Wilts	Yorks	Total
1279-1299	0:1	1:1	0:0	1:2	2:4
1300-1349	14:4	10:10	35:7	82:63	142:84
1350-1399	17:6	10:10	16:3	61:52	104:71
1400-1449	14:7	6:8	4:5	20:23	44:43
1450-1499	2:5	1:4	0:8	7:24	10:41
1500-1534	1:2	0:1	0:3	0:4	1:10
Total	48:25	28:34	55:26	171:168	301:253

Sources: *C.P.R.*; chantry certificates.

Note: The left-hand number in each ratio is the total of licensed chantries, stipendiary services, free chapels, and fraternities which were no longer extant in the 1540s. The right-hand number is the total of licensed chantries, etc., which were still actively functioning in the 1540s. The figures refer only to original foundations, and do not include refoundations or augmentations of institutions.

Table 3.4. Chantries, stipendiary services, free chapels, and fraternities founded by mortmain license and surviving in 1546-1548.

	Essex	Warwicks	Wilts	Yorks	Total
Surviving institutions at time of dissolution	92	55	86	576	809
Percent of surviving institutions founded by mortmain licenses	27.2%	68.1%	30.2%	29.2%	31.3%

Sources: see Table 3.3.

of the century prior to the dissolution (Table 3.5). This was a risky method, however, as those who referred to "the danger of the Statute of Mortmain" clearly recognized.[10] The numerous pardons on the patent rolls show that such illegal foundations were often detected by some alert escheator, and the pardon could on occasion be crushingly expensive to obtain. If the illegal foundation were discovered only after the original founder had died, when there might no longer be anyone with sufficient money or spiritual concern to secure the requisite pardon and amortization, there was real danger that the institution might collapse completely. The lands would then escheat to the king or some other lord, and the prayers for the founder would cease.[11]

An alternative device for evading the mortmain laws—granting lands to feoffees to the use of founding intercessory institutions—at least represented an attempt at legality. The use was one of the most important legal innovations of the later Middle Ages.[12] It was an extralegal instrument which, while vesting the full legal estate of certain properties in specified feoffees or trustees, enabled the user (or the *cestui que use*) who occupied and profited from the premises to have rights enforceable at equity. According to Sir Edward Coke, the use had been invented for two reasons—"fear and fraud." In an era of political uncertainty and strife, the former impelled prominent families to grant their lands to feoffees (while themselves retaining the use of them) to protect themselves against possible acts of attainder. The latter motive was also significant. By the 1330s numerous tenants of mesne lords were employing feoffments to avoid the payment of feudal incidents, a practice which by the late fifteenth century had become

Table 3.5. Numbers of Yorkshire chantries and stipendiary services of known foundation dates, 1450-1548, according to method of foundation.

Decade	Mortmain licenses	Feoffments	Conveyances, deeds, compositions, etc.[a]	Other and uncertain	Total
1450-1459	6	0	2	1	9
1460-1469	6	2	2	2	12
1470-1479	5	2	1	4	12
1480-1489	7	0	2	3	12
1490-1499	1	4	1	5	11
1500-1509	2	7	5	4	18
1510-1519	2	3	5	2	12
1520-1529	0	7	6	6	19
1530-1539	0	2	4	1	7
1540-1548	0	0	0	1	1
Total	29	27	28	29	113

Sources: *C.P.R.*; *Y.C.C.*; wills; local histories.

a. This category also includes wills, indentures, ordinances, and writings. The total may be somewhat inflated by a lack of precision of language in the chantry certificates which prevents classification of these foundations in the other categories.

even more widespread in response to Henry VII's fiscal feudalism.[13] It was likewise fraud—of a pious sort—which inspired Englishmen to evade the mortmain laws by this means, thereby enabling spiritual persons (including chantry priests) as the users to profit from the lands while celebrating masses for the soul of the original feoffor. Meanwhile the lands were technically exempt from the Statute of Mortmain since in the sight of the law the real owners were the feoffees. By 1391 this practice had become widespread enough to call forth a statute forbidding the employment of uses in evasion of the statute and requiring the ecclesiastics who had profited from these grants to obtain retrospective licenses of amortization.[14]

Although the 1391 statute brought about a brief flurry of mortmain licenses for chantries, it was not effective for long. Some founders may have noted that the statute specifically mentioned guilds and fraternities but nowhere referred to chantries.[15] Other founders may simply have chosen to ignore it. And a few founders made feoffments which, while cannily stating no use at all, were accompanied by the verbal understanding that the profits of the lands were to be used to support an intercessory priest.[16] At any rate, before long the employment of uses for the foundation of chantries began once again with renewed vigor, as the chantry certificates attest.[17] For example, the 1546 certificate for Gloucestershire reported that the lands of 68 out of 143 institutions were "put in feoffment." In 1548 the Suffolk chantry commissioners discovered that an even higher proportion of that county's intercessory institutions (24 out of 46) had been founded by feoffments.[18] In other counties it is impossible to be so precise, but the existence of numerous such foundations is confirmed by a late sixteenth-century law report which stated that "of these kind of reputed chantries [founded by feoffments] that were never incorporated by the king's authority there were thousands."[19] Typical of these was the foundation of the Chantry of Our Lady in the chapel of Rylstone in the parish of Burnsall (W.R., Yorks). In June 1524 Geoffrey Procter composed a lengthy, meticulously framed will in which he stipulated that Sir William Fairfax and other feoffees of his lands "should stand and be seised . . . to the use and intent that of finding of a priest to say mass in the said chapel, and pray for the said founder and all Christian souls."[20] From the vantage point of the founders, the spiritual consequences of the feoffees' stewardship of the donor's lands appeared momentous. As Sir Humphrey Stafford urged upon his feoffees in his will of 1463,

I put all my faith and soul is [sic] trust in you which have the guiding of all, desiring you and, in His Name, which all made, advertising you that you which in my life here have loved me and you both desire you no more but to love the poor soul which cannot help himself when he is departed from hence, but standeth in the mercy of God and looketh after refuge and comfort which should come from this world by the remembrance of executors and feoffees of trust made in this aforesaid world, which beeth so of very trust made will not forget the aforesaid poor soul, the pilgrim. And so I charge you as you will answer before the High Judge which shall deem both you and me. And that I have no cause to cry upon you at the dreadful day of doom.[21]

A third device used by founders to evade the mortmain laws was the foundation of institutions for carefully specified terms of years. This method, unlike that of feoffments to uses (in conjunction with which it was often used), was entirely legal, for the mortmain statutes were concerned only to prevent the *perpetual* alienation of lands into the possession of the Church. The long-term nonperpetual foundations seem first to have appeared around the middle of the fifteenth century.[22] Soon there were numerous intercessory institutions which were founded for periods of varying duration (typically thirty, eighty, eighty-nine, or ninety-nine years). In Suffolk, for example, on the eve of the dissolution there were sixteen nonperpetual foundations all established by

feoffments with a variety of life-expectancies.[23] For most of these institutions, the founders had left clear instructions about the disposition
of their assets at the end of the specified period. Generally the feoffees
were to sell the lands and to bestow the proceeds upon worthy projects
— the repair of churches, the purchase of ecclesiastical vestments, the
shoring up of bridges and highways, the marriage of poor maidens,
and other good works which were to benefit the founder's soul.[24]

Occasionally, however, founders slipped into illegality by attempting to make their limited-term foundations self-perpetuating. In 1530
Sir Walter Griffiths of Burton Agnes (E.R., Yorks), for example,
willed that for the term of forty years a succession of priests be employed to sing for his soul. However,

> supposing that by such space as these years shall be ended, my heirs, of their charitable
> mind, will devise for the health of their souls and ours in likewise; and so from heir to
> heir forever, so to be continued, which I pray God grant them grace for to do, accord-
> ing to the good example of my mother that this did begin.

Other founders likewise required that their institutions be renewed for
a similar period at the end of the allotted life-span, and so "to the end
of the world."[25]

Why, then, were the pious Englishmen who founded chantries so
reluctant to do so in the proper manner — by obtaining mortmain licenses? The procedure was certainly irksome: the would-be benefactor
had to contact an agent in London to petition the king, submit his
lands to the examination of the escheator in his shire, and then wait to
found his chantry until the slow machinery of government had done its
work.[26] An even more tempting reason to avoid the licenses was the
often considerable expense of obtaining them. Hiring an agent was an
expensive proposition, and the gifts that the applicant was expected to
make to the appropriate officials and intermediaries who were expe-
diting his application could add considerably to his costs. In addition,
there were substantial fees for making the necessary inquisitions *ad
quod damnum,* passing the seals, and enrolling the letters patent.[27]
Finally, and most important, there were the "gross fines" which many
licensees were required to pay into the Hanaper of Chancery in return
for the king's gracious willingness to waive the provisions of the mortmain statutes. There seems to have been no fixed principle governing
the severity of the fines charged during the reign of Edward III;[28] and
in the mid-fifteenth century the policy is still unclear. Certain licensees

were seemingly charged no fine at all, whether as a result of the special relationship between themselves and the king, because of some stated reason (that is, "for his good service in France and Normandy in the wars and . . . his impoverishment through payment to the king's enemies there, who took him"),[29] or for no discernible reason. Other licensees were charged modest sums, while a few were required to pay substantial fines.

As the fifteenth century progressed a general pattern seems to have emerged in the fluctuating severity of the fines, a pattern which makes the eagerness of the founders to evade the requirements of the mortmain laws all the more comprehensible (Table 3.6). In the middle decades of the century, although some fines were quite low and others were relatively high, the majority of the fines were between one and three times the annual value of the property being alienated.[30] Typical was the fine of twenty marks which the earl of Warwick was required to pay in 1461 to alienate into mortmain lands worth up to ten marks per annum for the support of a chantry in Olney (Bucks).[31] Around 1470, however, a new pattern becomes evident. Coinciding with and no doubt resulting from the reassertion of strong monarchical rule under Edward IV and his successors, this pattern seems to have reflected a determination to maximize crown revenues and to minimize the amount of land which would continue to flow into the dead hand of the Church.[32] As a result, the great bulk of the fines was now between three and five times the annual value of the property — markedly more expensive than the fines had been in previous decades. A few of the fines, such as the £300 exacted from Bishop Beauchamp of Salisbury, who wished to found a chantry in his cathedral, were truly crippling.[33]

In the mid-1480s it becomes suddenly more difficult to be certain about the severity of the fines. In 1485, and perhaps earlier, the crown began to require frequently that licensees pay their fines into the burgeoning center of royal finance and administration, the Chamber.[34] Sometimes the licensees continued to pay their fines into the Hanaper; on occasion they were compelled to pay fines into both! Since disappointingly few of the Chamber books of receipt have survived, it is impossible to be certain whether our findings constitute a representative sample.[35] But what appears to have happened is this. Under Henry VII, who throughout his reign showed astonishing resourcefulness in devising means to "get every legitimate penny out of his fiscal rights, as re-defined by himself,"[36] the gross fines rose to a level of unprecedented, almost extortionate severity. Thus in 1493 Roger Hebbys and others of Fenny Stratford (Bucks) were required to pay £13 6s. 8d. into the Hanaper and £48 into the Chamber in return for a license to endow a religious guild with lands worth £8 per annum.[37] In the ensuing years this trend towards extreme severity continued. Two Chamber books of receipt which have survived for the years 1503-1507 indicate that the crown was routinely requiring founders to pay fines of between 7½ and 10 times the annual value of their newly amortized lands in return for granting them mortmain licenses. For example, in 1505 the archdeacon of York, Henry Carnebull, was forced to pay 200 marks into the Chamber for the alienation to his two new chantries of lands worth 20 marks per annum, while a group of men from Bedford had to pay a fine of £48 for permission to endow a chantry there with lands worth £6 per year.[38] Mortmain fines could hardly become more crushing than this without being priced completely out of the market.

Unfortunately, since no useful Chamber accounts have survived for the reign of Henry VIII, there is no firm indication of what happened to the level of the fines.[39] In light of the fact that there "was very little change in Chamber policy during the early years of the new reign,"[40] it is probable that prospective founders continued to pay substantial sums. Yet an analysis of the gross fines which founders were on occa-

Table 3.6.   Multiples of fines for mortmain licenses to annual value of lands alienated for founding chantries, free chapels, and guilds, 1440-1534.

Decade	Less than 1	1 to 1.99	2 to 2.99	3 to 3.99	4 to 4.99	5 to 6.99	7 to 9.99	More than 10
1440-1449	2	12	10	4	3	2	0	0
1450-1459	3	10	7	6	2	0	0	0
1460-1469	3	7	8	2	0	0	0	0
1470-1479	1	2	3	17	7	2	0	0
1480-1489	3	1	5	9	5	6	0	0
1490-1499	4	1	0	1	1	3	1	0
1500-1509	0	0	0	0	0	0	4	3
1510-1519	0	0	1	1	1	0	1	0
1520-1529	0	0	0	0	0	1	1	0
1530-1534	0	0	0	0	1	1	0	0

Sources: *C.P.R.*, original patent rolls, hanaper accounts, chamber accounts.
Note: Not included are institutions for which evidence is lacking with respect to the value of the amortized land or the amount of the fine.

sion forced to pay into the Hanaper suggests that the new monarch may have slightly diminished their severity. Between 1516 and 1520 fines paid into the Hanaper for the foundation of five intercessory institutions ranged in cost from 3¾ to 7 times the annual value of the amortized lands. Similarly, in the mid-1530s each of three fines paid for mortmain licenses was approximately five times the value of the lands.[41] The evidence is admittedly incomplete, and our conclusions must be tentative. But there are ample indications that under the Yorkists, even more notably under Henry VII, and possibly under Henry VIII, the heavy fines imposed an additional burden on those who wished to alienate lands into mortmain.[42] Indeed, they must have been a powerful deterrent to the founding of chantries in the legal manner.

It is doubtful, however, that these exorbitant fines were the most compelling reason for founding intercessory institutions by devious means. Certainly it is significant that in 1505, a year in which unprecedentedly onerous mortmain fines were being charged, as many as seven founders were able to produce the necessary money to receive the elusive licenses when they were available.[43] Availability, in fact, seems to have been the crucial point. By the end of the fifteenth century the crown, in an apparent attempt to arrest the movement of lands into mortmain, had become exceedingly reluctant to grant mortmain licenses. In 1495 a Derbyshire founder recorded his doubt "if a mortmain might be gotten."[44] And during the ensuing years expression of this fear recurred frequently in wills and foundation deeds. Some founders seem to have counted on the intercessions of influential intermediaries to persuade the authorities to grant a license. Alderman John Gilliot of York, for example, in 1509 willed that his executors give money for a landed endowment "to an abbey such as hath sufficient authority of the king to take mortmain. And if they can find no such abbey nor other place, then mine executors to purchase the lands & it to make as sure as they can; and thereof to found a chantry in the new chapel in St. Saviour's Church."[45] Others, who lacked such powerful contacts, founded their chantries for specified periods of years to secure prayers while their executors could tender applications for the mortmain licenses. Typical of this latter group of founders was Robert Tonnerd of Frampton (Lincs), who in April 1527 willed

that Gray house, with two acres of pasture to the same belonging, be put in sure feoffment to the behalf of Skirbeck church [for] the space and term of ninety-eight years, on this condition, that the churchwardens keep or cause to be kept an obit yearly for my soul and my friends' souls to the value of 5s. by the year. And if they can obtain the king's license for the said house and pasture for amortizing of the same within the said years, then I will it so continue to the behalf of the said church forever; and if not, then I will that at [the] end of the said years the house and pasture be sold by the churchwardens, and the money thereof coming to be bestowed in the said church for my soul and all Christian souls. [46]

Tonnerd, like many founders who hoped to establish unimpeachably legal institutions, was well aware that it might not be possible for his feoffees to do what he desired. [47]

In sum, by the end of the fifteenth century the crown, by means of its coordinated policies of charging exorbitant fines for mortmain licenses and of granting them only in exceptional circumstances, had taken a position profoundly hostile to the founding of intercessory institutions. In fact, despite the overt expressions of piety of Henry VII and his son, some Englishmen began to fear that new legislation might soon be introduced to confiscate the chantries which had been founded by feoffments or for terms of years. William Curteis, who in 1500 founded a stipendiary priest's service in Necton (Norfolk) for the term of eighty years, felt compelled to provide for the eventuality that "it might fortune any law or statute to be made for the breaking and against the maintenance of the said priest's service." Similarly, John Leke in 1508 gave lands for the founding of a cantarist-schoolmaster in Nuneaton (Warwicks) "if they can be enjoyed without interruption by the king." Numerous other founders in this period established their institutions "as long as the laws of the realm will suffer." [48]

In the 1530s the expected royal initiative against the founding of chantries finally materialized. For on this issue Henry VIII, the latest of a succession of kings who had been frustrated by the disappearance of lands into mortmain, was now able to ally himself with an increasingly articulate anti-clerical party which was quite as opposed to the amortization of additional properties into the Church as he was. [49] According to many authorities, the primary vehicle of this anti-intercessory initiative was the 1529 statute against pluralism, one clause of which has been read as forbidding "any person after Michaelmas of that year to accept any stipend for singing masses for the dead." [50] Clause xix of this statute, however, reads:

no spiritual person, secular or regular, beneficed with cure as is before rehearsed, from the feast of St. Michael the Archangel next coming, by authority of any manner license, dispensation, or otherwise, shall take any particular stipend or salary to sing for any soul. [51]

Inasmuch as the general intent of the act was to prevent pluralism, the qualifying phrase "beneficed with cure" is clearly the key. In no sense was the clause an attempt — nor was it ever used — to impede the foundation of chantries. It was intended simply to prevent those "beneficed with cure" from accepting other ecclesiastical promotions (including chantries) which might interfere with their pastoral duties.[52]

The royal initiative did, however, consist of two components which have received little notice. The first of these was administrative: in the 1530s the crown finally put a complete stop to the granting of mortmain licenses for the founding of chantries. In the previous decade it had already been subjecting applications for mortmain licenses to a scrutiny which was less sympathetic than ever before, and had granted only nine such licenses (Table 3.1). In the 1530s it granted only two: one in 1530, and one — the 2,182nd such license, authorizing the foundation of the chantry of Robert Jannys in Aylsham (Norfolk) — in 1534.[53] Although there was no statute or proclamation forbidding the granting of further mortmain licenses for the founding of intercessory institutions, someone (Henry VIII, perhaps, at the urging of Thomas Cromwell) evidently decided that all future applications should be turned down. Therefore, after 1534 the legal channel for establishing intercessory institutions was no longer open to would-be founders.[54]

Nor would it any longer be possible for founders to utilize foundations by feoffments to uses or for lengthy terms of years. For in 1532 the second *legislative* component of the royal initiative took the form of a parliamentary act which limited these practices severely. According to an "Act for feoffments & assurances of lands & tenements made to the use of any parish church, chapel, or such like," numerous feoffments had in the past been made to the uses of chantries, guilds, and churches, whereby "there groweth and issueth to the king our sovereign lord and to other lords and subjects of the realm the same like losses and inconveniences, and it is as much prejudicial to them as doth and is in case where lands be alienated into mortmain." Henceforth all feoffments to religious uses should be void, except those made for terms of twenty years or less.[55]

This statute was of decisive importance in bringing to a conclusion the era of the perpetual chantry in England. Indeed, some Englishmen interpreted it as forbidding the founding of intercessory institutions for periods of longer than twenty years *by any method*.[56] They were in error in point of law, for the statute did not forbid the crown to grant mortmain licenses if it so desired. But in point of fact, these people were absolutely right. Henceforth some founders would ignore the new law, defiantly founding institutions in perpetuity or for lengthy terms of years.[57] Other founders would reluctantly comply with its provisions. But one detects, time and again, the desire for intercessions "for evermore after if the king's laws will suffer."[58]

Because of the manifest incompleteness and uncertainty of the information provided by the mortmain licenses, it is clear that we must turn elsewhere to obtain a satisfactory overview of the chronological patterns of chantry foundation in England. Fortunately, the chantry certificates themselves often give the dates of the initial feoffments and foundation deeds. Local histories, which sometimes draw upon diocesan records, wills, and unpublished local documents, provide still further information. By using these sources to supplement the mortmain licenses, a picture of the fluctuating enthusiasm of Englishmen for the founding of intercessory institutions emerges which is at once more complete, more complex, and more convincing than that provided by the mortmain licenses alone. The resultant composite list of foundation dates (Table 3.7) accounts for the origins of approximately one-half of the foundations still in existence in six representative shires at the time of the dissolution, providing sufficient evidence to identify several significant trends.

In the first place, it is notable that on one point at least the composite list and the mortmain licenses are in full agreement: in the fourteenth century there was a tremendous crescendo of new chantry foundations—at different rates in different areas. In Kent and Lincolnshire, for example, the greatest number of foundations took place in the second half of the century,[59] a fact which would seem to give credence to the hoary notion that the chantries were the response of piously petrified Englishmen to the terrors of the Black Death. In many instances this was almost certainly the case. But it is also striking that in Warwickshire and Yorkshire, as in the six counties collectively, the greatest number of chantry foundations took place in the first half of the century, before the plague had made significant incursions into the British Isles (Table 3.8 and Figure 2).[60] The enthusiasm for intercessory institutions may therefore have resulted quite as much from the famines, wars, and population pressures of the time as it did from the plague. It may also have been a product of what appears in the sermons and works of art of the early fourteenth century to have been a

Table 3.7. Number of chantries, stipendiary services, and guilds in existence at the time of the dissolution, by date of foundation (before 1299 to 1548).

	Before 1299	1300-1349	1350-1399	1400-1449	1450-1499	1500-1548
Essex						
rural	1	6	9	7	8	4
urban	—	—	—	—	2	—
Kent						
rural	3	4	13	5	6	2
urban	—	1	4	4	—	1
Lincs						
rural	5	20	25	4	7	14
urban	3	8	6	3	—	—
Warwicks						
rural	1	12	4	5	2	1
urban	2	4	2	2	—	2
Wilts						
rural	1	5	3	2	5	7
urban	—	3	1	4	5	1
Yorks						
rural	11	61	44	33	44	55
urban	9	24	18	14	14	4

Sources: For the four shires of Essex, Warwickshire, Wiltshire, and Yorkshire, this list is based upon the *C.P.R.*, the chantry certificates, and numerous local histories. For Kent, it is based upon Hussey, *Kent Chantries,* and for Lincolnshire upon Foster and Thompson, "Chantry Certificates for Lincolnshire," both of which make use of sources similar to those that I have utilized for the four other counties. I have preferred the evidence of the *C.P.R.* to that of the chantry certificates whenever their evidence conflicts, for the latter were occasionally inaccurate in reporting foundation dates.

Note: Where numerous foundations or augmentations were made of a single institution, I have chosen the first recorded foundation as indicative of the original impulse for foundation. I have recorded as a single entry the intercessory institutions of multiple priests. The institutions categorized as "urban" are those in Boston, Canterbury, Colchester, Coventry, Hull, Lincoln, Salisbury, and York, all of which were among the leading twenty-five provincial towns in the subsidy of 1523-1527 (W.G. Hoskins, *Provincial England: Essays in Social and Economic History* [London, 1963], 70). Most of these cities were "permeated by the countryside" and were hardly urban in the modern sense of the term (Peter Clark and Paul Slack, eds., *Crisis and Order in English Towns,* 1500-1700 [London, 1972], 6).

transformation of the pervading attitudes towards death—from hopeful idealism to horrific realism.[61]

However that may be, the statistics, which are clear enough, only partially reflect the strength of the impulse to found chantries during these years, for they include solely those foundations which had managed to survive until the dissolution. There is good evidence that con-

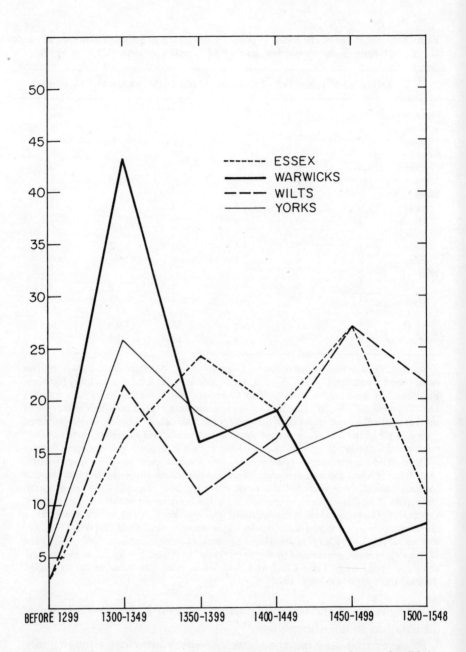

Figure 2. Proportionate distribution of chantries, stipendiary services, and guilds in existence at the time of the dissolution, by date of foundation (before 1299 to 1548).

Table 3.8. Proportionate distribution of chantries, stipendiary services, and guilds in existence at the time of the dissolution, by date of foundation (before 1299 to 1548).

	Before 1299	1300-1349	1350-1399	1400-1449	1450-1499	1500-1548
Essex	2.7%	16.2%	24.3%	18.9%	27.0%	10.8%
Warwicks	8.1%	43.2%	16.2%	18.9%	5.4%	8.1%
Wilts	2.7%	21.6%	10.8%	16.2%	27.0%	21.6%
Yorks	6.0%	25.7%	18.7%	14.2%	17.5%	17.8%

Source: Table 3.7.

siderably fewer than half of those institutions for which mortmain licenses had at any time been secured were still in existence in the 1540s (Table 3.3). In fact, it is axiomatic that the greater the chronological distance between the granting of a mortmain license for a chantry and the chantry surveys of the 1540s, the greater was the possibility that the chantry would disappear. Among the numerous reasons for this phenomenon was the decay in value of lands, which would force the cantarist to discontinue his ministrations or cause some sympathetic diocesan to amalgamate the chantry with another hard-pressed foundation. The resources of the chantry might be maladministered or even confiscated by the descendants of the original founders. Local men of greed and ambition might forcefully disseise the chantry priests and arrogate the lands to their own uses.

Whatever the reason, the fact that the intercessory institutions did decay and disappear in large numbers is incontestable. Fully 80 percent of the Wiltshire institutions and 78 percent of the Essex institutions for which mortmain licenses were obtained in the first half of the fourteenth century were no longer in existence in the 1540s. In Yorkshire the rate of attrition was somewhat less alarming (57 percent), while in Warwickshire, where only half of those institutions which were licensed disappeared, the survival rate for institutions of this period was actually quite good. In all four counties the rate of attrition becomes less extreme in the periods closest in time to the dissolution. In view of the heavy toll exacted of medieval institutions by the ravages of time, the number of chantries actually founded in the fourteenth century must have been even greater than appears from surviving documentary evidence.[62]

It is also significant that in the fifteenth century the composite list is at variance with the evidence of the mortmain licenses. Whereas the

latter had indicated a dramatic loss of interest in chantry foundation
in all parts of the realm, the composite list, which takes into account
more types of information, demonstrates that fifteenth-century founders in these six counties continued to evidence a lively if somewhat
diminished interest in establishing intercessory institutions. In the second half of the century, in fact, more chantries which were to survive
until the suppression were founded in two of our counties (Essex and
Wiltshire) than in any other fifty-year period. And in Lancashire the
movement for founding intercessory institutions was apparently just
getting under way.[63]

Furthermore, in striking contrast to the witness of the mortmain licenses by themselves, the composite list makes it abundantly evident
that numerous founders were still endowing chantries in the first half
of the sixteenth century. In Wiltshire eight chantries were founded between 1500 and thè dissolution, and thirteen in Lincolnshire. The
trend was even more notable in Yorkshire, where fifty-nine intercessory institutions were established in the same period.[64] This surge of
chantry foundations appears all the more remarkable when we recall
that it was taking place in a period that was effectively only thirty-two
years in length (prior to the statute of 1532) and that during these
years the government was doing a great deal to discourage the founding of chantries.

Certain geographical patterns are apparent in this eleventh-hour
enthusiasm for the foundation of intercessory institutions. My evidence
seems to indicate two crude but useful rules-of-thumb: that rural Englishmen were founding more chantries in the first half of the sixteenth
century than their urban compatriots; and that during this period the
people of the north and the west of England were establishing many
more institutions than their countrymen from the Midlands, the south,
and the east. In a few areas, economic forces may have militated
against the foundation of chantries. This was especially true in towns
such as Coventry, Lincoln, and York, which had flourished in the high
Middle Ages but which by the sixteenth century had entered into a
period of contraction and decay.[65] The capper in the *Discourse of the
Common Weal* eloquently expressed the plight of the once-prosperous
urban craftsmen: "Some time they had such superfluity as they could
. . . leave an other portion to find a priest or to found a chantry in
some parish church. And now we are scant able to live without debt."[66]
Economic factors could thus help to explain the precipitate decline in
the foundation of obits in York Minster: whereas no less than fifty obits

had been founded in the minster in the second half of the fourteenth century, only four were founded in the early sixteenth century.[67] For the most part, however, the chantry founders seem to have been oblivious of the movements of the economic indicators. In London, despite the fact that the city was prospering in the early sixteenth century as never before, the founders evidenced a marked loss of enthusiasm for establishing chantries, endowing only thirteen in the first four decades. In the fourteenth century, by contrast, an average of twenty-eight perpetual chantries per decade had been founded in the city.[68] Similar discrepancies between economic trends and the patterns of chantry foundations occur in other parts of the realm as well: in both prosperous Somerset and penurious Lancashire, founders were endowing numerous chantries on the eve of the Reformation.[69] In many of the more remote and less economically progressive parts of the realm founders appear to have been especially eager to found intercessory institutions. But, in general, economic forces were of only secondary importance in determining the number of chantry foundations in the era of the Reformation.

What, then, was primary? It was the intensity of people's belief in the existence of purgatory and the extent of their fear that an excruciating posthumous purgation was in store for them. That many people on the eve of the Reformation still fearfully believed in purgatory is a fact that emerges with striking clarity from a reading of the wills of the period. It is also clear from the pattern of chantry foundations. Chantries were expensive; to endow one required a substantial financial investment. Though the motives of the founders were admittedly not always devoid of this-worldly considerations, it seems certain that the vast majority of the sixteenth-century men and women who were willing to venture their money and to make the appropriate legal efforts (or to take the necessary legal risks) to found chantries were firmly convinced of the reality of purgatory. These people seem to have been more numerous in the north of England (despite its relative poverty) than in the south, more in the west than in the east, more in the countryside than in the cities. For in the southeasterly and urban segments of the realm the forces of anti-clericalism and secularism had undoubtedly done much to reduce the intensity of the popular belief in purgatory, although they had certainly not undercut the doctrine itself in the minds of many of the people or provided a reasonable alternative to it. These things were to happen only in the Reformation.

Yet when all this has been said, it remains striking that on the eve of the Reformation chantries were still being founded in all parts of the realm, even in London, that vortex of the life of this "earthy, selfish, grasping age," or within such counties as Essex and Kent.[70] It is certain that for rather more people in the south than in the north the belief in purgatory and in the intercession for souls had become a part of "conventional piety."[71] It is probable that this, in a highly generalized way, was also true of the English people as a whole compared with their fourteenth-century forefathers.[72] But even this conventional piety of purgatory was far from impotent or easily discardable. The conventions of every age which pertain to death are deeply rooted and notoriously difficult to alter or to set aside. So it was for the generation of the early sixteenth century. For many Englishmen from all parts of the realm the Reformation was therefore to be an intensely painful experience.

4 / "Extinguishing the Flames of Purgatory" (I): To the Ten Articles (1536)

Few topics of religious controversy in the Henrician Reformation were more fraught with emotion and more intensely argued than was the debate about the state of the departed souls.[1] Where were the souls of the faithful departed? Were they in purgatory, undergoing agonizing preparations for entry into the presence of an all-holy God? Or, having been justified by grace through faith, were they already in heaven, singing the praises of their Savior? Did masses, prayers, and almsdeeds alleviate their sufferings? Or were those activities unnecessary and sham-filled, detracting from the all-sufficiency of Christ's blood for the redemption of sinners? About questions such as these countless sermons were preached, scores of treatises were composed, and several doctrinal formularies were written during the first decade and a half of the English Reformation. And, as the years went by, these pronouncements made it increasingly clear that the civil and ecclesiastical powers in the realm were gradually espousing beliefs about the state of the departed which were distinctly nontraditional. These tenets were, in fact, almost Protestant, and they left no room for purgatory as late medieval Catholics had viewed it.

For some Englishmen, the government's gradual abandonment of the doctrine brought joyful release from an acutely existential dread. A young Kentish Protestant, for example, could greet the reformist tendencies of Henrician theology with the exultant exclamation that "the boiling flames of purgatory are extinguished amongst us!" And the theologian-diplomat Robert Barnes could confidently "vindicate the efficacy of the blood of Jesus Christ my Lord" against those who insisted that masses and almsdeeds were necessary for the salvation of departed souls.[2] But other Englishmen, who were unable so quickly to jettison traditional beliefs, reacted to the new ideas and their advocates with a mixture of shock and grief.[3] And understandably so, for a large number of Englishmen still believed heartily in the reality of a pain-filled purgatory. Furthermore, within the catena of Catholic presuppositions there was an excellent logical basis for its existence, even if its scriptural grounding was somewhat obscure. The conservatives therefore were convinced that the "liberated" reformers who railed so vehemently against purgatory were wantonly tampering with the welfare of precious souls. The reformers, on the other hand, were sure that the popish "superstitions" had been damning souls for centuries.

Conflict on the issue was inevitable, and it came in virulent form in the fifteen years between 1528 and 1543. Preachers arose to "deprave one another" about purgatory; bishops huddled behind closed doors to debate its existence; and the English people responded to the changes with a mixture of rage, eagerness, and bewilderment. Generally speaking, after the break with Rome in 1533, Thomas Cromwell and his associates tended to side with the reformers on this issue, for purgatory had long been closely associated with the papal power of binding and loosing. Their plans for dissolving the monasteries also impelled them to reject the Catholic conception of purgatory, for this had been one of the most imposing buttresses of monasticism.[4] Cromwell and his allies therefore often protected, and even sponsored, the radical preachers who were attempting to discredit purgatory in the minds of the people. In this process Henry VIII played his part too. The doctrinal formularies of 1536 and 1543 gave royal sanction to many of the radicals' views about the state of the departed souls. In comparison with the spine-tingling concreteness of traditional teaching, the purgatory of the Ten Articles of 1536 was a place of astonishing vagueness. Even more extreme was the King's Book of 1543, which admonished the English people to cease using the term altogether, for it had been merely a generator of romish abuses. As a result of the events of this tumultuous period, by the early 1540s the intercessory institutions had lost their raison d'être and were expendable. Later in the decade they were to disappear forever as a major force on the English scene.

For the roots of the heretical attitude toward prayers for the dead, as for the origins of English religious dissent in general, we must begin with the Lollards. At no stage of his career did John Wyclif, their prophet and founder, expressly denounce the doctrine of purgatory, but he was increasingly outraged by what he regarded as the Church's fiscally motivated exploitation of it. From his austere point of view, the founding of elaborate intercessory institutions was ostentatious folly. And the behavior of the priests who served in them seemed all too often to be offensively scandalous.[5] Some of Wyclif's early disciples, such as William Swinderby and Walter Brute, followed their mentor in these practical emphases. So also did the band of Lollards which in

1395 surreptitiously nailed "Twelve Conclusions" to the doors of Westminster Abbey and St. Paul's Cathedral. Although these statements were censorious of special prayers for the dead as a "false ground of almsgiving," they did not actually attack purgatory itself.[6]

By the early fifteenth century, however, some Lollards were denying outright the existence of a third place between heaven and hell.[7] In scattered instances throughout the century, and even more notably in the early sixteenth century, Lollards frequently included purgatory and the efficacy of prayers for the dead among the objects of their rationalistic disbelief. For example, John Blomstone of Coventry argued that "prayer and alms avail not the dead; for incontinent after death, he goeth either to heaven or hell; whereupon . . . there is no purgatory." A Buckinghamshire heretic was alleged to have claimed that there was no purgatory; but that even if there were, "and every mass that is said should deliver a soul out of purgatory, there should be never a soul there; for there be more masses said in a day, than there be bodies buried in a month."[8] Other Lollards were in some confusion on the matter. John Tyball of Steeple Bumpstead (Essex) in 1528 confessed that for a while he had thought that there was no purgatory. Now, however, he had come to believe that there was a place of painful posthumous purgation, but for sinners only: "the souls of good men which departeth this world . . . be in some place of joy and pleasure." Similar examples of Lollard disbelief and uncertainty also emerge from other parts of England.[9]

The striking thing about the accounts of the persecution of the Lollards is not that some of those detected for heresy did not believe in purgatory and prayers for the dead; rather it is that this particular deviation from the medieval theological norm occurred so infrequently among them. Although Bishop Blyth's careful heresy hunt of 1511-1512 in the diocese of Coventry and Lichfield ferreted out sizable communities of heretics, his court books do not indicate that their tenets included disbelief in purgatory. Similarly, Archbishop Warham, who at the same time was attempting to search out and destroy heterodoxy within his diocese, was able to detect only one person of heretical views on purgatory.[10] Far more often the authorities accused the Lollards of other things: of scoffing at pilgrimages, of denying the efficacy of holy water and holy bread, of refusing ostentatiously to venerate saints and images, of possessing the scriptures and devotional works in English, and, most serious of all, of disbelieving the doctrine of transubstantiation. Compared with these more characteristic points, the anti-purgatorial heresy appeared infrequently and insignificantly in the general catalogue of Lollard negations. From such dissenters might emanate criticism of the abuses of the chantry system and occasional unsystematic attacks upon purgatory itself. A full-scale onslaught against the doctrine of purgatory, however, would require a new theological mainspring which would go far beyond the simple piety, the works-righteousness notions, and the "popular materialist skepticism" of the Lollards.[11]

Such an impetus was supplied by the doctrine of justification by faith. It was this doctrine which began filtering into England from Germany in the early 1520s and which eventually supplied the theological rationale for the Edwardian dissolution of the chantries. It taught that men are granted salvation, not as a reward for their earthly endeavors, nor as a result of posthumous purgative suffering, but as God's free and sovereign gift to those who have faith. Humans cannot by their own efforts become righteous. But God in his mercy imputes Christ's righteousness to each repentant sinner. These bold insights, which came to Martin Luther over a period of years, had by 1520 forced him to reject the complex of traditional Catholic practices associated with the doctrine of purgatory.[12] His doubts about the doctrine itself were also growing. As his conflict with the Church intensified, and as the radical implications of his doctrine of salvation became increasingly clear to him, he became more and more convinced that purgatory was one of the pestilent products of the papist imagination. Throughout the 1520s, in interviews, letters, and sermons, he gave vent to his mounting impatience with the traditional belief. Finally, in 1530, armed with his most vitriolic pen, he declared war on it in *Ein Widderruff vom Fegefeur* [A Recantation of Purgatory].[13] Examining the most commonly cited scriptural texts supporting the existence of purgatory, Luther concluded that they prove purgatory only if twisted and interpreted beyond all semblance of their original meaning. In fact, "there was no purgatory in the Old Testament, nor in the New Testament at the time of the apostles, nor long thereafter." It was a later invention, inspired by the god Mammon, for the profit of covetous churchmen. Those who favored it he castigated as "liars, blasphemers, faithless enemies of God, betrayers of Christ, and murderers." Indeed, there was "no bigger lie on earth than purgatory."[14]

Several years before Luther wrote this blistering tract, a number of

Englishmen had begun to share his doubts. A few, such as William Tyndale, who actually made the pilgrimage to Wittenberg, may have acquired their anti-purgatorial convictions directly from Luther and his associates. Others, who bought Lutheran books in England on the clandestine market, were able logically to make the same inferences about purgatory from the doctrine of justification by faith as Luther himself had done. Possibly there were still other Englishmen who read and inwardly digested the "pestiferous errors" (several of which dealt with purgatory), a list of which Cardinal Wolsey in 1521 required the prelates to post on their cathedral doors.[15] The defenders of orthodoxy seem to have been aware that the new doctrine had implications for the traditional conception of purgatory and the practices which had been associated with it. Thus, although it is indisputable that Henry VIII objected primarily to Luther's treatment of the sacrament of the altar, he found room in his *Assertio septem sacramentorum* to charge that Luther's denial of papal control over purgatory by means of indulgences was in fact an impugning of purgatory itself.[16] The other redoubtable champion of medieval orthodoxy in the early 1520s, Bishop John Fisher of Rochester, also felt constrained to reassert the traditional doctrine of purgatory in response to mounting criticism, for he devoted an important section of his *Assertionis Lutheranae confutatio* (1523) to the matter. Fisher also returned to this theme in a number of sermons later in the decade, most notably in the first of *Two Fruytfull Sermons* (1526).[17]

The debate on purgatory did not get fully under way in England until the spring of 1529, when the vituperative gentleman of Gray's Inn, Simon Fish, entered the fray with his *Supplicacyon for the Beggers.* Although Tyndale's *Obedience of a Christian Man,* which said many of the same things, had arrived in England the previous year, it was Fish's work which seized the popular imagination. For the *Supplicacyon,* in accusing the clerical order of using the fear of purgatory to fleece a piously gullible nation, expressed brilliantly what many were beginning to suspect. Fish's charge that "this purgatory, and the pope's pardons, is all the cause of the translation of your kingdom so fast into [the clergy's] hands" was designed to appeal to those, including the king and many laymen, who were deeply concerned by the irretrievable disappearance of land down the sinkhole of mortmain. Similarly, his indictment of the clergy for simony—"if they will not pray for no man but for them that give them money, they are tyrants, and lack charity"—was expertly tailored to fit the prejudices of an increasingly anti-clerical populace.[18] Fish, as a friend of Tyndale, no doubt had theological grounds for denying the existence of purgatory, but he did not choose to develop them. In castigating the clergy and deriding the pope as a "cruel tyrant" he designed rather to shock, to anger, and to spur to action. If the issue were raised to this emotion-laden level, he could reasonably expect a systematic theological exposition of the Protestant view of the matter to follow.

It would have to. For Fish's libelous *libellus,* which had encouraged many Englishmen in their anti-clericalism and distrust of purgatory, also impelled Sir Thomas More to reply with a tract of equal brilliance. *The Supplycacyon of Soulys,*[19] which appeared later in 1529, began with a fierce and rather frightened counterattack against the "wily folly" of Fish's "pernicious book."[20] Not content to remain on the defensive, More then proceeded to restate eloquently the traditional case for purgatory and for prayers for the "silly, poor, pewling souls" suffering there.[21] His graphic recitation of the purgative "fire and torments intolerable" to which the souls were forced to submit was carefully calculated to give twinges of concern to all who had a vestige of orthodox piety left in them. What Catholic Christian could harden his heart to the anguished plea of his suffering kinsmen for the "prayers, pilgrimages, and other almsdeeds" which would ameliorate their lot?[22] More went beyond Fish in raising the discussion to a theological plane. Carefully, yet with caustic wit, he reviewed the citations from the scriptures and the arguments from the fathers which he thought would render the traditional concepts impregnable. But what most remains in the memory after reading the *Supplycacyon* is not the theological discussion but the heartrending cry of the "poor prisoners of God."[23]

This is certainly as More intended. Notable though his achievement was, however, its theological apparatus and emotional appeal were not sufficient to discourage further Protestant attacks on the belief in purgatory. Although Tyndale cast passing aspersions on it in many of his later works, the definitive Protestant refutation of More, Fisher, and John Rastell* was written by a youthful English exile on the Continent. John Frith, grieved at the thought "that this their painful purgatory

---

*In 1530 Rastell, More's brother-in-law, published his own defense of purgatory based on concepts of natural philosophy (*A New Boke of Purgatory*). For his later role as a left-wing Protestant promoter of rapid reformation, see below, n. 85, and A. W. Reed, *Early Tudor Drama* (London, Methuen, 1926), chap. 1.

was but a vain imagination, and that it hath of long time but deceived
the people and milked them from their money," attempted to prove as
much in *A Disputacion of Purgatorye,* which first appeared in 1531.[24]
Frith searched the scriptures diligently for the traditional concepts of
purgatory and failed to find them.[25] This, he maintained, was a result
of the fact that "to God can not all the world make satisfaction for one
crime. In so much that if every grass of the ground were a man, even as
holy as ever was Paul or Peter and should pray unto God all their lives
long for one crime, yet could they not make satisfaction for it." Instead, "it is only the blood of Christ" that could purge a man of his
sin.[26] Only God—not the pope and the clergy—could bestow the
merits of Christ's passion. Only Christ—not the Church or the saints—
could be a true "mid dealer" between God and man.[27] In Frith's writing, Luther's dynamic doctrine of justification by faith was thus
brought to bear systematically and convincingly upon the concepts
and practices associated with purgatory.

The effect of this achievement upon the coming generation of English Protestants was momentous. Years later John Louthe, the Elizabethan archdeacon of Nottingham, reminisced about the compelling
attractiveness Frith's book had had for him during his school days in
the early 1530s. He was at Wykeham's college "when Master Thomas
Hardyng [later to become a stalwart Catholic, but now a youthful
Protestant colporteur] delivered me John Frith's Purgatory to read for
two days; but I begged it and craved it for twenty-three days." It also
became required reading for humbler heretics.[28] Frith's *Disputacion*
did not supply the budding reformers with answers to all their questions about the afterlife, as the subsequent controversy between Tyndale and George Joye over "soul-sleep" was to demonstrate.[29] But it did
provide them with a boldly reasoned and charitably argued attack
upon a vital link in the Catholic armor.[30] John Frith died at the stake
in 1533 at the age of thirty. But his influence upon the arguments
marshaled against the doctrine of purgatory—and therefore indirectly
upon the dissolution of the English chantries—was immense indeed.

The tempo of theological disputation in England increased markedly in the 1530s. Lutheran ideas had begun to spread from the universities and the clandestine booksellers to society at large, where they
frequently intermingled with received Lollard notions in the minds of
simple folk confident of the need for reformation and eager to bring it
about. There are indications that in many parts of England the eccle-

siastical authorities were encountering heresy—especially that emanating from disbelief in purgatory and disapproval of the practices traditionally associated with it—on an unprecedented scale. Men of the social and educational elite were also for the first time openly asserting doubts about purgatory.

The members of the church hierarchy who were dedicated to the extirpation of all heresy reacted with predictable sternness. James Bainham, a Gloucestershire gentleman of impressive anti-purgatorial associations (he had married Simon Fish's widow), defended himself with "the authority of the scriptures" against the charge that he had spoken "against purgatory, that there was no such thing, but that it picked men's purses, and against satisfactory masses." For this heresy he was burned in 1532.[31] Nicholas Shaxton was also in trouble for having declared in 1531 that, although it is "evil and dangerous publicly to assert or preach that there is no purgatory, yet to believe that there is no purgatory is by no means damnable." The vice-chancellor of Cambridge University took him in hand and required Shaxton to sign a lengthy pledge listing in detail the heretical writings which he would refrain in future from reading.[32] The intensity of the ecclesiastical antipathy to those who impugned purgatory is further indicated by the posthumous fate of the body of another Gloucestershire gentleman.[33] William Tracy had died in 1530, leaving a will which dispensed with the accustomed funereal pomp and soul-masses for the eminently Protestant reason that "there is but . . . one mediator between God and man, which is Jesus Christ." Two years later Convocation pronounced the will heretical and ordered that the body which had shrouded Tracy's heterodox soul should be exhumed from consecrated ground. In an excess of zeal, Dr. Thomas Parker, the vicar general of Worcester diocese, ordered the body to be burned. But this could legally take place only upon royal orders, and in the protection of his own rights Henry VIII aligned himself—not for the last time in the decade—with the heretics. Parker was fined £300 for his temerity. And the will, which had been the origin of the whole fracas, was soon published, with annotations by Tyndale and Frith, and was circulated widely among those of reforming tendencies.[34]

Other influential and articulate men, who were reluctant to go so far as to disavow the doctrine of purgatory completely, were nevertheless willing to undermine public confidence in it. Some, such as the prominent lawyer Christopher Saint German, were cunningly cautious in their approach. Not only was he careful to publish his *Treatise concernynge the Diuision betwene the Spirytualtie and Temporaltie* anonymously; he also attempted to retain a spurious air of impartiality as he reported what "some" were saying about the Church. Was it his fault that people were bruiting about arguments that "because great riches have come to the Church for praying for souls in purgatory, [they] have by words affirmed that there is no purgatory"?[35]

Edward Crome and Hugh Latimer were bolder than Saint German. These men, alumni of the proto-Protestant cell group which met in the White Horse in Cambridge, soon made something of a specialty of denouncing the complex of pious practices associated with purgatory. In May 1530, as members of a commission assisting Archbishop Warham and Lord Chancellor More in compiling a list of heretical opinions contained in recent English books, both Crome and Latimer had concurred in the condemnation of the works of Tyndale and Fish. These writings, the commission reported, "totally do swarm full of heresies and detestable opinions" such as the denial of the existence of purgatory and the benefit of chantries and soul-masses to souls suffering there.[36] Crome, however, was soon railing from the pulpit against doctrines which he had affirmed on the commission. Early in 1531 he preached a sermon in London in which he attacked a whole catalogue of traditional Catholic practices and expressed cautious doubts about purgatory and the efficacy of prayers for the dead. When examined by Bishop John Stokesley and other ecclesiastics, Crome agreed to abjure his offensive notions and to express his newly corrected opinions in a sermon. However, although it was orthodox enough in word, Crome's sermon was apparently equivocal in tone. When the martyr-to-be, James Bainham, who was present, heard Crome assert that "he thought there was a purgatory after this life, he thought in his mind that the said Master Crome lied, and spoke against his conscience."[37] Before many years had passed, Crome was once again decrying the abuses associated with the doctrine of purgatory from the pulpits of London.

In 1531 Latimer too was in trouble with the ecclesiastical authorities for an outspoken sermon in London. Precisely what he said at St. Mary Abchurch that so offended Bishop Stokesley has not been recorded, but some of his indiscretions there almost certainly dealt with purgatory. It is striking that the first two of the sixteen articles which the bishops were soon requiring him to sign dealt with purgatory and soul-masses.[38] Latimer was at this time intensely concerned about the way in which folk were abusing such traditional practices as going on pilgrimages, using images, praying to saints, and interceding for souls in purgatory. In a remarkably candid letter to Archbishop Warham, he argued that all of these practices were lawful, but they were hardly matters of central importance to the Christian faith. The trouble was that many people tended to view them as such. "From a mistaken love of God and by a foolish devotion," simple folk were tempted to concentrate on these "voluntary" appendages of faith rather than upon its compulsory essentials, "which bring eternal life to those who keep them, and eternal death to those who neglect them." His preaching had been designed to correct this state of affairs and to bring about "a reformation in the judgment of the vulgar" which would instil in them a proper sense of Christian priorities. For these reasons, in his reluctant and partial submission to the bishops (March 1532), Latimer was willing merely to concede that he had indulged in undue "vehemence of speaking." Only two of the sixteen articles would he sign, neither of which could be construed as bestowing his blessing upon the practices which he felt were abused. The following month, however, after another rash outburst had once more got him into hot water, he made a complete submission to the king, acknowledging that he had erred "not only in discretion but also in doctrine," and begging the forgiveness of the bishops.[39]

Less than a year later the unabashed Latimer was again in the forefront of controversy. In March 1533, when invited by the mayor of Bristol to deliver a series of Lenten sermons in the city, he gave vent to the same inflammatory views. Among these controversial matters once again was purgatory. Exactly what Latimer said is uncertain, for his own highly interpretative reporting about his preaching dates from several months after the event. It is possible that John Hilsey, the prior of the Dominicans in Bristol, was correct in commenting that Latimer's "mind is much more against the abusing of things than against the things it self." The conservatives of the city, however, could not appreciate the distinction. From Latimer's point of view, preaching that "the souls that be in purgatory . . . have no need of our prayers, but rather . . . pray for us" may merely have been an attempt to rectify soul-destroying abuses while leaving purgatory itself intact. But to the conservatives such preaching was "schismatic and erroneous," threatening a whole complex of beliefs and observances which were inextricably bound up with purgatory, and impugning the authority of the Church. They responded with their own champions, and an orgy of pulpit-thumping ensued. The city was divided into two antagonistic camps: those who favored Latimer and "his new manner of preaching," and those who rallied to the support of the "old manner of preaching" of William Hubbardine, Edward Powell, and Nicholas Wilson.[40] Hubbardine was an especially unfortunate choice. That he would respond to Latimer by vehemently advocating the old faith at its worst was perhaps only to be expected. But, like so many defenders of the faith in the 1530s, he committed the cardinal error of punctuating his discourse with ill-timed assertions "that Rome cannot be destroyed nor can [it] err." Dr. Powell's indiscretion was at least as bad. By fulminating against "the king's proceedings," which were then well advanced, he went still further in identifying conservative preaching with treason.[41]

This, indeed, was the crucial point. For in 1533, following Henry's marriage with Anne Boleyn and the break with Rome, the English climate was more favorable for preaching such as Latimer's than it had been previously. The old guard, by the same token, would now have to be more cautious in their utterances. The outcome of the Bristol affair exemplified these new trends. Dr. Thomas Bagarde, the chancellor of the diocese of Worcester, who had taken what must have seemed to be the obvious step of inhibiting both Latimer and Hubbardine from preaching, was obliged by Thomas Cromwell to reinstate Latimer and, "with sorrowful heart and weeping tears," to protest his loyalty to the king.[42] Furthermore, when Cromwell appointed a commission to investigate the situation in Bristol, it is notable that his interest was "especially what words Hubbardine should have concerning the King's his majesty." Equally significant is the fact that the surviving depositions which the conservative-minded commissioners compiled dealt (with one exception) with the trespasses of Hubbardine and Powell rather than with those of Latimer. By the first week of July Hubbardine had been sent to the Tower, and within a year Powell and Wilson had also been incarcerated.[43] In contrast, Latimer, whose innovative utterances had started the whole embroglio, emerged scot-free with an enhanced reputation at court. And in January 1534, less than a year after the onset of the Bristol preaching crisis, Archbishop Cranmer appointed Latimer to preach another series of Lenten sermons — this time before Henry VIII.[44]

In the spread of the new attitudes towards purgatory, as in so many other areas of doctrine and policy, it was the severance of ties with Rome resulting from the royal divorce that made the decisive difference in preparing the way for reformation. It was not that the pope's control over the Englishmen's faith or observances had been in any way extensive. But the banishment of papal authority from England, which had finally become necessary if Henry were to get the divorce which he urgently required, provided an excellent opportunity for many Englishmen of a reforming bent to call for a thorough eradication of the vestiges of popery.[45] The very rhetoric of the break with Rome tended to further this tendency. Meanwhile, Henry's apologists and propagandists felt it necessary to present the papacy and all its works in the worst possible light. And if they were in fact correct in asserting that the papacy's power had been usurped and that it had committed "countless detestable enormities," then the whole complex of beliefs and practices which had been associated with it would of course come into question.

So it was with purgatory. Because the pope, as the descendant of St. Peter, was believed to have powers of "binding and loosing" in purgatory as well as on earth, the whole issue of purgatory was inextricably intertwined with the papacy. The early English reformers loved to describe purgatory as the creation of avaricious pontiffs for their own fiscal benefit. If purgatory really existed, they taunted, why did the pope not commit the charitable act of emptying the horrid place, since he purportedly had the power to do so?[46] But now the authority of the papacy was suddenly expelled from England. What effect would this remarkable development have on the future of the doctrine which had been so closely associated with it? The pope, Tyndale had argued, "is grounded in purgatory." Subsequent events revealed that purgatory (or at least the Englishmen's conception of it) was very much grounded on the pope.[47] And, despite the herculean efforts of some conservatives, the doctrine was to be swept away, along with many other remnants of popery, in the maelstrom of events called the English Reformation.

The link between the expulsion of papal authority from England and the inauguration of the official attack upon purgatory is clear. John Foxe correctly dated the process from 1534, "at what time purgatory and such trumpery began to grow in contempt."[48] For in the late spring of that year Archbishop Cranmer issued an order commanding all preachers to inveigh against the papacy and forbidding them to speak out in defense of purgatory.

Cranmer's order reflected the growing alarm of many influential Englishmen at the spread of disorderly and divisive preaching throughout the realm. The conservatives among them were outraged by the preaching of those who denied the real presence, the existence of purgatory, and the efficacy of almsgiving for the succour of the departed. The would-be reformers were equally offended by the widespread "railing against new gospellers [and] justification of faith." And both of these emerging camps — to say nothing of the king who arbitrated between them — were angered by the defiant temerity of those who continued to proclaim the power of the pope.[49] A lull in the homiletic storm seemed highly desirable, so in April 1534 Cranmer and several of his episcopal colleagues in the southern province* issued letters in their dioceses which were designed to produce it.[50] Sternly they required all previously accredited preachers to obtain new licenses and "in no wise to touch or intermeddle themselves to preach or teach any such thing that might slander or bring in doubt and opinion the catholic and received doctrine of Christ's Church, or speak of such matters as touch the prince, his laws, or succession." In issuing these letters, the primary concern of Bishops Stokesley, Gardiner, and Longland was undoubtedly to suppress all preaching of a Protestant coloration. This was not what Cranmer had in mind. As he wrote to Latimer, his intent was to impede "the malignity of divers preachers" who had been publicly censuring the king's "just cause of matrimony" and denouncing the recent parliamentary statutes.[51] If the letters were also intended to discourage innovative preaching, Cranmer gave no indication of the fact to Latimer.

Henry VIII and some of his lay and ecclesiastical advisers felt that the situation was critical enough to warrant an inhibition of more general incidence as well.[52] According to Cranmer, a group of bishops (some of whom may have remained in London following the March session of convocation) had an important hand in drafting it.[53] The "council" was also drawn into consultations about it. And the king himself, whom Archbishop Lee of York cited as the initiator of the whole project,[54] made a number of substantive contributions to the document — among them, that preachers be commanded to refrain

*John Stokesley of London, Stephen Gardiner of Winchester, and John Longland of Lincoln.

from holding forth on the subject of miracles. In early June 1534, following these consultations, Archbishop Cranmer issued the order "for
preaching and bidding of the beads in all sermons to be made within
this realm," which was to be binding in both ecclesiastical provinces.[55]
   This document was devoted in the main to ensuring that every
preacher should inveigh "in the presence of his greatest audience
against the usurped power of the bishop of Rome," and should at the
same time inform his parishioners of the "false and unjust handling" of
the said bishop in obstructing the royal divorce. To enable the preachers to expand on "the king's just cause of matrimony" in convincing
detail, the order provided a somewhat tendentious fourteen-hundred-
word-long history of the matter. In the bidding prayer, the preachers
were instructed to include Queen Anne and to omit the bishop of
Rome. The order also dealt with doctrine. It ordained that no preachers should rail against each other unduly "nor uncharitably deprave
one another in open audience." To avoid having cause for priestly
squabbling, it then decreed that for one year no preachers "shall
preach neither with nor against" such controversial topics as purgatory, the cult of saints, clerical marriage, justification by faith, pilgrimages, and miracles. On all of these subjects, the imperial ambassador Eustace Chapuys reported, the archbishop promised to pro-
nounce definitively within a year.[56] If by banning these hot issues from
the pulpits of England Cranmer was depriving the Protestant preachers of some of their favorite topics, he was at the same time muzzling
the vast bulk of the clergy of England from defending the practices
and doctrines of medieval orthodoxy. By virtue of this order, the highest ecclesiastical authority in England had also confessed that these
matters were subject to real uncertainty. Was there a purgatory or not?
For a year no one in England would know for sure.
   In fact, more than two years elapsed before the prelates made a definitive pronouncement on these ticklish issues. Yet this was hardly a
period of homiletic quiescence. Comparatively speaking, the first of
these years (ca. 1 June 1534 to ca. 1 June 1535) seems to have been
relatively uneventful. There were, to be sure, a few preachers who
strayed into forbidden territory, like the Franciscan friar who was carried away by his own eloquence in a sermon at Herne (Kent). Railing
against the "Judas fellows" who preached against pilgrimages, and
contending that if St. Thomas the Martyr "were a devil in hell if the
Church had canonized him he ought to worship him," he then pro-

ceeded to commit the cardinal sin of ostentatiously omitting the king and queen from the bidding prayer. In Mistley (Essex) another friar found himself in trouble when he vociferously attacked satisfactory masses and penance as a "superstitious robbery of the honor of Christ's blood."[57] Following the expiration of Cranmer's order in early June 1535, however, this comparative calm was disturbed by an increasing quantity of incendiary preaching. For it was now unclear what the official policy on preaching actually was. And given this uncertainty, many preachers felt constrained to speak out about the issues confronting the realm, thereby unsettling many of the people and threatening public order.

If Henry VIII was aware of this danger, he gave no indication of it. Instead, on 3 June he wrote a blistering circular to the bishops concerning the royal supremacy. Why had the bishops been so lukewarm in proclaiming it? Why had they not been tirelessly denouncing the bishop of Rome's usurped authority and ensuring that their subordinates did likewise? In the future they must be more vociferously vocal on these topics and be sure that all references to the bishop of Rome were "abolished, eradicated, and razed out" of the service books in their dioceses.[58] Perhaps Henry was correct in assuming that the most pressing necessity of the moment was the acceptance — by clergy and laity alike — of his recently acquired title as "supreme head in earth of the Church of England." Perhaps he also calculated that the preachers of the realm would continue to observe the restraints upon homiletic license which Cranmer's order had imposed, thus ensuring a continuation of the relative calm of the previous year. For whatever reason, having put into the hearts of the bishops the fear of the royal wrath about the supremacy, Henry was willing to leave the general oversight of preaching in the hands of his two chief lieutenants in matters ecclesiastical, Thomas Cromwell and Archbishop Cranmer.

These men were by no means aloof and disinterested executants of royal policy. By 1535 both had come to be partisans of the reforming cause in the midst of what Cranmer called "this world of reformation."[59] It is thus not surprising that both men promptly began to encourage the preaching of clerics of reforming tendencies. To some extent, of course, they had been doing this already. Several of Cromwell's remembrances of 1534 indicate that he was actively interested in preaching at that time, and he had apparently been toying with schemes "to appoint preachers to go throughout this realm to preach the Gospel and true Word of God."[60] Both he and Cranmer had also for some time been discreetly extending comfort and assistance to preachers who favored the Protestant cause. But in the period following Henry's letter to the bishops and the expiration of Cranmer's order on preaching they appear to have grown bolder. Within five weeks Cromwell suddenly licensed four preachers (including the martyr-to-be Thomas Garret) "to preach throughout the realm." Cranmer was also keeping preachers busy under his archiepiscopal license, both in his own diocese and throughout the rest of the country.[61] As they traversed the realm denouncing the pope, these preachers frequently found it impossible to keep from pontificating on issues dear to the reformers. Tense and bitter incidents ensued in numerous parishes, and at least one person concluded that "all those that preached at the king's commandment were heretics nowadays." But when one of Cromwell's preachers came under hostile fire in Kent, the archbishop, while confessing himself less than fully informed about the case, nevertheless came stoutly to the defense. For, Cranmer reasoned, to censure the erring preacher would be greatly to discourage "learned men which favoreth the truth, to take any pains on them in setting forth of the same."[62]

The activities of these preachers put the other bishops in a difficult spot. Cranmer's promised determination of disputed doctrinal points had not materialized, nor had he provided new instructions following the official expiration of his order on preaching. Had it in fact expired? Archbishop Lee of York, who chose to operate on the assumption that it had not, was especially exercised when in late October 1535 one of Cromwell's protégés flagrantly flouted its spirit by railing and jesting in Selby "that it is hypocrisy to fast." Lee was also disturbed by others who "preach against purgatory and other things, wherewith the people grudge." Nevertheless most priests in his diocese were obeying "the king's commandment" diligently. He had restrained a friar from preaching in favor of purgatory, "as we know not the king's pleasure." But he was eager for the ecclesiastical authorities to devise a book determining "all these matters of controversy . . . so that the preaching might be uniform, and that avowable and well grounded." In any case, Lee observed ruefully, because of the small size of the northern livings "we have here very few preachers."[63]

Bishop Stokesley of London, on the other hand, who could not bless the Lord for a paucity of powerful preachers, chose to assume that the inhibiting order had lapsed and that preaching would once again be subject to the regulation of the bishops, as it had been before Henry's divorce. Therefore, when in August 1535 Thomas Corthope, the staunchly conservative curate of Harwich, was accused of preaching in favor of purgatory, he was able to invoke the support of Stokesley. "Now," Corthope claimed, "I dare boldly speak of it and preach of it, too. For I have spoken with mine ordinary the bishop of London of late and he hath showed me so that it be not against no thing that is granted by act of Parliament we may preach as we have done in time past."[64]

Stokesley, however, had a difficult diocese to control. All types of theological opinion flourished in the capital, including Protestantism of varying degrees of virulence. Some London preachers declared that purgatory "was tribulations of this world, other [men said it was] punishments in another world, and some saith there is none."[65] Especially offensive to Stokesley was the fact that many of these views were being encouraged from the prestigious pulpit of Paul's Cross, which was formally under his jurisdiction. It was vital for the government to control the preaching there, no matter how much Cromwell's theological predilections differed from Stokesley's. Conflict was inevitable. Cromwell had appointed the fast-rising provincial of the Dominicans, John Hilsey, to preach at the Cross on 18 July. Stokesley was furious, for he was certain that Hilsey would embarrass him by maintaining "his undiscreet fashion of remembrance of the souls departed." He had good reason. For when he had required Hilsey "to conform himself in praying for the souls departed as Master Latimer and Master Crome and other men did," Hilsey had refused to respond. Exasperated with the situation, Stokesley grudgingly conceded that after his own departure from London Hilsey might be permitted (on Cromwell's express orders) to "contaminate my church." But he was grieved at the thought of the spiritual infection that would inevitably spread among his flock. As it happened, Cromwell and Hilsey retreated, and on 18 July the pulpit at Paul's Cross was occupied by Stokesley's nominee, the reliably conservative Simon Matthew.[66] But Stokesley, who had won this skirmish, lost the battle. Five months later, on 22 December 1535, Cromwell gave to the "contaminator" Hilsey (who had recently been preferred to the bishopric of Rochester) a broad commission to supervise preaching in London and its environs, including Paul's Cross.[67] And during the ensuing three years Hilsey used his powers to fill the pulpits of London with men whose views Stokesley found most uncongenial.

It was, in fact, during the first six months of 1536 that the discordant chorus of preachers came to a forte, despite the fact that on 7 January Henry VIII sent to the bishops another of his irritable circulars designed to prevent just this.[68] As in his letter of the previous June, Henry admonished the bishops resolutely to encourage preaching against "the filthy and corrupt abominations of the bishop of Rome." But this time he had a new concern. He had been informed that there "swarmeth abroad" a horde of preachers unencumbered with wisdom, learning, or judgment, who nevertheless were giving vent to their opinions on sensitive topics. Indignantly Henry ordered the bishops to revoke the licenses of such preachers as "treat and dispute such matters as do rather engender a contrariety than either touch things necessary or apt." Along with the king's letters Cromwell sent letters of his own, reproving "the pronunciation of novelties, without wise and discreet qualification," and obediently reinforcing the points which his master had made. A further order was issued by Cromwell on 20 January reasserting the clause of Cranmer's order of June 1534 which had commanded priests "to abstain from preaching anything either against or in favor of the existence of purgatory, images, the worship of saints, and other doubtful theological questions." It is possible that, as Chapuys suggested, this demonstration of the king's determination to harness the preachers was designed for diplomatic purposes.[69] Certainly it had little effect in England. During the coming months, prior to the issuance of the Ten Articles, the tempo and intensity of contentiously novel preaching increased markedly. And the poor bishops who had been hectored by Henry's letters received scant support from either Cromwell or the king as they combated "contrariety" in their dioceses.

The reforming preachers were by far the hardest for the bishops to control. In the diocese of York, for example, Archbishop Lee reported difficulty with a conservative friar, who had publicly been upholding the traditional notions about purgatory. Because the friar had done this "the king's pleasure not known," Lee had been forced to discharge him from preaching, and the friar had apparently complied willingly. The radical friars, however, were less accommodating. Despite Lee's insistence that no one preach "of any article mentioned in the order taken by the king's highness," a large-lunged "light friar" had been holding forth on a number of the forbidden topics in Doncaster. His hearers had been much offended, and when the vicar of the parish attempted to intervene, a nasty scene had ensued. In response to vigorous complaints from Doncaster, the archbishop had summoned the friar to discuss his preaching. But the light friar had been recalcitrant and had hurried instead to London to "ask counsel" (from Cromwell?). Since he had subsequently returned to the diocese and was continuing to preach as slanderously as ever, Lee promised to attempt to silence him. Also troublesome had been a certain grey friar who had been enthusiastically advocating new things, as had been two or three preachers "that pretended to have the king's authority." Generally, however, despite the grudging of the people at the preaching of novelties, the diocese was relatively quiet, and Lee promised to soldier on in the causes of order and orthodoxy.[70]

Four months later Bishop Longland of Lincoln was having even more trouble with the radical preachers in his diocese. He was somewhat irritated at Latimer's disciple Thomas Garret, who in May was touring Lincolnshire with the king's license, preaching with indiscreet enthusiasm, and purportedly arousing popular resentment. But with Thomas Swynnerton, Longland was utterly exasperated. This left-leaning Protestant publicist and preacher, who had also been licensed by Cromwell, was proclaiming his extreme views in southern Buckinghamshire, indecently close to the bishop's manor at Wooburn, and in the heart of Lollard country. Shockingly enough, Swynnerton was preaching to eager audiences not only on Sundays but also on weekdays, sometimes several times per day. People had been leaving their work and walking for miles to hear him, whereupon, Longland acidly commented, "they fall into poverty and much idleness." The bishop even feared a general disruption of society, and pointed to an increase in the number of robberies in the area to show the inevitable result of the mixture of under-employment and agitation.[71]

What were Garret and Swynnerton preaching? Longland did not say, but a list of articles against innovative preachers who had been active in Sussex gives some indications. According to deponents in Rye and Winchelsea, Garret had been holding forth "against purgatory and suffrages for souls departed, and against oblations to saints, and against pilgrimage." Swynnerton's messages in similarly inflammatory fashion had meddled with topics whose prohibition Cromwell had recently reasserted. He had allegedly declared "that our Lady was not of such honor as the people gave unto her, and preached against oblation done to saints in Church of God, and against pilgrimage, and against

prayer to be said for souls departed, and against purgatory."[72] Faced
with the vigorous expression of ideas such as these and deeply offended
by Swynnerton's effrontery in preaching from Longland's own pulpit
in Wooburn parish church, the bishop appealed to Cromwell to restrain his preacher. Cromwell complied, but with such deliberate haste
that Swynnerton had ample time to disappear into London or Essex.
Despite Longland's protests, both Garret and Swynnerton continued to
preach actively in other parts of the realm.[73]

Unlike his brother prelates of York and Lincoln, Hugh Latimer,
who was consecrated bishop of Worcester on 26 September 1535,
made no attempt to suppress the preaching of novelties. Indeed, Latimer's own chaplains were among the most vehement of the radical
preachers in his diocese. Consequently it fell to a conservative layman
— Thomas Bell, sheriff of Gloucester — to uphold the causes of order
and orthodoxy. Bell, who evidently felt that he could obtain no satisfaction from Cromwell, wrote to Bishop Stokesley in June 1536 to report the pernicious doctrines which preachers were belching forth.
Particularly offensive had been Latimer's chaplain Thomas Benet,
who had asserted on more than one occasion that soul-masses could
not help the souls of the departed: "if the purgatory priests do pray
with their tongues till their tongues be worn to stumps, yet their prayers shall not help nor prevail the souls departed." Bell had not lost
hope that someone might yet silence Benet and his like. If Stokesley
and the duke of Norfolk could convince the king of the disreputable
extremes to which the "disorderly and colorable preaching" had gone,
quiet might once again return to the shires of England.[74]

Stokesley, however, was scarcely in a position to intercede in behalf
of conservatives in the countryside, for he had virtually lost control of
the preaching in his own diocese of London. Since December 1535
Bishop Hilsey had been acting as the government's impresario of the
pulpit at Paul's Cross. And during the first half of 1536 he secured a
constant succession of preachers — either prominent reformers or notable conservatives — to advocate the royal supremacy.[75] Stokesley, who
had obediently set forth the supremacy on a previous occasion,[76] was
not among them, but Longland and Cuthbert Tunstall of Durham
were. So too, from another camp, were John Salcot of Bangor, Shaxton of Salisbury, and Hilsey himself. However, the real stars of Hilsey's
show were Latimer, unleashed once again in London, and Archbishop
Cranmer. Both railed against purgatory. Cranmer, in fact, allegedly

proclaimed Henry VIII to be "at a full point [precise moment for action] for friars and chantry priests, that they shall away all that, saving those that can preach."[77]

The imperial ambassador Chapuys watched in disbelief as the preaching campaign gathered momentum. He could understand, although it filled him with revulsion, that the preachers should attack purgatory as a prelude to a royal confiscation of ecclesiastical endowments. But what royal logic enabled the king in January to issue strict orders forbidding preaching on controverted issues and then in February to tolerate a governmentally organized propaganda campaign in the capital city in which these orders were systematically flouted? "The king's fickleness and inclination to new and strange things is such as I cannot describe!" he exclaimed.[78] A further indication of the change of policy came in March. While a renegade monk of Syon was preaching against purgatory in the presence of the king, another monk butted in and declared, "You lie!" By making public assertions about purgatory both monks had technically transgressed against the recent restatement of Cranmer's order on preaching. It was a sign of the times, however, that the monk who had blurted out his faith in one of the time-honored doctrines of the Church was arrested and threatened with execution, while the other monk completed his heretical sermon.[79]

Stokesley's loss of influence and control is well illustrated by another incident. On 23 February a certain John Stanton (probably an agent provocateur) went to confession at the Crutched Friars near the Tower of London. A remarkable dialogue ensued which revealed the confessor, George Rowland, to be an outspoken critic of recent religious developments. When Stanton confessed that there were several things "in my stomach which grieveth my conscience very sore"—all of them induced by Latimer's iconoclasm—the priest began repeatedly to damn Latimer as a "false knave" and "an heretic." While Stanton cleverly led him on, Rowland's confessional candor grew increasingly incriminating, as he affirmed the pope to be the head of the universal Church, avowed the value of images and the reality of purgatory, and vituperated upon the transitory shallowness of the new learning. Having received absolution, Stanton departed to make extensive notes of the interview, which he promptly sent to Cromwell. Cromwell did not wait long before taking action. On 7 March he dispatched his ecclesiastical factotum Hilsey to the Crutched Friars to inhibit "a doctor and three or four more" (no doubt including Rowland) from hearing confessions. To fill their places Hilsey installed several new priests, including John Cardmaker, a Franciscan friar whom Cromwell on 12 January had licensed to preach throughout the realm. Almost immediately the outraged Stokesley responded by sending his apparitor, who came and fulminated against Hilsey, saying that "no such as he is shall have jurisdiction within his lord's precinct." Hilsey reported this to Cromwell, who two days later summoned Stokesley to answer for the conduct of his apparitor. But Stokesley, as on another occasion, pleaded illness and failed to appear.[80] In the spring of 1536 illness— whether real or feigned—could not obscure the fact that in the diocese of London the real power to govern preaching and to combat heresy had passed from the conservative Stokesley to the reforming duo of Cromwell and Hilsey.

In the face of this explosion of innovative preaching, the conservative champions were strangely quiet in the first half of 1536. To be sure, a few of them found the courage publicly to protest against the trends of the times. In Oxford, for example, two dons delivered sermons in May which on point after point transgressed the preaching orders of Cranmer and Cromwell. The one don, William Weston of Lincoln College, after chiding the undergraduates for organizing teach-ins ("privy lectures") on heretical topics, went on to make "a most grievous exclamation against the heresy of such as should say there was no purgatory." The other don, Master [Richard] Smyth of Merton, apparently devoted most of his sermon to proving "that works did justify and not only faith." However, he also prayed for the souls in purgatory, which one listener deemed "contrary to the commandment."[81] It was, of course, perfectly permissible to pray for (but not to preach about) those in purgatory. As religious tensions mounted in the spring of 1536, however, rumors may well have been spreading in Oxford, as they were in London, which tempted hyper-enthusiastic reformers to give a selectively Protestant reading to the preaching orders. As early as March it was being noised abroad in London that a number of the most influential bishops did not believe in purgatory. When one Dr. Creukehorne was brought to Lambeth for questioning about his politically charged visions of the Virgin Mary, he compounded his difficulties by claiming that he could prove the existence of purgatory by a certain verse in the psalter. But under the hostile cross-examination of Bishops Cranmer, Latimer, and Shaxton, his defense collapsed. He had, he affirmed, been told about the verse by Bishop Stokesley, but now he could not recall which it was.[82] With so many powers in church and state thus arrayed against them, it is hardly surprising that most conservatives chose to look on in silent disbelief as the radical preachers peddled their controversial wares.

Some thoughtful observers were increasingly concerned by this argumentative wrangling in a theological vacuum. One such was Thomas Starkey, who since early 1535 had been advising the king and Cromwell on matters of state, and who was attempting to sketch the outlines of a moderate approach to religion and politics. In a memorandum entitled "Of Preaching," which was passed around in governmental circles in 1536, Starkey argued strongly for muzzling the preachers. He conceded that preaching is a necessary medium for proclaiming the truth of God's Word. But on obscure and arguable points many preachers had been tempted to "fantasy after their own pleasure, without any stay of judgment therein," to the destruction of the unity of Christian people. To avoid such "discord in preaching," Starkey proposed that the preachers be "directed and tempered by a certain rule of judgment, from which they may not square." The rule was to be this: on all obscure matters which were repugnant neither to God's Word, the power of the king, nor the laws of the realm, the preachers were to base their utterances upon the opinions of the ancient doctors and the "laudable custom of the Church of England." If they refused to be obedient and conformable, let "their bodies and goods . . . stand at the king's pleasure!"[83]

Why such severity? Because, as Starkey pointed out in a letter to Henry VIII, the innovating preachers, in their uncharitable assaults upon the beliefs and practices of traditional orthodoxy, had made it almost impossible either to salvage the worthy remnants of medieval Christianity or to construct a new orthodoxy for an obedient people. To illustrate his argument, Starkey singled out the effect of the antipurgatorial preaching which was so prevalent. The radicals, he commented,

under the color of driving away man's tradition and popishness . . . had almost set your people at such liberty from all old customs and ceremonies that they began . . . little to esteem other virtues or honesty. And with the despising of purgatory, they began little to regard hell, heaven, or any other felicity hereafter to be had in another life. For when the knot of obedience, wherein your people had lived many a day, was once broken and plucked away, then the multitude, which ever by their own nature are prone, and ever have been, to all pleasure and liberty, began to slip from all ancient customs and ceremonies, and to the contempt and despising of all traditions, moved chiefly . . . by the imprudent preaching of them which lacked judgment to see and perceive, how that in such a time, in the alteration of laws, people ought most specially to be contained in due obedience and restrained from lewd liberty.[84]

By the summer of 1536 Henry VIII and his chief advisers finally showed an awareness of the urgency of the situation. They must curb the homiletic altercations which had been disturbing the peace; they must guide the theological change which they had set in motion by breaking with the papacy; they must end the uncertainties which Cranmer's 1534 order on preaching had introduced. The means which they chose to accomplish these ends was a doctrinal statement, the Ten Articles, which was passed by convocation on 11 July. Though ambiguous and flexible in many respects, this statement represented a considerable departure from traditional orthodox teaching on purgatory. It had not been adopted without much soul-searching and anxious debate.

If a number of Cromwell's associates had had their way, the authorities would have moved at a far earlier date to redefine purgatory—or to have denied its existence altogether. As early as August 1534, a group of radical reformers—apparently led by that early Tudor jack-of-all-trades John Rastell, and including Sir Francis Bigod and probably Clement Armstrong—sent to Cromwell a comprehensive and rather fanciful blueprint for rapid reformation. Among its intriguing suggestions was the recommendation that before the next meeting of Parliament the government should supervise the compiling and printing of books advocating the marriage of priests, arguing against the veneration of images, and proving "that the prayers of men that be here living for the souls of them that be dead can in no wise be profitable to them that be dead." Later that year, while Parliament was in session (3 November to 18 December), a member of Cromwell's office composed a memorandum of "things necessary . . . to be remembered before the breaking up of the Parliament." For this anonymous clerk, uncertainty in matters of belief and practice was intolerable. Therefore he impatiently urged that "such things as be now of late confessed to be abused in time past be plainly confirmed by Parliament or wholly prohibited." Almost half of those items which he hoped that Parliament would proscribe dealt with purgatory:

That it cannot be proved by scripture that the bishops of Rome may deliver souls out of purgatory, nor that there is any purgatory. That if there be a purgatory, that there is neither pain of fire nor heat, nor sight of devils. That it is a more necessary and more charitable prayer to pray for them that be alive than for them that be dead.[85]

There is no record that Parliament discussed or took action on either of these proposals.[86]

Throughout the following year, however, the pressure continued. In March one of the king's Lenten preachers advised Henry to convoke the theologians to determine with finality "whether in the consecrated host was the real body of God, and whether there was a purgatory."[87] Some months later Clement Armstrong, who was hoping to become an adviser to Cromwell on the religious and economic problems of the commonwealth, sent Cromwell a fat volume containing his own sermons and treatises, at least one of which vigorously denounced purgatory.[88] Thomas Swynnerton, one of Cromwell's itinerant preachers, also found time to dedicate to his master a manuscript treatise on "The Tropes and Figures of Scripture." In it he repeatedly pointed to the "wild conjectural fantasy" of purgatory as an example of the truth-distorting potentialities of the allegorical approach to the scriptures.[89]

It is not clear at what point the government first decided to bend under this pressure. In June 1535 it had permitted the publication of William Marshall's English primer, which had had the temerity to declare that "there is nothing in the *dirige* [office of the dead] taken out of scripture, that maketh any more mention of the souls departed, than doth the tale of Robin Hood." Later that year it had allowed Marshall to continue his iconoclastic campaign with the publication of his own translation of Martin Bucer's attack on images. And, according to Chapuys, when the Reformation Parliament met for its last session on 4 February 1536 the government had supplied the members with books against both purgatory and the adoration of saints. Shortly thereafter Reginald Pole's English correspondents informed him — with a certain naiveté — that Parliament was about to abolish purgatory.[90] While members of this Parliament may well have discussed this and other controversial topics, the final decisions on the matter were obviously made elsewhere.

On New Year's Day 1536 the English emissary-theologians — Bishop Edward Foxe of Hereford, Robert Barnes, and Nicholas Heath — had begun negotiating about a number of doctrines with the Lutherans in Wittenberg. Despite a short disputation on private masses, it is doubtful that they spent much time discussing purgatory.[91] That doctrine was, however, one of the major items on the agenda in late March when a group of prelates met in Lambeth Palace "for the determination of certain articles and for the reform of ecclesiastical ceremonies."[92] At long last they were beginning work on the authoritative statement which Cranmer had promised two years earlier and which in July was to become the Ten Articles.[93]

Astonishingly enough, by 1 April Chapuys was reporting that the bishops "do not admit purgatory."[94] Improbable though this may at first seem, it is likely that Chapuys was correct. One possible indication of this is the sermon preached at Paul's Cross on 26 March by Robert Singleton. This flaming Protestant, who was in close touch with Cromwell during this period, spoke in favor of prayer for the souls of the departed, but made only deprecatory references to purgatory and the "earthly foundations" and practices associated with it.[95] An even more interesting and reliable insight into the ponderings of the prelates came from one of the newest and brashest of the Cromwellian bishops, William Barlow of St. David's. In trouble the following year for his inflammatory preaching against purgatory, Barlow now composed a lengthy defense in which he told of the deliberations of the assemblage of prelates "among whom as an inferior and least of learning I was one."[96] They had "seriously reasoned upon and earnestly debated by such places of authentic scriptures" which the churchmen had in the past used to prove the existence of purgatory (Matthew 5:25-26; I Corinthians 3:11-15). But "conferring our ingenuities with others it could not be tried that they formed any thing to the finding or establishment of purgatory." The prelates then turned to the apocrypha, especially to II Maccabees 12:40-45. It *did* refer to prayer and sacrifices for the departed, but, according to Barlow, was "most suspected to be of least authority." Finally, the bishops perused the writings of the Church fathers and discovered "no little contrariety among the most part of them all." Nevertheless, he concluded, because the views of some of the fathers were corroborated by "custom of long continuance," the bishops determined that "it was meet and expedient to pray for the souls departed." They had been concerned, however, that there be "no determination of any special place, or expressed assertion of any name, either to be called *sinus Abrahae* [Abraham's bosom] or other wise, referring it to God." By the consensus of the prelates, then, the Church would have ceased to use the word "purgatory." And churchmen would have to be on their guard lest the continued use of candles and the recitation of pater nosters might convince simple believers that purgatory actually existed.

Perhaps it was at this point that Henry VIII intervened. In March 1537 a Carthusian monk wrote to the duke of Norfolk, urging him to persuade the king to renounce the supreme headship as on the previous occasion "when he by your grace stayed purgatory."[97] Was he referring to this occasion in April of the previous year? We cannot be certain. But it is notable that in the articles which the bishops prepared at the conclusion of their sessions the word "purgatory" was still present, although much of the substance traditionally associated with it had disappeared. And at the end of the month Chapuys could report that the king had ordered the preachers to preach according to the old fashion. "He admits, as he did before, that there is a purgatory, or at least a third place besides paradise and hell, and owns that prayers and suffrages help the dead."[98]

Once again Chapuys' intelligence was accurate: the articles which the prelates compiled during their labors of March and April have survived, and the last of them is entitled specifically "Of Purgatory."[99] The episcopal origin of the articles is obvious, for the article, "Of Images," reads: "if the rude people take from henceforth such superstition as in time past it is thought that they have used to do, then *we bishops* do not our duties if we see not them punished."[100] The articles survive in two drafts, one of which is clearly a preparation for the other.[101]

It is not certain for what purpose the bishops prepared these draft articles. Perhaps they had originally intended them to be issued as an independent statement which would set forth their authoritative determinations about eight of the most hotly disputed religious issues of the day. Perhaps, on the other hand, the prelates had from the beginning intended merely to prepare a working document for the use of the coming session of convocation. The latter, at any rate, was the use to which the draft articles were put. Convocation took the preliminary work of the bishops very seriously. Except for the articles on salvation and on the salvation of infants[102] (which were omitted from the Ten Articles) and the article on justification (which was completely redrafted), the Ten Articles incorporate all of the remaining draft articles of the bishops—dealing with images, the honoring of saints, praying to saints, rites and ceremonies, and purgatory—with no more than minor verbal alterations.[103]

Convocation met on 9 June 1536 and sat for just over a month. The honor of preaching the first sermon to the convened clergy was given to Hugh Latimer, who used the opportunity to attack purgatory with all the colorful vehemence at his disposal. It was a "pleasant fiction," a "pick-purse" introduced by the bishop of Rome and his cowled minions for their own profit. Indeed, "there hath been no emperor that hath gotten more by taxes and tallages of them that were alive, than these [feigners of purgatory] got by dead men's tributes and gifts." Latimer was content that prayers should be said for the departed and, at the conclusion of his sermon, bade those present to pray for those "being departed out of this transitory life, and [who] now sleep in the sleep of peace, and rest from their labors in quietness and in peaceable sleep, faithfully, lovingly and patiently looking for that they clearly shall see when God shall be so pleased." He contended nevertheless that the word "purgatory," which had provided occasion for so many abuses, should be dropped from the vocabulary of the reformed Henrician church.[104]

In this sermon Latimer was advocating a position more radical than his king and many of his episcopal colleagues were willing to espouse. However, the irrepressible reformer was not easily discouraged. In fact, it was probably at about this time that he made his well-known attempt to convert Henry to his belief that there was no purgatory. Latimer sent to the king a memorandum of fourteen articles in which he argued his anti-purgatorial case, basing his conclusions upon logic and upon citations from the scriptures and from the fathers. His favorite device in disputation was the argument from silence. For example, after quoting a passage from St. Jerome, Latimer noted that "if Jerome had regarded purgatory, here had been occasion to have made mention of it." Henry was not impressed. He retorted, "Doth saints take occasion always to write where you think place is for them, or where they think it meetest?" Latimer's arguments smacked too much of "carnal wit," and Henry would have none of them.[105]

The leading participants in convocation seem to have been more receptive. To be sure, they had no choice but to lend an attentive ear on 23 June when the prolocutor of the lower house came to the upper house to present a list of sixty-seven "mala dogmata" which had been causing dissension among the faithful.[106] Four of these were notions of a strongly Protestant cast concerning the state of the departed which the governmentally licensed preachers had been expounding. But convocation did not respond by making the bishops' draft article on purgatory more specifically Catholic. On the contrary, when the tenth article emerged from convocation in its final form it had been emended in only one place; and that alteration, which introduced scripture as the final arbiter of doctrine, made the article if anything slightly more Protestant in tone.[107]

Since convocation was able to accept the articles of the bishops almost verbatim, it is likely that the greatest part of its debates dealt with other topics. The clergy indeed had a great deal to discuss. On 21 June they were confronted with a document nullifying the marriage between Henry VIII and Anne Boleyn.[108] They also had additional doctrinal business to transact. The bishops' draft articles had not dealt with the sacraments, and their article on justification was unacceptable to someone of influence, possibly to the king himself. In addition, the clergy had a new document to consider — the so-called Wittenberg Articles, which had recently been hammered out in discussions between the English and German theologians and which Robert Barnes had brought back to England in time for convocation.[109]

It is unclear how convocation made up its mind to include mention of only three sacraments: baptism, penance, and the eucharist. And although the last five of the Ten Articles had been written by the bishops in April, it is uncertain who prepared the drafts of the first five articles for presentation to convocation. By 19 November Henry himself was claiming authorship. "We were constrained to put our own pen to the book and to conceive certain articles which were by all you the bishops and whole clergy of this our realm in convocation agreed on as catholic, meet, and necessary."[110] According to the anonymous author of a draft introduction to the Bishop's Book of 1537, the king had indeed helped to write the Ten Articles, but his contribution had been limited to the three sacraments "most necessary to be known and to be for our salvation believed."[111] It is also conceivable that Henry's influence was responsible for the revision of the article on justification, which characteristically gives far more emphasis to the proposition that "our good works be necessarily required to the attaining of everlasting life" than either the bishops or the Germans had felt was necessary.[112] But if it was retrospective conceit upon Henry's part to claim authorship, then the articles were more probably the work of a small committee, over which the king may have presided.[113] It is also possible that Henry, who was gradually developing the habit of emending important documents, revised the articles after they had been passed by convocation but prior to their publication by Berthelet. For a few of the verbal infelicities in the printed text have an unmistakable Hen-

rician ring.[114] When it became clear how heavily the new articles on
the three sacraments and on justification borrowed from the concepts,
the scriptural citations, and the actual phraseology of the Wittenberg
statement, there was a heated debate between the reformers and the
conservatives.[115] Nicholas Heath, who had helped to negotiate the
Wittenberg Articles, reported that "there were many who assented to
the meaning of these articles only with great di'ficulty. And in the end
it was necessary to obtain consent by the intervention of royal authority." Henry implied as much in a letter to the bishops: "We have . . .
caused all you the bishops, with the clergy of our realm, in solemn
convocation deliberately disputing and advising the same, to agree."[116]

Agree to what? This is not the place to examine all the Ten Articles
in detail. But we must pause to look at the last of them entitled, "Of
Purgatory."[117] This article exhorted all bishops and preachers to urge
the people to pray for the souls of the departed, to commend them to
God's mercy, "and also to cause other to pray for them, whereby they
may be relieved and holpen of some part of their pain." It advanced a
wide variety of reasons for this recommendation, including the dictates
of Christian charity, the usage of the Church from time immemorial, a
passage in the book of [II] Maccabees, and the testimony of "divers
ancient doctors." Having said as much, however, the article proceeded
to make cautious reservations. The scriptures, it stated, contain no
certain references to the location or name of the place where the faithful departed remain, nor do they record the nature of the pains to be
suffered there. But these, like all other matters, Christians ought to
entrust to God, "unto whose mercy it is meet and convenient for us to
commend them [and] to whom is known their estate and condition."
The article closed on a note of warning. The abuses which had in times
past been foisted upon the English people under the name of purgatory could no longer be countenanced. Englishmen were therefore no
longer to believe that the bishop of Rome's pardons, or special masses
said at the Scala Coeli or before a special image, might "deliver them
from all their pain, and send them straight to heaven."

This tenth article, like the other nine, is difficult to evaluate. Like
many pronouncements of English bishops, it was sufficiently vague
that people of markedly differing viewpoints could coexist with it comfortably. A contemporary as orthodox as Reginald Pole could exult
that the article treated purgatory "much after the old manner." Archbishop Cranmer, however, who should have known, interpreted it to

mean that "purgatory . . . be not restored to [its] late accustomed abuses; but [men] shall evidently perceive that the Word of God hath gotten the upper hand of them all." More recent historians have echoed these disparate views.[118]

In a limited sense, perhaps, Pole was correct. Although certain of the Ten Articles were strongly indebted to the Wittenberg Articles, the article, "Of Purgatory" — reflecting a controversy which was particularly keen in England at the time — was a totally independent, and thus un-Lutheran, composition.[119] By Luther's standards its strictures against purgatory were also gentle. But certainly if, as Pole proposed, the "old manner" is used as the criterion for judging the new article, its substantial novelty is unmistakable. In the first place, its very location within the Ten Articles is significant. The articles are divided into two groups: the first five articles dealt with things which were "commanded expressly by God, and be necessary to our salvation;" and the concluding five treated of "such things as have been of a long continuance for a decent order and honest policy, prudently instituted and used in the churches of our realm, and be for that same purpose and end to be observed and kept accordingly, although they be not expressly commanded of God, nor necessary for our salvation."[120] The doctrine of purgatory, in a significant concession to adiaphorism which would have delighted John Frith, was placed at the end of the second category! The tone of the tenth article, furthermore, is markedly untraditional. No longer is there the lingering emphasis upon the torments of purgatory which was characteristic of the late medieval treatment of the subject. Gone also is the air of confident certainty about the doctrine. The contents of the tenth article are notably similar to its tone. Whereas former generations would have felt confident in spelling out the name, location, and tortures of purgatory on the authority of some of the fathers, custom, and legend, this the half-reformed authors of the tenth article would not do. Instead, they called upon the Bible to serve as the sole criterion by which all other sources of doctrine and practice were to be judged. By this standard, many of the traditional ideas and customs could not be sustained. Furthermore, although the new article recommended that Christians "pray for [souls departed] in masses," it completely ignored the unique efficacy which had traditionally been claimed for the *sacrifice* of the mass.[121] In so doing, it tacitly challenged the entire doctrinal groundwork upon which the chantry system had been founded.

The issuing of the Ten Articles was an important milestone in the English Reformation. Although it had implications for many teachings of the Church, its effect on the doctrine of purgatory was especially marked. For in the tenth article the Henrician government put an end to the officially sanctioned uncertainty about purgatory which had existed for over two years. More important, it also broke decisively with the traditional Catholic vision of purgatory. The purgatory of the tenth article was a lukewarm place, without flames, possibly without pains, and without any deep rooting either in scripture or in the consciousness of the people. Five years previously the government — with the king's blessing and with a good conscience — would have burned those who upheld such a doctrine. But now, after the divorce, the dissolution of the lesser monasteries, and the Protestant preaching campaign of 1535-1536, the government would reserve its greatest severity for those who deviated from the tepid norm of the tenth article by arguing for the "popish" purgatory. Much though he might protest the contrary, after 1536 Henry VIII was the defender of a different faith.

5 / "Extinguishing the Flames of Purgatory" (II): To the King's Book (1543)

Henry VIII had high hopes for the Ten Articles. As the product of the extended deliberations of temperate men, they appeared well designed to provide lasting doctrinal and practical guidelines for the moderate church which he envisaged. As articles "most catholic conceived," which nevertheless made substantial concessions to the reformers, they seemed ideally suited to restore religious "unity, concord, and agreement" to the realm. Therefore, on 12 July 1536, the day after the Ten Articles had been formally adopted by convocation, Henry issued firm orders establishing a new form of bidding prayer and prohibiting further theological discussion from the pulpits.[1] To prevent the preachers of either party from using their post-sermon prayers as an occasion to dwell on the state of the departed, Henry prescribed a lean and rather vague formula which, significantly, made no mention of purgatory: "ye shall pray for the souls that be departed, abiding the mercy of Almighty God, that it may please him the rather, at the contemplation of our prayers, to grant them the fruition of his presence." To muzzle the controversial preachers, Henry further ordered the bishops to revoke all licenses which they had issued to preachers. If the parochial clergy must continue to mount their pulpits to address their flocks, let them confine themselves until Michaelmas (29 September) to reading without comment from the Ten Articles. "Private communications, arguments, or disputations" about theology were also to stop. If Henry had had his way, "secret silence" on religious matters would have been the order of the day. And why not? For, as Thomas Starkey exulted, the realm finally had a "tempered doctrine, whereof all our country ought not a little to rejoice. For the doctrine of our country is now so tempered in truth, that it is both purged from the old abuses and foolish superstition and also defended from the errors of this time, and from all false religion."[2] What could be more likely to last than the unvarnished truth?

It was not easy, however, to restore unity to a country in the midst of a religious revolution, for there were a number of forces which worked together to keep the pot boiling. One of these was the deep cleavage which already existed between the reformers and conservatives of the realm. Thus when the conservative prelates attempted to use the Ten Articles and Henry's orders to the bishops to stem the tide of Protestant preaching, the reformers were quick to protest. Already in late July Bishop Longland of Lincoln was moving to silence Robert Wisdom, the vocally Protestant curate of All Hallows, Oxford. Wisdom, for his part, lost little time before appealing to Cromwell for help. He also rallied his parishioners (including the mayor of Oxford) to inform Longland of their support for their silenced curate and their sorrow that many years had gone by before they had been released from their "ignorancy" by proper instruction in "God's commandments and the articles of our faith."[3] At about the same time, Bishop Stokesley was attempting to reassert a measure of control over the pulpit at Paul's Cross. From Thomas Cromwell he exacted the concession that he might submit a list of suitable preachers for the Cross, from which Cromwell (no doubt working together with Hilsey) might select a "convenient mixture." This arrangement, though short-lived, lasted long enough to elicit a strenuous complaint from William Marshall at the retrograde railings which were going on at Paul's Cross.[4] In such an atmosphere of theological disunity, it was impossible completely to silence the preachers.

A further force for religious instability was the propensity of men in situations of tension and uncertainty to change their minds. Revolutions have generally been marked by incessant constitution-making, and for good reason. Having jettisoned the patterns and orthodoxies of the past, people tend to respond to situations of rapid change in an uncertain, opportunistic fashion. So it was in the English Reformation. Having left behind the certainties of medieval orthodoxy, Henry VIII and his advisers were flailing about in a sea of theological options. In 1536 they had committed themselves to a firm definition of religious truth in the Ten Articles. But as experiences accumulated and ideas changed, they were forced to make new attempts to discern and set forth Christian doctrine. The subsequent Henrician formularies of 1537 and 1543 were in many respects more conservative than the Ten Articles. The Bishops' Book of 1537 restored the four sacraments which had been "lost" in 1536; and the King's Book of 1543, which has justly been called "the handsomest monument of Henry's experiment in Anglo-Catholicism,"[5] eradicated much of the Protestant thought and phraseology from the Bishops' Book. This movement in the direction of conservatism was a natural reaction on the part of the king and an important group of his churchmen to theological change and social upheaval which had been greater than they had anticipated. The teaching on purgatory and prayers for souls, however, was a notable exception to this trend. While in most areas of theology the formularies were veering in a conservative direction after 1536, the teaching concerning the souls of the departed continued on its reformist course. By late 1537 Henry VIII was giving serious and sympathetic consideration to a statement "concerning the souls of them which be departed from this life" which dispensed altogether with the concept of purgatory. And in 1543 the King's Book officially dropped purgatory from the teaching of the English church.[6] Purgatory was evidently not to be an essential component of Anglo-Catholicism.

The purgatorial teaching of the Henrician church thus moved toward Wittenberg while the bulk of its teaching vacillated somewhat Rome-wards. The reasons for the shift are no doubt complex, but prominent among them must be the dissolution of the monasteries. For just as that upheaval gave the English people a vested interest in the Reformation, so it also gave to the English government a vested interest in disproving the existence of purgatory. The monasteries, like the chantries after them, had in large measure been founded to maintain continual intercession for the living and the dead. As Latimer pointed out to the king in 1536,

the founding of monasteries argued purgatory to be; so the putting of them down argueth it not to be. What uncharitableness and cruelness seemeth it to be to destroy monasteries if purgatory be. Now it seemeth not convenient the act of Parliament to preach one thing, and the pulpit another clean contrary.[7]

This argument, which was to become a Protestant commonplace, was persuasive because it was undeniable. It was clear to Thomas Starkey, who was hardly a reforming zealot. It was also evident to the conservative vicar of St. Paul's, Malmesbury (Wilts), who exclaimed with a touch of bitterness, "I trow if the king's grace did think that masses and diriges did good to the souls departed, he would not suppress so many houses or monasteries as he have done and take their livings from them, but rather to have given them more."[8] If the English government, which in 1536 had no clear rationale for the dissolution of the monasteries, wished to escape the stigma of covetousness, it would have to disprove the existence of purgatory.

Meanwhile, the government's plundering of the monasteries was dramatically diminishing the quantity of intercession for the departed. This was not only a matter of the loss of the suffrages of the monks.[9] The dissolution of the monasteries also reduced the size of the chantry system and impaired the functioning of many chantries which survived. A large number of the chantries had been founded to support secular priests within monastic churches. Precisely how many such "monastic chantries" there were can never be known, for the *Valor Ecclesiasticus* was not very informative about them, and most of them had disappeared by the time of the chantry surveys of the mid-1540s. But the patent rolls, which record 251 mortmain licenses for such foundations, indicate that their numbers, although perhaps only one-ninth of the total number of licensed chantries, were not negligible.[10] Though a few of these chantries managed to relocate themselves in neighboring parish churches after the dissolution of the monasteries which had housed them, most of them seem simply to have vanished without leaving a trace.[11]

The dissolution of the monasteries also threatened the existence of many of the chantries in the nonmonastic churches and chapels of the realm. The founders of many of these chantries had sought to provide their priests with reliable sources of income by bestowing landed endowments upon monasteries and by requiring the monks in turn to pay fixed stipends to the cantarists. In the 1530s, however, this source of income became extremely precarious. In frequent instances the Augmentations officials failed to honor the recurring financial obligations of the monasteries whose resources they were liquidating. In November 1537 Bishop Tunstall appealed to Cromwell on behalf of two cantarist-schoolmasters in Durham. Hitherto they had been paid by the monks of Jervaulx Abbey; now they hoped to receive their stipends out of the Court of Augmentations, but "the king's auditors not knowing the king's pleasure durst not allow any payment to be made unto them." Tunstall requested that the local Augmentations officials be authorized to make the payments, and Cromwell responded favorably.[12] Many chantry priests, however, had no powerful advocate of their interests and found themselves deprived of their livelihoods by the action of local government functionaries.[13] In some instances, it was the lay purchaser of the monastic estates who ceased paying the priest his stipend.[14] Other cantarists found their income markedly reduced, but not cut off altogether.[15]

Chantry priests whose incomes were threatened by the dissolution could fight for their livelihoods and jobs by suing in the Court of Augmentations provided they had sufficient financial reserves to bear legal costs. The court appears often to have given such men a sympathetic hearing, and in the early 1540s numerous priests were recovering their incomes by this means.[16] We must not exaggerate the impact of the suppression of the monasteries upon the chan.ries — the vast majority of the chantries continued to exist and to function normally, with no loss of funds and no necessity for litigation. Nevertheless, it is clear that the dissolution of the monasteries, while leaving the chantry system still functioning, dealt brutal blows to numerous individual chantries. In the process, the routine of masses and prayers for the departed was disturbed and the quantity of intercession, which was so important to the medieval mind, was diminished.

Fifteen hundred thirty-six, then, was the year in which the government, by adopting the tenth article and by beginning the dissolution of the monasteries, struck two of the severest blows at the traditional concepts and practices associated with purgatory. It was also the year in which opposition to these changes crystallized most formidably. The forces behind the Lincolnshire Rebellion and the Pilgrimage of Grace were many and complex, but discontent at the government's policies toward purgatory and the monasteries was certainly one of them. According to the vicar of Louth, where the troubles in Lincolnshire started, "all men . . . did grudge and murmur at the new erroneous opinions touching our Lady and purgatory."[17] The same fear of change in the age-old practices and beliefs concerning purgatory were present also in Yorkshire.[18] Although there was no mention of purgatory in the Pontefract Articles, the fifteen divines who drafted them asserted that

preaching against purgatory, worshipping of saints, pilgrimage, images, and all books set forth against the same, or sacraments and sacramentals of the Church, be worthy to be reproved and condemned by Convocation, and the pain to doers to the contrary and process to be made hereafter in heresy as was in the days of King Henry IV.[19]

Robert Aske, the leader of the Pilgrims, was himself much concerned that as a result of the dissolution "the divine service of Almighty God is much minished and great number of masses unsaid."[20] In Yorkshire, where several chantry priests were also concerned at the trends of the times, William Tristram of Lartington chapel near Romaldkirk

donned armor and spurred his horse across the countryside in the attempt to rally support and money for the Pilgrims. According to one
observer, he was the "busiest priest in these parts" in the cause of the
insurrection.[21]

In this troubled period criticism of the Ten Articles was also mounting. Richard Jackson, the newly appointed incumbent of Witnesham
(Suffolk), shook his copy of the Ten Articles at his parishioners and exclaimed, "Beware, my friends, of these English books!" And John Gale,
rector of the neighboring parish of Thwaite, refused to declare the
articles to his people, "for the one half of them were naught."[22] Similar
reports came from other parts of the realm as "divers contentious or
rather seditious persons" noised abroad the rumor that the Ten Articles had "clearly abolished and forsaken" the sacraments of marriage,
confirmation, holy orders, and extreme unction.[23]

How should the government respond to this crisis? The answer of a
radical Protestant such as the Scot Alexander Alesius was that of the
convinced revolutionary. "The real cause of the rebellion," he wrote to
Cranmer, "was no new doctrine but the papistical doctrine which
taught the Lincolnshire rustics to take arms against their king in defence of priestly and monkish insanities." The solution, therefore,
must be a fearless extirpation of the old ways and a more forthright
and consistent adoption of Reformation principles. "The real way to
promote the Gospel and the peace of the republic is to get rid entirely
of the papistical leaven, of the profanation of masses for the living and
the dead, unchaste celibacy, monastic vows, and other impious dog-
mas."[24] There was never the remotest chance that Henry VIII would
agree to such a program. In November 1536 he still seemed hopeful
that the Ten Articles might provide an adequate basis for the restora-
tion of "unity, quietness, and good concord."[25] Within a few months,
however, he had evidently thought better of this. Having used liberal
quantities of exemplary repression in dealing with the northern rebels,
Henry now called for a new doctrinal statement which would reinstate
the four "lost" sacraments, for the mollification of the conservatives
and "the satisfaction of all parts."[26]

In late February 1537[27] the king convened at Lambeth an assembly
of prelates and theologians who formulated the new doctrinal statement during the next six months. By the second week of Lent (25
February – 3 March) Dr. Marmaduke Waldby was able to report that
after much dissension "the four sacraments omitted in the king's book

of articles be now found by the bishops and shall be expressed in a new book."[28] During the coming months the prelates and divines went on to other hotly disputed topics. They found it hardest to agree on the article dealing with the sacrament of orders.[29] If Bishop Gardiner's report is at all accurate, it is clear that hard work and a determined willingness to compromise were necessary before Stokesley and Foxe, Tunstall and Cranmer, Sampson and Shaxton could come to an agreement on anything.[30] At first the divines seem to have had the lively interest and critical participation of the king.[31] But before the end of May— partly because he did not get his way on certain matters and partly because of the virulence of the plague in London—Henry withdrew to Hampton Court, leaving the clerics to thresh things out in Lambeth and reserving his critical judgment for the end product.

From the final text of the Bishops' Book one might conclude that the divines did not deal with purgatory in their debates, for the article "Of Purgatory" is almost identical to the last of the Ten Articles.[32] Other evidence, however, indicates that they did indeed discuss purgatory, although it must have been a relatively minor item on their agenda. On 24 March the king, who was still actively involved in the proceedings, summoned Dr. Richard Layton and Thomas Starkey to meet with the bishops to discuss the invocation of saints, clerical celibacy, satisfaction, and purgatory.[33] Bishop Sampson, reminiscing about the work on the Bishops' Book, wrote some years later that he had frequently ridden to Lambeth in Tunstall's barge with Stokesley and Tunstall. The two bishops, he recalled, had consulted old books in Greek dealing with the usages of the Eastern Church, which they took as a model in matters of current dispute. They "were fully bent to maintain so many of the old usages and traditions as they might, and so they said as was necessary to do, especially when they appeared by the Greek Church . . . One especial thing was for praying for souls and that by prayers they were delivered from pains."[34]

The bishops and doctors finished their arduous deliberations on 23 July. Exhausted by their labors and eager to depart from the plague-ridden capital, they were happy to leave to Bishop Foxe the tasks of preparing a satisfactory text and seeing the work through the printer. By 28 August the printed volume was ready for presentation to Henry VIII.[35] In their somewhat groveling introduction, the divines, although confident that their book was "concordant and agreeable to holy Scripture," nevertheless submitted their work to "the most excellent wisdom and exact judgment of your majesty, to be recognized, overseen, and corrected, if your Grace shall find any word or sentence in it meet to be changed, qualified, or further expounded."[36] The divines groveled for good reason. For some time the king had been holding himself studiously aloof from their deliberations, but in late July the bishops were still hoping that he would see fit to confer his blessing upon their book by issuing it in his own name.[37] Henry refused to cooperate. In August he authorized the royal printer Berthelet to publish the book, but he carefully dissociated his own name from it. Therefore, although the *Institution of a Christen Man* (as it was formally entitled) was published in five editions before the end of 1537, it appeared under episcopal — not royal — auspices and was popularly known as the Bishops' Book.[38]

The Bishops' Book was soon in widespread use, but Henry was not satisfied with it. On 10 October 1537 Cromwell's secretary Thomas Wriothesley wrote that it "shall be reformed as it had need in many points."[39] Overseeing the revision and doing an astonishing amount of the work was the king himself. During the remainder of 1537, in fact, he was engaged in his most concentrated and sustained effort as a royal theologian. With great care he read through the Bishops' Book, altering words, rewriting sentences, and deleting whole sections as his theological persuasions and personal whims dictated. From the theologians (and bishops-to-be) George Day, Nicholas Heath, Thomas Thirlby, and John Skip, Henry solicited advice on the sections dealing with the Ten Commandments, justification, and purgatory.[40]

By December he was ready to submit his revisions to the criticism of the experts. A secretary prepared a clean copy of the Bishops' Book with the king's alterations in the margins and between the lines; additional leaves were inserted into the volume to contain new statements on three of the sacraments, on the fifth petition of the Lord's Prayer, on justification, and on prayers for the departed.[41] The revised book was then sent for comment to Nicholas Heath, to the lawyer Christopher Saint German, and to Bishop Sampson.[42] By 14 January 1538 the volume "lately by us [bishops] devised, and now overseen and corrected by the King's Majesty" reached Archbishop Cranmer, who promised to give it his concentrated attention. Eleven days later he sent the book back to Cromwell along with no less than twenty-nine pages of his own outspoken commentary. "I trust," he wrote, the king's highness will pardon my presumption, that I have been so scrupulous and as it were a picker of quarrels to his Grace's book, making a great matter of every light fault, or rather where no fault is at all; which I do only for this intent, that because the book now shall be set forth by his Grace's censure and judgment, I would have nothing therein that Momus could reprehend. And yet I refer all mine annotations again to his Grace's most exact judgment. [43]

Shortly thereafter a secretary made a précis of the criticisms of Heath, Saint German, Sampson, and Cranmer for the use of the royal theologian. [44]

Henry, having studied these criticisms, went on to produce a final revision, which survives among the Royal Manuscripts in the British Library. It is a printed copy of the Bishops' Book, into which a secretary neatly inserted the hundreds of alterations which Henry had stipulated. [45] In addition to the numerous crossings-out and interlineations on the printed pages, there are sixty-three manuscript folios which were sewn into the volume to enable the inclusion of drastically revised treatments of the fifth article of the creed, the sacraments of penance, the altar, orders, the fifth petition of the Lord's prayer, justification, and prayer for the faithful departed. [46] In this volume Henry incorporated a few of the suggestions of his critics, the most notable of which was Cranmer's stately new translation "word for word according to the Latin" of the Apostles' Creed, which was later incorporated almost verbatim into the Book of Common Prayer. In the main, however, Henry preferred to cling to his own highly individual notions of theological orthodoxy and stylistic felicity. Five years before its time, here was a "king's book" in the fullest sense of the term, ready to "be set forth by his grace's censure and judgment." [47]

For some reason the "king's book" of 1538 was never published. Possibly some of the bishops found Henry's emendations theologically unacceptable and objected to its publication. [48] Perhaps Henry himself had second thoughts about issuing in his own name a book which was so palpably a revision of the work of the bishops. Perhaps more mature reflection convinced him that publication of a new doctrinal formulary ought not to take place until broader consultations and a more systematic reconsideration of the Bishops' Book had occurred. Conceivably Henry felt that for diplomatic or domestic reasons his own name ought for the time being to be kept out of the cockpit of theological controversy. At any rate, the bishops continued to enjoin their priests to acquire the unrevised Bishops' Book and to use it regularly. And in August 1538 Bishop Sampson indicated that Henry had deferred the publication of a revised formulary and was "content that the book lately put out by his grace's favor and licence by the prelates should be obeyed and may be taught till that his majesty shall otherwise order some things with a more mature and deliberate counsel."[49] It would be almost two years until that process began once again in earnest.

The "king's book" of 1538 remains a document of considerable importance. It had significance in its own time. In many respects it represented a faltering but necessary intermediate step between the two major formularies of Henry's reign. Contemporaries certainly knew of it, consulted it, and took it seriously. The divines Heath, Thirlby, and Day, who had provided advice and criticism in Henry's work of revision during 1537-1538, and who were shortly thereafter elevated to bishoprics, were among the most influential contributors to the successor King's Book of 1543.[50] It is not surprising, therefore, that the ultimate book incorporates so many of the phrases which Henry had laboriously scrawled in the margins of the Bishops' Book five years previously.[51] The "king's book" is also significant because of the insight it provides into the recesses of the royal mind in 1537-1538. Of particular interest is the "article concerning the souls of them which be departed from this life." It is probable that this was written by the team of Day, Heath, Thirlby, and Skip, who in December 1537 presented the king with a "determination" on a number of theological matters including purgatory.[52] But Henry was also at work on the article, and may well have included his emendations in the book which he sent to the theologians for comment.[53] Bishop Sampson had accepted most of Henry's revisions with pleasure or equanimity, but "the article of prayer for souls" offended him deeply. In response he penned a two-page memorandum reaffirming the reality of the pains suffered by the departed souls and the necessity of almsdeeds and masses ("not only at the time of the burial but also yearly with anniversaries") for their relief.[54] But Henry ignored Sampson's objections, and the "article concerning . . . souls" became the concluding article in the final version of the "king's book" of 1538.[55]

Several passages reveal similarities in phraseology between the "king's book" statement and the article of 1536-1537, which it was designed to supplant. In their final paragraphs, both statements condemn the abuses "which under the name of purgatory have been advanced." They are also equally unspecific about "the place where they [the departed] be" and "the name thereof." But the disparities are more striking than the similarities. Immediately apparent is the difference in the titles—the former entitled "Of Purgatory," and the latter referring merely to "the souls of them which be departed from this life." In fact, the 1538 article studiously avoided any reference to purgatory, except as it dealt with the abuses of the concept. The stated reason was that there exists no certain knowledge of the state of the departed "but only as farforth as the holy scripture speaketh of them," and because purgatory and the purgation of the departed "be undiscussed and undetermined in the *canon of the Bible* [italics mine]." The 1538 article, which is replete with scriptural quotations, becomes long and rambling; the pithier article of 1536-1537 refers only to a passage from the book of (II) Maccabees, which the 1538 statement labels extra-canonical.

The "king's book," unlike the 1536-1537 article, went into some detail concerning the fate of the departed souls. The wicked, whom the earlier article had failed to mention, are destined for perdition. They are in "the indignation and wrath of God" and will undergo everlasting torment in the lake of fire and brimstone. The righteous, in contrast, have pleasant prospects: their death is "precious in the sight of Our Lord"; the pains of death shall not touch them, nor shall they come into condemnation. We should not therefore

mourn nor weep much for them, for they be in peace and rest. Their souls be gone to the rest of Our Lord, and he is beneficial unto them. They be always in a joyful hope and expectation of the last day when Christ shall say unto them, "Come, ye blessed of my Father, inherit ye the kingdom prepared for you from the beginning of the world."

Nowhere, the 1538 statement claimed, do the scriptures indicate that any of the souls who are to be saved go to a place where they are continually cleansed "before they come to their final joy and glory." Nor do they specify the nature and duration of the purgative pains, if indeed there be any, which the departed suffer. Since these "curious questions" are thus uncertain by scripture, they are to be "left to the secret knowledge of Almighty God as things not necessary for us to know . . . And surely if the knowledge of these things had been necessary, the Scripture would not have overpassed them with such silence, but would have made some mention of them and taught them as it doth other necessary things." Here the "king's book" in essence adopted Latimer's primary argument against purgatory. Silence, Latimer and the "king's book" agreed, pointed to the fact that the Biblical writers had never heard of purgatory. And the concept must therefore have been a subsequent fabrication of the romish church.

The 1538 statement does not stop here, however, for it is intent on drawing a practical lesson of immediate concern to the commonwealth. Throughout Henry's revision of the Bishops' Book runs a strand of "law-and-order" moralism, of emphasis upon human effort and individual accountability.[56] Phrases such as "endeavoring themselves to live according to his precepts," "rejecting in my will and heart the devil and his works," "persevere in his precepts and laws" recur frequently in his emendations.[57] Henry emphasized that mercy must be tempered by justice, and that all subjects must strenuously apply themselves to their labors.[58] In its revised form, the article on the souls of the departed repeats this concern. Since there is no purgatory, those individuals are badly deceived who "during the time of this present life defer to do penance and to amend their lives vaguely trusting to be relieved and saved by good deeds which others shall do for them when they be dead." The scriptures are abundantly clear that "God will judge every man according to his own proper deeds." Therefore, since posthumous suffrages are of doubtful assistance to the departed, Christians must "endeavor themselves to live well and to keep the commandments of God while they be wholly here in this present life, for as their deeds and works be in this life, so every man shall be rewarded after this life." Such an approach completely undercut the traditional Catholic concept of intercession for the Church suffering; it also totally subverted the conceptual basis of the chantry system. Obedience and work, not masses and suffrages, would secure the eternal felicity of the departed.

The "king's book" of 1538 was nevertheless unable to make a total break with the practices of the Middle Ages. Since the book of (II) Maccabees, "which for divers things contained in it is to be read in the Church," made mention of prayers and oblations for the departed; since "divers ancient doctors" plainly showed that "it is a good and a charitable deed to pray for souls departed"; and since "the continual usage of the Church so many years" has sanctioned the practice—it is therefore convenient to teach the people that "no man ought to be aggrieved with the continuance thereof." Even though the state of the departed is "uncertain by scripture," it is a charitable deed for Christians to pray for them, "for it is the nature of love and charity to extend the self even unto things which be uncertain." Furthermore, our uncertainty about the condition and location of the departed souls whom we love "maketh us careful and fearful for them." For this reason, even though we trust that our friends and loved ones have died in the faith of Christ, because of our uncertainty about their condition "our charity and love towards them maketh us to wish well unto them to pray to God for them, to give alms, and to do such other things as be acceptable and pleasant to Almighty God."

The concluding article of the "king's book" of 1538 reveals the conflict which existed in Henry's mind in the late 1530s. It shows his ability to adjust his thinking on doctrinal matters when his personal and material interests were at stake.[59] A few years before, when confronted with the desirability of a divorce, Henry's mind had moved rapidly away from Catholic orthodoxy on the theology of matrimony and on papal authority. Now, while the monasteries were gradually falling into his hands, Henry's mind was once again on the move. He certainly had ample encouragement to depart from received notions. Luther's intimate, Georg Spalatin, dedicated to the king a beautifully copied manuscript Latin translation of the German reformer's *Widderruff,* entitled "De Purgatorio."[60] And Latimer was not the only Englishman to attempt to point out to Henry the logical implications of the dissolution of the monasteries. As one anonymous writer commented:

The very truth is that there is no purgatory. As long as praying for souls departed is suffered, the people will think that there is a purgatory. And that in process of time will cause many to think that it is pity that houses of religion should be decayed, whose prayers as they think profited much to souls departed. And that hereafter shall cause the king's deed in suppressing of houses of religion to be thought uncharitable . . .[61]

It is evident from the "king's book" that as early as 1538 Henry VIII had in large measure accepted the validity of this argument. He wanted the monasteries, and he wanted to feel justified in dissolving them as well.

The article on purgatory also demonstrates Henry's innate caution in matters touching the fate of his own soul. The German Protestants could not comprehend how a monarch who could so thoroughly bank the fires of purgatory could so tenaciously hold on to private masses.[62] Other contemporaries also remarked about the ostentatious solemnity of the royally sponsored exequies toward the end of the reign.[63] Henry's own rites were certainly as elaborate as any, and in his will he stipulated a lavish distribution of alms to worthy paupers who were to "pray heartily unto God for remission of our offenses and the wealth of our soul."[64] One can only conclude that Henry was planning for all contingencies. Having been forced for the sake of earthly treasure to accept the reformers' logic on purgatory, the king nevertheless continued to dread the loss of his treasure in heaven. Might there — the reformers' logic to the contrary — be an excruciating purgation in store for him after all? Not if his own foresightful action could prevent it!

Religious controversy throughout the realm did not cease while Henry and the theologians were laboring over their doctrinal formularies. It was all very well for the king to require his bishops to maintain "unity, quietness, and good concord" in their dioceses.[65] But in the midst of a religious revolution these were elusive goals, far easier to demand than to achieve. It was difficult to enforce respectful adherence to official doctrine when it was unclear to everyone — to laymen and clerics alike — what doctrine the government was sanctioning at the moment. The Royal Injunctions of August 1536 had compelled all preachers to set forth the Ten Articles of the previous month. But early the following year, when the divines were hard at work on yet another theological statement, and when the king himself made no secret of his dissatisfaction with the fruit of their labors, the Injunctions quickly lost much of their force. There was room for legitimate doubt as to what the Church of England really stood for. Nor did the second set of Royal Injunctions (issued in October 1538) make an attempt to fill the doctrinal void.[66] On the practical question of what to preach about purgatory, the best guidance was no doubt "no otherwise than according to the form of the beads appointed," as provided by Henry's order of 12 July 1536.[67] The order, however, was simply a formula for prayer, not a detailed exposition of doctrine, and the uncertainty remained. Radicals and conservatives meanwhile attempted to exploit the situation by peddling their controversial wares.

Between 1536 and 1539 the reformers, with the active encouragement of Vicegerent Cromwell, were continuing their struggle to effect a reformation in the Church of England. From their point of view, no weapon in their arsenal was more potent than that of preaching. Reforming bishops such as Shaxton and Latimer expressed this conviction in their injunctions to their own dioceses, which decreed that "preaching not be left off for any manner of observances in the church, as processions, or exequies of the dead." They could not, of course, trust all the bishops to appoint the right sort of preachers. In May 1537, for example, Cranmer complained to Cromwell that the bishop of Norwich William Repps "doth approve none to preach in his diocese that be of right judgment," and had unfairly silenced Master Gounthorp of Weeting St. Mary (Norfolk). Therefore he urged Cromwell to grant to the parson "as well the king's license to preach within this realm, as also that he may from time to time have recourse unto your lordship for your favourable aid and assistance in his right."[68] The surviving evidence does not tell us whether Cromwell acceded to Cranmer's plea. During the last years of his life, however, Cromwell was busy licensing preachers,[69] protecting reformers who had aroused the ire of the conservatives, and forcibly discouraging the preaching activities of those who favored the old religion. A bishop as formidable as Stokesley of London complained that he was "but a cypher for the Lord Privy Seal," for Cromwell's agent Hilsey persisted in appointing heretics to preach at Paul's Cross. Small wonder, therefore, that there was so "much contention for preaching in sundry parishes" and so little religious unity and concord in the realm.[70]

Cromwell's theological stance in 1536 is indicated by two incidents dealing with purgatory. In November the unbridled bishop of St. David's, William Barlow, who seems never to have taken to heart St. James's dictum that "the tongue is a fire," was in trouble with his flock for having "intermeddled further in my last preaching in the matter of purgatory than authority of scripture would sustain my purpose, and that I was unjustly noted to have contraried the King's Highness' determination in the same." If the report coming from the outraged Welshmen was correct, Barlow had indeed transgressed against the Ten Articles, for he had allegedly denied that "there is nor was any purgatory, but only a thing invented and imagined by the bishop of Rome and our priests to have trentals and other mundane lucre thereby only."[71] Bishop Rowland Lee, as president of the Council of the Marches of Wales, had general oversight over public order in Wales, and urged Cromwell to restrain Barlow "that further inconveniences do not ensue." Cromwell appears to have done nothing of the kind. And Barlow continued to preach against the "inveterate superstition" of his diocese, fortified "with the help of God and your lordship [Cromwell]."[72]

However safe it may have been to veer to the radical side of the Ten Articles, it was dangerous to err in the direction of conservatism. In July 1536 the warden of New College, Oxford, Dr. John London, learned that he had been accused, apparently by Latimer, of being inter alia a "defender of the papistical purgatory." What alarmed him especially was the rumor that for this reason Cromwell was about to deprive him of his wardenship. London therefore wrote frantically to Thomas Bedyll and to Cromwell protesting his opposition to the "old superstition." He had felt, he admitted to Cromwell, that some of the radical preachers were doing "more hurt than good," and he had spoken out against them. But no one in the whole realm was "more conformable to all such things as is or shall be determined by the king's Grace and his most honorable Council than I am." Apparently Cromwell was satisfied by this obeisance, for London kept his post — and an especially cautious relationship to Cromwell. Not until after Cromwell's fall did he receive further ecclesiastical promotion.[73]

In 1537 and 1538 reports of additional incidents concerning purgatory continued to come to Cromwell's attention. Some of those who were preaching against the doctrine seem to have viewed Cromwell as a sympathetic friend, who would champion them if they found themselves in difficulty. One of those who appealed to Cromwell was Thomas Wylley, the controversial vicar of Yoxford (Suffolk). The doctrine of the realm might be uncertain, but this had not deterred Wylley from composing and producing plays and interludes which debunked traditional beliefs and usages, much to the annoyance of his neighboring priests. They would no longer allow him to preach from their pulpits, "but have disdained me ever since I made a play against the pope's counselors, Error, Coll Clogger of Conscience, and Incredulity." He was at work on another play entitled "The Woman on the Rokke," whose faith was tested in the "true purgatory" of this life, and he promised to send it to Cromwell as soon as it was finished. Wylley did not seem concerned that by the standards of the tenth article, which had stated that there was a place of painful purgation *after this life,* his play would be heretical. His real worry was his hostile neighbors. "Fatherless and forsaken," he appealed for Cromwell's aid "that I may preach Christ."[74]

A number of the letters coming to Cromwell also show the intense pressure which pockets of would-be reformers could bring upon the conservatives in their area. In Worcestershire, for example, the sheriff

of the county Walter Walsshe, with the active support of Bishop Latimer and a number of local worthies, was seizing every possible opportunity to intimidate the vocal traditionalists. He was a leading partici-
pant in the investigation of a priest in Worcester who had ostentatiously persisted in venerating the town's image of the Virgin Mary. He
also witnessed and forwarded to Cromwell depositions concerning a
weaver in Northfield who had repeatedly flayed Bishops Hilsey and
Latimer for being "knave bishops, heretics, and Lollards" who had
"made thousands of heretics in England."[75] Walsshe and his confreres
even attempted to arrest the first Regius Professor of Divinity of Oxford, Dr. Richard Smyth. In 1537 Smyth was apparently no more able
to stomach the reformers' view of purgatory than he had been the previous year. Once again he spoke his mind on the issue, this time in the
bidding prayers with which he concluded a sermon in the Evesham
parish church. Walsshe and his associates reported to Cromwell that
Smyth had transgressed by praying for the king as "the supreme head
of this realm" (rather than as "the supreme head . . . of the spiritualty
and temporalty of the . . . Church"). He had compounded this error
by his highly selective intercession for the clergy — all of the seven bishops and abbots whom he singled out for prayer were prominent conservatives. For the redoubtable Bishop Stokesiey, whom he commended as "a founder of the faith of Christ," Smyth seems to have had
special concern. Finally, he had prayed "for all the souls that are departed out of this world abiding the mercy of God that lie in the pains
which is purgatory, and that you may have the grace to say some good
prayers that they may be the sooner relieved out of their pains." With
these words, Smyth had embellished in a dangerously retrograde manner the words of the bidding prayer which Henry had prescribed the
previous year — as Walsshe and his fellow informants were evidently
well aware.[76] When they moved to imprison Smyth for these manifold indiscretions, he fled back to Oxford where he would be out of
Walsshe's jurisdiction. Cromwell, however, was reluctant to take measures against Smyth, who continued to collect ecclesiastical promotions
during the remaining years of Henry's reign and who survived to preach
at Latimer's burning.[77] For the moment at least, Walsshe and his
friends seem to have forced the conservatives of Worcestershire into a
full-scale retreat.

A similar incident occurred in Oxford in May 1538. Richard Yakesley, a disgruntled monk from the nearby abbey of Thame, was unable

to contain his anger at the recent religious changes. Preaching in the church of St. Mary Magdalen, he heartily commended pilgrimages and the veneration of saints and encouraged his hearers to continue "to do as they have done in times past." He dwelt even longer on the existence of purgatory and offered to prove that "there was a purgatory as holy fathers hath declared it." At this a number of prominent citizens, including the mayor William Banastre and his predecessor William Freurs, took offense. When they confronted Yakesley with the enormity of his assertion, the monk became alarmed and "denieth the same and weepeth and waileth for the same." Although he expressed willingness to return to the pulpit and recant his offensively traditional views, Banastre and his colleagues chose to commit him to the custody of his abbot until they had heard from Cromwell.[78]

Cromwell was most likely to take action when the public advocacy of purgatory was linked with treason. One example of this comes from Calais. In the mid-1530s the reforming commissary John Butler was locked in mortal combat with the conservative royal representatives in the town. In July 1537 Butler reported the preaching of one William Mynstreley, who was contending that since priests were above angels "they ought to have no temporal prince over them nor pay any thing to them." These assertions he could prove by a book entitled the "Lauachrum conscientie" [The Font of the Conscience], which also "made for the probation of purgatory." After hearing about the case from Cranmer, Cromwell moved quickly. He ordered Mynstreley and another conservative priest (William Richardson) to be sent to London for examination, and fired off letters to Lord Lisle and the Council of Calais upbraiding them for their attachment to "superstitious old observations" and expressing the king's anger at those who were maintaining "the papistical fashion" in that town. In the autumn Mynstreley was shipped back to Calais for exemplary execution. If spending a few additional years in a Tudor prison was a fate better than death, Richardson was more fortunate. Although Cromwell was reported to have regarded him as a "false hypocrite knave," there were influential people who interceded in his behalf. It was therefore not until April 1540 — after he had allegedly committed additional acts of treason — that he was sent to Calais to face the hangman.[79]

Another person who combined treason with an overly vocal adherence to the old faith was the vicar of Newark, Henry Lytherland. As early as 1534 he had come to Cromwell's attention for declaring that if the reformers' opinions were correct, "holy Saint Francis is a devil in hell with many other saints." During the Lincolnshire Rebellion and the Pilgrimage of Grace he had also engaged in dangerously suspect activities among the rebels. It was apparently an outspoken sermon in March 1538 which once again brought him to the attention of the authorities and which finally sealed his fate. Protesting against Henry's efforts as a royal theologian, condemning all English translations of the scriptures, and claiming that "we be now in much more darkness than ever [our fathers before us] were," Lytherland went on to commend the whole catalogue of traditional beliefs and observances which the Reformation was threatening. Prominent among them was an insistence upon the necessity of praying for the souls in purgatory. Despite the tenth article, despite Henry's order for the bidding of the beads, despite the Bishops' Book, Lytherland

prayed for them that were dead after this fashion. You shall pray . . . for the souls departed, not for them that be in hell, for prayer doth not perfect them, nor for them that be in heaven, for they need no prayer, but pray for them that lie in pain, which had never so little help, nor so much need as they have now; and here he brought in this text *miseremini mei* etc. saying that every man ought at the least to pray for his friends' souls, for that we must needs be purged after this life in some place. In this matter he tarried long with much circumstance . . .

This outburst of unrepentant conservatism was Lytherland's last fling, and that summer he was executed in York.[80] A firm belief in purgatory also helped to seal the fate of two other conservative martyrs of the year 1538 — the last abbot of Woburn, Robert Hobbes, and the Observant friar John Forrest. The prosecution of Forrest, indeed, gave Latimer an opportunity to denounce from the pulpit at Paul's Cross the belief "that a priest may turn and change the pains of hell of a sinner, truly penitent, contrite of his sins, by certain penance enjoined him in the pains of purgatory." Forrest's doctrines, in sum, were "most abominable heresies, blasphemy against God and the country, to scripture, and the teaching of Christ and all his apostles."[81]

In the years following the issuance of the Ten Articles it is clear that those who stirred up opposition by preaching against purgatory were more likely to get a sympathetic hearing from Cromwell than were those who campaigned in its favor. The last abbess of Godstow, observing the trends of these years, wrote to Cromwell in terms which she must have calculated would be pleasing to him. In a pathetic attempt to persuade him to spare her house from the impending dissolution, she confessed in 1538 that "there is neither pope nor purgatory, image nor pilgrimage nor praying to dead saints used or regarded amongst us."[82] Unfortunately for her and her sisters, the dissolution of the monasteries was not governed by theological considerations alone. One cannot help pitying a religious woman who, in a frantic struggle to survive the cataclysmic changes which were sweeping the realm, had been driven to deny the original raison d'être of her house.

By the middle of 1538, however, the reforming movement superintended by Cromwell and Cranmer was beginning to lose momentum. It was not that the Protestants gave up trying. Their preachers continued to travel up and down the country, and in such unlikely places as Northumberland people were reported to be "very ready and glad to hear the Word of the Lord."[83] Protestants also continued to draft radical proposals for the reformation of the Church and commonwealth. One writer, assuming that the root cause of the "sore disease in Christ's Church" was the churchmen's departure from apostolic poverty, framed a draft bill giving the king the power to confiscate excess properties encumbering churchmen—from bishops to chantry priests.[84] Another writer submitted a proposal for change on numerous fronts, stating among other things that it ought finally and unequivocally to be determined "whether the holy scripture teacheth any purgatory to be after this life or not."[85]

Throughout the summer a delegation of Lutheran Germans was closeted with a high-powered team of English ecclesiastics. It quickly emerged that nothing was more offensive to the Germans than the obstinate retention by the English of four venerable "abuses"—enforced clerical celibacy, auricular confession, communion under one kind only, and private masses.[86] Why could the English not see that these matters, although perhaps not of the highest doctrinal importance, had practical ramifications of the most pestilent nature? Private masses, for example, were dangerous and ought to be proscribed, not because purgatory was a doctrine which made sense to any right-thinking person any more (the Germans assumed it did not), but because "there is an open fair or market made of celebration of masses," which time and again had led churchmen to succumb to the temptations of flagrant fiscality.[87]

Real though these forces were for tilting the Reformation in England further in the direction of Protestantism, there was an increasing number of powerful Englishmen to whom further reformation would have been anathema. Many of them, in fact, felt that for some time nothing had been decent and in order. What the situation really called for, these people sensed, was a firm application of governmental restraint and ecclesiastical discipline to restore to the realm many of the accustomed beliefs and practices. There must have been many lay peers who, like Lord de la Warr, never wavered in their adherence to the opinions of "old time holden touching praying to saints, pilgrimages, purgatory, free will and justification." And the eagerness with which the majority of the lay peers in 1539 accepted the Six Articles was unmistakable.[88] Many of the bishops were likewise eager to halt further religious change. Stephen Gardiner of Winchester, who had been abroad on diplomatic business while the formularies of 1536 and 1537 were being written, had returned to the realm in August 1538 to be a potent force for reaction. Of a similar mind was the triumvirate of Stokesley, Tunstall, and Sampson, all of whom Cromwell was watching closely for any hint of treason. Many of the bishops indicated their wariness at further reformation by their determined foot-dragging in the negotiations with the German reformers.[89]

By the autumn of 1538, Henry VIII was in many respects of a common mind with the conservatism of the lay and spiritual peers. He was of course still willing to lend his name to the practical reforms set forth in Cromwell's Injunctions of October. He was also delighted to preside over the decanonization of the "rebel and traitor" Thomas Becket. But Henry was increasingly alarmed at the spread of religious radicalism in the land. In September he received reliable evidence that Anabaptism was proving as contagious in England as it was in certain areas on the Continent.[90] Of even greater concern to the king was the spread (often associated with Anabaptism) of sacramentarian beliefs. In his emendations to the Bishops' Book he had derided the "natural wit" of those who attempted rationalistically to demean the mystery of the eucharist.[91] There were in 1538 increasing numbers of people who were doing just that, saying that the mass "was ordained to sing for dogs' souls and for hogs' souls, and some say for ducks' souls." Alarming reports were also coming from Calais about the allegedly sacramentarian preaching of Adam Damlip, which had the town in an uproar and which Cromwell was finding more and more difficult to ignore.[92] Much though Henry must have relished the opportunity to personify orthodoxy in his November 1538 confrontation with John Lambert, there was obviously something about sacramentarianism which genuinely horrified him.[93] In fact, Henry's frame of mind is well expressed by the proclamation of 16 November, which exiled these "strange persons called Anabaptists and Sacramentaries," and which referred repeatedly (at his insistence) to the "most blessed" sacrament of the altar.[94] As the Reformation thus appeared to be sliding from moderation into radicalism, Henry also began to lose much of his stomach for negotiating with the Germans. For political—even marital—reasons he must keep the discussions from breaking down; but his annotations to the documents relating to the embassy showed his distaste for the Lutheran position on communion under both kinds and on private masses. He was also increasingly irritated by the censorious insistence of the German princes and theologians that they knew better than he what constituted an abuse.[95]

In the early months of 1539, therefore, Henry began to toy with the idea of issuing a short doctrinal statement, touching only the most dangerously controverted verities, which would stop the theological rot before it was too late, and which would put the impudent Germans in their place. In May he acted. When a committee of reforming and conservative bishops failed to agree on a statement, Henry submitted to convocation six questions, each one dealing with a doctrine which required definitive formulation. One of the questions was "whether private masses may stand with the Word of God or not?" On this the bishops and abbots were in unusually full agreement—all of them, including the reformers, joined to state that private masses were indeed congruent with the Word of God.[96] It is doubtful, however, that the king was greatly influenced by the opinions of the clerics. For while they were considering his questions, he himself was busy revising a bill for the enforcement of doctrinal uniformity.[97] On article after article, Henry emended the rather sparsely matter-of-fact original statements (the work of Cromwell?)[98] to make them more elaborately enthusiastic. The original formulation of the fifth article, for example, was simply "that private masses be agreeable to the law of God." This was not wholehearted enough for Henry, who painstakingly rewrote the article to read:

that it is meet and necessary that private masses be continued and admitted in this our English Church and congregation, whereby good Christian people (ordering themself accordingly) do receive both godly and goodly consolations and benefits; and it is agreeable also to God's law. [99]

When the reforming bishops stubbornly voiced their opposition to a number of the articles, Henry came to the House of Lords to confound them with "God's learning." By 13 June both houses of parliament had passed the Six Articles bill substantially as Henry had revised it, and on 12 July it became law.[100]

The continental reformers were choleric when they received news of the act. Martin Bucer of Strassburg responded by sending an indignant missive to Cranmer attacking the articles as "monstrous . . . partly popish, partly evangelical, and . . . partly intended to appear in conformity with the ancient government of the Church." And Melanchthon took the bull by the horns by writing two letters directly to Henry, whom he was privately calling "the English Nero," which attempted methodically to demolish the Six Articles, article by article. Melanchthon's irritation may be gauged by the fact that he promptly gave permission for the publication of the second of his letters in an English translation. Much to the consternation of the Privy Council, it was soon being widely circulated among the English radicals.[101] But, for all the outraged excitement of the reformers, the Six Articles was by no means a return to pre-Reformation doctrine. As Professor Scarisbrick has observed, Henry's affirmation of private masses, although enthusiastic, is "still cryptic and avoids the assertion, perhaps intentionally, that the 'private' mass avails, as a sacrifice, for the benefit of the souls of the dead." The article on auricular confession, furthermore, urges its continued use not, as Tunstall had argued, because of its rooting in divine law, but simply on grounds of expediency.[102]

The passing of the Six Articles was, however, part and parcel of a general reaction against the reforming initiative of the mid-1530s. One of the primary purposes of the act was, according to Bishop Sampson, to provide a "bridle" for preachers. As Lord Lisle's London agent John Husee observed smugly, "men will not be so liberal of preaching as they hath been time past."[103] Sampson and Husee were indeed correct, less perhaps because of the operation of the act itself than because of the way in which it encouraged the conservative forces of the realm to reassert their control over the preachers. In June and July 1539 Lord Lisle and his associates in Calais were emboldened to move against the alleged sacramentary Damlip and the local protector of radical preaching, commissary John Butler. And Bishop Stokesley, who had been attempting for some time to get Cromwell to restrain Hilsey and his preachers, at last found it possible to regain his long-lost control over the pulpit at Paul's Cross. As Bishop Hilsey, who had been superintending the preaching there since 1535, complained to Cromwell, "since the Parliament I could not get one to preach a sermon there saving myself or one of my chaplains." Amidst the mood of outraged orthodoxy which was prevalent, it was dangerous for a known reformer to preach. On 20 July, for example, one of Hilsey's chaplains had preached at the Cross, only to find himself cited to appear before Stokesley for erroneous doctrine. And Hilsey himself, who was scheduled to preach the following Sunday, confessed that the prospect filled him "with more fear than ever I did [have] in my life." Stokesley was once again conveniently indisposed, and would not agree to see Hilsey or even to receive letters from him or from Cromwell. Having been humiliated by the reformers in the past, Stokesley was savoring his revenge.[104]

During 1540 the conservative reaction continued. Symbolic of this trend was the beheading in June of the arch-agent of moderate reformation, Thomas Cromwell. So also was the burning a month later of Thomas Garret and William Jerome, and of Robert Barnes, who had been unwisely engaging in a public controversy with Bishop Gardiner about justification by faith and purgatory. The following year the irrepressible and indestructible Dr. Crome was more fortunate. Although he was once again arrested and forced to renounce a series of inflammatory statements—attacks upon chantries, private masses, and prayers for the departed—Crome lived to preach and recant again.[105] In this period numerous other heretics—mostly of little note—were made to feel the intensity of the government's new-found commitment to the protection of orthodoxy.[106] From the vantage point of a zealous Protestant such as Richard Hilles, the situation in 1541 appeared hopeless. "At last," he lamented,

God has taken them all [godly preachers] away from us, and has inflicted upon us such a want of sincere ministers of the Word, that a man may now travel from the east of England to the west, and from the north to the south, without being able to discover a single preacher, who out of a pure heart and faith unfeigned is seeking the glory of our God.[107]

To Hilles, at least, the conservative triumph seemed complete.

It was not so, of course. Religious revolution, once loosed, could not be totally controlled by any power, whether civil or ecclesiastical. In the early 1540s many Englishmen were becoming persuaded of the

Protestant version of the Gospel regardless of the dearth of powerful preaching.[108] Cranmer continued to work unmolested by the hostility of the Howards, Bishop Gardiner, and the Canterbury canons, exerting steady but diplomatic pressure for further reformation. Even doughty conservatives such as Germain Gardiner could get in trouble when they hallowed palms on Palm Sunday "without declaring the ceremony" or "plainly affirmed the state and condition of the souls departed."[109]

Even in these dark days for the reformers, it is clear that Henry and his churchmen were uncertain which orthodoxy they were upholding. In the spring of 1540 the king submitted to his theological advisers seventeen penetrating and often fundamental questions about the sacraments. Henry studied collations of their answers closely, annotating them copiously.[110] At about the same time the bishops began meeting in London. Their assignment was apparently to compose yet another new formulary of faith which would come up to the king's idiosyncratically exacting requirements. This time—unlike 1537— Henry was in charge of the proceedings, "examining reasons and deciding for himself." The French ambassador Charles de Marillac was even able to predict that Parliament would shortly be issuing a book, "in which will be determined all that is to be held in religion; not according to the doctrines of the Germans or of the pope, but of the ancient councils of the Church; by which this king shall be known . . . as a searcher and lover of truth only."[111] Marillac did not identify the documents which were the basis of this royal-episcopal search for truth. It is unlikely, however, that the king had ordered the churchmen to start again from scratch. The debates probably revolved around the Bishops' Book and the alterations to it which Henry had suggested. The opinions concerning the sacraments which the bishops and theologians had recently expressed may also have suggested certain emendations and refinements. But unanimity, which the bishops had achieved the previous year on six points of doctrine, was vastly harder to attain on the whole gamut of beliefs and practices comprising a formulary. Therefore, despite the daily exertions of the bishops, which continued for some months,[112] someone (no doubt Henry VIII) grew impatient and called a halt to their deliberations. With the fall of Cromwell and his own growing passion for Catherine Howard, Henry had other things to think about.

In 1543 the saddened and aging king, having been disappointed in love and unsuccessful in war, returned once again to his quest for doctrinal purity. To Heath, Thirlby, and Day, who in 1537 had assisted him with his revision of the Bishops' Book and whom he had by now made bishops, Henry assigned the major task of hammering out the text of the new formulary. Assisting them were three learned doctors: Richard Cox, John Redman, and Thomas Robinson. Whatever may have been the inner convictions of these six men, overtly they were all obedient Henrician catholics—men of "indifferency for judgment in learning," as Henry complacently described them.[113] He nevertheless showed a keen interest in their efforts. Several of their drafts have survived, with extensive additions and corrections in the hamfisted royal hand. And the theologians, demonstrating that the experiences of the previous years had taught them to be duly subservient to the whims of their royal colleague, prudently chose to utilize a large proportion of his emendations.[114] They were also careful to refer back to the interpolations and alterations to the Bishops' Book which Henry had made five years previously, and many of which they now found it possible to incorporate.[115] As a result of Henry's contributions and of their own original work, the end-product of their labors, though obviously indebted to the Bishops' Book, was substantially a new formulary. During the last ten days of April it was presented article by article to convocation, whose lower house on 30 April accepted it with a profuse expression of gratitude. A week later the "nobility of the realm" was given a preview of it, as apparently was the House of Commons, both of whom (according to the king) did "like [it] very well."[116] Finally, on 29 May, under the title *The Necessary Doctrine and Erudition of any Christen Man,* the new formulary was published by Berthelet, who was soon printing numerous copies of it.[117]

The *Necessary Doctrine,* or the King's Book as it has been popularly called, was controversial from the first. Henry's aim was to set forth a "perfect doctrine," and an observer as hypercritical as Chapuys was forced to agree that he had largely succeeded.[118] The Scots, however, were unimpressed by it—the reformers because of its conservatism, and the Catholics because of its anti-papalism and because they thought (quite incorrectly) that it reeked of the influence of Cranmer.[119] In more recent years reactions to the King's Book have continued to vary. For Father Hughes, it was, although perhaps not Lutheran, most emphatically not Catholic; Professor Lacey Baldwin Smith, on the other hand, has contended that it is more Catholic than Protestant; and Professor E. Gordon Rupp has detected within it numerous hints of compromise and ambivalence.[120] However this may be, there can be no doubt that, with one significant exception, the articles comprising the King's Book are more conservative in tone and less indebted to Lutheranism than those of the Bishops' Book.

The exceptional article, however, is the one that concerns us here. Entitled "Of Prayers for Souls Departed," it gave further impetus to the movement away from the orthodox position on purgatory which the Ten Articles of 1536 had begun and the "king's book" of 1538 had continued.[121] Although it spends less time than does the 1538 statement in arguing from "manifest scripture," its contents are in many respects significantly more Protestant than either of its predecessors. In the first place, like the 1538 statement but unlike the tenth article, the King's Book drops the word "purgatory" from the title of the article concerning prayers for the dead. It went beyond the 1538 statement, however, in admonishing the English people to "abstain from the name of purgatory, and no more [to] dispute or reason thereof. Under color of which have been advanced many fond and great abuses." In the second place, also like the statement of 1538 but unlike that of 1536, the King's Book studiously avoids all mention of "pain." Instead, it enjoins prayer for the dead, not because of their pains (1536), nor because of our uncertainty about their state (1538), but because they are part of the mystical body of Christ in which all members — both quick and dead — are bound by charity to intercede for one another.

Equally interesting are the inserted passages which are unique to the 1543 statement. The various abuses associated with purgatory, we are now informed, "were brought in by the supporters and maintainers of the papacy of Rome, and their complices." Furthermore, several sentences state unequivocally that those notions and customs which led men to "fantasy" that their prayers would be more efficacious in one location than another were "utterly to be abolished and extinguished." Finally, and most interesting of all, the 1543 statement contains a paragraph which insists that "it is not in the power or knowledge of any man to limit and dispense how much, and in what space of time, or to what person particularly the said masses, exequies, and suffrages do profit and avail." No longer might masses be offered solely, or even primarily, for the soul of a specified person. Henceforth all such services, "though their intent be more for one than for another," were to be performed for "the universal congregation of Christian people." For only God has the power and knowledge "which alone knoweth the measures and times of his own judgment and mercies."

Although the tenth article of 1536, with its calculated vagueness about the state of the souls in purgatory, must have shaken the confidence of many Englishmen in the customs and practices associated with the chantry system, the section of the King's Book which dealt with "Prayers for Souls Departed" went substantially further in an innovative direction. Within several months it was being used against a canon of Canterbury Cathedral who had bequeathed 20d. to every vicar choral "that had a pair of beads and would say Our Lady psalter for his soul," for such practice was "thought to be against the King's Book last set forth in the article of prayer for the souls departed."[122] Indeed, it is reasonable to claim that the statement of 1543 effectively cut the ground from beneath the chantry system. The nightmarish vision of awesome torments awaiting souls after death, which had been so graphically depicted by Fisher and More and even more sensationally by the preaching friars, would now slowly recede from men's consciousness. Henceforth it would be impossible for many Englishmen to believe in a God who would mechanistically remit the agonizing pains of a given soul in purgatory in direct proportion to the number of masses which were said specifically on his behalf. And without these beliefs, the primary impetus which had led men to found chantries would disappear.

In sum, between 1521, when Henry VIII published his *Assertio,* and 1543, when he ascribed his approval to the *Necessary Doctrine,* the theological stance which he and his government took on the many controversial issues associated with purgatory underwent a remarkable transformation. In the 1520s, Fisher and More had joined the king in defending the faith. But by 1543, the position of Henry and his councillors was closer to Fish than to Fisher, closer to Tyndale than to More, closer to Wittenberg than to Rome. As a result of this theological revolution, a dissolution of the chantries would now be a live option for the English government.

It would not, however, be a necessary and inevitable outcome of the King's Book. The English clergy were still to urge people to pray for the faithful departed. The English people were still to regard masses and exequies as laudable works. Inasmuch as individual chantries offered up prayers and celebrated masses on behalf of the whole mystical body of Christ, they would continue to have a useful function. But since the King's Book now declared it to be impossible to specify "what person particularly the said masses, exequies, and suffrages do profit and avail," no one could view the continued existence of any one chantry as essential. Therefore, if the King's Book did not provide a mandate for the suppression of all the English chantries, it did provide a rationale for a selective dissolution of individual institutions. And this, as I shall indicate in the next two chapters, is precisely what Henry VIII had in mind.

6 / Anticipatory Dissolutions

The period between the break with Rome and the death of Henry VIII was one of distressing uncertainty for the English people. After centuries in which imperceptible change had been the fact but immutability the rule, Englishmen suddenly found themselves thrust into a situation of almost uncontrollable volatility. The theological changes which I have recounted in the previous chapters produced an atmosphere in which the most venerable doctrines and usages could be questioned and discarded with impunity. The monastic dissolutions of the late 1530s and the omnipresent rumors of additional confiscations to come both resulted from and intensified this unstable atmosphere. Who could predict which doctrine, which practice, which institution would be the next to be swept into the maelstrom of change, forever to be sucked under? It was in this climate of uncertainty that people in all parts of the realm moved on their own initiative to dissolve intercessory institutions. Some of them did so selfishly, for private gain. Others did so simply to keep these foundations from falling into the hands of their unpredictable monarch and his predatory courtiers. Numerous borough corporations took similar steps for similar reasons. And the Henrician government, which was unable to restrict its confiscatory appetite to the monasteries and was likewise unwilling that private subjects should reap a harvest of ecclesiastical spoils without its consent, moved on its own to dissolve individual intercessory institutions. Thereby it began to prepare the way for a more systematic suppression of them at an appropriate date. For this reason, the dissolution of the chantries and colleges, of the hospitals and free chapels, did not begin with the Chantries Acts of 1545 and 1547. Instead, it began—unofficially—approximately a decade earlier with these piecemeal dissolutions.

The private confiscation of chantry endowments was by no means a new phenomenon in the late 1530s. Indeed, this activity had been going on ever since chantries were first founded in England. Large numbers of chantries had vanished during the course of the late Middle Ages. Some had simply collapsed or were combined with other chantries owing to a marked decline in the value of their endowments.

Others had disappeared as a result of the improvident or even dishonest administration of their incumbents. Still others had found their resources exhausted as a result of extended litigation about their endowments. A substantial proportion of those chantries which disappeared in the course of the late Middle Ages, however, were suppressed by the initiative of their patrons or of the descendants of their founders. Good examples of this come from Archbishop Warham's visitation of his Kentish diocese in 1511. Warham discovered, among other things, that in Waldershare a son was withholding funds from a priest who had been hired for one year to sing for his father's soul. In Herne, certain lands were withdrawn from the local chantry, and another rent of 23s. was not being paid. A group of feoffees in Ivychurch were not providing sustenance for a chantry in the parish as they had been required to do. And in Dover there should have been a cantarist singing daily services in the Maison Dieu, but since the hospital had evidently ceased to support him, the services were going unsung.[1]

The chantry certificates provide additional evidence that the private dissolution of intercessory institutions was not limited to the dissolution-obsessed Englishmen of the late 1530s. In 1531, for example, Edmund Specott, gent., a descendant of William Cornne, ceased to support one of the two stipendiary priests' livings in Thornbury (Devon) that Cornne had endowed, despite the fact that ample funds remained for the sustenance of both of the stipulated two priests. Similarly, William Percye, esq., in 1534 seized the endowments of St. Mary Magdalen Chantry in Scarborough (N.R., Yorks), which one of his forefathers had founded 140 years previously. Additional examples of a similar nature in 1534 come from Stockerston (Leics) and from Dursley (Glos).[2] Under normal late-medieval conditions, therefore, it was likely that a certain proportion of the patrons of chantries would be graspingly indifferent to the state of their forebears in purgatory.

With the beginning of the Henrician dissolutions came another and still more potent motive for private action. Many Englishmen quickly came to the conclusion that Henry would not be content with the suppression of the lesser monasteries and that he would soon be confiscating many of the other ecclesiastical institutions of England as well. Rumors concerning the king's intentions spread wildly,[3] and the steady surrender of monasteries, hospitals, collegiate churches, and even of some chantries seemed to lend credence to them. Under such circumstances, it is hardly surprising that a number of intercessory priests began to exploit their institutions' resources for personal gain. In Nottingham the master of St. John's Hospital in 1542 or 1543 had taken £9 16s. 8d. worth of lead off the hospital's roof and had "made a new roof for the same and covered it with slate." The profits from the sale of the lead had gone into his own coffers.[4] The patrons of many institutions, similarly sensitive to their own self-interest, had likewise begun to consider suppressing the foundations in their charge for their own use before the king could appropriate them. For those patrons who had been converted to Protestantism, it could scarcely have been difficult to decide to preempt the king.[5] Nor would it have been an agonizing decision for those of a materialistically secular disdain for the well-being of the souls of their forefathers.

For many others, who remained convinced by the traditional concepts of purgatory, and in whom the normal quota of human greed contended with a sense of propriety towards the founder, it must have been well-nigh impossible to decide privately to suppress a chantry. Although these individuals might attempt to console themselves with the thought that the founder would prefer that the endowments of the institution remain within the family rather than be seized by a king who was determined to commit sacrilege, how could they be certain that the current rumors were well founded? How could these individuals be sure that Henry actually envisaged a wholesale suppression of the chantries? What if he intended only a partial or selective dissolution which would leave their chantry intact? And if there were any chance of the foundation continuing to exist, of the ceaseless rhythms of masses and prayers extending "to the end of time," how could they justify expelling the priest and seizing the lands to their own use? To those who were devoted to the old ways and who cherished each mass that was said for the members of the "Church suffering," the answer must have been clear—a privately initiated dissolution should take place, if at all, only as a very last resort.

It is therefore an eloquent commentary upon the land-hungry secularism of the age, and surely also upon the gradual diffusion of Protestant ideas, that in the decade from 1536 to 1545 there appears to have been a substantial increase in the number of private suppressions of chantries. Henry VIII and his advisers were acutely aware of this trend, and, at least in part to prevent individuals "of their avaricious and covetous minds and of their own authority" from expropriating chantries, they secured the passage of the Chantries Act of 1545.[6] The commissioners who in pursuance of the act surveyed the chantries of the realm in the following year were given special instructions to make note of those institutions which were so suppressed.[7] They uncovered a large number. In Warwickshire, for example, they found two institutions which had been privately dissolved prior to the chantries acts (a chantry in Chelmscote and a stipendiary priest in Coventry), while in Nuneaton they learned that in 1542 the parishioners had connived with the descendants of the founder to convert the local stipendiary priest's service into a grammar school.[8] In Wiltshire they discovered six chantries and a light (in Bromham, Chute, Market Lavington, Ogbourne St. George, Ramsbury, Salisbury Cathedral, and Warminster), whose endowments various private persons had confiscated.[9] The Earl of Hertford, who was eager to rebuke Lord Hungerford for attempting to force the surrender of a chantry in Chippenham, himself apparently suppressed three Wiltshire chantries.[10] In Yorkshire, the commissioners learned that three chantries (in Halifax, Metham, and Northallerton) had been totally confiscated by their patrons during this period while chantries in four other parishes had lost varying amounts of land as a result of land seizures.[11] Parishioners in Badsworth had decided to convert funds which they hitherto had used for the support of a stipendiary priest to the maintenance of their parish church and the "reparation of the bells, thatching, and other necessaries."[12]

Other counties gave evidence of similar trends. There were at least four unauthorized dissolutions in Essex, four in Sussex, eleven in Devon, and thirteen in Somerset.[13] And in many parishes, as in Nuneaton and Badsworth, the parishioners moved to find fruitful alternative uses for the threatened chantry endowments. In Monmouth they converted chantry funds to the finding of an "organ player"; in Walkeringham (Notts) to a maintenance fund for the "Trent banks and a highway leading unto the same"; in Harwich (Essex) and Henbury (Glos) to the support of "sea walls."[14] The evidence, although fragmentary, seems also to indicate that there was a cumulative accelerando in the tempo of private dissolutions during the decade 1536-1545. It is probable that this tempo would have continued to quicken had Henry VIII and his advisers not detected the danger and intervened with the Chantries Act of 1545.

The clandestine dissolutions were often the work of municipalities and boroughs as well. In Canterbury the radical leaders of the borough from 1538 onwards attempted to ease the strain upon borough fi-

nances by a discreet confiscation of chantry properties and goods.[15] In
other towns, as in Godmanchester (Hunts), fear of imminent royal expropriation was the primary motive for the furtive suppression of intercessory institutions. According to a tip sent to the officers of the Duchy
of Lancaster, a certain Henry Frere, at the instigation of the local bailiffs, "did burn all such deeds, writings, and evidences" referring to the
town's two guilds; thereafter the bailiffs had quietly diverted the profits from the guild endowments into the borough's treasury.[16] The
elaborate and successful subterfuge of the borough of Richmond
(N.R., Yorks) was motivated not simply by a desire to keep local endowments out of the hands of the king, but by a determination to save
the prayers of most of the town's chantries as well.[17] On 8 December
1544 the bailiffs and burgesses, sensing that a royal suppression of the
intercessory institutions was near at hand, quietly took for their corporate use the land and properties of six chantries, two chapels, and
ten obits which were then active in the borough. The chantry priests,
who were evidently party to the procedure, were then given pensions
from the borough's incomes to support them in their continuing intercessory activities. When the chantry commissioners arrived (in 1546
and 1548) to survey the institutions which had been granted to the king
by the chantries acts, the inhabitants cooperated with the conspiracy
of concealment. The commissioners were thus able to record the existence in Richmond of only one chantry, one hospital, one grammar
school, and a handful of obits,[18] all of which the borough had left
undissolved because the prior connections of these foundations with
the crown would have facilitated their detection. Sooner or later someone was bound to discover a concealment of this magnitude, and late
in Edward's reign an informer brought it to the attention of the Court
of Augmentations. Legal bickering ensued which (a respite in Queen
Mary's reign notwithstanding) did not finally cease until the crown in
1567 granted the disputed lands to the borough for the endowment of
a grammar school.

Other boroughs sought by more legal means to secularize the property of various chantries for municipal purposes. An excellent example of this process was Colchester, which in 1539 received a grant of
several of its urban chantries and chapels for the founding of a free
grammar school within the borough.[19] Also interesting was the case of
Lincoln, where the mayor and commonalty, who had long been greatly
concerned by the decayed lands and shaky finances of the city, in 1536

sought remedy from parliament. In that year they dispatched the municipal recorder to London in an effort to obtain a grant of "chantries in this city" by a private act. He was evidently unsuccessful. But the city was more fortunate in receiving a gift in 1545 of all the lands and tenements of the Guild of St. Mary, which must have been a welcome windfall.[20]

York too was keenly aware of its declining fortunes in the early sixteenth century. References to the poverty of the city and the "great ruin and decay" of its tenements recur frequently in the York House Books.[21] This woebegone verbiage was not simply a rhetorical device to elicit pity and benevolence from benefactors; rather, it reflected the economic realities of the day. York's population had fallen dramatically since the pinnacle of the city's fortunes in the fourteenth century. Her foreign trade and clothmaking industry had likewise contracted markedly.[22] Municipal revenues were declining while expenses, the heaviest of which were a rent to the Earl of Rutland, an annuity to St. Stephen's Chapel, Westminster, and £42 per annum for the maintenance of nine chantries and three obits, continued to be onerous.[23] In 1527 the mayor and aldermen appealed to Cardinal Wolsey in a futile attempt to secure his assistance in reducing the Rutland rent and in releasing the city from the stipends which it was required to pay to the cantarists. Three years later the city council, taking advantage of the death of one of the chantry priests, took matters in its own hands, refusing to provide further support for one chantry and one annuity which had formerly burdened the common chest.[24] This offered merely a temporary respite, however, and the municipal leadership continued to work for more adequate relief. In 1531 they supplied the up-and-coming Thomas Cromwell with "a paper of certain articles of the principal decay of the city of York." In the following year they instructed the city's M.P.'s to work for "remedy as touching the charge going forth of the Common Chamber of the city of York yearly to divers chantry priests."[25] Finally, after lengthy negotiations between the city's representatives and Cromwell, parliament in 1536 passed a private bill which provided the monetary alleviation that the city had so long desired.[26] The burdens on the Common Chamber, the act alleged, had been so great—owing to the "ruin and decay" of the city—that the citizens of York would have been forced to "refuse their habitations in the said city and leave it desolate into the king's hands" unless some remedy were provided. Therefore the act proceeded to reduce consider-

ably the rents which the city had previously owed. Even more remarkably, it also authorized the Common Chamber to suppress all of the
obits and seven of the nine chantries whose priests it had hitherto been
required to support. The act thus lifted a substantial financial burden
from the shoulders of the Common Chamber. But what of the wills of
the benefactors whose cherished foundations it was now allowing to
disappear? What of the cessation of the prayers for their souls which
these dissolutions would necessarily entail? The authors of the act do
not seem to have raised these questions. Unlike their medieval forebears, who over the centuries had been compelled by economic realities to amalgamate numerous chantries, they appear not to have considered the plight of the suffering souls.[27] In an age of incipient inflation, decaying cities, and crassest materialism, the men of York—like
their counterparts in Canterbury, Colchester, and Lincoln—had other
things on their minds.

It was not only private individuals and corporations who in the early
1540s were dissolving intercessory institutions. The 1539 act for the
dissolution of monasteries had not been limited in scope to religious
houses; it had also granted to the king all such colleges and hospitals
"which hereafter shall happen to be dissolved, suppressed."[28] It is not
surprising, therefore, that from 1539 until the passing of the 1545
Chantries Act the government intervened to dissolve a considerable
number of colleges and hospitals, and a handful of chantries and free
chapels (Table 6.1).

Although the total number of institutions which the government dissolved was not large in absolute terms, the institutions which it selected

Table 6.1. Royally initiated dissolutions of intercessory institutions; 1540-1545.

Year	Colleges	Hospitals	Free chapels	Chantries & fraternities	Total suppressions
1540	2	4	0	0	6
1541	2	0	0	2	4
1542	4	0	0	1	5
1543	0	1	1	6	8
1544	6	2	0	2	10
1545	11	3	5	8	27
Total	25	10	6	19	60

Sources: see Appendix 1.

for suppression were generally sizable establishments. Since the dissolution of a college could bring substantial dislocation to the life of its parish, the dissolution of twenty-five colleges (to say nothing of other institutions) was of itself sufficient to have a discernible effect upon the realm. Furthermore, the relative impact of the early dissolutions upon the group of larger intercessory institutions was a significant one. Although our figures for the smaller institutions dissolved during these years are undoubtedly low, it is nevertheless clear that the government suppressed only a small number (and a still smaller proportion) of all of England's chantries and free chapels. Our figures for the governmentally instigated suppressions of colleges and hospitals are at once more complete and more startling. Within this six-year span the government secured the dissolution of over one-quarter (25 of 96) of the colleges of the realm and not quite one-tenth (10 of 110) of the hospitals.[29] As a result of these "pre-dissolution dissolutions," by the time the chantry commissioners began touring the realm in the latter half of the 1540s, the larger intercessory institutions of the realm had been markedly weakened.

Very little information has survived concerning the methods which were used to secure the surrenders of these institutions. In most instances, no doubt, royally appointed visitors were present to accept the surrenders. We know little of their modes of operation, for the surviving evidence is sparse. It is possible that the inmates of certain institutions, sensing the mood of the times and being seized by "a seasonable spirit of voluntary surrender," may have made their submissions to the crown without the intervention of a visitor.[30] In some instances, we know, financial inducements were offered to the collegiate clergy in return for their willingness to surrender their houses. We get a hint of this practice from Lord Maltravers, the deputy of Calais and heir of the Earl of Arundel, who in 1542 was attempting to persuade Henry VIII to grant Arundel College to him. The fact that the college had not yet surrendered didn't worry Maltravers. If the king's gracious pleasure were known, Maltravers was confident that he could persuade the master and fellows to capitulate, "compounding with them at my own charges for the same." Even more specific about this practice was Dr. Matthew Parker, the future archbishop. In 1545 he was resisting with his considerable diplomatic skill the surrender of the college of Stoke-by-Clare (Suffolk), of which he was master. Writing to the Council of Queen Catherine Parr in the hope that his recently reformed institution might continue to exist, Parker conceded that he had "hitherto resisted such suit for surrender as might (by the occasion offered) have been both beneficial to me for the present commodity, as for a liberal pension with good assurance to have been obtained."[31]

The most illuminating insights into the process of obtaining the "voluntary" surrenders come from the records of the commissioners who secured the dissolutions of the colleges of Crediton, Ottery St. Mary, and Burton upon Trent.[32] In the case of Burton upon Trent, the college which Henry VIII had founded only four years previously— with considerable fanfare—on the site of the recently suppressed abbey,[33] the king in November 1545 dispatched two commissioners to accept its surrender. John Scudamore and Richard Goodrich were experienced administrators who were to have important careers as functionaries of the Court of Augmentations.[34] By easy stages they traveled to Burton, where they remained for four days. While in Burton they procured the surrender of the college; they sold and made inventories of its vestments and ornaments, paid its corporate debts, appointed one of the petty canons to serve as the curate of the parish; and— together with the priests and lay servants—they consumed (in this center-to-be of British brewery) forty-seven gallons of ale and one pottle of wine.[35] Of greatest interest to us is the financial persuasion which they seem to have exercised. To the highest-ranking clerics (the dean and three prebendaries) and to those who were ex-religious who had not previously been pensioned (three of the petty canons and the epistoler) they granted stipends, ranging from the munificent £40 per annum of the dean to the serviceable £5 per annum of the epistoler. None of the other clergy—not even the "petty canons never religious" —received pensions, but they were not sent empty away. Not quite. Instead, the commissioners paid their wages for the following quarter and gave them supplementary "rewards" (of between one-third and two-thirds of their quarterly incomes) to support them while they sought other employment. Having thus presided over the demise of the college, Scudamore and Goodrich leisurely retraced their steps to London, where they collected £10 for their labors.

From this account, and from the similar records of the suppressions of the colleges of Crediton and Ottery St. Mary, it is evident that the Henrician government, unlike its Edwardian successor, felt no obligation to pension all of the collegiate clergy. For the lesser clergy it might, as a humanitarian or ameliorating gesture, provide "rewards" or "payments."[36] But the government was primarily concerned to obtain the compliant goodwill of the priests who really counted—those fellows who had votes in the process of capitular decision-making.

The statutes of many English ecclesiastical corporations provided that the fellows of that institution could take action on a major matter of business only if they were in unanimous agreement.[37] It is probable that in some cases a cantankerous, conservative, or unusually scrupulous fellow, being less accustomed to relinquishing venerable institutions than Dr. Thomas Magnus,[38] chose to rebuff the government's blandishments and to vote against making a "voluntary" surrender. In 1542, however, the government urged through Parliament an "Act for Leases of Hospitals, Colleges . . . to be good and effectual with the consent of the more party."[39] No longer could the vote of a single priest block the surrender of his house. Henceforth a majority vote of the fellows would suffice to decide any item of corporate business. By the same token, a majority would still have to be persuaded to capitulate. In this process the masters of the colleges and hospitals were clearly of pivotal importance, and the government seems generally to have accorded them pensions—some of them at 100 marks or £80 per annum, very generous by any standards.[40] In some of the colleges, the government felt it advisable to provide perpetual stipends for the other senior clerics also.[41] But for the majority of the collegiate clergy—no doubt totaling well over one hundred priests—whose foundations were dissolved before 1548, the government seems to have provided no pensions whatever.[42] For those priests who seem not even to have received the "rewards" and "payments" that served as severance pay, the future must have been bleak indeed.[43]

The pace of the "voluntary" surrenders steadily increased throughout the early 1540s (Table 6.1). The apogee of the governmentally sanctioned capitulations did not come until 1545, when twenty-seven institutions came into the hands of the crown. It is difficult to say why these particular institutions were dissolved (see Appendix 1). There is certainly no evidence that dissolution was an especially severe retribution for the lax discipline or cold spirituality of an institution. Nor is any geographical or chronological pattern discernible. Many of the collegiate foundations were, of course, extremely well endowed, despite Matthew Parker's rather lame protest that his college was worth "but three hundred pounds."[44] Generally speaking, however, it seems that the government demanded the "surrender and gift" of these par-

ticular foundations because of a single, highly persuasive consideration
— someone influential coveted their endowments and properties. From
the fragmentary information which survives it is clear that the properties of five colleges and two chantries which made their surrenders during this period were soon granted to courtiers or to influential men in
the immediate vicinity.[45]

Taken individually, none of these dissolutions or surrenders was of
earthshaking importance. But when viewed collectively and in the
context of the theological upheavals and private dissolutions, the governmental suppressions were highly significant. Insofar as they revealed Henry's ambivalent attitude towards the continued existence of
the intercessory institutions, they could not but increase the general
mood of uncertainty and instability.

By 1545, as a result of the events of the previous ten years, it was no
longer possible to view the chantries, colleges, fraternities, and hospitals as an immutable part of the English ecclesiastical scene. Change
must come, but it was uncertain in what form. Henry Brinklow, who
was never reticent in making prescriptions for the health of the commonwealth, in 1542 proposed a simple remedy. "You must first," he
advised the king,

down with all your vain chantries, all your proud colleges of canons, and specially your
forked wolfs the bishops . . . Now for the goods of these chantries, colleges, and bishops, for the Lord's sake take no example at the distribution of the abbey goods and
lands; but look rather for your erudition to the godly and politic order of the Christian
Germanies in this case. Which divided not such goods and lands among the princes,
lords, and rich men, that had no need thereof; but they put it to the use of the commonwealth, and unto the provision for the poor, according to the doctrine of the
Scripture.[46]

Henry VIII and the councillors of Edward VI would indeed carry out
part of the program that Brinklow had advocated. They would do so,
however, not because of Brinklow's influence (it is doubtful that any of
them read his *Complaynt*), nor because of the godly example of the
"Christian Germanies." They would do so rather for the eminently
practical reasons which I shall detail in the following chapters.

7 / The Henrician Chantries Act, 1545: Selective Suppression

No one knows when Henry VIII began to contemplate a second wave of dissolutions. By the mid-1540s, however, rumors had been circulating for almost a decade that a suppression of the chantries and colleges was imminent. Most of these reports were not based upon knowledge of the actual intentions of Henry and his councillors; they were extrapolations from policies which the government had pursued in the past. After all, the king had dissolved the lesser monasteries and then moved to obtain the surrenders of the greater ones. What should now prevent him from seizing the rest of the ecclesiastical institutions of England as well? In 1536 it was easy to give credence to the rumors which were circulating in Yorkshire, that royal agents were about to "pull down all chapels dependent and many parish churches as that they would leave but in every ten miles one parish church." It was likewise easy to believe that the government was about to confiscate all silver and gilt church plate, leaving only tin substitutes in their places.[1] Another result of recent events was the growing fear that the intercessory institutions would soon be going the way of the monasteries. The municipalities and individuals who dissolved chantries on their own initiative were giving expression to this fear. James Crawford, a chantry priest from Ipswich, enunciated their reasoning well. When accused in 1538 of wasting his chantry's properties by selling its woods, he exclaimed, "I had rather sell than the king should have it!"[2]

These fears were not wholly unjustified. To be sure, prior to 1544 the government does not seem to have been seriously weighing plans for a general dissolution of the chantries. But during the 1530s enough people with well-established governmental connections were either plotting such a dissolution or preaching openly in its favor to lend substance to things dreaded. As early as 1534 an associate of Cromwell's was advocating legislation which would have seriously undermined the intercessory institutions. According to one of the proposals contained in an omnibus collection of drafts for possible use in parliament, all parochial incumbents and cantarists should be compelled to say a monthly *dirige* and requiem mass for the departed souls of their parishes and of the whole realm—without receiving any monetary compensation for so doing. The parish priests should also be required to celebrate—likewise without charge—obsequies for those of their parishioners who had just died. A second proposal, also emanating from governmental circles and dating from the autumn of 1534, recommended the transfer of half of the revenues of all collegiate churches into the king's hands. In 1539 a third proposal for the "reform" of the intercessory institutions came to the government, but was evidently the work of an outsider. This document reminded the king that "many colleges, many chapels, and chantries have not yet tasted of the wholesome medicine and treacle which your Grace prepareth for their souls' health." It urged Henry therefore to confiscate large portions of their endowments in order to assist them in their return to the "humility, temperance, continence, and virtuous study" of the early Church.[3]

The governmentally sanctioned oral onslaught against the chantries was quite as hostile to the continued existence of these institutions as were these confidential drafts. The verbal blasts seem, however, to have been confined to the first half of 1536. The first such attack was made by Archbishop Cranmer himself. Preaching at Paul's Cross on 6 February, he was alleged to have declared "that the King's Grace is at a full point for friars and chantry priests, that they shall away all that, saving those that can preach." The full intent behind Cranmer's sermon is unclear, but Chapuys interpreted it as being part of a governmental scheme to prepare the people for the seizing of "all ecclesiastical endowments."[4] Two months later the enthusiastic Protestant Robert Singleton preached another vigorously anti-chantry sermon at the Cross. Singleton, who was frequently communicating with Cromwell during this period, asserted baldly that "every good man" knew that it would be best for the realm "to have the whole fashion and manner of illusion of such hypocrites [the intercessory priests] clean abrogate and avoided."[5] In spite of these threatenings by the reformers, the crisis year of 1536 passed without a dissolution of the chantries. Five years later the crown was once again founding intercessory institutions. Admittedly, the colleges of Thornton (Lincs) and Burton upon Trent (Staffs) were founded on the sites of recently suppressed monasteries. There was nothing, however, either in their foundation ordinances or in their lavish endowments, to indicate that their life-expectancy was to be short.[6]

It was not until July 1544 that the government gave unambiguous indication that it was carefully weighing the merits of a possible dissolution. It proceeded to send a commission to require four Yorkshire worthies to make a survey of six free chapels and chantries in the East Riding, to report "to what purpose the same chapels do now stand, continue, or be necessary," and to list the "lands, profits, commodities, jewels, ornaments, bells, lead, goods, or other things" that belonged to the chapels. In response to this commission, two of the four men (including Sir Leonard Beckwith, who was to serve on the 1546 chantry commission for Yorkshire) visited the specified institutions and compiled what was virtually a prototype chantry certificate. The commissioners evaluated the contributions of the free chapels to the cure of souls in their parishes and admitted candidly of four of them that they were "not necessary or requisite to stand." One of the institutions, in fact, they unsympathetically adjudged to be a nuisance, for "divers beggars and vagabonds do lie there in the night time." Two others were worthy of continued existence because of the services which they were providing for "the old and impotent persons that cannot go to the parish church to hear mass there."[7] If there were similar exploratory surveys in other parts of the realm, no evidence of the fact has survived. But the wording of this East Riding survey by itself, so strikingly anticipatory of the chantry certificates of the later 1540s, is portent enough that in 1544 the days of the English chantries were numbered.

It was in 1545 that the initial blow finally came. The frequency with which intercessory institutions were "voluntarily" capitulating to the king increased to an unprecedented level; in fact, that year produced far more such surrenders than any previous year had done (see Table 6.1 and Appendix 2). By late spring rumors had begun to circulate that the government was on the point of deciding definitely to attack the chantries and colleges. In May these reports had even reached Stephen Vaughan, the English ambassador in the Netherlands. "If any colleges be put down," he wrote hopefully to Sir William Paget at court, "I would I had a piece of some good thing for my money." A month later Chapuys confirmed the existence of rumors that Henry would seize the revenues of the collegiate churches. But it was probably not until 15 December, when the government introduced in the House of Lords a bill "for the dissolution of chantries, hospitals, and free chapels," that anyone knew with certainty what its intentions were.[8]

It is not clear why the government waited until the last ten days of the session to introduce its chantries bill. The 1545 Parliament had convened at Westminster on 24 November. On that day, the lord chancellor, speaking on behalf of the king, reminded the Lords and Commons of the king's great expenses for the defense of the realm. There were, he charged, "certain bishops in the realm who are usurping the exercising prerogatives belonging to the king; and that this evil must be remedied."[9] Henry, who had good reason to fear that certain bishops might oppose his projected chantry legislation, may have been attempting to cow them into passive acquiescence. It was hardly coincidental that two of the most formidable of conservative bishops—Tunstall and Gardiner—were at this very moment out of the country on diplomatic missions.[10] Since the mightiest of the ecclesiastical guns were thus silenced, it was most probably dissension within the government, fear of a lengthy debate, or simply the flood of parliamentary business which caused the government to delay three weeks before introducing the chantry legislation.

The bill was read a second time and engrossed on 16 December, and was passed with no dissenting votes (though Cranmer was notably absent) on 17 December.[11] The ease with which the measure had passed the Lords contrasts strikingly with the evidently stubborn opposition which had been encountered by a bill for the implementation of the Six Articles, "the abolition of heresies and of certain books, infected with false opinions." The Lords subjected it to the unusual scrutiny of five readings before sending it to the House of Commons where, despite the fact that it was "at the beginning set earnestly forward," it was thrown out.[12]

The chantries bill, which had had such an uneventful passage through the House of Lords, had its moments of excitement in the Commons. According to William Petre, it "escaped narrowly, and was driven even to the last hour, and yet then passed only by division of this House." It had, however, escaped major revision. The bill which received the royal assent on 23 December was in the very form which the Lords had sent to the Commons six days earlier, without additions or corrections.[13]

Henry was immensely gratified with the results of this full session of parliament—his last, as it turned out. After having given his assent to the bills which it had passed and having listened to the speaker's eloquent address, he indicated his pleasure by giving the speech of prorogation himself, rather than following the usual custom of delegating this task to the lord chancellor. In a memorable oration, the king thanked his subjects for their generosity in granting him yet another subsidy. He then spoke at length of the Chantries Act which parliament had just passed:

I cannot a little rejoice when I consider the perfect trust and sure confidence which you have put in me, as men having undoubted hope and unfeigned belief in my good doings and just proceedings for you, without my desire or request, have committed to mine order and disposition all chantries, colleges, hospitals, and other places specified in a certain act, firmly trusting that I will order them to the glory of God and the profit of the commonwealth. Surely if I, contrary to your expectation, should suffer the ministers of the Church to decay, or learning (which is so great a jewel) to be minished, or poor and miserable people to be unrelieved, you might say that I, being put in so special a trust as I am in this case, were no trusty friend to you, nor charitable man to mine, even Christian, neither a lover of the public wealth, nor yet one that feared God, to whom account must be rendered of all our doings. Doubt not, I pray you, but your expectation shall be served more godly and goodly than you will wish or desire, as hereafter you shall plainly perceive. [14]

In this speech, which moved many of those present to weep openly, [15] Henry set a high standard for the stewardship of the institutions which parliament had committed to his care.

The act which had inspired the king's rhetoric — catalogued 37 Henry VIII, c. 4 — may be divided into two sections, each of which dealt with a particular category of institutions. [16] The first section began by bewailing the fact that many patrons and founders of chantries, "of their avaricious and covetous minds and of their own authority," had physically seized and dissolved to their own use various colleges, chantries, free chapels, hospitals, fraternities, brotherhoods, guilds, and services. In addition, many of the incumbents of these institutions had cooperated in this nefarious process by selling or leasing properties and profits to the patrons and founders without stipulating in return the payment of the traditionally accustomed rents. The result of both of these techniques, the act alleged, was identical: the promotions had thereby become extinct, contrary to the intents of the original founders and without regard to the interests of the king. Finally, after noting "the exceeding great and inestimable charges, costs, and expenses" of the wars against France and Scotland and of the defense of the realm, the first section proceeded to order the dissolution and seizure to the king's hands of all those institutions (which were subject to the payment of the clerical First Fruits and Tenths) which had been confiscated by private action at any time between 4 February

1536 and 25 December 1545.* All surrenders or gifts of any of these institutions to the king, however, were declared valid, as were the leases and grants which he had made of their premises.

The second section of the act alleged that "a great number" of chantries, hospitals, free chapels, fraternities, brotherhoods, guilds, and stipendiary priests having livings in perpetuity and subject to payment of the First Fruits and Tenths, and all colleges whether subject or not to the same taxes, had various lands and other hereditaments which had been assigned by their founders "to the intent that alms to the poor people and other good, virtuous, and charitable deeds might be made, done, and executed" by the incumbents of the same. It was notorious, however, that these incumbents had been poor stewards of their resources and had failed to devote the incomes of these lands according to the intention of the founders, "to the great displeasure of Almighty God and to the discontentation of the king." Furthermore, since the king intended "to have the premises used and exercised to more godly and virtuous purposes, and to reduce and bring them into a more decent and convenient order," this section provided that Henry might from time to time during his life direct his commissioners under the Great Seal—"upon a warrant signed with his Grace's hand" to appropriate persons who were to have full power and authority—to enter into and seize into the king's hands all or any part of the chantries or other institutions named in their commissions. The transaction having been completed, the commissioners were to return their commissions into Chancery. All the institutions thus seized were to be within the jurisdiction of the Court of Augmentations.

The preamble to the Chantries Act cites three reasons why Henry VIII desired the passage of such a measure. The most pressing of these was pinpointed by Chapuys in mid-1545: Henry's government was in serious fiscal difficulty.[17] This financial distress was not peculiar to the government of England. All over Europe, at this time, governments were being plagued by economic troubles which, though relatively new to some countries, were strikingly similar. The impact of inflation was being felt universally, though nowhere was it yet understood. The structures of national taxation were often obsolete and were becoming more inadequate with each passing year. Revenues were scarcely sufficient to support medieval household government, let alone to finance

*4 February 27 Henry VIII had been the date on which the act for the dissolution of the lesser monasteries came into force.

the growing bureaucratic apparatus of modern government or the opulence of the Renaissance court.[18] The most important cause of the financial difficulties of the governments of mid-sixteenth-century Europe, however, was war, which had preoccupied the leading continental powers almost constantly for half a century.[19]

England, protected by the Channel from attack and distracted by an internal religious upheaval of major proportions, had been less at war than most countries. As of 1542 it was nearly two decades since Henry VIII had mounted a major military expedition. Thanks to the dissolution of the monasteries and the slow capitulation of other ecclesiastical institutions, the rent rolls of his Court of Augmentations were burgeoning. The gradual alienation of crown lands provided yet further ready income. Henry's financial position appeared strong indeed. Its strength, however, was contingent on the maintenance of peace. It was comparatively inexpensive to fortify the realm against possible attack, or even to wage war against the Scots. But it was prohibitively costly to send expeditionary forces to France, to lay siege to French towns and, once captured, to fortify them. Therefore, as wars broke out with Scotland (1542) and with France (1543), Henry's financial position began to deteriorate rapidly. His government was forced to spend incredible sums of money on arms, men, and fortifications. The total cost of the campaigns against the French and the Scots in Henry's later years came to the staggering sum of £2,134,784 1s. 0d.[20] In the frantic search for funds to pour into the bottomless sinkhole of war, Henry's government was driven from one expedient to another.

One of the most important of these expedients was taxation. In the 1540s parliamentary taxation was heavier and more productive than it had ever been before. Between 1540 and 1546 an increasingly unwilling parliament granted to the king six fifteenths and tenths and three subsidies. These parliamentary taxes were supplemented by extra-parliamentary loans and also by benevolences, in spite of the fact that they had been declared illegal by an act of 1483.[21] While Henry's ability to raise large sums by taxing his subjects was a convincing demonstration of his personal prestige, no king could continue indefinitely taxation of this magnitude. The profuseness of Henry's gratitude for the subsidy granted by the 1545 Parliament may betray a feeling on his part that he had taxed his subjects to the limit of their tolerance. In addition, it is notable that in Edward VI's first parliament the members "were induced the rather and franklier to grant those said colleges and free chapels, chantries, and other things . . . that they might thereby be relieved of the continual charge of taxes, contributions, loans, and subsidies, the which by reason of wars they were constrained in the late king of famous memory, his Majesty's father's reign to abide."[22]

Other expedients were hardly less important than taxation in bolstering the sagging royal finances. In 1544 the government sent Stephen Vaughan to Antwerp to negotiate for borrowing substantial sums at high interest rates on the money market there. Even more ominously, in that same year the government ordered a substantial debasement of the English coinage.[23] Still another expedient was the sale of crown lands on a large scale. Fortunately for Henry's plans for martial glory, in 1542 the bulk of the monastic lands still remained in his possession. In the course of the next three years he sold these at an accelerated rate.[24] These expedients may have alleviated the financial pressure on the government in the short run, but unfortunately they entailed serious long-term consequences. A war of dubious benefit to the realm had forced Henry's government to adopt measures which diminished the goodwill of the people, weakened the English currency, exacerbated the inflationary tendencies of the times, and depleted the capital reserves of the crown. It is hardly surprising, therefore, that by November 1545 the Lord Treasurer Thomas Wriothesley "was at his wit's end as to how to shift for the next three months."[25]

In this situation of severe stress, Henry and his councillors turned to a final expedient: the confiscation of still more Church lands. There was nothing new in this. Henry had already dissolved the monasteries. Individual colleges, hospitals, and chantries had for some time been making their surrenders to the king as well, a process which was expedited by a statute of 1542.[26] The Chantries Act of 1545 was designed to make it still easier for the king to plunder the ecclesiastical institutions. The act stated its fiscal purpose almost from the outset: to support the king in "the exceeding great and inestimable charges, costs, and expenses which your Majesty hath had . . . as well for the maintenance of these present wars . . . and for the preservation and defense of us your said subjects against the invasions and malice of your enemies . . . as also for the maintenance of your most royal estate."[27] The need for money, which the act thus admitted with such disarming candor, was a major impetus behind its introduction by the government.

A second motivation, also stated in the preamble, was to deal with the growing number of private dissolutions of intercessory institutions. This was no trumped-up charge on the part of the government; it was a very real fact, a natural outgrowth of the fears and rumors which had been epidemic since the mid-1530s. The government was on weaker ground, however, when it accused the incumbents and priests of these institutions of making leases for long periods of time at low rates in an attempt to defraud the crown. Some of the monasteries, to be sure, had done this with enthusiasm during their last years,[28] but there is little evidence of similar activity by intercessory priests. In his studies of Yorkshire leases for the 1540s Dr. Kitching found "no trend to longer terms which might indicate fraud. Indeed, many of the longest leases . . . may represent little more than the established practice of the colleges."[29] The government, however — on the basis of the precedents of the 1530s — obviously felt that such chicanery was taking place and that it must be outlawed, along with the private dissolutions, by statutory means.[30] If the chantries and colleges were to be dissolved, or if their endowments were to be plundered, it must be done by the government for the benefit of the king and of the whole realm, not by private subjects for private gain.

The preamble to the act cited still another motivation. Although many of the chantries and colleges had originally been endowed for the express purpose of doing charitable deeds and distributing alms, their recent priests and incumbents had allegedly been lax in carrying out the intentions of the founders. Therefore the king should be given the power to seize these institutions, inasmuch as he "of his most godly and blessed disposition intendeth to have the premises used and exercised to more godly and virtuous purposes, and to reduce and bring them into a more decent and convenient order."[31] In his prorogation speech, Henry returned to this theme, promising to order the institutions in his care "to the glory of God and the profit of the commonwealth" in such manner that education, the cure of souls, and the relief of the poor might all be fostered.[32] Similarly, in his recent refoundations of cathedrals and colleges he had insisted on generous allocations for the poor. And only a few months before the passage of the Chantries Act, he had appointed commissioners to enquire whether these sums were being honestly distributed.[33] In the remaining months allotted to him, however, Henry made no move to ensure that the institutions which the act now placed at his disposal were actively engaging in good works. He failed to instruct the commissioners who surveyed the chantries and colleges in 1546 to make special note of their charitable functions. The commissions and the visitation injunctions which the chantry commissioners administered on the government's behalf reflect an almost total preoccupation with the lands, goods, and ornaments of the doomed institutions.[34] To the extent that some of the 1546 chantry certificates do contain useful information about the charitable activities and parochial contributions of the institutions, they reflect the personal concern of the commissioners themselves rather than the terms of their commissions. The fiscal motive was dominant with the king until the very end.[35]

There were two additional, if unstated, incentives which may have prompted the government to seek the dissolution of these miscellaneous foundations. The desire of certain influential men to purchase the confiscated lands of the Church was almost certainly one of these. Without a doubt, historians unfriendly to the expropriation of ecclesiastical property have exaggerated its importance. It is worth noting, however, that in 1546 Richard Cox, a man with intimate connections at court and tutor to Prince Edward, bewailed the existence of "such a number of importune wolves that be able to devour colleges, chantries, cathedral churches, universities, and your lands, and a thousand times as much." The existence of these men — the "greedy gripers," as Harrison termed them — was an accepted fact. Henry Brinklow's enthusiasm for the dissolution of the chantries and colleges was tempered by the realization that these men — "the princes, lords, and rich men, that had no need thereof" — would profit, and not the poor. For much the same reason Cranmer attempted to stay the sale of chantry properties until Edward VI came of age.[36]

How many men sought to influence the government to dissolve the chantries for their own private profit, it is impossible to say. But is is striking that immediately upon passage of the Chantries Act English ambassadors began writing to privy councillors in the hope of acquiring land. Other individuals in the entourage of the court shared the same hope.[37] In fact, the eventual recipients of chantry properties were in numerous instances those men who were in a position to influence decisions in Henry's last years as well as during Edward VI's reign.[38]

A final, possible rationale for the Chantries Act may have evolved from Henry's religious intentions in the winter of 1545-1546, although it is difficult to assess these with certainty. If the dissolution of the

chantries and colleges was a part of a larger program for the reformation of the English Church which was just beginning to unfold as
Henry passed from the scene, that program would undoubtedly have
involved the abolition of the mass and the institution of a reformed
liturgy. Specifically religious considerations may thus have been con-
joined with other motives in persuading the king and his councillors to
attack the chantries. Such an interpretation is an interesting and
plausible conjecture.[39] After all, in his last years Henry had shown continuing interest in Cranmer's projects for reform. And in August 1546
he had proposed to the French admiral that within a half year the
kings of both France and England should convert the mass in their
realms into a communion service.[40]

In this most confusing of periods, on the other hand, it is possible
persuasively to argue the opposite point of view and to cite facts which
indicate that Henry could not have been an eleventh-hour convert to
Protestantism. His remarks to the French admiral may have been
nothing more significant than "great clouds of verbal dust," while his
true convictions may have been revealed in the persecutions of Anne
Askew and Dr. Edward Crome.[41]

It seems highly improbable that Henry VIII had any coherent doctrinal rationale for dissolving the English intercessory institutions in
December 1545. Although the official doctrine of the English government had moved sufficiently far in the direction of Protestantism to
make a selective dissolution justifiable, it had not reached the point of
denying outright the value of prayers and masses for the well-being of
the departed, thus necessitating a wholesale dissolution. On this subject the government's circumspectly ambivalent position was demonstrably also that of Henry VIII. For the king had shown himself to be
in agreement with the innovative "purgatorial" doctrine of the King's
Book.

At the same time, evidence of Henry's sustained conviction in the
efficacy of prayers and masses for the souls of the departed (which the
King's Book had also affirmed) recurs frequently in his later years. In
the 1530s the depth of his belief in this doctrine had become clear in
his unsympathetic scrawling in the margins of Latimer's treatise on
purgatory and in his corrections to the Ten Articles.[42] In the mid-1540s
Henry was still actively advocating suffrages for the departed. Thus in
1546 he reacted with considerable irritation to a typically impolitic
sermon by Dr. Edward Crome. Parliament had been quite right,

Crome asserted, in exorcising papal power from England and in abolishing the pope's "pardons, pilgrimages, purgatory, Peter Pence, feigned religious foundations of monasteries and chantries." But Parliament had not yet taken the logical next step—it had failed to condemn the mass and the popish notion that the sacrifice of the mass was "a satisfaction for sins of the quick and dead." Crome was fortunate on this occasion to escape lightly. After a month in prison and repeated grillings by the Council, he was forced to recant at Paul's Cross and to admit that the mass "is available and profitable both to the quick and to the dead." Later in the year a similar recantation was required of Nicholas Shaxton.[43] Even in the king's last will and testament, which was fully revised only a month before his death, he was quite as insistent upon the full complement of traditional masses and intercessions for his own soul as he had been a decade earlier for the soul of his beloved Queen Jane.[44] It is therefore unlikely that a dramatic doctrinal shift on the part of the king lay behind the Chantries Act of 1545.

In the act itself, moreover, there is no indication of religious motivation. Its professed rationale ("the maintenance of these present wars . . . and [the] defence of us . . . against the invasions and malice of our enemies the Frenchmen and Scots") was secular and pragmatic. The institutions which it dissolved were, like all medieval institutions, devoted to intercession for the souls of the departed. But no attempt systematically to attack all such foundations was implicit in the act. The Chantries Act of 1547, by contrast, firmly asserted its fundamental doctrinal basis and authorized the suppression of all institutions in light of it.[45] Thus, it is notable that whereas the Henrician act gave into the king's hands only certain sizable institutions (colleges, chantries, guilds, hospitals, and free chapels), the Edwardian act also dissolved the minor intercessory institutions—obits and anniversaries, lamps and lights—as indeed it had to if its statement of doctrinal purpose were to carry conviction.

It was not simply that the government was more rapacious in 1547 than in 1545. On the contrary, if the Edwardian government had been solely interested in making money from the sale of the dissolved institutions, it would have been well advised to concentrate on the major foundations (as the 1545 act did), which it might more easily have surveyed and suppressed.[46] By the same token, good business sense would have dictated that the government ignore the obits and other such minor institutions with their minuscule and scattered plots of land, which would have added more to its administrative difficulties than to its rent rolls. Whereas the Edwardian government was interested in maintaining doctrinal consistency as well as in obtaining profit, the Henrician act was motivated by Mammon alone.

If its proposed attack on the chantries and colleges had been based on religious presuppositions, the government would have had every reason to proceed immediately with the wholesale destruction of the theologically offensive institutions. Indeed, the Edwardian act reasoned in this manner, and set a definite date (Easter of the following year, just over three months following the prorogation of parliament), at which time the foundations were to be vested in the king. The 1545 act, however, set no fixed date for a dissolution. It did not even assume that all of the institutions mentioned would be suppressed. While granting certain institutions to the king at once — those which had already been dissolved by private initiative — it allowed the other institutions to stand until the king expressed his pleasure. A wide range of options remained open to Henry, and only those institutions which he had expressly selected might be dissolved.

The terms of the 1545 act thus give no indication that the government intended a complete dissolution of the chantries and colleges. In fact, its framers assumed that some of the institutions would continue to exist and that some might be dissolved only partially. For example, the clause on fines and recoveries refers not only to the current incumbents of the institutions but also to "the successor and successors of every such chantry priest, governors, rulers, and other having any of the said promotions." Another special clause points out that the commissioners selected by the king might be directed to enter into part of the said institutions, or into any of their lands and tenements, which seizure was to be as valid in law as "if the said commissioners . . . had entered into all and every part and parcel of the same chantries . . . and other the said promotions."[47] In contrast to the Edwardian act, the 1545 act does not order the pensioning of dispossessed incumbents. Nor does it allow for the continuance of the essential pastoral, educational, and eleemosynary services which some of the intercessory institutions were providing. Its failure to make arrangements for the consequences of a wholesale dissolution is manifest.

It is apparent, therefore, that in 1545 Henry VIII and his advisers had no intention of dissolving all of the colleges, chantries, and other intercessory foundations of England and Wales. Their intention was more diffuse, more opportunistic than that. They wanted only to penalize those individuals who had been dissolving chantries on the sly, to suppress a few selected foundations for quick income, and to reward impatient courtiers with the lands which they coveted. As such, Henry's Chantries Act represented a marked escalation from the 1542 act which smoothed the way for "voluntary" surrenders of colleges.[48] But it still fell far short of the systematic, principled decisiveness of the 1547 Chantries Act.

This conclusion is reinforced in part by the fact that in 1545, somewhere within government circles, someone was proposing an immediate, doctrinally motivated dissolution of the intercessory institutions. Among the government's papers for that year there survives a roughly drafted proposal for a chantries bill.[49] The provenance of the document is uncertain, although from its repeated references to God's "most holy Word" one may perhaps infer that the author had Protestant leanings. It is a fascinating document, one which differs intriguingly on a number of matters from the Chantries Act of 1545 and anticipates the Chantries Act of 1547. For one thing, in order to raise money for the defense of the realm, it proposed a complete and immediate dissolution; all institutions specified in it were to be vested at once in the king and his heirs. Secondly, the institutions to be suppressed were those which had been "given to the use of the finding of priests to sing for the souls of the dead." This dissolution, then, was to be based on clear doctrinal principle. Thirdly, also similar to the 1547 act and in contrast to that of 1545, the document showed concern that the priests who had been dispossessed should have "competent livings or augmentations of livings and assurance of the same." And finally, it made provision for the continuance of the useful non-intercessory contributions of the intercessory institutions. It would require the government to ensure that lands be set aside to provide continuing support according to "the mind of the giver" of

the premises [which were] assigned and given to the relief and sustentation of the poor or impotent, or to the bringing up, nourishing, or maintaining of the ministers of the Word of God or of any liberal science, or for the amendment of highways, maintenance of bridges or common passages, or for the unburdening of any of the King's Highness his subjects from tax, tallage, or other like imposition.

Since the proposal remained in sketchily outlined form and was not decked out in the intricate formalisms of an actual draft bill, it is unlikely that the government seriously considered using it as the kernel of its parliamentary legislation on the chantries.[50]

The government's implementation of the Chantries Act during the thirteen months between its passage and Henry's death provides further confirmation of the implications inherent in the act itself. There seems to have been a leisurely air about the proceedings—with no threat of an immediate or imminent dissolution of the institutions which were in its grasp—which contrasts markedly with the purposeful atmosphere of 1547-1548. The government waited until 14 February 1546 before addressing its letters patent to the men in the various shires who were to survey the institutions. These commissioners were in no apparent hurry to be about the job. Such evidence as we possess indicates that the chantry surveys were compiled during the months of March and April.[51] None of the final chantry certificates which were submitted to the Court of Augmentations indicate the date when the survey was completed, but it is probable that by May 1546 most of them had been turned in. By that date the king had a fairly accurate notion of the number and extent of the institutions which were within his power to confiscate.

What were these institutions? According to the 1545 Chantries Act, the king was empowered to dissolve only those chantries, free chapels, hospitals, guilds, and stipendiary priests which were contributory to the First Fruits and Tenths, that is, which were included in the *Valor Ecclesiasticus*. It is not clear why this limitation was imposed, but it had a number of important consequences. It would exempt all institutions under purely lay control, thus protecting the hospitals controlled by municipal corporations and the craft and municipal guilds.[52] In addition, the numerous intercessory institutions which the compilers of the *Valor* had overlooked were not within the compass of the act. A specialist or two within the Court of Augmentations may have had a vague realization that there were in reality hundreds of unlisted chantry foundations. But not until the chantry commissioners began their rounds in 1546 did anyone know how great the disparity actually was. The commissioners, who carried with them "an abstract taken out of the Court of First Fruits and Tenths,"[53] seem generally to have approached their task with flexibility, recording the existence of numerous institutions which would definitely have been covered by the act if the *Valor* commissioners, working eleven years earlier, had done their job better. Thus the chantry certificates of 1546, although not as inclusive as those of 1548, give the particulars of many more institutions than the 1545 act had in fact placed within the king's power. Apparently Henry VIII respected this legal technicality, and seized none of the foundations which had not been included in the *Valor Ecclesiasticus.*

The act treated the colleges according to a different principle, however. Whereas other institutions were subject to dissolution only if they were chargeable to the First Fruits and Tenths, *all* colleges — regardless of whether they were so chargeable — were now to be eligible for suppression at the will of the king.[54] This inconsistency arose from an earlier parliamentary act (1536), which gave special exemption from payment of the First Fruits and Tenths to the colleges in the universities, along with the colleges of Eton and Winchester.[55] The 1545 Chantries Act, however, would accept no such limitations. Thus the clause in question was inserted for the express purpose of threatening the universities, and no colleges of any sort were to be exempt from its provisions.

Dr. Matthew Parker, who was vice-chancellor of Cambridge at the time, had an explanation for this stringent provision. "Certain officers in the Court and others then in authority under the king," he charged, were "importunately suing to him to have the lands and possessions of both universities surveyed, they meaning afterward to enjoy the best of their lands and possessions by exchange of impropriated benefices and such other improved lands." It is also conceivable that Henry may have desired (as his letters patent of January 1546 to the commissioners for the survey of the university of Cambridge put it) to "order, alter, change, and reform" all the colleges of the realm — those in the universities as well as those elsewhere. The university authorities, however, were quick to scent danger. Immediately upon receiving news of the passage of the Chantries Act, the authorities at Cambridge anxiously rushed letters to two of their most influential contacts at court, Sir Thomas Smith and Sir John Cheke. Smith, who seems to have been especially active in representing the interests of his university, is known to have pleaded its cause with Queen Catherine, who termed him a "discreet and learned advocate." It was he who also made the formal presentation of Cambridge's concerns to the king. Conceivably it was he who further succeeded in persuading Henry "for avoiding the great charges that should be sustained therein, not to send any of his costly officers" to survey the Cambridge foundations, when trusted and able men within the university could do the job more cheaply (and, of course, more sympathetically to the university).[56]

On 16 January 1546, scarcely three weeks after the passage of the act, the king commissioned three such men—Matthew Parker, John Redman, and William May (vice-chancellor of the university and masters of Trinity and Queens Colleges respectively)—to survey the institutions within Cambridge University which were within the compass of the Chantries Act. With "all goodly speed and diligence" they were to report their findings to the king on a special certificate.[57] Henry had given the universities and their representatives precious little time to correspond and negotiate. That they nevertheless accomplished so much in such a short time is clear evidence of the resolute dispatch with which they had acted.

Why was Henry in such a hurry with the universities? After all, it was not until almost a month later that he moved to survey the other institutions which the act had delivered into his power. He would no doubt have protested that zeal for educational reform had motivated his swift action. But this was not the way Parker and the university men saw things. Their fears were probably justified,[58] for it appears almost certain that the avaricious climbers at court were urging the king on in the hope of obtaining the best of the university lands for themselves.[59] Henry may have had reason enough to listen to them. A martial king must reward his successful lieutenants, and it must have appeared attractive to Henry—who was particularly hard-pressed at the moment—to enrich them at no cost to himself. Furthermore, Henry, like many subsequent politicians, may have been under the impression that the universities were far more amply endowed than was educationally necessary. Why not therefore compel them to exchange certain lands with his courtiers or even to surrender certain superfluous properties? Indeed, Henry may have persuaded himself that a judicious pruning of their resources would not only benefit the kingdom financially; it would also encourage the universities to concentrate upon learning rather than belly-cheer.

The Cambridge commissioners went to work with care and thoroughness. They consulted with Bishop Goodrich of Ely, to make sure that they had missed no chantries, hospitals, or free chapels within Cambridge; and they examined carefully the properties and financial health of the colleges. The Oxford commissioners, among them Dr. Richard Cox, apparently performed a similar task. Once their surveys were completed, each group of commissioners prepared certificates which turned out to be sizable volumes. The Cambridge commissioners at least were assisted in engrossing their lengthy returns by two clerks of the Court of Augmentations.[60]

It is not certain how long the period of anxious waiting lasted for the universities. By 10 February Oxford University could write enthusiastically to the king that "their confidence in his encouragement of letters is gratefully confirmed, and . . . that in England under Henry VIII, even in so great heat of wars, good letters may flourish no less than they did at Rome under Octavius in time of peace." The Cambridge authorities, however, had still not received word as to the fate of their colleges, and they were becoming worried. On 13 February Vice-Chancellor Parker sent two letters, one to Henry VIII protesting the university's readiness to place its possessions at the king's disposal, and the other to Secretary Paget trying desperately to forestall that eventuality. It was probably not until the end of the month that Cambridge received firm indication of Henry's intentions. On 26 February, Queen Catherine, whom the university had also approached to intercede in its behalf, wrote to Parker that, "notwithstanding his Majesty's property and interest through the consent of the high court of Parliament," he would rather erect new colleges than "confound those your ancient and godly institutions."[61]

Fortified with this knowledge, Parker and May were able confidently to travel to Hampton Court to present an abstract of their findings to the king. After having perused their document carefully, Henry listened sympathetically as they pleaded that the colleges be allowed to continue as they were and that the university not be compelled to make disadvantageous exchanges of land with courtiers. Henry expressed astonishment that the universities were able to support the livings of so many persons by "so little land and rent." When he perceived that most of the colleges were actually forced to engage in deficit spending to maintain their programs, he exclaimed, "Pity it were these lands should be altered to make them worse!" (At these words, Parker reported, some courtiers "were grieved, for that they [Henry's words] disappointed *lupos quosdam hiantes*.") Henry concluded by saying that he would of course need to write to "his servants and others doing the service for the realm in wars and other affairs." Before making any grants involving university lands, however, he would ask Parker and May "whether we should gratify them or no." With this promise, Parker concluded, "We were well armed and so departed."[62]

During the coming months the din of building-wrecking was indeed heard in Cambridge, but not in the colleges. The structures being demolished were those of the erstwhile Franciscan friary, which was being converted into Trinity College (formally founded by Henry on 19 December 1546).[63] Meanwhile the colleges and their lands remained intact. They had had a narrow escape. For in all probability Henry had seriously contemplated at least the partial confiscation of the endowments of the universities as well as the forcible exchange of collegiate lands to the advantage of his courtiers. Only the well-organized flurry of petitions had apparently restrained him from putting the educational colleges onto his list of foundations to be plundered at will.

The survey of the non-university foundations had scarcely been completed when the dissolutions, which had been halted since the previous year's parliament, began again. On 11 May 1546 commissioners were dispatched to Arundel, Sussex, to suppress Holy Trinity Hospital there.[64] During the nine months before the king's death a total of seven colleges, eight chantries, three hospitals, and two free chapels were seized into the king's hands.[65] The tempo of the dissolutions, like that of the non-university surveys, was leisurely. In fact, the tenor of the proceedings seems to have been much the same as it had been prior to the passage of the Chantries Act, except that the king could now aggressively effect confiscations through his commissioners rather than wait for the institution "voluntarily" to surrender. Once again there were comparatively few dissolutions, coming at irregular intervals and scattered seemingly at random all over the realm. In this period, too, the motivation behind the choice of institutions for dissolution remained generally obscure. It almost certainly had little to do with the spiritual state of the foundations. It is far more probable that the king, in dissolving specific foundations, was responding to requests for land from his hangers-on and from their friends. Such was certainly the case with the decision to dissolve the college of Tong, Shropshire. Sir Richard Manners, who was especially interested in purchasing the college and its lands, made "special suit" to Sir Anthony Denny, a courtier who was close to the king and interceded with him for its dissolution. Henry agreed to send a commission to four local men, who reported on 20 October 1546 that they had completed the suppression of the college and of two chantries, one in Tong and the other in Bakewell (Derbys). The king's death stopped the sale proceedings, but in July of Edward's first regnal year the Privy Council agreed to complete the transaction, and Sir Richard finally got his college for a sizable sum.[66]

A similar case is that of St. Edmund's College, Salisbury. In 1543, after having been governed by ecclesiastics for almost three centuries, the college received a lay provost in the person of William St. Barbe, esq., a gentleman of the privy chamber. At the time of St. Barbe's collation to the benefice, the bishop of Salisbury bound him to ensure "that divine service and the cure of souls were not neglected."[67] Perhaps St. Barbe found these conditions too onerous to tolerate, or perhaps he simply became vexed at the thought of having to devote £26 13s. 4d. of the collegiate revenues to the support of four chaplains, when he might receive the entire £88 himself. At any rate, on 6 June 1546 the king's commission was directed to the mayor and three prominent residents of the city, to seize the college and two free chapels in Whiteparish to the king's use. This they did on 16 and 17 June, receiving the surrender of the college from the understandably cooperative St. Barbe. Four months later, for the ridiculously low sum of £400 "and his services," the dispossessed provost received a grant of the three foundations.[68] Others who benefited from the post-1545 Henrician dissolutions were Sir Philip Hoby, John Gate, Sir Richard Lee, and the judge Sir Edward Montagu, not one of whom paid any fees whatever for their substantial grants.[69] Whatever else the Henrician Chantries Act accomplished, it enabled the king to reward his sycophants at the expense of others.

Perhaps this was all that Henry had ever intended. The act of 1542 had made it easier for him to secure the surrenders of various corporate bodies; and the Chantries Act now made the process even less complicated by obviating the necessity for the consent of any of the incumbents. The era of the elaborately engineered "voluntary" surrenders was now past. If Henry needed money for a special purpose, or if some courtier were being especially importunate in his efforts to secure certain collegiate or chantry lands, the king could now simply direct his commissioners to seize the lands and dissolve the institutions supported by them. Some historians have contended that Henry was planning a dissolution which would go much further than this, and which would eventually make a clean sweep of the institutions included in the act. Only the king's untimely death, they have maintained, prevented him from effecting this total dissolution.[70] Some contemporaries, indeed, seem to have been aware that the continued existence of the intercessory institutions was a precarious one. Furthermore, two ambassadorial letters of December 1546, if rather obscurely worded, may indicate that Henry was planning additional action against the chantries. Concerning the impending session of parliament, the imperial ambassador Van der Delft predicted that it would "deal with the employment of the proceeds" of the chantries which the previous parliament had placed in the king's hands. The French ambassador Selve, without referring directly to the chantries, reported that parliament would "treat of some other great changes in this realm."[71]

It is doubtful, however, that in his last months Henry was preparing decisively and totally to dissolve the chantries and colleges of the realm. The evidence is small in quantity and uncertain in meaning.[72] In addition, other aspects of the situation tell against it. Certainly the wording of the Henrician Chantries Act had not indicated that a total dissolution was being contemplated. Nor did the efforts to carry out the act point in this direction. The Henrician dissolutions were random, sporadic, and unhurried. They were dictated by the desire of specific suitors for land, not by any general underlying principle. There was no indication of an acceleration in the tempo of dissolutions in the months following the survey of the chantries. Although Henry's days were numbered, at the time of the passage of the act he had thirteen months left to live. Yet in this amount of time he moved to secure the dissolution of a mere handful of institutions.

The contrast with the Edwardian dissolution is striking. In a period of just over three months, Edward's government moved resolutely to secure the dissolution of the whole system of intercessory foundations. Basing its suppression of these institutions on a coherent doctrinal rationale, the Edwardian government was to be as self-confidently purposive and consistent in its approach as the Henrician government had been uncertain, ad hoc, and dilatory.

8 / The Edwardian Chantries Act, 1547:

Systematic Dissolution

At long last—in December of 1547—the government of Edward VI took steps definitively to dissolve the chantries. It was obvious that the Henrician Chantries Act, which had authorized the dissolution of intercessory institutions solely upon the signed warrant of Henry VIII himself, was no longer effective; that act had lapsed with the old king's death. That Edward's government would sooner or later replace it with chantry legislation of its own was almost inevitable. From the doctrinal standpoint alone it would have been hard to avoid doing so. As early as the end of July 1547, by publishing the book of *Certayne Sermons or Homilies,* the government gave public indication of its theological predispositions.[1] Throughout the realm, the parish clergy were commanded to mount their pulpits, to denounce purgatory, and to condemn the complex of observances which had grown up around it.[2] In following these orders they were backed by the full weight of ecclesiastical and civil authority. By early September the imperial ambassador was sure that in the future masses were "not to be allowed on behalf of the dead." The old heresy had thus become the new orthodoxy.[3] In such a hostile doctrinal climate, the intercessory institutions could not be expected to survive for long.

The injunctions, which the royally appointed visitors carried with them as they traversed the realm in the autumn of 1547, contained signs which pointed in the same direction. One of the most striking of these was the new form of bidding the common prayer. The time-honored bidding prayer had implored that God lessen the temporal pains of the departed souls and ensure their present felicity. The new formula which the injunctions introduced, however, in consonance with the anti-purgatorial doctrine of the *Homilies,* confined its attention to the future destiny of the dead. Emphasis was now put upon the day of judgment. In preparation for the inexorable parting of the ways which would occur on that day, believers were ordered to implore "that they [the departed] with us, and we with them at the day of judgment, may rest both body and soul with Abraham, Isaac, and Jacob in the Kingdom of Heaven."[4]

The injunctions introduced changes which were visible as well as verbal. They prescribed that all images which had been abused by pilgrimages and censings be taken down; and all lights (with the exception of two upon the high altar) were to be removed from the sanctuary.[5] A more utilitarian injunction ordered each parish within three months to provide "a strong chest with a hole in the upper part thereof . . . which you shall set and fasten near unto the high altar, to the intent the parishioners should put into it their oblation and alms for their poor neighbors."[6] The clergy were to remind their parishioners to keep the poor chests in mind, especially when making their wills. For "whereas heretofore they [testators] have been diligent to bestow much substance otherwise than God commanded upon pardons, pilgrimages, trentals, decking of images, offering of candles, giving to friars, and upon other like blind devotions, they ought at this time to be much more ready to help the poor and needy." Furthermore, all monies which belonged to religious guilds and fraternities, and all rents and lands which had been given to lamps and lights, were to be transferred to the use of the poor. It was in effect the injunctions which began the dissolution of the minor intercessory institutions by converting them, under ecclesiastical supervision, to charitable projects in the parishes. And before long, as the royal visitors went from parish to parish, the lights began to go out all over England.[7]

If the *Homilies* and injunctions gave practical expression to the gradually unfolding program of reform of the Edwardian government, they also made it clear that in July 1547 the government had not yet decided to introduce a chantries bill of the sort that it was eventually to frame. Although the injunctions did indeed order a marked change of function for the guilds and lights, they did not hint at tampering with the endowments. Nor were the changes of function to be compelled by extra-parochial intervention; the conversion of endowments to the relief of the poor was to be carried out by local men. The Edwardian Chantries Act, in contrast, required the compulsory confiscation of the guilds and lights by government functionaries. In seizing the endowments of these institutions to fill its own empty coffers, the government was depriving the parochial poor-boxes of their primary source of income. Between 31 July, when it issued the injunctions, and 6 December, when it introduced a chantries bill in the House of Lords, the government had thus demonstrably changed its plans for the future of the intercessory institutions. It had fancied itself to be caught in the eternal dilemma between butter and guns, between the poor and war, between idealism and realism. That the latter won out — after several months, during which the Edwardian government had seriously considered more beneficent policies — is hardly unprecedented.

The injunctions reinforce this contention. They enjoined all chantry priests "within three months after this visitation" to obtain Latin and English versions of the New Testament in addition to Erasmus's *Paraphrases*. In addition, they ordered these clerics in the future to "exercise themselves in teaching youth to read and write, and bring them up in good manners, and other virtuous exercises." Similarly, the Articles of Inquiry which were issued for the same royal visitation included a number of queries which the visitors were to address specifically to the chantry priests.[8] Were they resident upon their chantries? Were they pluralists or men of ill fame? Were they active in assisting the parish priest in the ministration of the sacraments and the celebration of divine services? Did they distribute money, food, and drink to the poor as required by the foundation ordinances of some of their chantries? There is no hint in these articles and injunctions that within five months' time (during which the cantarists would have dutifully acquired their New Testaments and *Paraphrases*) the government would be proposing the wholesale dissolution of the institutions which it now seemed eager to reform for parochial services.

There are several possible explanations for the posture of the government in July 1547. In making its proposals for the poor chests, the cantarist schoolmasters, and the assistant curates, the government may simply have been conducting an elaborate charade to mask its confiscatory intentions. This seems unlikely. Two other possibilities, both of which credit Somerset and Cranmer with a modicum of honesty in their reforming professions, seem more credible. The government may have been planning to introduce a chantries bill which would selectively expropriate those intercessory institutions which were either hopelessly unreformable or especially desirable to some importunate courtier; it would at the same time permit the bulk of the intercessory institutions, after having been purged of their popish perversions and reordered according to Protestant notions, to continue to exist. Such a bill would have been consistent with the tradition of Henry VIII's chantry legislation. It would also have been congruent with the plans for reform as revealed in the *Homilies*, the injunctions, and the articles of inquiry. Or, on the other hand, it is possible that in

July 1547 the government had simply not made up its collective mind on the matter. If so, it is understandable that one faction might have been working for the reform of the intercessory institutions for charitable and educational purposes, while another faction might have been bent on securing a wholesale dissolution for fiscal reasons.

One can first ascertain the intentions of the government when it introduced a chantries bill into the House of Lords on 6 December 1547.[9] By that date the party advocating the reform and conversion of these institutions to charitable purposes—represented most eloquently by Cranmer—had clearly got the worst of the argument. The dissolution was to be total and immediate, thereby reflecting the government's Protestant aversion to "superstition" in all its guises. It was also to be more heavily fiscal than philanthropic in motivation, with the result that the good works which the injunctions and articles had anticipated were never to be performed. Perhaps it was partly this change in emphasis that caused the government's chantry legislation to have so tumultuous a passage through parliament.

The traditional sources for the 1547 Parliament, if scanty by late-sixteenth-century standards, are significantly more instructive than those for most of the earlier parliaments of the Tudor period. Fortunately, the Commons Journal made its initial appearance in this session—though hardly yet a journal in the accepted sense of the term.[10] It does nevertheless provide a listing of the bills which the Commons read and passed in their daily sessions, and it is a most useful supplement to the more informative Lords Journal. The journals of neither house, however, provide any record of speeches made, compromises reached, crises precipitated or averted, which their later counterparts contain and which the parliamentary diaries for the Elizabethan and Stuart parliaments provide. A minute of the Privy Council for 6 May 1548 has also survived, which provides some illuminating detail about an acrimonious assault on the chantries bill which threatened to prevent the passage of any chantries legislation whatever.[11] The act did, of course, pass and remains a vitally important source.[12]

From these materials it is possible to construct a relatively full chronology for the passage of the Chantries Act through the 1547 Parliament. Although the session opened on 4 November, more than a month elapsed before it became apparent that the government was planning to attack the intercessory institutions. The first indications of impending government-backed chantry legislation may have prompted the introduction — presumably by private members — of bills in the House of Commons on 30 November and 1 December "for Chantry Lands and Church Lands" and "for Colleges, Chantries, and other Spiritualities." Neither of these bills was given a second reading. Far more important was the bill "for Chantries" which was introduced, almost certainly at the instigation of the government, in the House of Lords on 6 December. It was read a second time on 12 December, a third time two days later "with a proviso annexed unto the same," and was passed by the Lords as the first item of business on 15 December.[13] The bill's passage through the Lords had been stormy. Cranmer is known to have opposed it,[14] and on the fifteenth he was joined by seven of his episcopal colleagues — of both conservative and reforming convictions — in voting against it. Despite this futile demonstration of clerical discontent, the lay lords voted for the measure to a man, and it was sent to an uncertain fate in the House of Commons.

The Commons were quick to give the Lords' bill their attention. After having considered six other measures on the morning of 15 December, they gave it its first reading. It was read for a second time on 17 December, but for three days thereafter there is no sign in the journals of any chantry legislation. Then, on the twenty-first, "The new bill for Chantries, Colleges, and Free Chapels" was given three readings — a most unusual procedure — and was passed on the following day. The Lords received the new Commons' bill on 23 December, and on the twenty-fourth they passed it, once more over the protests of several bishops.[15] Later that day the king gave his assent to the act, and a scribe wrote at the top of it the words which were reserved for subsidy bills: "Le roi remercie sez loyallez subiectez, accepte leur benevolence et ainsi le veult."[16] Thus the Chantries Act of 1547 became the law of the land.

It was an impressive and lengthy document which parliament had just passed. At many important points it differed from the Henrician Chantries Act of 1545. Most immediately apparent is its professed motivation. In contrast to the Henrician preamble, which presents a pragmatic rationale for the legislation,[17] the Edwardian statement concentrates on religious and educational matters. It alleges that

a great part of superstition [18] and errors in Christian religion hath been brought into the minds and estimation of men by reason of the ignorance of their very true and perfect salvation through the death of Jesus Christ, and by devising and fantasying vain opinions of purgatory and masses satisfactory to be done for them which be departed, the which doctrine and vain opinion by nothing more is maintained and upholden than by the abuse of trentals, chantries, and other provisions made for the continuance of the said blindness and ignorance. [19]

It then proceeds to claim that parliament might most expediently commit these institutions, which self-evidently need "alteration, change, and amendment," to the king, who with the advice of his council could convert them to educational and charitable purposes. Thus, if the preamble was to be believed, there was to be nothing crass or materialistic about the Edwardian Chantries Act. It was to be a statesmanlike measure designed to carry out charitable functions on a basis of Reformation doctrine. [20]

Surprisingly enough, much of the rest of the act is in keeping with the idealistic desire for responsible reform based on religious principles, as alleged in the preamble. The aim was to dissolve or to convert to godly uses all those institutions which had been founded to foster prayers for the dead. The 1545 act had included some of these institutions, but there remained many small foundations and institutions for short terms of years which Henry and his councillors had apparently not deemed it worthwhile to suppress. In 1547, however, because of the theological rationale expressed in the preamble and carried consistently throughout the act, all of these intercessory institutions were to be confiscated regardless of the administrative difficulties which would be involved.

The list of these institutions is imposing: all colleges, free chapels, and chantries which had been in existence during the preceding five years;[21] all lands devoted to the finding of a priest in perpetuity or for a term of years (the Henrician act had not concerned itself with non-perpetual foundations); all rents which had been paid to stipendiary priests; all lands and rents which had supported anniversaries and obits, lamps, and lights; all fraternities, brotherhoods, and guilds; and all the goods and plate of any of these institutions. The hospitals, which the Henrician act had included, were now conspicuously absent, perhaps because their "superstitious" practices were deemed to be less essential than their charitable functions.[22] It seems likely that the framers of the Henrician act had assumed that many of the intercessory institutions cited would continue to exist and that the dissolutions, each of which could take place only by virtue of a warrant signed by Henry himself, would be sporadic and selective. The Edwardian act, by contrast, provided that all of the specified institutions would be vested in the king on a fixed date (Easter [1 April] 1548), to dispose of as he saw fit. There would be no selectivity. The suppression would be total, immediate, and unconditional.

Perhaps because it expected Henry to use his benevolent discrimination in dissolving foundations, the 1545 Parliament, in its Chantries Act, had placed whole categories of institutions at the king's disposal. The 1547 act, however, which envisaged the immediate dissolution of all the institutions which it mentioned, had to be more careful. For example, although the king was to be seized of all the free chapels in the realm, he was not to receive those which were chapels of ease. Likewise, certain educational colleges were exempted from the ruling that all colleges were to be vested in the king. The continued existence of the colleges in both universities and of the foundations at Winchester and Eton, which had been threatened by the Henrician statute, was now guaranteed by specific clauses. The Edwardian act was indeed so solicitous of the welfare of the universities that even the chantries and obits within the colleges were withheld from the king, although he might alter their names and foundation ordinances at will. The cathedrals were less fortunate. Although a special clause protected their endowments, the large number of chantries which had been founded within them were to be confiscated to the king's use. Finally, the act exempted from dissolution St. George's Chapel in Windsor Castle and the free chapel in Newton (Cambs).[23] Through the insertion of such clauses, the drafters of the act had shown their sensitivity to the necessity of protecting certain ecclesiastical institutions which had particular usefulness to the religious and educational life of the realm.

The statesmanlike qualities of the 1547 Chantries Act are especially evident in the sections dealing with the commissioners who were to carry out its purposes. The 1545 act had said very little about these men, save that upon instruction from the king they were to suppress the particular institutions which he had specified in his letters of commission. The Edwardian act, however, gave the commissioners tasks of considerable importance for the responsible implementation of the act. They were to survey all lay corporations and craft guilds to ascertain which of their revenues had been devoted to superstitious purposes. They were to re-endow all grammar schools and preachers who had formerly been supported by institutions now to be dissolved, so that their useful functions might continue. Similarly, in parishes which had been deprived of priests by the dissolution, they were to appoint vicars and assistant curates and to endow them with lands and tenements. To incumbents who had lost their livings entirely because of the dissolution, they were to grant adequate pensions and annuities. The act expressed especial concern for the poor who had been supported by the intercessory institutions, and ordered the commissioners to assign pensions or to set aside certain lands which might support them in the future. Finally, the act noted that certain guilds and fraternities had made payments for the maintenance of seawalls and piers; and it ordered that endowments be assigned for the continuance of these useful services.

The commissioners, in short, were charged with minimizing the hardships which the suppressions would cause. If they had carried out these farsighted provisions, the period of social and educational transition would have been comparatively smooth and uneventful. That it was, in reality, eminently rough and painful was not, generally speaking, the fault of the commissioners. Nor was it the fault of the act. It was the fault of the Edwardian government which, financially crippled by war, could not afford to empower the commissioners to implement the idealistic intentions which it had professed.

The second half of the act is chiefly concerned with matters of detail. One significant proviso barred the king from seizing any copyhold lands. Others affirmed that the act was not to be prejudicial to the general corporations of boroughs or to confiscate any of their lands, and stated that the dissolved lands were to be administered by the Court of Augmentations and the Court of the Duchy of Lancaster. The remaining clauses served either to limit the competence of the act or to protect the interests of various parties involved. In sum, the 1547 Chantries Act was less generous than measures for the reformation of the chantries which the government had been contemplating during July. When examined in detail, however — especially when compared with the Henrician Chantries Act — it stands out as a carefully drafted, prudent measure of reformation.

The chantry legislation passed only after encountering intense opposition in the House of Commons. The Commons Journals hint as much; and a minute of the Privy Council of 6 May 1548 makes it absolutely clear.[24] On that date the Council ordered that letters patent be issued granting to their respective boroughs the guild lands which had formerly belonged to two churches in Coventry and to the guild of King's Lynn, despite the newly passed chantries act. As background

for this action, the Council minute records an episode which had occurred in the previous year's parliament. At the time (the minute does
not specify the exact date) when the House of Commons was debating
"the act for Colleges and Chantry lands," a clause "was also inserted
that the lands pertaining to all guilds and brotherhoods within this
realm should pass unto his Majesty by way of like gift." Thereupon,
trouble erupted, and "divers then being of the Lower House did not
only reason and argue against that article made for the guildable
lands, but also incensed many others to hold with them, amongst the
which none were stiffer nor more busily went about to impugn the said
article than the burgesses for the town of Lynn . . . and the burgesses
of the city of Coventry." The members for Lynn were concerned that
their town might lose the guild lands, which had been used for the
"maintenance and keeping up of the pier and sea banks there, which
being untended to would be the loss of a great deal of low ground of
the country adjoining"; and the Coventry burgesses were fearful that
the loss of their city's immense agglomeration of guild lands would ac-
celerate its seemingly inexorable decline and decay. The opposition
stirred up by the Lynn and Coventry burgesses was extremely fierce, so
fierce in fact that the privy councillors in the House thought it likely
"that not only that article for the guildable lands should be dashed,
but also that the whole body of the act might either sustain peril or
hindrance, being already engrossed, and the time of the parliament
prorogation hard at hand."[25]

At this prospect Somerset and his colleagues became alarmed and
decided to intervene. They were determined to secure passage of the
whole act, for they knew the value of the lands of the religious guilds
would be considerable. They further hoped to avoid a situation in
which every member would scamper to add a proviso to protect his
local guilds. In "weighing in a multitude of free voices what moment
the labor of a few setters on had been," they calculated that if some
kind of extra-parliamentary agreement could satisfy the agitators (the
"setters on" from Lynn and Coventry), the opposition in general might
subside; then the bill, with the guild lands still intact, might be saved.
That is what happened. The privy councillors in the Commons were in
fact able to bargain with the cantankerous burgesses from Lynn and
Coventry, whom they persuaded to cease their opposition in return for
grants to their boroughs of local guild lands which they were so determined to save.[26]

These dramatic events probably took place on 21 December, which must have been one of the longest, busiest, and noisiest days of the session. On that day the Commons transacted so much business, in fact, that one suspects that it may have sat well into the afternoon, despite its general custom of meeting only in the mornings.[27] This long session, the sixteenth-century equivalent of the modern all-night sitting, was necessary to secure the required three readings for the chantries bill. And that bill, as the events of the day demonstrate, the government was desperately eager to pass. Although the House gave eight bills a total of ten readings on the twenty-first, it certainly devoted most of its time to the chantries bill, which had two readings early in the day. It then turned its attention to five less significant measures. Late in the day the House was ready once again to deal with the intercessory institutions, and it then gave a third reading to the chantries bill.[28] It is not clear at what point the explosive criticism took place. If, as seems possible, the bill was initially introduced on parchment,[29] the Coventry-Lynn battery must have fired its broadsides during the first two readings. Several hours would then have been necessary for feverish negotiating before the government felt safe in submitting the bill for a third reading. If, on the other hand, the chantries bill was introduced on paper, it may then have had its two initial readings. The long pause which preceded the third reading may be explained by the need to have the bill immediately and hastily engrossed.[30] If this is so, the explosion then occurred towards the end of the day, which may explain why the bill did not pass until it had a fourth reading on the following day. However that may be, it is certain that at some point on the twenty-first, when the bill was "already engrossed, and the time of parliament prorogation hard at hand," the "multitude of free voices," with the men from Coventry and Lynn as soloists, directed a chorus of criticism at the bill.[31] Later still, five members offered amendments to the bill, which the House debated and adopted.[32] The House of Commons can seldom have witnessed a stormier sitting.

It seems probable, however, that there had been a tumult of even greater tempestuousness earlier in the parliament of which no record has survived. It is hard to imagine the members bottling up their hostility to chantry legislation until it finally bubbled forth on 21 December. As Professors Lehmberg and Elton have demonstrated, the early Tudor parliament had a history of recurrent assertiveness.[33] Edward VI's first parliament, under the lenient guidance of Somerset, was

probably no more restrained than its Henrician predecessors. The
Commons of the 1545 Parliament had not hesitated to vent their displeasure with the Chantries Act of that year.[34] And in 1547, when a
bill was introduced on 1 December (very likely by a private member
who was trying to head off a full-scale governmental attack on the
intercessory institutions) "for Colleges, Chantries, and other Spiritualities" as the second of two items of business for the day, the House probably took a considerable amount of time to debate the whole issue.

Presumably it was the fear that a chantries act would threaten their
guild and chantry lands which prompted the burgesses of Lynn to introduce a bill on 10 December. This fear was not allayed by the chantry bill which arrived in the Commons from the Lords on 15 December, for on the sixteenth the bill for Lynn was given a second reading.[35]
The Lynn bill was never read again, however. Perhaps the volatile
burgesses, rejoicing in the fact that the Commons on 17 December had
thrown out the Lords' bill, decided to wait for the government to introduce a new and more acceptable chantries bill. Indeed, the vociferous-
ness of the opposition of the Lynn burgesses earlier in the session may
be deduced not only from their bill, but also from the fact that the
government's bill of 21 December, in guaranteeing the maintenance of
"piers, jetties, walls or banks against the rages of the sea," was respon-
sive to the specific concerns of Lynn in a way that the Lords' bill had
not been.[36] Even this verbal concession was evidently not enough to
pacify the angry men from Lynn, who saw that without a private
agreement the government would still confiscate their guild lands. It is
also probable that the portions of the Lords' bill which had been objectionable to the members for Lynn were offensive to other members
as well. Governmentally sponsored bills were not dashed simply because of the opposition of the testy burgesses of one Norfolk borough.
It is likely, therefore, that on 17 December, when the House of Commons read the Lords' chantry bill for the second time and threw it out,
there was a parliamentary fracas of the first magnitude.

What was so objectionable about the Lords' bill which had, after
all, been introduced by the government? Fortunately the bill, which
had been presumed lost, has survived in the House of Lords Record
Office; its apparent similarity to the Edwardian Chantries Act had
misled the compiler of the *Statutes of the Realm* into listing it as "a
Duplicate of this Act, but to which the Royal Assent does not appear to
have been given." Similar the two documents certainly are. Both are so

lengthy that they fill several sizable pieces of parchment. Both contain numerous internal provisos.[37] The wording of the first forty-three lines of the draft is with one insignificant exception identical to that of the act. And large subsequent segments of the draft were incorporated either completely or in slightly modified form into the act.

As one systematically compares the texts, however, numerous differences appear. Some, although intrinsically of minor importance, shed useful light on the meticulous examination that the Edwardian House of Commons gave to major legislation. The Commons were concerned, for example, that the act be worded with precision and that its consequences be specified as clearly as possible. Thus the final version of the act stipulated that the king receive the goods, jewels, plate, and ornaments of *all* the dissolved institutions, not only of the dissolved colleges (as in the Lords' bill). Similarly, a clause, notably missing from the Lords' bill, was added, empowering the king to distrain and enter into property in case of a default in the payment of a rent from a dissolved institution. The act differed from the Lords' bill also in securing the interests of special groups: of the towns;[38] of those members concerned about preaching;[39] of those places whose institutions supported dikes against the sea; of the cathedrals. As a result of these minor alterations, which reflected criticisms of the Lords' bill, the act emerged a more carefully drafted, tightly worded, and intelligently considered measure than the original version had been. Parliamentary criticism and additional thought by the government had paid rich dividends.

Another difference was of vastly greater significance. The 1547 Chantries Act, though dissolving the religious guilds and fraternities, was more lenient with the lay guilds, corporations, mysteries and crafts — it merely stripped them of the sums which they had devoted to "superstitious" purposes. The Lords' bill, however, differed markedly on precisely this point. The bill had not attacked only the pious, intercessory appendages of these secular guilds and corporations; it had attacked their very existence. If parliament had passed the Lords' bill, the secular guilds and corporations of England and Wales would have lost their properties; to all intents and purposes, they would have been as dissolved as the chantries. The phraseology is circuitous, but when read closely the intent of the bill is unmistakable. It begins — in words identical to the Chantries Act — by ordering the dissolution of all colleges, free chapels, chantries, sums devoted to the perpetual finding of priests, stipendiary priests in perpetuity and for terms of years, obits, and lights. The bill then proceeds in an interesting fashion all its own. It empowered the king to dispatch commissioners into various counties to survey "all brotherhoods, fraternities, guilds, mysteries, and crafts" and all manors, lands, and tenements belonging to them "or to the corporation of any of them." These commissioners were also to ascertain "what money, meat, drink, wood, coal, livery, and other things" had within the previous five years been given or distributed to poor persons out of the incomes of any of these secular corporations. Having completed their investigations, the commissioners were then to assign to the poor "as much money and other things" as had been (or ought to have been) distributed, paid, or delivered — to continue forever. The commissioners were further commanded to appoint specific manors, lands, and rents (which the act had given to the king) to support these and many other kinds of charitable work:

the payment of any fifteenth and tenth, fee farms, wages of knights or burgesses of the parliament, repairing of common gaols, finding or keeping of schools, or for finding of any beadmen, poor folks, or scholars in any college or in any other the premises, or for the reparation, amending, or maintaining of any bridges or highways, as to their discretion shall be thought meet and convenient for that purposes and intents to remain and continue forever.

In terms similar to those of the act, the draft then proceeds to ensure that the commissioners appoint lands for the support of grammar schoolmasters (though not, like the act, of preachers) who had been supported out of the dissolved secular corporations, and ordain vicars and appoint assistants to the cures in parishes (the act adds "great towns") where they were needed. Then comes the critical clause:

And that done, to seize into the king's hands the overplus and residue of all manors. lands, tenements, rents, tithes, portions, pensions, and other hereditaments and things appertaining or belonging to any of the said brotherhoods, fraternities, guilds, mysteries, or crafts, or to the corporations of any of them, being in the counties, cities, and places mentioned in the commission to them directed, the messuage or house called the common hall and garden and orchard adjoining to the same of the said brotherhoods, fraternities, guilds, mysteries, and crafts or of the corporation of them or any of them only excepted.

In other words, having made provision for the continuance of all the charitable activities of the secular guilds and corporations, the bill would have empowered the king to seize the remainder of their lands and tenements. By being allowed to keep their common halls with their adjacent gardens, the guilds would have been able to maintain a shadowy existence. But their endowments—and their splendor and their vigor—would have been gone.

The remainder of the Lords' bill several times refers to the dissolution of the lay corporations and craft guilds. Pensions were to be paid to the incumbents of the "colleges, free chapels, chantries, brotherhoods, fraternities, guilds, mysteries, crafts . . . which hereafter shall be dissolved, determined, or diminished by virtue of this act." In the Duchy of Lancaster they were to be within the survey of the Duchy's court. Throughout the Lords' bill these institutions—guilds, mysteries, crafts, and corporations—are mentioned again and again in places where the Chantries Act notably omits them. The full extent of the confiscatory appetite of the Edwardian government is therefore clear. In December 1547 it intended not only to suppress the intercessory institutions of England and Wales, but to mount a full-scale attack on the lay corporations and secular guilds as well.

In view of the gravity of the issues at stake, there can be little room for doubt that a second tumult about chantry legislation erupted in the 1547 Parliament. The members for London must have fought furiously to save the livery companies; many burgesses would have exerted themselves for the protection of local craft guilds; and all the burgesses would have sensed the threat which the bill posed to their borough corporations. So the members from Lynn and Coventry, who also had craft guilds and municipal corporations to protect,[40] would certainly have had company in opposing the sweepingly destructive bill which the Lords had passed. It would therefore not be at all surprising if the greatest uproar of the session had come at the time of the assault upon the Lords' bill on 17 December rather than at the time of the recorded fracas on the twenty-first.

Such an attack must have forced the government to reconsider its position. Somerset and the privy councillors evidently decided to accommodate their critics by scuttling the Lords' bill. They instructed Sir James Hales to draft in its place a new bill which would bring the maximum possible profit to the government and still withstand the scrutiny of the Commons.[41] Hales's new bill (which, with a few amendments, was to become the 1547 Chantries Act) was more carefully drafted than its predecessor. He included in it passages designed to meet the general criticisms which the Commons had heaped on the Lords' bill. And he inserted certain provisions which were formulated specifically to appease some of the most vocal opponents of chantry legislation. The most striking area in which the new bill differed from the old was in its treatment of the guilds. Hales added clauses which specified which guilds were to be dissolved and which were to remain intact. The king was not to be entitled to any of the lands, tenements, or other properties of the "corporations, guilds, fraternities, companies, and fellowships of mysteries or crafts." The "sums of money, profits, commodities, and emoluments," however, which these institutions had bestowed within the past five years upon the maintenance of priests, obits, and lights were in the future to be paid to the king. The new bill further empowered the chantry commissioners to search the records of these lay guilds and corporations to make certain that the king was getting his due.

There was to be no respite for the "fraternities, brotherhoods, and guilds" of a religious nature, however. Having distinguished these carefully from the lay corporations, the new bill ordered them to be suppressed completely, although it made careful provision for the continuance of the charitable works which they had performed. Finally, an interesting proviso towards the end of the new bill (which had not been in the Lords' bill) stipulated that the new measure should not "in any wise extend or be prejudicial or hurtful to the general corporation of any city, borough, or town." These careful reservations in Hales's revised chantry bill are a monument to the vigilance of the House of Commons, which saved from dissolution the lay corporations and craft guilds of England and Wales.

With the exception of these institutions, however, the chantries bill which finally received the royal assent gave to the government practically everything it had originally hoped to receive. The list of institutions to be dissolved—all of them a familiar part of English religious and social life for centuries—was a long one. Now, at Easter 1548, the colleges and chantries, free chapels and stipendiary priests, obits and lights, guilds and fraternities, were to disappear, victims of the revolutionary process which was transforming England into a secular, modern society.

Notwithstanding the nonmaterialistic tone of the preamble and the statesmanlike regulations set forth in the Edwardian Chantries Act, the attack which Somerset and his associates mounted on this widely varied group of institutions was both massive and unrelenting. Two explanations for its intensity have been advanced, both of which are rooted in man's acquisitive drive. The first is the desire for land. This consideration can hardly have been less important in 1547 than it had been two years earlier when the Henrician Chantries Act was passed. Henry VIII had suppressed only a handful of intercessory institutions (Appendix 2); and the demand for land, which had been growing in his later years, was therefore unsatisfied. It is impossible accurately to measure the intensity of this demand, or to assess its influence on the formation of policy in either 1545 or 1547. There are, however, several indications that this motivation was an important one. Several members of Somerset's faction were unabashedly eager to acquire the intercessory institutions and their lands. One among them was Sir Michael Stanhope, Somerset's brother-in-law, who in July 1547 used his position as lieutenant of Hull to arrange for the "spontaneous" surrender of six substantial institutions in the East Riding.[42] Somerset's brother Thomas Seymour, the Lord Admiral, was equally impatient for the spoils of suppression. Before the properly accredited chantry commissioners could manage to get to Fotheringhay College, Seymour's servants had already conducted their own private survey, thereby making such a shambles of the college that the commissioners were "not able to make any perfect certificate of the state of the same house."[43] Land-hunger was not confined to the Seymour clan. The imperial ambassador was convinced that "all the gentry, large and small" — not just the courtiers — were "on the look out to receive rewards and benefits from the King." There were reports of long queues at the home of Sir Walter Mildmay as people attempted to clinch deals which would bring them the lands and goods of the chantries.[44] Under Edward VI the disposition of the chantry properties heavily favored the new nobility and the upper gentry who had governmental connections. As a result, the social orders which had not managed to profit in a significant way from the Henrician dissolutions were now able to harvest a rich yield of properties.[45]

Another likely motive for dissolution was the government's need of money. Edward VI's advisers were in deep financial trouble from the outset. From Henry VIII, who had himself inherited a vast accumulation of treasure, the Edwardians received an empty treasury, a debased currency, a Flemish debt of £100,000, and a depleted royal demesne.[46] War had been the source of Henry's fiscal embarrassments, and the fruits of his wars were a steady drain on Edward's slender resources. Boulogne must be defended; Berwick, Calais, and the other garrison towns must be fortified; and the fleet must be supplied and maintained. Unfortunately, from September 1547 on, Edward's advisers had a war of their own to finance — with the Scots. As a result, the government's already precarious finances were strained to the breaking point. In his last years Henry had exhausted the traditional sources of additional money. Even more disastrously, he had also imposed taxation in a heavy-handed manner which Somerset would find impossible to emulate.

In this fiscal emergency, the dissolution of the intercessory institutions must have appeared seductively lucrative to the government. They were now doctrinally outmoded and thus expendable. If the properties of the lay corporations might also be "nationalized," so much the better for a hard pressed regime. Furthermore, in advocating such a measure to skeptical members of parliament, the councillors were able enticingly to argue that if parliament granted these institutions to the king, the realm might be relieved of the burdensome taxes which Henry had imposed upon it.[47]

In a minute of 17 April 1548 ordering the sale of chantry lands, the privy council admitted that financial considerations were indeed of primary importance in motivating the government to suppress the chantries. The dissolution, it stated, had been animated by various considerations expressed in the act; but "specially" important was "the relief of the King's Majesty's charges and expenses, which do daily grow and increase by reason of diverse and sundry fortifications, garrisons, levying of men and soldiers, which at this present is so chargeable and costly unto his Highness."[48]

There is some justice in the charge of some historians that the act's stated intentions are "somewhat hypocritical."[49] Land-hunger and financial desperation were two eminently weighty realities which were impelling the government towards the dissolution. Furthermore, it should hardly surprise us that there was hypocrisy in governmental circles in the late 1540s. But to stop there would be to oversimplify. For there were two — or possibly three — other considerations of varying significance which prompted the government to attack the chantry foundations in 1547.

The most problematic of these non-economic motives is legal in origin. The 1547 act contained clauses which two scholars have construed as threatening the secular guilds and corporations as well as the religious guilds. Its intent, in their view, was to suppress all corporate bodies—whether religious or secular—whose very existence was seen by civil lawyers as "impugning the sovereignty of the State."[50] As I have indicated, the act was worded with great care to ensure that it would *not* threaten the existence of the lay corporations. Furthermore, in implementing the act the chantry commissioners appear to have been similarly cautious. For example, in the returns for 1548 for London and Middlesex they meticulously detailed the "superstitious" appendages of the "Corporations and Companies" of the city, but gave no information about their secular endowments.[51] The Lords' bill, however, sheds new light upon the government's original intentions, and for this reason the argument of these historians is eminently worth exploring.

On several counts, however, the case for the decisiveness of civil law theory in governmental thinking appears weak.[52] The Edwardian government of 1547 was made up of a preponderance of men trained in the common law rather than in the civil law. Furthermore, men with influence upon the government though not themselves members of it —such as Sir James Hales—seem often to have been either common lawyers or men trained in the Inns of Court. It is also notable that two powerful personages who had been trained as civilians—Bishops Bonner and Tunstall—twice voted against the chantries legislation in the House of Lords.[53] The primary exception to this pattern is Sir Thomas Smith. A brilliant young Cambridge scholar, Smith was appointed in 1540 to the newly founded Regius Professorship of Civil Law. After a brief study and prestige-building tour in Orleans, Paris, and Padua, he returned to Cambridge to lecture enthusiastically about the work of the civil law reformers on the Continent. His talents soon attracted the attention of the court, where by the last years of Henry VIII's reign he had achieved some influence. Under Edward VI his rise was even more rapid. In February 1547 he entered the service of Protector Somerset. Thereafter in rapid succession a number of posts and perquisites were showered upon him, culminating in April 1548 in his appointment as one of the two principal secretaries.

In 1547, Smith was the chief civil lawyer within earshot of the government; he was also Protector Somerset's companion on the Scottish expedition of August and September 1547.[54] It is, however, impossible to estimate his influence. For lack of further evidence on Smith's and the civil lawyers' role, therefore, we must view the government's decision to attack the secular corporations and guilds as another indication, not of its devotion to the principles of Roman law, but of its financial desperation.

The 1547 act itself alleges yet another motive for the dissolution — the necessity that "superstitious" institutions and practices be eradicated for the ongoing work of religious reformation. Critics of the act, who have regarded the undoubted desire of the government for money as the only "real" motive for the suppression, have been eager to dismiss this statement as hypocritical.[55] They have done so too quickly, however, for they have not been willing to see the Edwardian chantry legislation in the setting of its times.

In 1547 Somerset and Cranmer were cautiously but inexorably beginning the reformation of the Church of England. They were not doing so according to the Henrician model, which had substantially retained tradition in rite and thought while eradicating "abuses." Instead, they were attempting a reformation of the theology of the English Church according to Protestant principles; and they intended that this reformation should effect profound changes at every level of religious life in the realm. According to the new theology, there could be no room for any doctrine which seemed to deny the all-sufficiency of Christ's sacrificial death for the purgation and justification of each believer. Nor could there be continued toleration for the practices traditionally associated with this doctrine which "do not only injury to Christ, but also commit the most detestable idolatry."[56]

The approach of Somerset and Cranmer was not impulsive. The *Homilies* of July 1547, which fiercely attacked purgatory and the observances which had grown up around it, had made clear the general theological predilections of the government. The injunctions of the same year, on the other hand, which impugned many of the customary practices of the Church, made only partially manifest the practical ramifications of the new doctrine. Further action was therefore necessary to bring the chantries and the other intercessory institutions into conformity with Reformation theology, for the continued existence of these foundations in their traditional form "would have placed an impossible burden upon the meagre fund of Protestant tolerance."[57] It appears that some reformers, no doubt including Cranmer, favored a non-destructive approach, one which involved simply the reordering and restructuring of these offending institutions for "non-superstitious" purposes. The injunctions testify that in the late summer of 1547 the government was seriously considering this possibility.[58] At some time in the ensuing months, however, Somerset and his colleagues decided that the almost total suppression of the intercessory foundations was essential. In making this decision, they were without question influenced by financial considerations. They also had good theological reasons for following the dictates of fiscal advantage. The chantries had been founded for reasons that were now deemed "superstitious"; it would soon have become evident that many of the cantarists were men of slender learning who would have made deplorable schoolmasters;[59] and it is possible that, in the Protestant view, the chantries were essentially unreformable. At any rate, a dissolution was quite as congruent with governmentally sanctioned doctrine as a reordering of the institutions would have been.

The argument for a religious motivation for the Chantries Act is further bolstered by the provisions of the statute itself. Whereas the 1545 act had contented itself with insuring the right of the king to dissolve at will any substantial institution which he might specify, the 1547 act vested *all* intercessory foundations in the king immediately. The range of these institutions was extremely broad, extending from the magnificence of Beverley Minster to the multitude of minuscule endowments which supported the obits and lights throughout the realm. It is obvious that the "four kine very old," which provided a few shillings for a penurious Somerset priest, and the "stock of bees" which maintained a light on the altar of a Gloucestershire church, were not selected for dissolution because of the ease with which they could be surveyed, seized, and sold.[60] Some of their endowments were so complex and at the same time so minute that the difficulties and expenses of administration jeopardized the profits which the government could hope to realize from them. It was hardly an economic proposition to dissolve the endowments of lamps and lights in Little Yeldham, Foxearth, Radwinter, and Great Bardfield (Essex), which amounted respectively to 2d., 4d., 5d., and 6d. per annum.[61] But because they had been founded according to the same "superstitious" presuppositions as the larger institutions, they had to suffer the same fate. Theological principle thus governed the demise of the intercessory institutions quite as much as prudential calculation.

In the preamble to the 1547 act the government eloquently professed a final motive for chantry legislation — its desire to alter the suppressed institutions "to good and godly uses, as in erecting of grammar schools to the education of youth in virtue and godliness, the further

augmenting of the universities and better provision of the poor and
needy."[62] The body of the act, however, was rather less idealistic than
the propagandistic preamble. Instead of providing mechanisms whereby the suppressed foundations might be converted to more godly uses,
it specified simply that the chantry commissioners should provide for
the continuance and re-endowment of all existing grammar schools
and other good works which the intercessory institutions had been required by their foundation ordinances to provide. Yet the government
failed to reach even this limited goal. By mid-1548 it appeared to have
wholly forgotten its beneficent purposes. For this reason, some scholars
have seen in this passage yet another example of Edwardian cant.
There was, however, almost certainly purpose behind it. Within the
government there were fervent idealists as well as crass opportunists.
The Edwardian privy council was composed of men most of whom
"had been well and formally educated . . . Never before had the principal officers of state as a body enjoyed as high a degree of literacy and
of intellectual competence." Their concern for education may be seen
in the school and university foundations which a number of them later
made.[63] It may also be inferred from the scrupulousness with which
the Chantries Act protected the colleges of the universities and of Eton
and Winchester.

The educational idealism of these men was tempered by the realities
of the situation in which they found themselves when the time came to
implement the act. In 1548 England was at war. With armed forces
and fortifications gobbling up immense sums of money, the financial
situation, which was already embarrassing enough, was steadily deteri-
orating. It was therefore exceedingly difficult for Somerset and his
associates to prevent the immediate sale of the chantry properties to
meet the government's need of ready cash. The government did not
exempt from sale even those lands which had comprised the endowments of the chantry schools. Therefore, instead of re-endowing these
schools according to the provisions of the act, the government simply
kept them going by the expedient of awarding perpetual stipends to
the masters.[64]

As a desperate measure of war finance, such a policy is understandable: whereas the government was immediately able to realize the full
capital value of the chantry properties, it generally needed to pay out
annually only a fraction (averaging perhaps one-twentieth) of that

amount in stipends.[65] One is, moreover, bound to sympathize with a government whose financial plight was exacerbated by its inability to tap the real wealth of the country on any regular basis. At the same time, the policy of selling off chantry/school endowments and granting annual stipends had a number of unfortunate side-effects. Somerset and his colleagues, who were beginning to experience the early stages of a "price revolution" which they had no means of comprehending, could hardly have predicted the ultimate effects of inflation upon stipends of fixed value. Another implication, however, they should have foreseen: by granting stipends to the schoolmasters, they were binding their successors to the payment of annual charges for which they would be liable long after the capital received for the properties had been expended. The extent of this fiscal irresponsibility is indicated by the fact that the English government was still saddled with many of these charges three centuries later. In Lancashire, for example, the crown was still paying out £500 5s. 7d. per annum to schoolmasters and curates in 1837, when the annual income of the remaining chantry lands was only £14 16s. 8d.[66] The government also procrastinated in founding and endowing the new schools which the preamble to the Chantries Act had promised.[67]

Under the Protector Somerset there was often a gap between vision and practice. It was unfortunate that the endowments of the chantry schools were caught in this gap and channeled into wars which in the long run have appeared less than vitally important. The fault was in reality one of execution, not of intention. And in the course of the following century the schools of England would emerge from this temporary setback with renewed strength and vigor. In fact, before many years had passed, Sir Francis Bacon was commenting acidly that "of grammar schools there are too many."[68]

Once the Chantries Act of 1547 had received the royal assent, the intentions of its framers and the turbulences of parliament must suddenly have seemed considerably less important than the immediate tasks of implementing its provisions. This time there could be no turning back, no tarrying for the will of an imperious but dilatory monarch. At Easter of the following year all of the doomed foundations would become part of the royal demesne. Commissioners must therefore begin touring the realm to survey the lands and properties of these institutions, to order the continuance of the most urgent of their good works, to pension the priests who were being forced into retirement. Thereafter, for better or for worse, the chantries and other intercessory institutions, in which many late-medieval Englishmen had given fervent testimony to their faith, would recede into the mists of the English past.

Appendixes, Notes, Bibliography, Index

Appendix 1 / Royally initiated dissolutions of
intercessory institutions, 1540-1545

1540

12 April	Hospital of St. Giles, Norwich (*L.P.*, XV, 506).
19 May	Hospital of St. James, Northallerton, N R., Yorks (ibid., 691).
20 May	Hospital of St. Wolstan, Worcester (ibid., 695).
2 June	Hospital of St. Nicholas, Portsmouth (ibid., 743).
5 July	College of Thompson, Norfolk (ibid., 834).
17 November	Collegiate Church and Vicars Choral of Southwell, Notts (*L.P.*, XVI, 275). The college was refounded in 1543 by act of parliament, 35 Henry VIII, c.45 (*L.P.*, XVIII, i, 66 [45]). Apparently there had been no cessation of services.

1541

6 February	Chantries (2) of Sir John Villiers, Tuxford, Notts (E 301/13/18).
6 December	College of St. John the Evangelist, Rushford, Norfolk (*L.P.*, XVI, 1417).
(?)	College of St. Martin le Grand, London (*L.P.*, XVII, 74, 258).

1542

8 April	College of St. Mary, Mettingham Castle, Suffolk (*L.P.*, XVII, 243).
2 June	College of St. Mary, Wingfield, Suffolk (ibid., 366).
18 July	College of St. Mary, Higham Ferrers, Northants (ibid., 509).
2 August	College de Vaux, Salisbury (ibid., 563).
(?)	Chantry of Haverhill, Suffolk (E 301/45/28).

1543

15 April	Hospital of St. Leonard, Newport, Essex (*L.P.*, XVIII, i, 982, p. 548; *V.C.H., Essex,* II, 190-191).
(?)	Free Chapel of St. Thomas the Martyr, Sittingbourne, Kent (Hussey, *Kent Chantries,* 293).
(?)	Chantries (3) of Thomas Gumby, George Windham, and William Wroo, Danbury, Essex (*Valor,* I, 450; Newcourt, *Repertorium,* II, 204; Morant, *History,* II, 30).
(?)	Chantries (3) of Hugh Fetherston, William Finch, and John Parker, Maldon, Essex (*Valor,* I, 446; Newcourt, *Repertorium,* II, 204).

1544

18 February	College of the Holy Trinity, Westbury on Trym, Glos (*L.P.*, XIX, i, 120).
4 March	Hospital of St. John the Baptist, Bristol (ibid., i, 157).

17 March	College of St. Elizabeth of Hungary, Wolvesey, Winchester (ibid., 209).
26 April	College of St. Peter, Lingfield, Surrey (ibid., 403).
25 July	Chantry of St. Mary, Brundish, Suffolk (ibid., 983; E 301/45/42).
11 November	Fraternity of St. Mary Rouncivall, Charing Cross, London (*L.P.*, XIX, ii, 590).
9 December	College of St. Gregory, Sudbury, Suffolk (ibid., 718).
11 December	Hospital of St. Mary (Maison Dieu), Dover, Kent (ibid., 728; E 301/116).
12 December	College of the Holy Trinity, Arundel, Sussex (*L.P.*, XIX, ii, 734).
(?)	College of St. Mary, Warwick (*L.P.*, XX, i, 557, p. 270; ibid., 846 [41]; E 315/492, f. 79; *V.C.H., Warwickshire*, II, 129).

1545

14 January	Hospital of St. Giles, Kepier, Durham (*L.P.*, XX, i, 60).
19 January	College of SS. Gregory and Martin, Wye, Kent (ibid., 68; E 322/272).
27 January	College (Domus Dei) of St. Ethelbert, Herringby, Norfolk (*L.P.*, XX, i, 102).
29 January	College of St. Mary in the Fields, Norwich (ibid., 112).
4 February	College of the Holy Trinity, Tattershall, Lincs (ibid., 140).
4 March	Hospital of St. John the Baptist, Coventry (E 322/64; *L.P.*, XX, i, 307).
10 March	College of St. Michael, South Malling, Sussex (*L.P.*, XX, i, 333).
17 April	College of St. Peter, Sibthorpe, Notts (ibid., 534).
28 April	Chantry of St. Mary, North Wingfield, Derbys (ibid., 595).
12 May	Chantry of Elmley Castle, Worcs (ibid., 718).
16 May	Free Chapel of Tokyngton (?), Middx (ibid., 748).
18 May	Hospital of St. John the Baptist, Lynn, Norfolk (ibid., 762).
25 May	College of the Holy Cross, Crediton, Devon (E 301/81, m. 1).
28 May	College of Ottery St. Mary, Devon (E 301/92, m. 2).
5 June	Chantry of Stretton on Dunsmore, Warwicks (E 322/228; *L.P.*, XX, i, 874).
27 June	Free Chapel of St. John the Baptist, Great Baddow, Essex (E 322/11; *L.P.*, XX, i, 793).
17 July	Fraternity of the Holy Trinity, Walsoken, Norfolk (*L.P.*, XX, i, 1211).
3 September	Free Chapel of St. James, Whipstrode, Hants (*L.P.*, XX, ii, 282).
24 October	Free Chapel of Monkton, Wilts (E 322/157; *L.P.*, XX, ii, 644).
17 November	College or Chantry of St. Mary, Slapton, Devon (*L.P.*, XX, ii, 744).
20 November	College of St. Mary, Astley, Warwicks (E 322/6; *L.P.*, XX, ii, 825).
21 November	College of Christ and St. Mary, Burton upon Trent, Staffs (E 315/400, pp. 62-86; *L.P.*, XXI, i, 1538, p. 778).
29 November	Chantry of Kedington, Suffolk (*L.P.*, XX, ii, 892).
30 November	Chantry of Great Bardfield, Essex (E 322/12; *L.P.*, XX, ii, 902).
(?)	Chantry of Bishop John Grandisson, Exeter Cathedral (dissolved "by

reason of the suppression of the College of Ottery Saint Mary which
was chargeable with the payment of the pension belonging to the
said chantry" [Snell, *Chantry Certificates for Devon,* 9-10]).
(?)   Free Chapel of Le Graces, Little Baddow, Essex (E 301/20/39).
(?)   Stonehouse Chantry, East Tilbury, Essex (E 301/20/57).

Appendix 2 / Foundations dissolved by virtue of the 1545 Chantries Act

Chantries

Bakewell, Derbys: Chantry of St. Mary. Letters of commission for seizure, 17 September 1546; return of commission reporting seizure, 20 October 1546 (C 47/7/3, mm. 3-4; *L.P.*, XXI, ii, 200 [16]).

Tong, Salop: Vernon's Chantry. Commission, 17 September 1546; report of seizure, 20 October 1546 (C 47/7/3, mm. 3-4; *L.P.*, XXI, ii, 200 [16]).

Aldwinkle, Northants: Chantry of William Aldewyncle. Commission, 18 December 1546; report of seizure, 22 December 1546 (C 47/7/3, mm. 7-8; *L.P.*, XXI, ii, 648 [39]).

Lowick, Northants: Chantry (of two chaplains) of St. Peter. Commission, 18 December 1546; report of seizure, 22 December 1546 (C 47/7/3, mm. 7-8; *L.P.*, XXI, ii, 648 [39]).

South Mimms, Middx: Frowicke's Chantry. Granted on 4 January 1547 (*L.P.*, XXI, ii, 771 [6]).

Stanford-le-Hope, Essex: Chantry. Surrendered into the hands of Henry VIII, n.d. (E 301/83, m. 4).

Treadington, Worcs: Chantry of St. Nicholas. Although Henry VIII had allegedly intended to award this chantry to Sir Philip Hoby, the grant was not finally made until 2 July 1547 (*C.P.R., Edward VI*, I, 238).

Grineston (Grimston Hill?), Northants: Chantry. Surrender, which was accomplished under Henry VIII, was reported on 9 July 1547 (*A.P.C.*, II, 107-108).

Collegiate Churches

Thornton, Lincs: College of St. Mary. Surrendered 7 May 1546 (*L.P.*, XXI, i, 760).

Salisbury, Wilts: College of St. Edmund. Commission, 6 June 1546; report of seizure, 20 June 1546 (C 47/7/3, m. 2; *L.P.*, XXI, i, 1166 [16]).

Tong, Salop: College of St. Bartholomew. Commission, 17 September 1546; report of seizure, 20 October 1546 (C 47/7/3, mm. 3-4; *L.P.*, XXI, ii, 200 [16]).

Hastings, Sussex: College of St. Mary in the Castle. Commission, 16 October 1546; report of seizure, 1 November 1546 (C 47/7/3, mm. 11-12; *L.P.*, XXI, ii, 332 [42]).

Pleshy, Essex: College of the Holy Trinity. Commission, 29 October 1546; report of seizure, 2 November 1546 (C 47/7/3, mm. 9-10; *L.P.*, XXI, ii, 332 [84]).

Fotheringhay, Northants: College of St. Mary and All Saints. Surrendered 24 January 1547 (*L.P.*, XXI, ii, 738).

Cothercott, Salop: College. Crown granted lands of this foundation to Sir Robert Kirkham, n.d. (*A.P.C.*, II, 107-108).

Free Chapels

Whiteparish, Wilts: Free Chapels of St. James and Whelpley. Commission, 6 June

1546; report of seizure, 20 June 1546 (C 47/7/3, m. 2; *L.P.*, XXI, i, 1099, 1166 [16]).

Hospitals

Arundel, Sussex: Hospital of the Holy Trinity. Dissolved on 11 May 1546 and granted on 6 June 1546 (*L.P.*, XXI, i, 791, 1166 [15]).

Kendal, Westmorland: Hospital of St. Leonard. Granted on 2 September 1546 (*L.P.*, XXI, ii, 200 [4]).

London: Hospital of St. Bartholomew, West Smithfield. Commission, 21 December 1546; report of seizure, 23 December 1546 (C 47/7/3, mm. 5-6).

Abbreviations

A.A.S.R.P.	*Associated Archaeological Societies of Lincoln, York, Leicester, Reports and Papers*
A.P.C.	*Acts of the Privy Council of England*
B.I.H.R.	*Bulletin of the Institute of Historical Research*
B.J.E.S.	*British Journal of Educational Studies*
B.L.	British Library
Burnet	Gilbert Burnet, *The History of the Reformation of the Church of England*
Cal.S.P.Span.	*Calendar of State Papers, Spanish*
C.C.C.C.	Corpus Christi College, Cambridge
C.J.	*Journals of the House of Commons*
C.P.R.	*Calendar of Patent Rolls*
D.N.B.	*Dictionary of National Biography*
Ec.H.R.	*Economic History Review*
E.E.T.S.	Early English Text Society
E.H.R.	*English Historical Review*
Ellis	Henry Ellis, ed., *Original Letters Illustrative of English History*
E.R.O.	Essex Record Office
Fac. Off. Reg.	D.S. Chambers, ed., *Faculty Office Registers*
Foxe	John Foxe, *Acts and Monuments*
Frere and Kennedy	W.H. Frere and W.M. Kennedy, eds., *Visitation Articles and Injunctions*
H.J.	*Historical Journal*
H.L.R.O.	House of Lords Record Office
H.M.C.	Historical Manuscripts Commission
J.E.H.	*Journal of Ecclesiastical History*
L.J.	*Journals of the House of Lords*
Lloyd	Charles Lloyd, ed., *Formularies of Faith*
L.P.	*Letters and Papers, Foreign and Domestic, of the Reign of Henry VIII*
L.P.L.	Lambeth Palace Library
O.E.D.	*Oxford English Dictionary*
P.R.O.	Public Record Office
S.R.	*The Statutes of the Realm*
S.T.C.	*A Short-Title Catalogue of Books Printed in England, Scotland, and Ireland, and of English Books Printed Abroad*
Strype	John Strype, *Ecclesiastical Memorials*
T.R.H.S.	*Transactions of the Royal Historical Society*
Valor	*Valor Ecclesiasticus*
V.C.H.	*Victoria County Histories*
W.A.N.H.M.	*The Wiltshire Archaeological and Natural History Magazine*
Whole Workes	John Foxe, ed., *The Whole Workes of W. Tyndall, J. Frith, and Doct. Barnes*
Wilkins	David Wilkins, ed., *Concilia Magnae Britanniae et Hiberniae*
Wood-Legh	K.L. Wood-Legh, *Perpetual Chantries in Britain*

Wright	Thomas Wright, ed., *Three Chapters of Letters Relating to the Suppression of the Monasteries*
W.R.O.	Worcestershire Record Office
Y.A.J.	*Yorkshire Archaeological Journal*
Y.A.S.R.S.	Yorkshire Archaeological Society, Record Series
Y.C.C.	William Page, ed., *The Certificates of the Commissioners Appointed to Survey the Chantries . . . in the County of York*
Y.M.L.	York Minster Library

Notes

Introduction

1. *Journals of the House of Lords* (henceforth *L.J.*), I (London, [1888]), 312-313.
2. The Seamer (N.R., Yorks) rising of 1549, a relatively minor affair, was an exception. See A. G. Dickens, "Some Popular Reactions to the Edwardian Reformation in Yorkshire," *Yorkshire Archaeological Journal* (henceforth *Y.A.J.*), 34 (1939), 151-169.
3. "The chief interest in chantries today is that afforded by the splendid series of chapels that remain in our cathedrals and greater churches" (G. H. Cook, *Mediaeval Chantries and Chantry Chapels*, rev. ed. [London, 1963], 80).
4. See especially K. L. Wood-Legh, *Perpetual Chantries in Britain* (henceforth Wood-Legh) (Cambridge, 1965). Many of the shorter writings on the chantries by Miss Wood-Legh and by Professor Hamilton Thompson—especially the latter's numerous editions of the chantry certificates—are listed in the Bibliography. My debt to both of these outstanding scholars is immense.
5. A. Hamilton Thompson, ed., "The Certificates of the Chantry Commissioners for the College of Southwell in 1546 and 1548," *Trans. Thoroton Soc.*, 15 (1911), 65; T. M. Parker, *The English Reformation to 1558* (London, Oxford University Press, 1950), 126-127; H. J. Hanham, "The Suppression of the Chantries in Ashburton," *Trans. Devonshire Assn.*, 99 (1967), 111; A. G. Dickens, *The English Reformation* (London, 1964), 207; W. K. Jordan, *Edward VI, The Threshold of Power* (henceforth Jordan, *Edward VI*, II) (Cambridge, Mass., 1970), 181.
6. Dickens, *English Reformation*, 207.
7. For brief treatments of the Edwardian dissolutions in these counties, see James E. Oxley, *The Reformation in Essex to the Death of Mary* (Manchester, 1965), 152-162; I. T. Shield, "The Reformation in the Diocese of Salisbury, 1547-1562" (B.Litt. diss., Oxford University, 1960); A. G. Dickens, "A Municipal Dissolution of Chantries at York, 1536," *Y.A.J.*, 36 (1944-1947), 164-173.
8. For an indication of what can be done, see Dr. C. J. Kitching's important thesis, "Studies in the Redistribution of Collegiate and Chantry Property in the Diocese and County of York at the Dissolution" (Ph.D. diss., University of Durham, 1970).

Chapter 1: The Intercessory Institutions and Their Priests

1. *The Statutes of the Realm* (henceforth *S.R.*), 11 vols. (London, 1810-1828), III, 988; ibid., IV, 24-33; A. Hamilton Thompson, *The English Clergy and Their Organization in the Later Middle Ages* (Oxford, 1947), 132.
2. See Wood-Legh, chap. 2 passim, and pp. 273-284; Thompson, *English Clergy*, chap. 5. The cantarists were occasionally elected, especially in the cities (H.M.C., *Fourteenth Report*, app. VIII, 27-28).
3. Wood-Legh, 16-21; Thompson, *English Clergy*, 136-137.
4. The best discussion of the religious guilds is H. F. Westlake, *The Parish Guilds of Mediaeval England* (London, S.P.C.K., 1919).
5. A. Hamilton Thompson, "The Collegiate Churches of the Bishopric of Durham," *Durham University Journal*, 26 (1944), 35-36, 40, and *English Clergy*, chap. 3;

Margaret Bowker, *The Secular Clergy in the Diocese of Lincoln, 1495-1520* (Cambridge, 1968), 155-156; E. F. Jacob, *The Fifteenth Century, 1399-1485,* Oxford History of England, VI (Oxford, 1961), 291-292.

6. On the monumental scale of the ecclesiastical activities in the classical colleges of Beverley and Ripon, see William Page, ed., *The Certificates of the Commissioners Appointed to Survey the Chantries, Guilds, Hospitals, etc., in the County of York* (henceforth *Y.C.C.,* I and II), 2 vols., Surtees Soc. 91-92 (1892-1893), 348-364, 524, 539; A. F. Leach, "The Inmates of Beverley Minster," *Trans. East Riding Antiquarian Soc.,* 2 (1894), 100.

7. *Y.C.C.,* I, 201; *Calendar of the Patent Rolls Preserved in the Public Record Office* (henceforth *C.P.R.*), 48 vols. (London, 1901-1973), *1476-1485,* 252.

8. Richard Burn, *The Ecclesiastical Law,* ed. Robert Phillimore, 4 vols. (London, 1842), II, 299; Emanuel Green, *The Survey and Rental of the Chantries, Colleges and Free Chapels, Guilds, Fraternities, Lamps, Lights, and Obits in the County of Somerset,* Somerset Rec. Soc., 2 (1888), ix-x. Cf. J. H. Denton, *English Royal Free Chapels, 1100-1300: A Constitutional Study* (Manchester, Manchester University Press, 1970).

9. J. W. Walker, "St. Mary's Chapel on Wakefield Bridge," *Y.A.J.,* 11 (1891), 144-168.

10. Cf. Rotha Mary Clay, *The Mediaeval Hospitals of England* (London, 1909), and Margaret A. Seymour, "The Organization, Personnel and Functions of the Medieval Hospital in the Later Middle Ages" (M.A. diss., London University, 1946).

11. Clay, *Mediaeval Hospitals,* 158-162.

12. Cf. Daniel Rock, *The Church of Our Fathers,* ed. G. W. Hart and W. H. Frere, 4 vols. (London, 1903), III, 80-84.

13. W. H. Frere and W. M. Kennedy, eds., *Visitation Articles and Injunctions of the Period of the Reformation* (henceforth Frere and Kennedy, vols. I, II, and III), Alcuin Club, 14-16 (London, 1910), II, 301n.; C. L. Kingsford, ed., "Two London Chronicles," *Camden Misc.,* 12 (1910), 29; SP 1/86, f. 25.

14. Rock, *Church,* III, 70-76.

15. E 301/1/13; Green, *Survey of Somerset,* 46, 136; Sir John Maclean, ed., "Chantry Certificates, Gloucestershire," *Trans. Bristol and Gloucestershire Archaeol. Soc.,* 8 (1883-1884), 300, 304.

16. William Camden, *Britannia, or a Chorographical Description of Great Britain and Ireland,* 4th ed., ed. Edmund Gibson, 2 vols. (London, 1772), I, 122. These figures were cited by John Speed (*History of Great Britaine* [London, 1611], 801), and by John Weever (*Ancient Funerall Monuments* [London, 1631], 192). They appear again in an anonymous mid-nineteenth-century query ("Suppressed Chantries," *Notes and Queries,* 1st ser. 3 [1851], 24). More recent scholars (Cook, *Mediaeval Chantries,* 78; Dickens, *English Reformation,* 207; Jordan, *Edward VI,* II, 191n.; and M. S. Giuseppi, *A Guide to the Manuscripts Preserved in the Public Record Office,* 2 vols. [London, H.M.S.O., 1923-1924], I, 141) have quoted the same totals, save that they have recorded only 90 colleges instead of the original 96. In this they have followed Lord Herbert of Cherbury (*The Life and Reign of King Henry the Eighth* [London, 1683], 506) who, while citing Speed as his authority, inaccurately transcribed the number "96."

17. B.L. Cotton MSS., Cleopatra E IV, ff. 458-474; transcribed by the Jacobean antiquary Nicholas Wanton (Bodleian Library, Rawlinson MS. B. 450, f. 322) and by Weever (*Ancient Funerall Monuments,* 185-192).

18. B.L. Cotton MSS., Cleopatra E IV, f. 471v.

19. John Caley and Jos. Hunter, eds., *Valor Ecclesiasticus,* 6 vols. (London, 1810-1834) (henceforth *Valor*).

20. B.L. Cotton MSS., Cleopatra E IV, f. 200; Richard Bulkeley to Thomas Cromwell, 27 April 1535, ibid., ff. 372v-373 (*Letters and Papers, Foreign and Domestic, of the Reign of Henry VIII* [henceforth *L.P.*], ed. J. S. Brewer, J. H. Gairdner, and R. H. Brodie, 21 vols. [London, 1860-1920], VIII, 599).

21. Dom David Knowles, *The Religious Orders in England,* III, *The Tudor Age* (Cambridge, 1959), 244-245, 247.

22. Ibid., 244.

23. *Y.C.C.,* II, 430, 487; E 301/102, m. 4v; E 301/31/2; E 301/53/1.

24. E 301/18/46; E 301/13/5; E 301/25/46; E 301/31/82; E 301/32; *Y.C.C.,* I, 113.

25. A. Hamilton Thompson, ed., "The Chantry Certificates for Northamptonshire," *A.A.S.R.P.,* 31 (1911), 126. The *Valor* had omitted two chantries in Essex and one in Nottinghamshire (E 301/30/28, 50; E 301/13/38; *Valor*, I, 435-450; ibid., V, 147-200); for Wiltshire, see E 301/58; *Valor*, II, 86-151; for Yorkshire, *Y.C.C.,* I and II, passim; DL 28/27/18; DL 29/564/8945, mm. 22, 22v, 23, 41, 52, 55v, 58v, 69, 70v; DL 42/135, f. 124.

26. *Valor,* II, 297-403. B.L. Cotton MSS., Cleopatra E IV, f. 465, found 47 chantries and free chapels in the *Valor*'s reporting of the Exeter diocese. For the chantry certificates, see Lawrence S. Snell, ed., *Documents towards a History of the Reformation in Cornwall,* I, *The Chantry Certificates for Cornwall* (Exeter, 1953), and *Documents towards a History of the Reformation in Devon: The Chantry Certificates for Devon and the City of Exeter* (Exeter, 1961).

27. *Valor,* II, 439-503, also lists ten stipendiary priests and fraternities. By including all minor intercessory institutions under the rubric of "chantries and free chapels," 46 foundations in this category are noted in B.L. Cotton MSS., Cleopatra E IV, f. 465. For the chantry certificates, see E 301/21; Maclean, "Chantry Certificates, Gloucestershire," 229-308.

28. B.L. Cotton MSS., Cleopatra E IV, ff. 370-371; B.L. Cotton MSS., Titus B i, f. 480.

29. 26 Henry VIII, c.3 (*S.R.,* III, 494-495).

30. *Valor,* II, 86-152. For Wiltshire fraternities, see E 301/58/12, 13, 17, 18, 29, 46, 56; and for stipendiary priests, E 301/58/35, 36, 44, 47, 48, 49, 53; for Exeter, see *Valor,* II, 312, 390; for Essex, see ibid., I, 438, 439, 440, 442, 445, 447; for the West Riding, see ibid., V, 51, 61, 62, 75, 77.

31. *L.P.,* XXI, i, 302 (30); *C.P.R., Edward VI,* II, 135-137.

32. E 301/110, 111, 130; E 315/68, ff. 512-513; DL 38/5.

33. DL 38/5; B. Cozens-Hardy, ed., "Chantries in the Duchy of Lancaster in Norfolk, 1548," *Norfolk Archaeology,* 29 (1946), 201-210; E 301/13; Snell, *Chantry Certificates for Devon;* A. Hamilton Thompson, ed., "The Chantry Certificates for Leicestershire . . . under the Act of 37 Henry VIII, Cap. IV," *A.A.S.R.P.,* 30 (1909-1910), 463-570; E 301/11 (the 1546 certificate for Cumberland [E 301/99] is drastically truncated); C. W. Foster and A. Hamilton Thompson, eds., "The Chantry Certificates for Lincoln and Lincolnshire," *A.A.S.R.P.,* 36 (1921-1922), 183-294; 37 (1923-1925), 18-106, 247-275; Green, *Survey of Somerset.*

34. The surviving chantry certificates (*Y.C.C.*) do not provide a complete listing of the intercessory institutions in Yorkshire on the eve of the dissolution. See C. J. Kitching, "The Chantries of the East Riding of Yorkshire at the Dissolution in 1548," *Y.A.J.,* 44 (1972), 178-194.

35. Maclean, "Chantry Certificates, Gloucestershire," 262.

36. C. J. Kitching, "The Quest for Concealed Lands in the Reign of Elizabeth I," *T.R.H.S.*, 5th ser. 24 (1974), 63-78. When it became clear that there had been so many concealments in Staffordshire that the substantial accuracy of the 1548 chantry certificate was doubtful, the government early in 1549 appointed commissioners to conduct yet another survey of the intercessory institutions in the shire (E 301/43, m. 1).

37. For examples, see Snell, *Chantry Certificates for Cornwall,* 40, 52, and see below, Table 2.2, note a.

38. SP 1/213, f. 80 (Wilkins, III, 875-876); E 301/126; Theodore Craib, ed., "Surrey Chantries," *Surrey Archaeological Collections,* 25 (1912), 12-14. At the end of the entry for each parish in Worcestershire, for example, the engrosser of the 1548 certificate wrote in large letters, "Preachers, school masters, to the poor," next to which he allowed sufficient space to enter the appropriate names and sums (E 301/60).

39. For examples of Henrician certificates which give insight into the pastoral functions of the chantry priests, see *Y.C.C.,* I-II, passim, and E 301/4. Edwardian certificates which give considerable detail about chantry endowments are E 301/1, 27, 30.

40. These documents are interspersed with the chantry certificates of 1546 and 1548 in the E 301 category in the P.R.O. They were probably compiled after the end of June 1548 (E 301/102, m. 1; E 315/68, f. 189v). For the commission to Mildmay and Keilway, see C 66/811, mm. 23v-25v (*C.P.R., Edward VI,* I, 417-419).

41. John E. Ray, ed., *Sussex Chantry Records,* Sussex Rec. Soc., 36 (1931). Cf. above, n. 34, for Kitching's list of the chantries of the East Riding based upon the "Brief Declaration" (E 301/119).

42. Ministers' accounts are located in the SC 6 and DL 29 categories in the P.R.O., warrants for the continuance of various institutions in E 319 (except for the warrant for Essex, which is inexplicably located in E 315/30, f. 44). For the records of land sales, see E 315/67, 68; E 36/258-259;/LR 2/65; B.L. Harleian MSS. 605-606.

43. Jordan, *Edward VI,* II, 192n.; A. G. Dickens, *Thomas Cromwell and the English Reformation* (London, English Universities Press, 1959), 139.

44. Sir Thomas More, *The Workes of Sir Thomas More Knyght . . . Wrytten by Him in the Englysh Tonge,* ed. William Rastell (London, 1557), 333. See also chap. 3, below, n. 69.

45. The parishes in Yorkshire, especially in parts of the West Riding, were substantially larger than those in counties such as Suffolk; cf. Hughes, *Reformation,* I, 35.

46. Wood-Legh, *Perpetual Chantries;* K. L. Wood-Legh, *A Small Household in the Fifteenth Century, Being the Account Book of Munden's Chantry, Bridport* (Manchester, 1956).

47. Thompson, *English Clergy,* 72-73.

48. The term is A. F. Leach's (*V.C.H., Yorkshire,* I, 454n.). Cf. Philip Tyler, "The Status of the Elizabethan Parochial Clergy," in G. J. Cuming, ed., *Studies in Church History,* IV, *The Province of York* (Leiden, 1967), 80.

49. Josiah Cox Russell, "The Clerical Population of Medieval England," *Traditio,* 2 (1944), 179; W. A. Pantin, *The English Church in the Fourteenth Century* (Cambridge, Cambridge University Press, 1955), 28-29; Wood-Legh, 191. The ecclesiastical subsidy lists of the 1520s and an episcopal visitation of the 1540s show that these unbeneficed priests were to be found in almost all parishes, often in considerable numbers. See B.L. Lansdowne MS. 452, ff. 7v-12v; T. M. Fallow, "The Fallow Papers," *Y.A.J.,* 21 (1911), 243-252; T. M. Fallow and W. Brown, eds., "The East Riding Clergy in 1525-1526," *Y.A.J.,* 24 (1917), 62-80; H. E. Salter, ed., *A Subsidy Collected*

in the Diocese of Lincoln in 1526, Oxford Hist. Soc., 63 (1909); H. D. Eshelby, ed., "The Episcopal Visitations of the Yorkshire Deaneries of the Archdeaconry of Richmond in 1548 and 1554," *Y.A.J.,* 14 (1898), 390-421.

50. F. W. Weaver, ed., *Somerset Medieval Wills, 1383-1500,* Somerset Rec. Soc., 16 (1901), 58, 65, 80, 168; N. H. Nicolas, ed., *Testamenta Vetusta,* 2 vols. (London, 1826), I, 370-371; Peter Heath, *The English Parish Clergy on the Eve of the Reformation* (London, 1969), 25.

51. G. Montagu Benton, ed., "Essex Wills at Canterbury," *Trans. Essex Archaeol. Soc.,* n.s. 21 (1937), 234-269. Early sixteenth-century wills from Lincolnshire, Yorkshire, and Somerset reveal that the median incomes of stipendiary priests in those shires was £5, £4 13s. 4d., and £6 respectively (C. W. Foster, ed., *Lincoln Wills,* I-II, Lincoln Rec. Soc., 5 [1914], 10 [1918]; James Raine, Jr., ed., *Testamenta Eboracensia,* V, Surtees Soc., 79 [1884]; J. W. Clay, ed., *Testamenta Eboracensia,* VI, Surtees Soc., 106 [1902]; F. W. Weaver, ed., *Somerset Medieval Wills, 1501-1530,* Somerset Rec. Soc., 19 [1903], and *Somerset Medieval Wills, 1531-1558,* Somerset Rec. Soc., 32 [1905]).

52. *Y.C.C.,* I, 114; Thompson, "Certificates of the Shropshire Chantries," 347-348; cf. Redstone, "Chapels, Chantries, and Gilds in Suffolk," 40.

53. W. K. Jordan, *Philanthropy in England, 1480-1660* (London, 1959), 59, and *The Charities of Rural England, 1480-1660* (London, 1961), 11.

54. Eric Kerridge, "The Movement of Rent, 1540-1640," *Economic History Review* (henceforth *Ec.H.R.*), 2nd ser. 6 (1953-1954), 24-25; for an account of the way in which certain cantarists used their lands, see Wood-Legh, *Small Household,* xxi-xxii. On the extent of the inflation, see Y. S. Brenner, "The Inflation of Prices in Early Sixteenth-Century England," *Ec.H.R.,* 2nd ser. 14 (1961-1962), 227-228.

55. "Mansion houses" appear frequently in the chantry certificates. In certain areas the commissioners seem to have assumed that the cantarists would have such a house; e.g., the 1548 commissioners for Buckinghamshire thought it worth mentioning that the chantry priest of Aston Chapel, Ivinghoe parish, "hath no mansion house" (E 301/5/50). In Nottinghamshire and Derbyshire in 1546, the commissioners noted those who possessed mansion houses (E 301/13). Of 118 cantarists, 70 possessed "mansion houses" worth over 2s. per annum; 12 had chambers or mansion houses worth less than 2s. per annum; and 26 apparently had no housing provided by their foundations. Many of the houses seem to have been commodious structures. See W. A. Pantin, "Chantry Priests' Houses and Other Medieval Lodgings," *Medieval Archaeology,* 3 (1959), 218, 257; C. E. Ponting, " 'The Chantry,' Marlborough," *W.A.N.H.M.,* 36 (1909-1910), 585-589.

56. Some chantries which originally had been well endowed had decayed by the early sixteenth century, often as a result of the decline of urban rents and the peculation of patrons or incumbents. Some chantries managed to survive through being united with other institutions, intercessory or parochial (Wood-Legh, 111-117); cf. E 301/54/7; Maclean, "Chantry Certificates, Gloucestershire," 232-233, 234, 243-244; E 301/27/3; E 301/31/12.

57. Mrs. Bowker (*Secular Clergy,* 144) estimated the average wage of a curate in the diocese of Lincoln in 1526 at £5 3s. 2d., and found very few instances in which curates earned more than that. For the East Riding Peter Heath has recorded only 28, out of 298 chaplains, receiving more than £4 (*English Parish Clergy,* 24). In the *Valor,* I have found five perpetual curates in Yorkshire whose average wage was £3 18s. 7d. per annum (median £4), and six in Warwickshire whose average wage was £4 16s. 10d. (median £4 13s. 4d.).

Working with figures for a "hypothetical arable farm" of the early *seventeenth* century, Dr. Peter J. Bowden has calculated that, when public holidays and periods of unemployment are taken into account, "it is doubtful whether the wage-earnings of even the fullest employed agricultural labourers [whose wage-rate was 8d. per day] were more than about £9 per annum." Slightly higher up the economic scale, the arable farmer with holdings of 30 acres "in times of moderate plenty" might expect to have profits of £14 to £15 per year ("Agricultural Prices, Farm Profits, and Rents," in Joan Thirsk, ed., *The Agrarian History of England and Wales,* IV, *1500-1640* [Cambridge, Cambridge University Press, 1967], 657). In the 1530s, when the wage-rate in southern England was 4d. per day, the most fully employed laborer must therefore have earned approximately £4 10s. per annum and the 30-acre farmer approximately £7. (For information about wage-rates, see ibid., 864, and E. H. Phelps Brown and Sheila V. Hopkins, "Seven Centuries of Building Wages," *Economica,* n.s. 22 [1955], 195-206). Cf. F. W. Brooks, "The Social Position of the Parson in the Sixteenth Century," *Journal of the British Archaeol. Assn.,* 3rd ser. 10 (1945-1947), 28, 32, 35.

58. John Longland to Cromwell, 14 October 1532, SP 1/71, f. 112 (*L.P.,* V, 1423); Edward Lee to Cromwell, 29 October 1535, SP 1/98, f. 103v (*L.P.,* IX, 704).

59. *Fac. Off. Reg.,* passim. In the registers numerous dispensations for pluralism are justified on grounds that "the above [living] does not yield £8 per annum."

60. Hugh Latimer, *Seven Sermons before Edward VI,* ed. Edward Arber (London, 1869), 40.

61. Many persons thought a parochial incumbent ought to receive more. In 1515 Roger Eyre of Holme (Derbys) bequeathed to his son Michael (who was in holy orders) an annual stipend of 5 marks until he should receive an adequate living of 20 marks (£13 6s. 8d.) yearly (Raine, *Testamenta Eboracensia,* V, 66), and in 1519 Thomas Welby of Stixwould (Lincs) provided £8 per annum for his son until "he be promoted to a benefice of £20 yearly if he be disposed to be a priest" (Foster, *Lincoln Wills,* I, 86).

62. *Y.C.C.,* I, 51-52, 92; II, 217; E 301/13/71; E 301/18/9; E 301/93/4.

63. Longland to Cromwell, 14 March 1534, SP 1/82, f. 283 (*L.P.,* VII, 322). For similar letters to Wolsey and Cromwell, see *L.P.,* IV, i, 2101; *L.P.,* V, 486; *L.P.,* IX, 279; *L.P.,* X, 362; *L.P.,* XII, i, 961; *L.P.,* XV, 601.

64. *L.P.,* V, 15; *L.P.,* VI, 1625. No chantry in this parish was worth less than £8 per year; several were worth a great deal more (E 301/34/46-47; B.L. Harleian MS. 601, ff. 23v, 26).

65. Any study of the ages of sixteenth-century men which is based on their own testimony will be only approximate. This was "an age that dealt grandly in round numbers" (Jordan, *Philanthropy,* 36), and inevitably some of the priests must have exaggerated their venerability (Peter Laslett, *The World We Have Lost* [London, Methuen, 1965], 99). In some cases the priests must have understated their ages (E 301/117; E 310/119, m.8; *Y.C.C.,* II, 446; Y.M.L., Torre MS. L 1(7), 1414; E 301/57/44-46; Reg. Silvestro de Gigli, f. 124v; Reg. Latimer, f. 4). Dr. Kitching ("Studies, " I, 45) has noted a glaring inconsistency with reference to Avery Bingham, incumbent of Trinity Guild, Bawtry (W.R., Yorks). The Yorkshire commissioners reported in 1548 that Bingham was 40 years of age, the Nottinghamshire commissioners that he was 62! Dr. Rose Graham noticed a tendency for the Oxfordshire commissioners to report ages in round numbers: only two priests in their certificate were not aged either 30, 40, 50, or 60 (*Chantry Certificates,* xiii).

66. DL 38/3, m. 39; E 301/39/5; *Y.C.C.,* II, 467.

67. Mark H. Curtis, "The Alienated Intellectuals of Early Stuart England," *Past and Present,* no. 23 (1962), 31-32.

68. Oxley, *Reformation in Essex,* 153; Heath, *English Parish Clergy,* 185.

69. Chaucer praised the good parson for not following in the footsteps of the purportedly typical cleric who

> Sette . . . His benefice to hyre,
> And leet his sheep encombred in the myre,
> And ran to London, un-to seynt Poules,
> To seken him a chaunterie for soules.

For examples of rectors and vicars who left their paroch al duties to become chantry priests, see the six-volume alphabetical index of sixteenth-century Yorkshire clergy in the Borthwick Institute of Historical Research, York, "Tudor Crockford," s.v. "Henry Raynecoke"; *Valor,* V, 21, 26; "Tudor Crockford," s.v. "Richard Barwyk"; Y.M.L., Torre MS. L 1(8), I, 558; *Y.C.C.,* II, 471; "Tudor Crockford," s.v. "Richard Otterborne"; *Valor,* V, 102; "Tudor Crockford," s.v. "Robert Greenewood"; *Valor,* V, 101. See also G. M. Platt and J. W. Morkill, *Records of the Parish of Whitkirk* (Leeds, 1892), 27; Christopher Wordsworth, "Marlborough Chantries and the Supply of Clergy in the Olden Days," *W.A.N.H.M.,* 36 (1909-1910), 560; Arthur Rowntree, ed., *The History of Scarborough* (London, J.M. Dent, 1931), 83; Sir John Maclean, "Notes on the Greyndour Chapel and Chantry in the Church of Newland," *Trans. Bristol and Gloucestershire Archaeol. Soc.,* 7 (1882-1883), 125; and Wood-Legh, *Small Household,* xii. Cf. Rosalind Hill, " 'A Chaunterie for Soules': London Chantries in the Reign of Richard II," in F. R. H. Du Boulay and C. M. Barron, eds., *The Reign of Richard II: Essays in Honour of May McKisack* (London, 1971), 245.

70. On this phenomenon, see Knowles, *Religious Orders,* III, 408-410; G. W. O. Woodward, *The Dissolution of the Monasteries* (London, Blandford, 1966), 149; and Lawrence S. Snell, *The Suppression of the Religious Foundations of Devon and Cornwall* (Marazion, Wordens of Cornwall, 1967), 110. By collating the names of priests listed in the chantry certificates of the four sample shires with the *Fac. Off. Reg.,* I have found many cantarists who had been in religious orders: Essex, 10 cantarists probably or certainly ex-religious, 4 possibly ex-religious; Warwickshire, 5 probably, 7 possibly; Wiltshire, 8 probably, 2 possibly; Yorkshire, 45 probably, 20 possibly. This evidence, along with the 1554 report on pensioners in the diocese of Lincoln (G. A. J. Hodgett, ed., *The State of the Ex-Religious and Former Chantry Priests in the Diocese of Lincoln, 1547-1574,* Lincoln Rec. Soc., 53 [1959], 75-125), indicates that Professor Knowles's estimate that "one in a dozen" former monks became chantry priests may be somewhat low.

71. E.g., Nicholas Collys, monk of Roche Abbey, who was promoted to a chantry in Tickhill (W.R., Yorks) within five months of the dissolution of his house. Other Yorkshire monks such as William Swanne and William Modie had to wait longer— four and a half and nine years respectively—(Dom David Knowles and R. Neville Hadcock, *Medieval Religious Houses: England and Wales,* 2nd ed. [London, 1971], 125, 235; *Fac. Off. Reg.,* 76, 144, 160; Joseph Hunter, *South Yorkshire: The History and Topography of the Deanery of Doncaster,* 2 vols. [London, 1828-1831], I, 243; *Y.C.C.,* I, 183, and II, 306; J. W. Walker, *Wakefield, Its History and People,* 2nd ed. [Wakefield, 1939], I, 208; Y.M.L., Torre MS. L 1(10), 684; E 301/119, m. 6).

72. Knowles, *Religious Orders,* III, 409; R. B. Walker, "Reformation and Reaction in the County of Lincoln, 1547-1558," *Lincolnshire Archit. and Archaeol. Soc. Reports and Papers,* 9 (1960), 61, 61n. The decreasing number of ordinations was also a result of the suppression of the monasteries, which for centuries had been the primary guarantor of titles.

73. Wood-Legh, 232.

74. I owe this phrase to Mrs. Bowker (*Secular Clergy*, 71).

75. Raine, *Testamenta Eboracensia*, V, 288. For a similar provision in a Lincolnshire will, see Foster, *Lincoln Wills*, I, 85.

76. Reg. Bainbridge, f. 104v; Raine, *Testamenta Eboracensia*, V, 53; B.L. Lansdowne MS. 452, f. 11v; *Valor*, V, 72-73; *Y.C.C.*, II, 276-277; DL 28/27/18.

77. Reg. Wolsey, f. 204; G. D. Lumb, ed., *Testamenta Leodiensia*, Thoresby Soc. 19 (1913), 96-97; *Y.C.C.*, II, 263-264; DL 28/27/18.

78. Reg. Bainbridge, f. 112; Raine, *Testamenta Eboracensia*, V, 111-112; B.L. Lansdowne MS. 452, f. 5; Y.M.L., Torre MS. L 1(8), I, 580; *Valor*, V, 29; *Y.C.C.*, II, 450, 455.

79. R. L. Storey, *Thomas Langley and the Bishopric of Durham, 1406-1437* (London, S.P.C.K., 1961), 181, has suggested that some clerics used their posts as chantry priests for this purpose. Examples of this practice occur, for example, in B.L., Stowe Charter 583; *L.P.*, I (rev. ed.), 924(26); Heath, *English Parish Clergy*, 46-47; P. A. Bill, "Five Aspects of the Medieval Parochial Clergy of Warwickshire," *University of Birmingham Historical Journal*, 10 (1966), 99-100; Maclean, "Greyndour," 125; Hussey, *Kent Chantries*, 290-291. Although this was probably not a general pattern, the whole matter needs thorough investigation.

80. E.g., John Cancefield, who between 1520 and the dissolution moved from one chantry in York Minster to another and acquired a prebend in the college of St. Sepulchre, thereby quintupling his original income; and Uhtred Johnson, who from a chantry in the city of York worth £1 per annum climbed to a chantry and a prebend in York Minster, which together were worth almost £19 annually (Y.M.L., Torre MS. L 1(7), 1462, 1548, 1636; *Y.C.C.*, II, 429, 431, 435-436; *Valor*, V, 29).

81. Bowker, *Secular Clergy*, 72-73.

82. Foster and Thompson, "Chantry Certificates for Lincolnshire," passim.

83. William Bewell of Lowthorpe College, instituted in 1504 (Y.A.S.R.S., 129 (1967), 107; E 301/119, m. 8); Christopher Rocke of the Stapleton Chantry in the chapel of East Haddlesey within the parish of Birkin, instituted in 1507 (Y.M.L., Torre MS. L 1(8), II, 380; *Y.C.C.*, II, 220-221); John Sturtyvaunt of the St. Mary Chantry in Todwick, instituted in 1508 (Y.M.L., Torre MS. L 1(8), II, 1178; *Y.C.C.*, II, 383); William Sheffeld (Y.M.L., Torre MS. L 1(8), II, 269; DL 28/27/18); William Colte (Y.M.L., Torre MS. L 1(8), I, 374; *Y.C.C.*, II, 467).

84. Heath, *English Parish Clergy*, 81.

85. *Y.C.C.*, II, 415; Hussey, *Kent Chantries*, 227; Foster and Thompson, "Chantry Certificates for Lincolnshire," *A.A.S.R.P.*, 36 (1921-1922), 261.

86. In the four sample counties I have found only four university graduates among the intercessory priests (E 301/19/36; E 301/58/3, 9; *Y.C.C.*, II, 392-393). Many of the priests presented by the crown to chantries seem to have possessed university degrees; see *L.P.*, I (rev. ed.), ii, 2055 (77); *L.P.*, II, ii, 3903; *L.P.*, III, i, 154 (17), 405 (29), 1186 (1); *L.P.*, IV, iii, 6542 (5); *L.P.*, VI, 929 (46).

87. Foster and Thompson, "Chantry Certificates for Lincolnshire," *A.A.S.R.P.*, 36 (1921-1922), 195. In Wiltshire the commissioners adjudged that numerous priests in their sixties or older were "not able to serve a cure by reason of . . . age" (E 301/58/44).

88. Oxfordshire was ostensibly an exception, for the commissioners described the majority of the priests as men "of honest behaviour and well learned, meet to keep a cure" (Graham, *Chantry Certificates*, passim). I am inclined to believe that this reflected more lenient standards on the part of the commissioners rather than superior learning on the part of the incumbents.

89. A. R. Myers, "Richard III and the Historical Tradition," *History*, 53 (1968),

183; M. W. Beresford, "The Deserted Villages of Warwickshire," *Trans. Birmingham Archaeol. Soc.*, 66 (1945-1946), 53-55; John Leland, *Itinerary*, ed. Lucy Toulmin Smith, 5 vols. (London, 1906-1910), II, 42; Thomas Warly to Lady Lisle, 2 May 1536, SP 3/14, f. 54v (*L.P.*, X, 789); Heath, *English Parish Clergy*, 89; Clay, *Testamenta Eboracensia*, VI, 289-290; B.L. Harleian MS. 1710; A. G. Dickens, "Aspects of Intellectual Transition among the English Parish Clergy of the Reformation Period: A Regional Example," *Archiv für Reformationsgeschichte*, 43 (1952), 58.

90. Quoted in Cook, *Mediaeval Chantries*, 63.

91. *Y.C.C.*, II, 460; E. Brunskill, "Two Hundred Years of Parish Life in York," *Yorkshire Archit. and York Archaeol. Soc., Annual Report* (1950-1951), 23-24.

92. A. G. Dickens, *Lollards and Protestants in the Diocese of York, 1509-1558* (London, 1959), 40; see also *L.P.*, XII, ii, 436.

93. SP 1/123, f. 118 (*L.P.*, XII, ii, 353); Dickens, *Lollards and Protestants*, 39; *L.P.*, XII, ii, 357; W. H. Jones, "Bradford-upon-Avon: General History of the Parish," *W.A.N.H.M.*, 5 (1859), 40; *Valor*, II, 147; *L.P.*, XV, 498 [59]; SP 1/93, ff. 80, 82 (*L.P.*, VIII, 862); Robert Colens to Cranmer, 26 April 1536, SP 1/103, f. 183 (*L.P.*, X, 735); Cranmer to Cromwell, 12 June 1538, in Thomas Cranmer, *Works*, ed. J. E. Cox, 2 vols. (Parker Soc., Cambridge, 1846), II, 369-371; SP 1/117, f. 205 (*L.P.*, XII, i, 786); A. G. Dickens, "Sedition and Conspiracy in Yorkshire during the Later Years of Henry VIII," *Y.A.J.*, 34 (1939), 389-390.

94. Dickens, "Sedition and Conspiracy," 381.

95. C.C.C.C., MS. 128, p. 269; Hussey, *Kent Chantries*, 65-66.

96. Wentworth to Cromwell, 15 December 1538, B.L. Cotton MSS., Vespasian F XIII, f. 211 (*L.P.*, XIII, ii, 1063).

97. John Foxe, *Actes and Monuments* (henceforth Foxe), ed. Josiah Pratt, 8 vols. (London, 1870), IV, 233; Anthony Sawnders to Cromwell, 3 February 1535, SP 1/89, f. 145 (*L.P.*, VIII, 171); J. Horsfall Turner, *The History of Brighouse, Rastrick, and Hipperholme* (Bingley, Yorks, 1893), 216; Lumb, *Testamenta Leodiensia*, 99-100; *Y.C.C.*, II, 275, 299; Snell, *Chantry Certificates for Cornwall*, 51; Phillipps, "Institutiones," I, 207.

98. Thompson, *English Clergy*, 157-158. Cf. *C.P.R., 1476-1485*, 252, and W. S. Simpson, "On a Newly-Discovered Manuscript Containing Statutes Compiled by Dean Colet for the Government of Chantry Priests . . . in St. Paul's Cathedral," *Archaeologia*, 52 (1890), 147, 155.

99. *Y.C.C.*, II, 456. "Mean," which could in sixteenth-century parlance signify "mediocre," appears in this case, as in other instances in the chantry certificates, to signify its other contemporary meaning, "inferior" (*O.E.D.*, s.v. "mean").

100. Thompson, "Chantry Certificates for Northamptonshire," 161; E 301/52/49.

101. Sir Thomas Tempest to Cromwell, 11 May 1535, SP 1/92, f. 168 (*L.P.*, VIII, 700); Reg. Warham, ff. 47, 54; Beresford, "Deserted Villages of Warwickshire," 89; J. G. Nichols, ed., *Chronicle of the Grey Friars of London*, Camden Soc., orig. ser. 53 (1852), 35; Reg. Warham, f. 56v; A. Hamilton Thompson, ed., *Visitations in the Diocese of Lincoln, 1517-1531*, I, Lincoln Rec. Soc., 33 (1940), 74, 85; *V.C.H., Wiltshire*, VIII, 229; Bowker, *Secular Clergy*, 117; Canterbury Cathedral Library, MS. CCL, X/10/2, ff. 90v-92v (for this reference I am indebted to my friend Peter Clark); SP 1/152, ff. 235, 237-238 (*L.P.*, XIV, i, 1333 [2-3]); Cranmer, *Works*, II, 37-38.

102. Wood-Legh, 186.

103. *Fac. Off. Reg.*, xi, xvi-xvii. For examples of papal dispensations for chantry pluralism in England, see B.L., Stow Charter 583; J. A. Twemlow, ed., *Calendar of Entries in the Papal Registers Relating to Great Britain and Ireland*, 14 vols. (London, H.M.S.O., 1893-1960), XIII, i, 463-465; XIII, ii, 796, 836-837; XIV, 9-10, 217.

104. *Fac. Off. Reg.*, 18, 51, 52, 71, 81, 82, 105, 115, 134, 146, 176, 197, 223, 225, 227, 230, 234, 252, 261, 282, 283, 293, 298.

105. In Essex, there were three free chapels and one chantry which were held in plurality (E 301/19/38, 39; DL 38/4; DL 28/27/18). In Warwickshire there was one nonresident cantarist (E 301/31/48). In Wiltshire there were three pluralist chantry priests (E 301/58/7, 8, 27), two nonresident chantry priests (E 301/58/33 and E 301/ 101, m. 3) and eleven free chapels held by nonresident or pluralist priests (E 301/58/ 57, 59, 62, 64, 69, 74, 77, 78, 79, 80). In Yorkshire thirty-eight cantarists were pluralists (*Y.C.C.*, I, 21; II, 301-303, 403, 404, 407, 431, 432, 436, 437, 438-439, 440-441, 442, 443, 445, 448, 448-449, 450, 451, 453, 455, 456, 459, 460-461, 462, 462-463, 465, 469-470, 471, 472, 473, 475, 479, 480, 481, 495, 496, 511; E 301/102, m. 1v; DL 28/27/18; E 301/119, mm. 6, 8) and ten cantarists were nonresident (*Y.C.C.*, I, 51- 52, 92, 103, 118, 143, 205; II, 217, 293-294, 498). I have not considered as pluralism the simultaneous holding of positions as chantry priests and as vicars choral in such churches as the York and Beverley Minsters. For Topcliffe, see *Y.C.C.*, II, 479-480.

106. A comparison of the "Tudor Crockford" (see above, n. 69) with other sources indicates the following cases of certain pluralism: Robert Baynton (*Y.C.C.*, I, 135); Henry Clough and Anthony Florence (ibid., II, 304, 458); John Geffryson (DL 28/27/ 18); Thomas Raper (*Y.C.C.*, II, 482); Robert Rome (ibid., I, 128-129). Cases of possible pluralism are: William Arnarde (ibid., II, 487); John Bereby (ibid., I, 138); Thomas Cooke, Robert Day, William Robinson (ibid., II, 249, 425, 434); John Thompson (DL 28/27/18); Thomas Tyson (*Y.C.C.*, II, 537-538).

107. Reports of "far decay" and "magna ruina" come from all parts of the realm, but perhaps most insistently from such venerable cities as Coventry and York. See E 301/53/1; Angelo Raine, ed., *York Civic Records*, I-VI, Y.A.S.R.S. 98, 103, 106, 108, 110, 112 (1939-1948); J. N. Bartlett, "The Expansion and Decline of York in the Later Middle Ages, *Ec.H.R.*, 2nd ser. 12 (1959-1960), 28.

108. See Table 1.4.

109. E 301/53/1-3.

110. *Y.C.C.*, I, 53; II, 440-441, 445, 448-449, 450, 451, 453-455, 456, 459, 460- 461, 462, 463, 465, 472, 473.

111. Ibid., II, 442, 448, 469-472.

112. Cf. Wood-Legh, 197.

113. Augustus Jessopp, ed., *Visitations of the Diocese of Norwich, 1492-1532*, Camden Soc., n.s. 43 (1888), xxxvii-xxxviii; Thompson, *English Clergy*, 98-99, 158- 159; Bowker, *Secular Clergy*, 174-178; D. M. Loades, "The Collegiate Churches of Durham at the Time of the Dissolution," in Cuming, *Studies in Church History*, IV, 70-75; Peter Heath, ed., *Bishop Geoffrey Blythe's Visitations, c. 1515-1525*, Staffordshire Rec. Soc., 4th ser. 7 (1973), lxii-lxiii.

114. E 301/19/34; E 301/56/3; Philip Morant, *The History and Antiquities of the County of Essex*, 2 vols. (London, 1768), II, 259-260; *V.C.H., Wiltshire*, III, 385-388; Leland, *Itinerary*, I, 46; Latimer to Cromwell, 14 October 1537, in Hugh Latimer, *Works*, ed. George Elwes Corrie, 2 vols. (Parker Soc., Cambridge, 1844-1845), II, 384.

115. Namely, Acaster Selby (*Y.C.C.*, II, 240-241, 378; E 301/103/9); Beverley (E 301/119, m. 3); Coventry (E 301/53/1; E 301/57/1-5; E 319/6); Ripon (*Y.C.C.*, II, 361); Rotherham (*Y.C.C.*, I, 200-204; ibid., II, 380-382; E 301/103/14); Stratford- on-Avon (E 301/31/42); and Warwick (A. F. Leach, *History of Warwick School* [London, 1906], 87, 94). The school at Stratford was a song school, and that at Beverley was "not by the foundation." I have found no evidence that a school was actually functioning in the college of Howden in the 1540s (*Valor*, V, 137; E 301/119, m. 4v; E

178/2552, f. 10; *V.C.H., Yorkshire*, I, 439); but cf. Leach, *English Schools*, I, 12, and John Lawson, *The Endowed Grammar Schools of East Yorkshire*, East Yorkshire Local History Series, 14 (1962), 5-11.

 116. W.R.O., MS. B.A. 2764/802, ff. 111-111v.

 117. Latimer to Cromwell, 17 June 1538, SP 1/133, ff. 55 and 57 (*L.P.*, XIII, i, 1202 [1] and [2]).

 118. Latimer to Cromwell, 2 October 1538, SP 1/137, ff. 78-78v (*L.P.*, XIII, ii, 515), and 28 October 1538, SP 1/138, f. 48 (*L.P.*, XIII, ii, 709); Benet to Latimer, 31 March 1539, SP 1/144, f. 199 (*L.P.*, XIV, i, 638); Latimer to Cromwell, 11 April 1539, SP 1/150, f. 116 (*L.P.*, XIV, i, 740); John Wattwood and three canons of Warwick to Cromwell, 13 September 1539, SP 1/153, f. 123 (*L.P.*, XIV, ii, 159).

 119. Although two of the seven prebendaries were formally bound to be resident (*Y.C.C.*, II, 348), it is clear that by 1537 only the treasurer was complying with this requirement (SP 1/127, f. 13 [*L.P.*, XII, ii, 1175]).

 120. J. T. Fowler, ed., *Memorials of the Church of SS. Peter and Wilfrid, Ripon*, II, Surtees Soc., 78 (1884), 167-175.

 121. *L.P.*, X, 711; Frere and Kennedy, II, 25-29; Fowler, *Memorials*, II, 180-181.

 122. J. T. Fowler, ed., *Acts of the Chapter of the Collegiate Church of SS. Peter and Wilfrid, Ripon*, Surtees Soc., 64 (1874), 351; Fowler, *Memorials*, II, 305-308; DL 42/135, f. 125; Lucius Smith, *The Story of Ripon Minster* (Leeds, 1914), 144, 151-166; Fowler, *Memorials*, I, 257-258, 308-309.

 123. *Valor*, III, 61; E 301/119, m. 1; *Y.C.C.*, II, 349-351, 525-527; E 301/119, m. 4v. Cf. Loades, "Collegiate Churches of Durham," 68-70.

 124. E. 301/57/1-5; *Y.C.C.*, II, 326-327.

 125. For an impassioned narrative of the dissolution of Rotherham College by one who had witnessed it, see Michael Sherbrook's "The Fall of Religious Houses," in A. G. Dickens, ed., *Tudor Treatises*, Y.A.S.R.S., 125 (1959), 126-127.

 126. The Duke of Norfolk, who was considering the conversion of a monastery into a collegiate church, on 19 August 1538 wrote to Parker asking him for a copy of the statutes which had been instrumental in Stoke-by-Clare's resurgence (C.C.C.C., MS. 114, p. 105). See also Jessopp, *Visitations*, 233-239, 299-300; Robert Shorton to Cromwell, 27 June 1535, SP 1/93, f. 183 (*L.P.*, VIII, 934).

 127. For Parker's statutes, see C.C.C.C., MS. 108, pp. 155-160. These have been fully summarized in John Strype, *The Life and Acts of Matthew Parker,* 3 vols. (Oxford, 1821), I, 16-18, and more briefly in V. J. K. Brook, *A Life of Archbishop Parker* (Oxford, Clarendon Press, 1962), 18.

Chapter 2: The Intercessory Priests' Practical Contributions

 1. More, *Supplicacyon of Soulys*, in *Workes*, 288-339; A. G. Dickens, "South Yorkshire Letters, 1555," *Trans. Hunter Archaeol. Soc.*, 6 (1944-1950), 278-284; Edmund Bonner, ed., *Homelies Sette Forth by the Righte Reuerende Father in God, Edmunde Byshop of London* (London, John Cawood, 1555), 41v-42; Robert Crowley, *Select Works*, ed. J. Meadows Cowper, E.E.T.S., extra ser. 15 (1872), 12; Thomas Lever, *Sermons, 1550*, ed. Edward Arber (London, 1870), 123.

 2. Cf. Leach, *English Schools at the Reformation*, his most authoritative statement; Hughes, *Reformation in England*, II, 151; Francis Aidan Gasquet, *Parish Life in Medieval England* (London, 1906), 96; Augustus Jessopp, *Before the Great Pillage* (London, T. Fisher Unwin, 1901), 62; Toulmin Smith, *English Guilds*, E.E.T.S., 40 (1870), xlii n.

 3. Erasmus to Charles V (?), n.d., in James A. Froude, *Life and Letters of Eras-*

mus (London, 1894), 311; Robert Singleton, *A Sermon Preached at Poules Crosse* (London, Thomas Godfraye, 1536; *S.T.C.* 22,575), sig. Biiii, of which the sole surviving copy is in the Lincoln Cathedral Library); Cranmer, *Works*, II, 37-38; Jean Veron, *Huntynge of Purgatorye to Death* (London, John Tysdale, 1561; *S.T.C.* 24,683), ff. 185v-186. See also Henry Brinklow, *The Lamentacyon of a Christen agaynst the Cytye of London*, E.E.T.S., extra ser. 22 (1874), 88.

4. Joel T. Rosenthal, *The Purchase of Paradise: Gift Giving and the Aristocracy, 1307-1485* (London, 1972), 37; H. Maynard Smith, *Pre-Reformation England* (London, 1938), 82; H. F. Carpenter, "The Reformation," in W. R. Matthews and W. M. Atkins, eds., *A History of St. Paul's Cathedral* (London, Phoenix House, 1957), 110; Rosalind Hill, "Two Northamptonshire Chantries," *E.H.R.*, 62 (1947), 208; Miss Hill quotes a conversation with Professor Sykes in " 'A Chaunterie for Soules,' " 245; R. S. Arrowsmith, *The Prelude to the Reformation: A Study of English Church Life from the Age of Wycliffe to the Break with Rome* (London, S.P.C.K., 1923), 39; A. L. Rowse, *Tudor Cornwall: Portrait of a Society* (London, Jonathan Cape, 1941), 261.

5. Thomas Fuller, *The Church History of Britain*, ed. J. S. Brewer, 6 vols. (Oxford, 1845), III, 468.

6. More, *Workes*, 335. Professor Knowles considered the foundation of chantries to be a symptom of the "purely material and personal" interests of the late medieval Englishmen (*Religious Orders*, III, 5).

7. *C.P.R., 1436-1441*, 137; *C.P.R., 1446-1452*, 244; *C.P.R., 1485-1494*, 152-153 (cf. Wood-Legh, 267-268, 275); *C.P.R., 1441-1446*, 408-409; Leland, *Itinerary*, V, 144.

8. *Die Religion in Geschichte und Gegenwart*, 3rd ed., ed. Kurt Galling (Tübingen, J. C. B. Mohr, 1958), s.v. "Fegfeuer"; St. Catherine of Genoa, *Treatise on Purgatory*, ed. Charlotte Balfour and Helen D. Irvine (London, Sheed & Ward, 1946), 18-19, esp. 32. See also C. S. Lewis, *English Literature in the Sixteenth Century Excluding Drama*, Oxford History of English Literature, III (Oxford, Clarendon Press, 1954), 163-165, 172-173; and J. W. Blench, *Preaching in England in the Late Fifteenth and Sixteenth Centuries* (Oxford, Basil Blackwell, 1964), 236.

9. John Fisher, *Hereafter Ensueth Two Fruytfull Sermons* (London, W. Rastell, 1532; *S.T.C.* 10,909), sigs. C2-C3; *Here Begynneth a Lytell Boke, That Speketh of Purgatorye* (London, Robert Wyer, n.d.; *S.T.C.* 3,360), sig. A. This colorful, noncontroversial exposition of the pains of purgatory in rhymed verse has survived in a single copy in the Huntington Library, San Marino, California. It was first brought to my attention by Dr. C. J. Kitching, who kindly lent me his microfilm of it. Its author is unknown, and it is undated. The late F. S. Ferguson, who had studied Wyer's publications carefully, dated the volume ca. 1534, and it will be entered at [1534] in the revised *S.T.C.* (letter from Miss K. F. Pantzer of Houghton Library, Harvard University, 11 May 1973). However, it can hardly have been published after Cranmer's June 1534 order which forbade preaching on purgatory (Cranmer, *Works*, II, 460-462).

10. Fisher, *Two Fruytfull Sermons*, sig. C3; *Lytell Boke*, sigs. Bii, Di; Raine, *Testamenta Eboracensia*, V, 29; Charles Cotton, ed., *The Canterbury Chantries and Hospitals in 1546*, Kent Records 12, Supplement (1934), 11.

11. Glanmor Williams, *The Welsh Church from Conquest to Reformation* (Cardiff, University of Wales Press, 1962), 289; Wood-Legh, 69, 312-313; G. G. Coulton, *Five Centuries of Religion*, 4 vols. (Cambridge, Cambridge University Press, 1929-1950), I, 127.

12. John Foxe, ed., *The Whole Workes of W. Tyndall, J. Frith, and Doct. Barnes* (henceforth *Whole Workes*) (London, John Daye, 1573; *S.T.C.* 24,436), 309; William Allen, *A Defense and Declaracion of the Catholike Churchies Doctrine, touching Purgatory* (Antwerp, John Latius, 1565), f. 215v.

13. Leach, *English Schools*, I, 68.

14. *C.P.R., 1436-1441*, 137; for other examples, see above, n.7, and E 301/58/71; *Y.C.C.*, II, 419.

15. Even the cantarist or stipendiary priest who participated dutifully in all the choir offices of his church in addition to his own "private" services would hardly have found himself occupied more than three or four hours a day. For the duration of the services held in medieval parish churches, see Christopher Wordsworth and Henry Littlehales, *The Old Service-Books of the English Church* (London, Methuen, 1904), 20, 23-24.

16. Gasquet, *Parish Life*, 95; cf. Heath, *English Parish Clergy*, xii.

17. Wood-Legh, 272. That there were "variances . . . in many places betwixt curates and chantry priests . . ." was a contention of Christopher St. German, for which there is some evidence in the sources (*Salem and Bizance* [London, T. Berthelet, 1533; *S.T.C.* 21,584], 22v; Reg. Warham, f. 47; Thompson, *Visitations*, I, 61, 100; but cf. Cotton, *Canterbury Chantries*, 59).

18. SP 1/131, f. 28v (*L.P.*, XIII, i, 686); Anthony Sawnders to Cromwell, 3 February 1535, SP 1/89, f. 145 (*L.P.*, VIII, 171); Thompson, *Visitations*, I, 102.

19. *Y.C.C.*, I, 113, and II, 496. See also ibid., 491 (Kirby Wiske, N.R., Yorks), from which the brief certificate (E 301/102, m. 4v) differs markedly.

20. *Y.C.C.*, II, 503, 505-506.

21. C 66/811, mm. 23v-25v (*C.P.R., Edward VI*, I, 417-418). The letter of commission (20 June 1548) does not actually refer to the continuance of assistants in the cure of souls, which Mildmay and Keilway may have included under the evidently elastic rubric of "preachings." For South Cowton, see *Y.C.C.*, II, 494; E 301/102, mm. 4v-5; see also *Y.C.C.*, II, 491; E 301/102, m. 4v; for Malmesbury, see E 301/58/36; E 301/101, m. 4.

22. Wood-Legh, 275; W. E. Tate, *A. F. Leach as a Historian of Yorkshire Education*, St. Anthony's Hall Publications 23 (York, 1963), 11.

23. *L.P.*, XXI, i, 302(30); *C.P.R., Edward VI*, II, 135-137; and cf. Hanham, "The Suppression of the Chantries in Ashburton," 117-120.

24. E 301/74/37; John E. Ray, ed., *Sussex Chantry Records*, Sussex Rec. Soc. 36 (1931), 51; Graham, *Chantry Certificates*, 54.

25. E.R.O., DP 27/5, f. 42; DP 11/5/1, ff. 39, 41v; E 315/67, ii, f. 454; Green, *Survey of Somerset*, 25, 131. Surviving examples of these draft certificates are in E 301/89, 90, 91, 110, 111, 120, 121, 123, 125, 127, 129, 130; Cotton, *Canterbury Chantries*, passim.

26. E 301/13; E 301/32/1; E 301/25/46; E 301/37/52; Green, *Survey of Somerset*, 22-23.

27. E 301/46; Maclean, "Chantry Certificates, Gloucestershire," 244.

28. E 301/52/54; DL 38/7; Thompson, "Chantry Certificates for Northamptonshire," 129, and "Certificates of the Shropshire Chantries," 333; Maclean, "Chantry Certificates, Gloucestershire," 262. See also E 301/13/28; DL 38/7 (Monmouth).

29. C 66/777, m. 1v (*L.P.*, XXI, i, 302 [30]); C 66/814, m. 13v (*C.P.R., Edward VI*, II, 135).

30. Craib, "Surrey Chantries," 12-14, from the Loseley MSS.

31. E.g., E 301/27/13; E 301/34/71, 74, 85, 101, 107; E 301/76/22; *Y.C.C.*, II, 398-399, 476; Green, *Survey of Somerset*, 116.

32. E 301/4/18; E 301/3/3; Maclean, "Chantry Certificates, Gloucestershire," 301.

33. *Y.C.C.*, II, 476.

34. Eshelby, "Episcopal Visitations," 408; *Y.C.C.*, II, 506-507.

35. For other examples, see Eshelby, "Episcopal Visitations," 397, 402, 411

(*Y.C.C.*, II, 491, 492, 496).

36. An examination of evidence from a random selection of 15 parishes from 7 shires has shown substantial agreement between the chantry certificates and the *Valor*, with one exception: in the parish of Christchurch (Hants), the vicarage was appraised in the *Valor* at £14 8s. 0d. (after subtraction of the tenth), in the chantry certificate at £26 (*Valor*, II, 18; E 301/52/53).

37. Many of the warrants of continuance have disappeared; enough have survived, however, to indicate that the continuance of institution in our sample counties was not exceptional; cf. E 319/7, 9, 12, 17, 24.

38. E 301/76/22; E 301/23/27; Snell, *Chantry Certificates for Cornwall*, 16.

39. It was impossible, for example, for the vicar of Sheffield adequately to serve his parishioners if assisted only by the single cantarist whom the commissioners assigned to serve as assistant to the cure. Upon the petition of the burgesses and inhabitants, Queen Mary on 8 June 1554 granted back to the town the rent which had formerly supported three stipendiary priests, without whom the vicar "cannot administer the sacraments and divine services to the parishioners" (*C.P.R., Philip and Mary*, I, 170-172). The chaplain of Garsdale in the parish of Sedbergh (W.R., Yorks) was continued by order of the Court of Augmentations on 24 November 1551, at the intercession of the parishioners (E 315/105, f. 175v). The collegiate churches of Beverley and Ripon also faced serious difficulties as a result of the dissolution (E 315/105, ff. 256v-257; DL 5/19, ff. 81-84).

40. Horton Davies, *Worship and Theology in England*, I, *From Cranmer to Hooker, 1534-1603* (Princeton, Princeton University Press, 1970), 32.

41. E 301/56/23; E 319/1.

42. E 301/103/83; E 301/119, m. 1; for Edlesborough, see E 301/4/6; for Kempsey, see E 301/25/10.

43. These ratios could on occasion be as low as 190:1 (Henley-in-Arden, Warwicks) and 264:1 (Marlborough, Wilts) (E 301/53/21; E 301/58/54; E 319/6, 1).

44. For Rotherham, see E 301/103/14; for Scarborough, E 301/102, m. 6; E 319/22; for Tewkesbury, E 301/23/52, 129.

45. E 301/103/54; *Y.C.C.*, II, 400; *C.P.R., Philip and Mary*, I, 170-172; Joseph Hunter, *Hallamshire*, 239.

46. Wood-Legh, 276. Cf. Christopher Haigh, *Reformation and Resistance in Tudor Lancashire* (Cambridge, Cambridge University Press, 1975), 33.

47. *Y.C.C.*, II, 508; E 301/80; *Y.C.C.*, II, 383; E 301/60/15.

48. *Y.C.C.*, I, 175; E 301/19/36; E 301/13/11, 56; *Y.C.C.*, II, 299, 273-275; *Y.C.C.*, I, 61.

49. Smith, *Pre-Reformation England*, 95-96; Gasquet, *Parish Life*, 181-182.

50. *Y.C.C.*, I, 175; E 301/89, f. 3v; E 301/31/28; B.L. Harleian MS. 594, f. 166v; and cf. E 301/13/69, for the situation in Chesterfield, Derbys.

51. Redstone, "Chapels, Chantries, and Gilds in Suffolk," 39; E 301/25/1.

52. E 301/53/1, 2; E 301/54/7; E 301/103/14; *Y.C.C.*, II, 442, 448, 469, 471, 472.

53. *Y.C.C.*, II, 454 (St. Peter the Little). For a similar situation, cf. J. E. Brown and F. A. Page-Turner, eds., *Chantry Certificates for Bedfordshire* (Bedford, 1908), 11-12.

54. *Y.C.C.*, I, 180; ibid., II, 312-313; E 301/31/43; E 301/53/20; E 301/31/6, 29.

55. *Y.C.C.*, II, 306-316, 414-418; Walker, *Wakefield*, I, 223-227; E 301/103/83.

56. SP 1/219, f. 141 (*L.P.*, XXI, i, 966); and cf. E 321/19/61 for a similar petition from Carlton chapelry, Snaith parish (W.R., Yorks).

57. E 301/31/41; B.L. Harleian MS. 594, f. 104; Maclean, "Chantry Certificates, Gloucestershire," 292.

58. *Y.C.C.*, II, 253, 266-267, 411; B.L. Harleian MS. 594, f. 104; *Y.A.J.*, XIV, 414.

59. For a good example, see Dugdale, *Antiquities*, II, 806-807.

60. E 301/53/54; *V.C.H., Warwickshire*, IV, 98; *Y.C.C.,* II, 389. For other examples, see E 301/119, m. 7v (Foston-on-the-Wolds, E.R., Yorks); *Y.C.C.*, II, 280 (Kellington, W.R., Yorks); DL 38/4 (Brentwood, Essex); E 315/68, f. 301v (Billinghay, Lincs).

61. E 301/31/44; *V.C.H., Warwickshire*, III, 211; *Y.C.C.*, I, 209; ibid., II, 380; E 301/103/13; Y.A.S.R.S., 107 (1943), 138-139.

62. E 301/18/95; *Y.C.C.*, II, 269, 413; B.L. Harleian MS. 594, f. 105. On the difficulties of traveling in the Archdeaconry of Richmond, see Archbishop Lee to Cromwell, 30 June 1535 (SP 1/93, f. 199v [*L.P.*, VIII, 952]): "It is a wild country . . . It is a hard country to ride in, ne can be ridden in many places in the winter, ne afore April."

63. E 301/18/95; *Y.C.C.*, II, 413. Certain parishes alleged the dangerously exposed location of local hamlets as justification for the continued existence of their chapelries. The parishioners of Saltash (Cornwall) and Weymouth (Dorset) contended that if the inhabitants were forced to leave their chapelries to attend the parish churches, certain "enemies" (or, as the Cornishmen unambiguously put it, "the Frenchmen") "might invade the same to their great loss and hindrance" (Snell, *Chantry Certificates for Cornwall*, 46; E 315/68, ff. 108-108v). The great fear of the parishioners of Aldenham (Herts) was indigenous foes—robbers lurking in "a suspect place called Bushy Heath"—who might loot the homes of the villagers while they were in church (E 301/27/1).

64. E.g., the chapel of St. Bartholomew in the manor of Erleigh (Sonning, Berks), whose incumbent was the provost of Queen's College, Oxford (E 301/3/15; E 301/51/24). For examples of "lost village chapelries" in the four sample shires, see M. W. Beresford, "The Lost Villages of Yorkshire," *Y.A.J.*, 38 (1952-1955), 64, 66, 69, 234, 237, 238, 298, 302, 303, 304, 306; Beresford, *The Lost Villages of England* (London, Lutterworth Press, 1954), 390; *V.C.H., Wiltshire*, VII, 64-65, and VIII, 88.

65. E 301/56, 58, 59, 101; E 319/1.

66. Lee to Cromwell, 30 June 1535, SP 1/93, f. 199 (*L.P.*, VIII, 952).

67. E 301/58/44; E 301/101, m. 5. The Corsham vicarage was worth £9 14s. 4¾d. after deduction of the clerical tenth (*Valor*, II, 138).

68. E 301/31/70; *Valor*, IV, 148; *Y.C.C.*, II, 395-397; E 301/103/44-47.

69. Cf. Tyler, "The Status of the Elizabethan Parochial Clergy," 81.

70. Beverley had 2,878 housling people, Hemingbrough 1,200, Howden 2,500, and Stratford-on-Avon 1,500 (*Y.C.C.*, II, 529; E 301/119, mm. 4v, 1; E 301/31/42); Ripon also had a large number of communicants (*Y.C.C.*, II, 353; Smith, *Story of Ripon Minster*, 168-169.

71. *Y.C.C.*, II, 528-529; E 301/119, m. 8; E 301/57/22; B.L. Harleian MS. 605, ff. 57-57v; DL 42/135, f. 125; E 301/119, mm. 2-3; E 319/6.

72. Wood-Legh, 276.

73. *Y.C.C.*, I, 167; a common phrase in the chantry certificates.

74. For examples of their musical contributions, see E 301/34/9; E 301/31/20, 42; E 301/53/55; E 301/57/27; E 301/83, m. 1; Maclean, "Chantry Certificates, Gloucestershire," 286; *Y.C.C.*, II, 402-403, 496. See also Dorothy M. Owen, *Church and Society in Medieval Lincolnshire* (History of Lincolnshire, ed. Joan Thirsk, V) (Lincoln, 1971), 97, 100.

75. For a full discussion of the cathedral cantarists, see Kathleen Edwards, *The English Secular Cathedrals in the Middle Ages*, 2nd ed. (Manchester, 1967), 285-303.

76. E 301/34/108; E 301/56/1; E 301/58/1-10; *Y.C.C.*, I, 1-42; ibid., II, 431-449, 524-536; SP 10/4, ff. 11-12; Bodleian MSS., Rawlinson B. 235, f. 1; E 301/31/19; E 301/57/23; *V.C.H.*, *Warwickshire*, IV, 98.

77. R. E. G. Cole, ed., *Chapter Acts of the Cathedral Church of St. Mary of Lincoln*, I, Lincoln Rec. Soc. 12 (1915), 142-144; Edwards, *English Secular Cathedrals*, 301-302.

78. See the forceful criticisms of Leach by Mrs. Joan Simon, "A. F. Leach on the Reformation," *B.J.E.S.*, 3 (1954-1955), 128-143, and 4 (1955-1956), 32-48. Mrs. Simon's article, which was a response to a two-part article by W. E. Tate ("Sources for the History of English Grammar Schools," ibid., 1 [1952-1953], 164-175, and 2 [1953-1954], 67-81), has led to some not very illuminating controversy. See W. N. Chaplin, "A. F. Leach: A Reappraisal," ibid., 11 (1962-1963), 99-124; Joan Simon, "A. F. Leach: A Reply," ibid., 12 (1963-1964), 41-50; W. N. Chaplin, "A. F. Leach: Agreement and Difference," ibid., 173-183; P. J. Wallis, "Leach—Past, Present and Future," ibid., 184-194. The most adequate treatment of the chantry schools at the dissolution is in Nicholas Orme, *English Schools in the Middle Ages* (London, Methuen, 1973), 272-289, which, like Mrs. Simon's *Education and Society in Tudor England* (Cambridge, Cambridge University Press, 1966), is based chiefly on secondary sources and *printed* primary sources. In order finally to supersede Leach's writings on the dissolution, an equally assiduous examination *de novo* of the manuscripts in the P.R.O. must be undertaken.

79. Leach, *English Schools*, I, 68-69, 91-92.

80. Bowker, *Secular Clergy*, 43-44.

81. Frere and Kennedy, II, 17, 56, 63, 85; Wilkins, III, 722-723.

82. Cf. Wood-Legh, 268.

83. E 301/102, m. 5. See also the Guild of the Holy Ghost, Basingstoke (Hants) (E 301/52/2; cf. Leach, *English Schools*, II, 322); E 301/58/43-45.

84. Jordan, *Philanthropy*, 286.

85. *Y.C.C.*, II, 381; E 301/57/24; *Y.C.C.*, II, 520; E 301/19/36.

86. For example, the 1548 chantry certificate for Gosfield (Essex) informs us that John Hornesey "teacheth a grammar school there and hath to the number of forty scholars and hath taught the said school by the space of seven years" (E 301/19/41). Yet Bonner's Register (f. 148v) indicates that Hornesey had been instituted to the Gosfield chantry less than four years earlier (on 13 October 1544). Since there is some evidence that the school continued to function following the chantry's dissolution (*V.C.H.*, *Essex*, II, 553), it is likely that the school had an independent endowment and that Hornesey was simply using his chantry income to augment the stipend that he was already receiving for teaching the school.

87. Cf. Table 1.3.

88. For example, the income of the schoolmaster of Middleton near Pickering (N.R., Yorks) was a miserable 18s. 4½d. per year (DL 42/135. f. 124).

89. E 301/58/26. The donor who replenished the stock of sheep may have been William Birde, vicar of Bradford-on-Avon (Wilts) in the 1520s and 1530s (*V.C.H.*, *Wiltshire*, VII, 25-26). For other examples, see *Y.C.C.*, II, 492; Raine, *Testamenta Eboracensia*, V, 21.

90. *Y.C.C.*, II, 410; E 301/103/74. See also ibid., 496; E 301/102, m. 5.

91. But cf. Leach's comments on the chantry schools (*English Schools*, I, 6).

92. Walker, *Wakefield*, I, 210; *Y.C.C.*, II, 416; LR 2/65, f. 117.

93. E 301/19/36; *Y.C.C.*, II, 520.

94. E 301/19/2; *Y.C.C.*, II, 251-252, 407.

95. For example, the school supported by the Lupton Chantry in Sedbergh (W.R., Yorks) (*V.C.H., Yorkshire*, I, 466-468).

96. E 301/58/43, 45.

97. For continuance warrants in other counties, see E 319/5, 11, 12, 13, 18, 24; and cf. Jordan, *Edward VI*, II, 196.

98. Borthwick Institute, MS. R.VI.A.1, ff. 39, 39v, 40v, 42v-43v, 45-46, 48-49, 50v, 55v-56, 60, 63v, 83v-84, 85-86v, 87v; Simon, *Education and Society*, 311-313; Lawrence Stone, "The Educational Revolution in England, 1560-1640," *Past and Present*, no. 28 (1964), 52, 46-47.

99. Seymour, "Medieval Hospital," 24; Jordan, *Philanthropy*, 257-258.

100. 2 Henry V, c.1 (*S.R.*, II, 175); Clay, *Mediaeval Hospitals*, 226.

101. Simon Fish, *A Supplicacyon for the Beggars*, ed. F. J. Furnivall, E.E.T.S., extra ser. 13 (1871), 13; Seymour, "Medieval Hospital," 317-318.

102. Leland, *Itinerary*, I, 47, and II, 45; E 301/58/30; cf. *V.C.H., Wiltshire*, III, 334-335; *Y.C.C.*, I, 42; E 301/57/52.

103. E 301/58/54; in January 1549 the government granted their request (E 36/258, f. 98).

104. E 301/20/46 (Ilford); *Y.C.C.*, I, 141 (Richmond); ibid., II, 338 (Hull); E 301/58/85 (Salisbury); *Y.C.C.*, II, 326-333 (Pontefract); E 301/102, m. 4v (Kirkleatham). Cf. Jordan, *Charities of Rural England*, 256, 256n.

105. E 301/31/28; E 301/53/55; E 301/57/29; E 301/20/43; E 301/83, m. 2; DL 38/4; E 301/13/62; Jordan, *Philanthropy*, 146.

106. J. W. Clay, *Testamenta Eboracensia*, VI, 40.

107. *Y.C.C.*, II, 419 (Chantry of Our Lady, Normanton, W.R., Yorks).

108. E 301/19/195.

109. *Y.C.C.*, I, 201, 161.

110. Gasquet, *Parish Life*, 97-98, 266-268; E 301/19; Maclean, "Chantry Certificates, Gloucestershire," passim; E 301/1; E 301/58; E 301/17.

111. Cf., for example, Essex (E 301/19) with Suffolk (E 301/45), or Cambridgeshire (E 315/68, ff. 512-513) with Bedfordshire (E 301/1); and cf. Table 2.2, note a.

112. E 301/58; E 301/17.

113. Among Essex wills, one of seven endowing obits provided for alms for the poor (Benton, "Essex Wills," 234-269); in Yorkshire, seven of thirty-two (Raine, *Testamenta Eboracensia*, V); in Somerset, one of ten (Weaver, *Somerset Medieval Wills, 1383-1500*, 164-398, and ibid., *1501-1530*).

114. C. W. Foster, *Lincoln Wills*, I, 121; Foster and Thompson, "Chantry Certificates for Lincolnshire," *A.A.S.R.P.*, 36 (1921-1922), 294.

115. Brinklow, *Lamentacyon*, 88; E. G. C. F. Atchley, "The Halleway Chauntry at the Parish Church of All Saints, Bristol," *Trans. Bristol and Gloucestershire Archaeol. Soc.*, 24 (1901), 84; E 301/19/193.

116. *Y.C.C.*, I, 56; Maclean, "Chantry Certificates, Gloucestershire," 252-253; E 301/83, m. 4; E 301/53/20; Leland, *Itinerary*, II, 27, 49-50. See also a similar case in Langport (Soms) (Green, *Survey of Somerset*, 115); E 301/31/35; E 301/58/85; E 301/3/9; Maclean, "Chantry Certificates, Gloucestershire," 239-240; *Y.C.C.*, I, 82, and II, 273, 316; E 301/53/55.

117. For Houghton Regis, E 301/4/20; for Ashburton, Snell, *Chantry Certificates for Devon*, 39; Hanham, "The Suppression of the Chantries in Ashburton," 113; for a similar example in Milverton, see Green, *Survey of Somerset*, 38. For London, E 301/

34/77 (St. Mary-le-Bow), E 301/34/107 (St. Bride's). For Birmingham, E 301/31/28.

118. Thomas S. Kuhn, *The Structure of Scientific Revolutions* (Chicago, University of Chicago Press, 1962), chap. 10.

Chapter 3: The Founding of the Chantries: Chronological Contours

1. 7 Edward I (*S.R.*, I, 51). For discussions of this statute, see K. L. Wood-Legh, *Studies in the Church Life under Edward III* (Cambridge, 1934), 60-61, and J. M. W. Bean, *The Decline of English Feudalism, 1215-1540* (Manchester, 1968), 52-54.

2. Bean, *Decline,* 55. The first license authorizing the foundation of an intercessory institution was granted on 18 January 1281 to Robert de Castre for a stipendiary priest's service in Caister-on-Sea (Norfolk) (*C.P.R., 1272-1281*, 423).

3. The number of mortmain licenses granted for the founding of chantries (calendared in the *C.P.R.*) rose from 10 in 1390 and 6 in 1391 to 77 in 1392.

4. Hill, " 'A Chaunterie for Soules,' " 252-253.

5. Some chantries disappeared when their endowments were seized by impious patrons or self-interested descendants of the founders.

6. For the chantries in our four sample shires which had disappeared by the time of the chantry surveys, see:

Essex: St Ch 2/18/166; B.L. Harleian MS. 133, ff. 17v, 28; Reg. Fitzjames, ff. 26v, 55v, 78, 81v; Reg. Bonner, f. 158v; W. G. Benham, ed., *The Red Paper Book of Colchester* (Colchester, Essex County Standard, 1902), 74-75; Newcourt, *Repertorium*, II, 181; Morant, *History*, I, 243; ibid., II, 166, 195, 226, 231, 314, 389, 486; Hill, " 'A Chaunterie for Soules,' " 249.

Warwicks: Reg. Ghinucci, f. 62v; Reg. Rowland Lee, f. 3; Dugdale, *Antiquities*, I, 61, 121, 172, 173, 178, 438-439, 466, 467; II, 807; *V.C.H., Warwickshire*, III, 146; V, 39, 67, 83, 116, 165; VI, 25-26, 29-30, 56; Benjamin Poole, *Coventry: Its History and Antiquities* (London, 1870), 136, 183.

Wilts: J. E. Jackson, "Ancient Chapels," *W.A.N.H.M.*, 10 (1867), 285, 288, 321; *V.C.H., Wiltshire*, VII, 26, 64; VIII, 56, 83, 87, 176-177, 247, 260; Hoare, *Modern Wiltshire*, I, iii, 182; ibid., V, i, 25; John Aubrey, *Topographical Collections for Wiltshire*, ed. J. E. Jackson (Devizes, 1862), 196n.-198n., 436.

Yorks: SP 1/37, ff. 175-177; Y.M.L., Torre MS. L 1(7), 1423, 1431-1432, 1435, 1440, 1467, 1497, 1498, 1503, 1513, 1520-1521, 1539, 1586, 1611, 1625-1626, 1631, 1645, 1651, 1671, 1693; Torre MS. L 1(8), I, 25, 33, 34, 90, 106, 146, 159, 160, 205, 234-236, 268, 299, 317-318, 478, 557, 615, 646, 739-740; II, 374, 396, 572, 596, 1028; Torre MS. L 1(9), 35, 119, 287, 337, 393, 479, 862, 870, 998, 1001, 1019-1020, 1450; Torre MS. L 1(10), 97, 1520, 1552, 1594; *Y.A.J.*, 24(1917), 69; ibid., 33(1938), 251, 281-284; Y.A.S.R.S., 129(1967), 115; George Poulson, *The History and Antiquities of the Seigniory of Holderness*, 2 vols. (London, 1840-1841), I, 412; Whitaker, *History of Craven*, 41-42; John Tickell, *History of Hull* (Hull, 1798), 798-802, 809-811; R. B. Dobson, "The Foundation of Perpetual Chantries by the Citizens of Medieval York," in Cuming, *Studies in Church History*, IV, 24. Cf. Wood-Legh, 207.

7. Cf. Wood-Legh, *Church Life*, 91.

8. E.g., according to the 1548 chantry commissioners the chantry of Biddenham Bridge in Bromham (Beds) "doth appear by a license" to have been founded on 2 June 1473 (E 301/1/10). I could find no reference to this in the *C.P.R.* For other examples, see *Y.C.C.*, II, 260; E 301/13/52.

9. *S.R.*, III, 988.

10. Foster, *Lincoln Wills*, II, 28, 190.

11. Wood-Legh, *Church Life*, 69.

12. For what follows, see Sir William Holdsworth, *A History of English Law*, IV

(London, 1924), 407-443; J. L. Barton, "The Medieval Use," *Law Quarterly Review,* 81 (1965), 562-577; and E. W. Ives, "The Genesis of the Statute of Uses," *E.H.R.*, 82 (1967), 674-675.

13. Ives, "Genesis," 674, quoting Sir Edward Coke, *Reports* (London, 1738), I, 121v; Bean, *Decline,* 180, 220-234; S. E. Thorne, ed., *Prerogativa Regis* (New Haven, 1949), viii.

14. 15 Ric. II, c.5 (*S.R.,* II, 79-80); Bean, *Decline,* 126.

15. Holdsworth, *History,* IV, 443-444.

16. For typical cases, see E 301/13/28 and E 301/25/54.

17. Some of the chantries founded by deeds of feoffment had also been duly licensed by the crown, e.g., the Robert Thirsk chantry in Thirsk (N.R., Yorks) (*Y.C.C.,* I, 90-92; *C.P.R., 1413-1416,* 361).

18. E 301/21; E 301/45.

19. B.L. Hargrave MS. 4, f. 297. Professor L. W. Abbott kindly drew my attention to this anonymously authored report.

20. *Y.C.C.,* II, 255-256. For Procter's will, see Raine, *Testamenta Eboracensia,* V, 182-188. For similar examples, see J. W. Clay and E. W. Crossley, eds., *Halifax Wills, 1389-1544* (Leeds, n.d.), 34, 78-79; W. H. Jones, "Terumber's Endowments at Trowbridge," *W.A.N.H.M.*, 10 (1867), 247-252; Foster, *Lincoln Wills,* II, 80-81; and Weaver, *Somerset Medieval Wills, 1501-1530,* 52-57.

21. Weaver, *Somerset Medieval Wills, 1383-1500,* 197.

22. The first certain example that I have found dates from 1464, from the parish of St. Clement Danes, London (E 315/67, ii, f. 320).

23. E 301/45.

24. For examples, see E 301/54/15; E 301/95, f. 8v; Maclean, "Chantry Certificates, Gloucestershire," 287; Foster, *Lincoln Wills,* I, 154.

25. Raine, *Testamenta Eboracensia,* V, 288; E 36/258, f. 115v; Weaver, *Somerset Medieval Wills, 1531-1558,* 14; Foster, *Lincoln Wills,* I, 70; ibid., II, 78; Clay, *Testamenta Eboracensia,* VI, 135.

26. H. C. Maxwell-Lyte, *Historical Notes on the Use of the Great Seal of England* (London, 1926), 358-359.

27. Ibid., 332-338. Sandra Raban has shown that in one mid-fourteenth-century itemization the expenses for an amortization "amounted to a surcharge of five per cent." This figure could vary considerably; the fees might also be remitted or substantially reduced by order of the king ("Mortmain in Medieval England," *Past and Present,* 62 [1974], 18).

28. Wood-Legh, *Church Life,* 62.

29. *C.P.R., 1446-1452,* 65.

30. The crown required a fine of five times the annual value of the land which Sir John Fastolf was amortizing for his proposed collegiate foundation in Caister (Norfolk) (Henry Fylungley to Fastolf, 17 July [1456?], James Gairdner, ed., *The Paston Letters,* new ed., 3 vols. [Westminster, 1896], I, 397). This fine was exceptionally severe for the 1450s (Table 3.6). Fastolf felt that his long service to the crown entitled him to more favorable treatment. He therefore wrote to his cousin to see whether the archbishop of Canterbury or the bishop of Winchester would intercede with the authorities for permission to amortize lands "without any great fine" (Fastolf to John Paston, 18 November 1456, Gairdner, *Paston Letters,* I, 411).

31. *C.P.R., 1461-1467,* 47.

32. Thorne, *Prerogativa Regis,* xxxvii.

33. He was licensed to amortize lands worth up to £50 p.a. (*C.P.R., 1476-1485,* 276).

34. The earliest mention I have seen of a mortmain fine being "paid in the king's

chamber" is dated May 1485 under Richard III (*C.P.R., 1476-1485*, 524-525).

35. Those which have survived are E 101/413/2/1, 2, 3; E 36/123; and B.L. Lansdowne MS. 127.

36. G. R. Elton, "Henry VII: Rapacity and Remorse," *H.J.*, 1 (1958), 22.

37. E 101/413/2/2, f. 50v; *C.P.R., 1485-1494*, 465. See also E 101/413/2/2, f. 51; *C.P.R., 1485-1494*, 450.

38. B.L. Lansdowne MS. 127, f. 4; *C.P.R., 1494-1509*, 394-395; *Y.C.C.*, I, 24, 205. See also E 101/413/2/3, f. 24; E 36/123, f. 9v; *C.P.R., 1494-1509*, 416.

39. E 36/123, which does contain Chamber records from the reign of Henry VIII, records only the receipts of the fifteenth and tenth which were raised in 1512 (f. 61 to end of the document).

40. W. C. Richardson, *Tudor Chamber Administration, 1485-1547* (Baton Rouge, Louisiana State University Press, 1952), 219.

41. C 66/628, m. 2 (*L.P.*, II, i, 2660); C 66/630, m. 17 (*L.P.*, II, ii, 3149); E 101/ 220/14 (*L.P.*, III, i, 105 [5]); E 101/220/16 (*L.P.*, III, i, 967 [17]); E 101/220/20 (*L.P.*, III, ii, 2411); E 101/222/4 (*L.P.*, VI, 929 [18]); *L.P.*, VII, 1026 (20); E 101/ 222/8 (*L.P.*, X, 226 [13]).

42. Cf. the codicil on the 1517 will of John Lord Zouche: "And when there shall arise and grow of the same as much money as will get a license of Our Sovereign Lord the King to amortise the said manors, or as much thereof as will serve for a perpetual chantry for two priests" (Weaver, *Somerset Medieval Wills, 1501-1530*, 246).

43. *C.P.R., 1494-1509*, 394, 395, 416, 418, 452, 461; E 101/413/2/3, f. 24; B.L. Lansdowne MS. 127, ff. 4, 5, 9v, 11v, 35v, 49v.

44. E 301/13/68. In a document referring to a London foundation of 1464 (E 315/67, ii, f. 320) there is already a hint that founders may have had difficulty in persuading the crown to grant mortmain licenses ("if the rulers & governors of the said fraternity purchase a license within the said term [of ninety-nine years] to amortise a livelihood of the said fraternity"). To the best of my knowledge this was an isolated incident, and the frequent assertion of unambiguously stated fears that the crown might not grant mortmain licenses does not begin until the 1490s. But perhaps additional research into fifteenth-century wills would demonstrate that the crown, some years earlier than I have suggested, became restive at the amount of land which was being alienated into mortmain and decided to take preventive counter-measures. If so, this might help explain why there appear to have been so few licensed chantry foundations for many of the decades of the fifteenth century (Table 3.1).

45. Raine, *Testamenta Eboracensia*, V, 15. For similar cases, see Foster, *Lincoln Wills*, I, 162; Foster and Thompson, "Chantry Certificates of Lincolnshire," *A.A.S.R.P.*, 37 (1923-1925), 56; *L.P.*, I (rev. ed.), i, 381 (69).

46. Foster, *Lincoln Wills*, II, 29.

47. E 301/1/24, 35-36; E 301/11/17; Foster and Thompson, "Chantry Certificates for Lincolnshire," *A.A.S.R.P.*, 37 (1923-1925), 103; Snell, *Chantry Certificates for Devon*, 12-13; Weaver, *Somerset Medieval Wills, 1501-1530*, 159-160; Foster, *Lincoln Wills*, II, 28, 190-191; Nicolas, *Testamenta Vetusta*, II, 543.

48. E 36/258, f. 115v; M.A. Farrow, ed., *Index of Wills Proved in the Consistory Court of Norwich, 1370-1550*, Norfolk Rec. Soc., 16 (1943), pt. i, 112; *V.C.H., War-wickshire*, II, 342. See also E 301/45/16; E 36/258, ff. 16, 111; B.L. Harleian MS. 601, f. 47v; Foster, *Lincoln Wills*, II, 75, 127-128; Foster and Thompson, "Chantry Certificates for Lincolnshire," *A.A.S.R.P.*, 37 (1923-1925), 254.

49. See the omnibus anti-clerical draft of 1531, one clause of which would have forbidden any additional alienations into mortmain, although it was revised to allow the king to make new foundations if he so desired (SP 6/7, f. 31). For comment on this

draft, see G. R. Elton, *Reform and Renewal: Thomas Cromwell and the Common Weal* (Cambridge, 1973), 71-76; Stanford E. Lehmberg, *The Reformation Parliament, 1529-1536* (Cambridge, 1970), 120-121.

50. Cook, *Mediaeval Chantries*, 76; E. L. Cutts, *Parish Priests and Their People in the Middle Ages in England* (London, S.P.C.K., 1917), 471; Thompson, "Certificates of the Shropshire Chantries," 289.

51. 21 Henry VIII, c.13 (*S.R.*, III, 295). On this statute see also Dickens, *English Reformation*, 103.

52. For example, the act was invoked against the parson of Benacre (Suffolk) for having accepted an annual stipend of 4s. for singing for the souls of the members of the guild in his parish (SP 2/P, ff. 137-138).

53. *L.P.*, IV, iii, 6264; C 82/686/8 (*L.P.*, VII, 1026 [20]).

54. In spite of this, there were still people who wanted to obtain mortmain licenses for chantries (cf. Nicolas, *Testamenta Vetusta*, II, 661-663).

55. 23 Henry VIII, c.10 (*S.R.*, III, 378). On this statute, see Jordan, *Philanthropy*, 115, and Lehmberg, *Reformation Parliament*, 141-142.

56. E 321/32/14; Foster and Thompson, eds., "Chantry Certificates for Lincolnshire," *A.A.S.R.P.*, 37 (1923-1925), 79, 103.

57. For foundations contrary to the 1532 statute, see E 301/17/10; E 301/45/12, 14; E 301/54/50; E 36/259, f. 269v; Hussey, *Kent Chantries*, 1-2; Thompson, "Certificates of the Shropshire Chantries," 378; Clay, *Testamenta Eboracensia*, VI, 135, 170-171; Weaver, *Somerset Medieval Wills, 1531-1558*, 14; Snell, *Chantry Certificates for Devon*, 7-8.

58. James Raine, Jr., ed., *Wills and Inventories from the Registry of the Archdeaconry of Richmond*, Surtees Soc., 26 (1853), 59; Clay, *Testamenta Eboracensia*, VI, 62.

59. Owen, *Church and Society in Medieval Lincolnshire*, 94.

60. Miss Wood-Legh (*Church Life*, 125) also dates the period of the greatest popularity of chantry foundations in the nation as a whole in the first half of the fourteenth century.

61. David S. Gillespie, "The Changing Outlook of Chaucerian England" (Ph.D. diss., Michigan State University, 1971), 203, 220, 236-238.

62. Cf. Jordan, *Philanthropy*, 51; Wood-Legh, 128-129.

63. W. K. Jordan, *The Social Institutions of Lancashire*, Chetham Soc., 3rd ser. 11 (1962), 77.

64. Jordan, *Charities of Rural England*, 365-366.

65. Clark and Slack, *Crisis and Order*, 10-11; Bartlett, "Expansion and Decline," 27-31.

66. Elizabeth Lamond, ed., *A Discourse of the Common Weal of this Realm of England* (Cambridge, 1893), 18.

67. Frederick Harrison, *Life in a Medieval College* (London, John Murray, 1952), 165. For the decline of the urban chantries of York, see D. M. Palliser, *The Reformation in York, 1534-1553*, Borthwick Papers, 40 (York, 1971), 4; Dobson, "Foundation," 34-35.

68. *V.C.H., London*, I, 205. Cf. W. K. Jordan, *The Charities of London, 1480-1660* (London, George Allen and Unwin, 1960), 273-276; J. A. F. Thomson, "Piety and Charity in Late Medieval London," *J.E.H.*, 16 (1965), 191-192. That as many as thirteen chantries were founded in London in this period may reflect the belief, alluded to by Sir Thomas More (*Workes*, 333), that "in the city of London, to which there is granted by authority of parliament, that men may there devise their lands into mortmain by their testaments." It is unclear to what act of parliament More was re-

ferring. Cf. H. M. Chew, "Mortmain in Medieval London," *E.H.R.*, 60 (1945), 1-15.

69. W. K. Jordan, "The Forming of the Charitable Institutions of the West of England," *Trans. American Philosophical Soc.*, n.s. 50, pt. 8 (1960), 69; Jordan, *Social Institutions of Lancashire*, 77; R. S. Schofield, "The Geographical Distribution of Wealth in England, 1334-1649," *Ec.H.R.*, 2nd ser. 18 (1965), 504-507.

70. Knowles, *Religious Orders* III, 6; W. K. Jordan, *Social Institutions in Kent, 1480-1660 (Archaeologia Cantiana*, 75 [1961]), 99, 103.

71. Thomson, "Piety and Charity," 194.

72. For examples of the decline of other medieval beliefs and observances by the eve of the Reformation, see Keith Thomas, *Religion and the Decline of Magic* (London, Weidenfeld & Nicolson, 1971), 29, 74; Royal Commission on Historical Monuments, *A Guide to Saint Albans Cathedral*, 7th ed. (London, H.M.S.O., 1967), 16; Dickens, *English Reformation*, 5.

Chapter 4: "Extinguishing the Flames of Purgatory" (I)

1. Jordan, *Edward VI*, II, 181; A. J. Mason, *Purgatory* (London, Longmans, Green, 1901), 1, 3.

2. Nicholas Partridge to Heinrich Bullinger, 17 September 1538, in Hastings Robinson, ed., *Original Letters Relative to the English Reformation*, 2 vols. (Parker Soc., Cambridge, 1847), II, 612; Barnes to Johannes Aepinus, 21 May 1540, ibid., 617.

3. E.g., SP 1/130, f. 141v (*L.P.*, XIII, i, 604).

4. Cf. Sadler to Henry VIII, 9 April 1543, B.L. Add. MS. 32,650, f. 146v (*L.P.*, XVIII, i, 391).

5. John Wyclif, *The English Works*, ed. F. D. Matthew, E.E.T.S., original ser. 74 (London, 1880), 81-82, 201; idem, *Tracts and Treatises*, ed. Robert Vaughan (London, 1845), 74; idem, *Polemical Works in Latin*, ed. Rudolf Buddensieg, 2 vols. (London, 1883), I, 148; Foxe, III, 21. Cf. Herbert B. Workman, *John Wyclif: A Study of the English Medieval Church*, 2 vols. (Oxford, 1926), II, 18-19; Wood-Legh, 305, 305n.

6. Foxe, III, 118, 181-183; James Gairdner, *Lollardy and the Reformation in England*, 4 vols. (London, 1908-1913), I, 43, 45.

7. Foxe, III, 345, 597; J. A. F. Thomson, *The Later Lollards, 1414-1520* (London, 1965), 31-32, 128.

8. Foxe, IV, 133, 584.

9. Strype, I, ii, 51-52. And cf. SP 1/38, ff. 16v-17 (*L.P.*, IV, i, 2073 [1]); Foxe, IV, 181-182; Dickens, *Lollards and Protestants*, 19; Thomson, *Later Lollards*, 89, 136.

10. J. Fines, "Heresy Trials in the Diocese of Coventry and Lichfield, 1511-1512," *J.E.H.*, 14 (1962), 160-174; Thomson, *Later Lollards*, 108-109, 112-113; Reg. Warham, ff. 179-179v.

11. Claire Cross, "Popular Piety and the Records of the Unestablished Churches, 1460-1660," in Derek Baker, ed., *Studies in Church History*, 11 (Oxford, 1975), 274, 278; E. G. Rupp, *Studies in the Making of the English Protestant Tradition* (Cambridge, 1947), 5; Dickens, *Lollards and Protestants*, 12-13.

12. Julius Köstlin, *Luthers Theologie in ihrer geschichtlichen Entwicklung und ihrem inneren Zusammenhange*, 2nd ed., 2 vols. (Stuttgart, J.F. Steinkopf, 1901), I, 207-209, 270, 314, 373-376; II, 340-341.

13. Martin Luther, *Ein Widderruff vom Fegefeur* (Wittenberg, Hans Lufft, 1530), in Luther, *Werke*, Weimarer Ausgabe, XXX, ii, 367-390.

14. Ibid., sigs. Eiij^v, Bij-Bij^v, Fiij^v, Eij^v.

15. Strype, I, i, 56-61.

16. Henry VIII, *Assertio septem sacramentorum; or An Assertion of the Seven Sacraments, against Martin Luther,* trans. T[homas] W[ebster] (London, 1688), 3.

17. According to John Frith, Fisher was the "first patron and defender of this fantasy [purgatory]" (*Whole Workes,* II, 51); Edward Surtz, *The Works and Days of John Fisher* (Cambridge, Mass., Harvard University Press, 1967), 106-107, 313; Fisher, *Two Fruytfull Sermons,* sigs. C-D4^v.

18. William Tyndale, *Doctrinal Treatises,* ed. Henry Walter (Parker Soc., Cambridge, 1848), 158-159, 236-238, 302-303; Fish, *Supplicacyon,* 11; cf. chap. 3 above, n. 50.

19. More, *Workes,* 288-339.

20. Ibid., 289, 306. More noted ruefully that the then-anonymous *Supplicacyon for the Beggers* was "nameless" and that it "neither was put up to the king, nor beareth any date" (ibid., 289, 297). His antagonist, irritatingly enough, was not playing by the rules.

21. Ibid., 299.

22. Ibid., 316, 334, 338.

23. Ibid., 288.

24. John Frith, *Disputacion* (in *Whole Workes,* II, 3-60), 5.

25. Ibid., 12, 17, and esp. 34-36.

26. Ibid., 23.

27. Ibid., 18, 22, 27, 79.

28. John Gough Nichols, ed., *Narratives of the Days of the Reformation,* Camden Soc., orig. ser. 77 (1859), 55; and cf. Foxe, IV, 683, 700; ibid., V, 38; *L.P.,* V, 583; ibid., XVIII, ii, 546 (p. 312); John Harryson [John Bale], *Yet a Course at the Romyshe Foxe* (Zürich, Olyuer Iacobson, 1543), f. 47v; William A. Clebsch, *England's Earliest Protestants, 1520-1535* (New Haven, Conn., 1964), 281.

29. *L.P.,* VI, 402; J. F. Mozley, *William Tyndale* (London, 1937), 271-272; Allen G. Chester, *Hugh Latimer: Apostle to the English* (Philadelphia, 1954), 94; Clebsch, *England's Earliest Protestants,* 219-223; Norman T. Burns, *Christian Mortalism from Tyndale to Milton* (Cambridge, Mass., Harvard University Press, 1972), 106-111.

30. The *Disputacion* was not Frith's last word on purgatory. In response to Rastell's *New Boke,* replying to his arguments, Frith—although in prison—in late 1532 wrote a brief rejoinder which was published posthumously (*An Other Boke against Rastel* [Antwerp, M. de Keyser, after 1537; *S.T.C.* 11,385]; reprinted in *Whole Workes,* 60-76; cf. Clebsch, *England's Earliest Protestants,* 110n., 324). Frith not only defended his contentions against Rastell's criticisms, but also continued his attack on his major antagonists by pointing out the multiple discrepancies between their descriptions of purgatory as a place (*Whole Workes,* II, 67). He also discussed the subject of purgatory with Rastell in person. It was apparently Frith, more than any other person, who was responsible for Rastell's conversion to Protestantism (anonymous introduction to *An Other Boke,* 61; John Bale, *Illustrium Maioris Britanniae Scriptorum* [Ipswich, John Overton, 1548], f. 222; Clebsch, *England's Earliest Protestants,* 109).

31. B.L. Harleian MS. 422, f. 90 (*L.P.,* V, App., 30).

32. Strype, III, i, 572; Foxe, IV, 680; *L.P.,* V, 297.

33. Clebsch, *England's Earliest Protestants,* 107-108; Dickens, *English Reformation,* 96; see also Charles Wriothesley, *A Chronicle of England during the Reigns of the Tudors,* Camden Soc., n.s. 11 (1875), 72-73.

34. Edward Hall, *Chronicle* (London, 1809), 796-797; Foxe, V, 31-32; *The Testament of Master Wylliam Tracie esquier expounded both by William Tindall and Ihon*

Frith ([Antwerp?], 1535). Thomas Cromwell was among those who possessed a copy (E 36/139, f. 12 [*L.P.*, VII, 923, vii]).

35. Christopher Saint German, *A Treatise Concernynge the Diuision betwene the Spirytualtie and Temporaltie* (London, R. Redman, 1532), sigs. Aiij^v-Aiiij^v.

36. Wilkins, III, 727-737.

37. Strype, III, i, 157-158; ibid., III, ii, 194, 199; Chester, *Hugh Latimer*, 70; Foxe, IV, 699.

38. Chester, *Hugh Latimer*, 71-72; Latimer, *Works*, II, 219-220.

39. Latimer to Warham, [March ?] 1532, Latimer, *Works*, II, 353; Wilkins, III, 747; Harold S. Darby, *Hugh Latimer* (London, Epworth Press, 1953), 78-79.

40. For an excellent study of the Bristol preaching crisis, see G. R. Elton, *Policy and Police: The Enforcement of the Reformation in the Age of Thomas Cromwell* (Cambridge, 1972), 112-117; Latimer to Ralph Morice, [dated May/June by Elton] 1533, Latimer, *Works*, II, 357-366 (*L.P.*, VI, 247); Hilsey to Thomas Bagarde, 2 May 1533, SP 6/1, f. 82 (*L.P.*, VI, 433); John Bartholomew and other commissioners to Cromwell, 11 July 1533, B.L. Cotton MSS., Cleopatra E IV, f. 73v (*L.P.*, VI, 799).

41. Hubbardine's doctrinal statements allegedly included: "The Church knoweth those things that Christ preached and did which were not written in scripture"; "it was not necessary for scripture to be written"; "the blood of Christ is not sufficient for us without the blood of martyrs" (SP 6/3, ff. 56-57).

42. Bagarde to Cromwell, 28 May 1533, SP 2/P, f. 161 (*L.P.*, VII, 722, which is incorrect in dating this letter 1534).

43. B.L. Cotton MSS., Cleopatra E IV, f. 73 (*L.P.*, VI, 799); SP 2/0, ff. 196-199 (*L.P.*, VI, 799 [2]); SP 1/94, f. 3 (*L.P.*, VIII, 1001).

44. Cranmer to Richard Sampson, 9 January 1534, Cranmer, *Works*, II, 309; Sampson to Cranmer, 10 January 1534, SP 1/82, f. 47 (*L.P.*, VII, 32).

45. Lacey Baldwin Smith, *Tudor Prelates and Politics, 1536-1558* (Princeton, 1953), 161-165.

46. For developments of this argument, see John Frith, *Disputacion*, in *Whole Workes*, II, 59; Fish, *Supplicacyon*, 10-11; Latimer, *Works*, II, 332; and an anonymous treatise against the "power of Rome" (SP 1/105, ff. 61-62). This argument, which Frith and Tyndale doubtlessly picked up from Luther, did not in fact originate with the German reformer — certain of the medieval scholastics had already hazarded it, as had Wyclif and the early Lollards. See Walther Köhler, *Luthers 95 Thesen samt seinen Resolutionen* (Leipzig, J. C. Hinrichs'sche Buchhandlung, 1903), 87-88; Roland H. Bainton, *Here I Stand: A Life of Martin Luther* (Nashville, Abingdon-Cokesbury, 1950), 81-82; Wyclif, *English Works*, 81-82; Foxe, III, 118.

47. Tyndale, *Doctrinal Treatises*, 303. Cf. the case of Nicholas Came, who in 1537 at Saint Faith's fair in Norwich exclaimed, "Rome shall up again, and purgatory is found!" (SP 1/125, f. 163 [*L.P.*, XII, ii, 864]).

48. Foxe, V, 601.

49. SP 2/P, ff. 139-140, 142-143 (*L.P.*, VII, 155); Cranmer, *Works*, II, 280; SP 1/82, ff. 273-274 (*L.P.*, VII, 308); SP 1/83, f. 38 (*L.P.*, VII, 406); SP 2/P, ff. 158-159 (*L.P.*, VII, 449).

50. Cranmer to a bishop, Easter week [5-11 April] 1534, Cranmer, *Works*, II, 283-284.

51. Cranmer to Latimer, [May?] 1534, ibid., 296-297.

52. This paragraph is based on Cranmer's letter of 24 May 1534 to Thomas Thirlby (ibid., 292-293). That the "billet from the king's highness" mentioned in the letter is the order for preaching is indicated by several considerations mentioned by J. E. Cox (ibid., 292n.) and by the following manuscript evidence: Cranmer's letter notes that

the third of the questionable passages in the billet "is on the second side in the fourteenth line, whereof I would have known . . . if the king's grace would have left out 'miracles' which all the bishops do think good to be left out." In the final version of the order (B.L. Cotton MSS., Cleopatra E V, ff. 294-297), the phrase concerning miracles occurs on line 13 on the dorse of the first folio (f. 294v).

53. Cranmer reported that "all the bishops" had preferred that the order not prohibit preaching about miracles (*Works*, II, 292). It is not clear, however, to which bishops he was referring. According to the occasional references to various bishops in the *L.P.*, it is apparent that some of the bishops (such as Gardiner of Winchester and Sherburn of Chichester) returned to their dioceses soon after the 31 March prorogation of convocation (*L.P.*, VII, 441, 525). Bishop Longland of Lincoln, on the other hand, seems to have remained in the London area until well into May (ibid., 639), and other bishops may have done likewise.

54. Edward Lee to Henry VIII, 14 June 1535, in Henry Ellis, ed., *Original Letters Illustrative of English History* (henceforth Ellis), 3 series, 11 vols. (London, 1824-1846), 3rd ser., II, 326 (*L.P.*, VIII, 869).

55. B.L. Cotton MSS., Cleopatra E V, ff. 294-297; Cranmer, *Works*, II, 460-462. The exact dating of the document is problematic. As Cranmer indicated in his letter to Thirlby (n. 52 above), the document was substantially complete on 24 May. But Chapuys, who wrote to Charles V on 7 June, first mentioned it in his next letter of 23 June (*L.P.*, VII, 809, 871). Furthermore, a year later Archbishop Lee wrote to the king (14 June 1535, in Ellis, 3rd ser. 2, 327) that the final version of the order had not reached him in Yorkshire until the week prior to "the second Sunday after Trinity Sunday" (14 June 1534). Thus it is probable that Cranmer issued the order on preaching in the first or second week of June. Archbishop Lee was clear in his assertion that Cranmer's order was binding on the province of York; cf. Gairdner, *Lollardy and the Reformation*, II, 35.

56. Chapuys to Charles V, 23 June 1534, *L.P.*, VII, 871.

57. SP 1/91, f. 176 (*L.P.*, VIII, 480); SP 2/R, f. 21 (*L.P.*, VIII, 625); see also *L.P.*, VIII, 570, 626.

58. Although no copy of this circular has survived, one can learn a great deal about it from other sources. Cranmer and Tunstall both noted that it was sent from Greenwich on 3 June (Cranmer, *Works*, II, 307; *L.P.*, VIII, 849); other bishops also acknowledged receipt of it (ibid., 821, 832, 833, 835, 836, 839, 869). From the king's letter of 25 June to the justices of the peace, and from Archbishop Lee's letters of 14 June and 1 July, we get useful indications of its tone and contents (Strype, I, ii, 210 [*L.P.*, VIII, 921]; Ellis, 3rd ser. 2, 324-332, 338-339 [*L.P.*, VIII, 869, 963]).

59. Cranmer to Cromwell, 8 October 1535, Cranmer, *Works*, II, 311. Cromwell's attitude to purgatory at this time may be deduced from the letters to him of various of his supplicants (*L.P.*, IX, 134, 135, 723, 740).

60. B.L. Cotton MSS., Titus B I, ff. 466-467 (*L.P.*, VII, 420); E 36/139, ff. 59v, 64, 66 (*L.P.*, VII, 923).

61. SP 1/87, f. 114 (*L.P.*, VII, 1537); SP 1/92, f. 132 (*L.P.*, VIII, 637); *Fac. Off. Reg.*, 7, 39; Cranmer to Cromwell, 18 January 1536, B.L. Cotton MSS., Vespasian F XIII, f. 152 (*L.P.*, X, 120).

62. SP 1/94, f. 2 (*L.P.*, VIII, 1000 [2]); SP 1/94, ff. 24-25 (*L.P.*, VIII, 1025); B.L. Cotton MSS., Cleopatra E V, ff. 397-398 (*L.P.*, IX, 230); Cranmer to Cromwell, 12 October 1535, Cranmer, *Works*, II, 311.

63. Lee to Cromwell, 2 November and 29 October 1535, SP 1/98, ff. 194, 103-103v (*L.P.*, IX, 742, 704).

64. SP 1/99, ff. 202v-203 (*L.P.*, IX, 1059).

65. SP 3/14, f. 14 (*L.P.*, IX, 583); Antony Waite to Lady Lisle, 12 November 1535, SP 3/14, f. 25 (*L.P.*, IX, 812).

66. Stokesley to Cromwell, 17 July 1535, SP 1/94, ff. 98v-99 (*L.P.*, VIII, 1054); Hilsey to Cromwell [17 July 1535], SP 1/88, f. 82 (*L.P.*, VII, 1643, which places this letter at the end of 1534); Thomas Bedyll to Cromwell, 15 July 1535, ibid., VIII, 1043.

67. B.L. Add. MS. 48,022, ff. 87-88.

68. Henry VIII to the bishop of Llandaff, 7 January 1536, SP 1/101, f. 33 (*L.P.*, X, 45). That this was in fact a general letter to all the bishops is indicated by a corrected draft in Wriothesley's hand which is endorsed, "The king's writ to the bishops commanding them to have regard to place good preachers in their dioceses" (SP 6/2, ff. 126-129 [*L.P.*, VII, 750, which erroneously dates this document at the end of May 1534]).

69. B.L. Cotton MSS., Cleopatra E IV, f. 8; ibid., Cleopatra E V, f. 310 (*L.P.*, X, 46); Chapuys to Charles V, 21 January 1536, *C.S.P.Span.*, V, ii, 20.

70. Lee to Cromwell, 24 January 1536, B.L. Cotton MSS., Cleopatra E V, ff. 101-101v (*L.P.*, X, 172). According to Dr. L. P. Fairfield, this friar "certainly sounds like John Bale" (*John Bale: Mythmaker for the English Reformation* [West Lafayette, Ind., Purdue University Press, 1976], 37).

71. Longland to Cromwell, 5 May 1536, SP 1/103, ff. 234-235 (*L.P.*, X, 804); *Fac. Off. Reg.*, 39; *V.C.H.*, *Buckinghamshire*, III, 109. On Swinnerton, who had already had an eventful career as a writer and itinerant preacher, see C. H. Cooper and T. Cooper, eds., *Athenae Cantabrigienses* (Cambridge, 1858), I, 124; *L.P.*, VII, 1067 (2); *L.P.*, VII, 923 (7).

72. SP 1/113, f. 108v (*L.P.*, XI, 1424). Although the Sussex articles refer to *John* Swynnerton, it is probable that he was the same man as the Thomas Swynnerton about whom there is considerable evidence, and who is known to have traveled widely as an itinerant preacher under the pseudonym of *John* Roberts (Cooper, *Athenae*, I, 124). Longland unfortunately never saw fit to refer to "Sir Swynnerton" by his Christian name.

73. Longland to Cromwell, 12 and 16 May 1536, SP 1/103, ff. 274, 304 (*L.P.*, X, 850, 891); SP 1/104, f. 157 (*L.P.*, X, 1099); SP 1/113, ff. 108v-109 (*L.P.*, XI, 1424).

74. Bell to Stokesley, 9 June 1536, SP 1/104, f. 157 (*L.P.*, X, 1099).

75. See Millar Maclure, *The Paul's Cross Sermons, 1534-1642* (Toronto, 1958), 185-186; Elton, *Policy and Police*, 214-215.

76. *L.P.*, VIII, 1043, 1054.

77. Thomas Dorset to the mayor of Plymouth and others, 13 March 1536, Thomas Wright, ed., *Three Chapters of Letters Relating to the Suppression of the Monasteries* (henceforth Wright), Camden Soc., orig. ser. 26 (1843), 38 (*L.P.*, X, 462); M. A. S. Hume, ed., *Chronicle of Henry VIII of England* (London, 1889), 87-88.

78. Chapuys to Charles V, 10 February 1536, *L.P.*, X, 282, and to Granvelle, 17 February 1536, ibid., 308.

79. Dr. Pedro Ortiz to the Empress, 22 March 1536, *C.S.P.Span.*, V, ii, 70.

80. SP 1/102, ff. 73-74 (*L.P.*, X, 346); Thomas Dorset to the mayor of Plymouth and others, 13 March 1536, Wright, 37-38; B.L. Add. MS. 48,022, ff. 88-88v. On Cardmaker's subsequent career (he was to be burned at the stake in 1555), see J. Venn and J. A. Venn, *Alumni Cantabrigienses*, pt. 1 (Cambridge, 1922-1927), I, 291; Hughes, *Reformation*, II, 66, 298n.; Foxe, VII, 77-80.

81. SP 6/2, f. 106 (*L.P.*, X, 950). Although the document does not supply his Christian name, the don was certainly the Richard Smyth of Merton who in 1535 had been named the first Regius Professor of Divinity at Oxford (Joseph Foster, *Alumni Oxonienses, 1500-1714* [Oxford, 1891-1892], IV, 1378; *D.N.B.*).

82. Wright, 36-37.

83. SP 1/100, f. 130 (*L.P.*, IX, 1160).

84. Starkey to Henry VIII, n.d., SP 1/105, ff. 123-124, esp. 123v (*L.P.*, XI, 156). Professor Elton (*Reform and Renewal*, 52) dates this letter "about July" 1536. Starkey himself did not believe in purgatory. See his *Exhortation to the People Instructynge Theym to Vnitie and Obedience* (London, Berthelet, 1536; S.T.C. 23,236), sigs. X iii-X iv^V.

85. Rastell to Cromwell, 17 August 1534 (SP 1/85, f. 129 [*L.P.*, VII, 1071]); for the proposal, see SP 1/85, ff. 99-100 (*L.P.*, VII, 1043); B.L. Cotton MSS., Cleopatra E VI, f. 330 (*L.P.*, VII, 1383).

86. Lehmberg, *Reformation Parliament*, 215.

87. Chapuys to Charles V, 7 March 1535, *L.P.*, VIII, 355.

88. E 36/197, pp. 199-200. For Armstrong, see S. T. Bindoff, "Clement Armstrong and His Treatises of the Commonweal," *Ec.H.R.*, 14 (1944), 64-73. There is no study of his religious writings.

89. E 36/193, p. 78; see also pp. 6-8, 12-13, 79. For other anonymously authored tracts which dealt with purgatory, see SP 6/11, ff. 145, 156, 157-158.

90. Charles C. Butterworth, *The English Primers, 1529-1545* (Philadelphia, University of Pennsylvania Press, 1953), 112; Martin Bucer, *A Treatise declarying . . . that Pyctures & other Ymages . . . are in no Wise to be Suffred . . .* (London, T. Godfray for W. Marshall, 1535; *S.T.C.* 24,238); Chapuys to Charles V, 10 February 1536, *L.P.*, X, 282 (it is inconceivable that one of these books was the anonymously authored *Lytell Boke, That Speketh of Purgatorye* [see above, chap. 2, n.9; cf. Lehmberg, *Reformation Parliament*, 221]); Pole to Alvise Pruili, 3 April 1536 (*L.P.*, X, 619). Pole's intelligence was based on letters posted in England on 25 February.

91. Georg Mentz, ed., *Die Wittenberger Artikel von 1536*, Quellenschriften zur Geschichte des Protestantismus, no. 2 (Leipzig, 1905), 8.

92. Chapuys to Charles V, 1 April 1536, *L.P.*, X, 601. The fact that an abnormally small number of episcopal letters has survived for the month 22 March-21 April may indicate that many of the bishops were in London during this period. The only surviving letters are two by Cranmer, from Lambeth, and one by Bishop John Clerk of Bath and Wells, dated 5 April from Wells (ibid., 547, 577, 625).

93. The Ten Articles were thus the result of many months of reflection and deliberation by the bishops. They were not, as some scholars have maintained, a *Diktat* sprung upon convocation in early July 1536 by Bishop Foxe at the behest of the king. Cf. Lacey Baldwin Smith, *Tudor Prelates*, 189-190.

94. *L.P.*, X, 601.

95. Robert Singleton, *A Sermon Preached at Poules Crosse the Fourth Sunday in Lent, the Yere of Our Lorde God 1535* (London, T. Godfray [1536]; *S.T.C.* 22,575), sigs. Bii^V, Biii^V. The date of the sermon can hardly have been 2 April 1536 (Maclure, *Paul's Cross Sermons*, 186), since in that year the fourth Sunday in Lent fell on 26 March, and on 2 April Singleton was in Dover (*L.P.*, X, 612). The title as published contributes to the confusion, because there *was* no fourth Sunday in Lent in old style 1535! (The fourth Sunday in Lent in n.s. 1534 fell on 15 March, and thus was within o.s. 1533; in n.s. 1535 it fell on 7 March, within o.s. 1534.) Because of the general tenor of the Paul's Cross preaching campaign in the early months of 1536, I am confident that the compositor of the title really meant to write "1536." For Singleton's communications with Cromwell during this period, see *L.P.*, X, 612, 640.

96. SP 1/101, ff. 101-102 (*L.P.*, X, 225). The editors of the *L.P.* attributed this document to Barlow's predecessor at St. David's, Richard Rawlins (d. 18 February 1536), though its contents, as well as the contrasting characters and careers of the two

bishops, point to Barlow. For Rawlins, see G. C. Brodrick, *Memorials of Merton College*, Oxford Hist. Soc., IV (1885), 162-163.

97. John Rochester to Norfolk, March 1537, SP 1/117, f. 183v (*L.P.*, XII, i, 778). "To stay": "to support, sustain, hold up" (*O.E.D.*).

98. Chapuys to Charles V, 29 April 1536, *L.P.*, X, 752. See also ibid., 831, 1043.

99. SP 6/1, ff. 1-5; SP 6/11, ff. 147-153.

100. SP 6/1, ff. 2v; SP 6/11, f. 149. Italics are mine.

101. Of the two drafts, the earlier (SP 6/1, ff. 1-5) is more formally and cleanly written; the latter (SP 6/11, ff. 147-153), which has ample spaces between the lines for further emendation, is in several places more similar to the Ten Articles. Significant differences between the drafts occur in the article "Of Praying to Saints," in which the second draft reflected the concern of some prelates that the people should not believe that any saint "will hear us sooner than Christ," whereas the first draft did not mention the problem; and the article "Of Purgatory," the first draft of which had asserted that prayers, masses, and almsgiving might deliver departed souls out "of their pains or of some part of their pains," whereas the second draft deleted the first four words which had suggested that earthly efforts might relieve more than a fraction of the pains (SP 6/1, ff. 4, 4v; SP 6/11, ff. 151, 152v).

102. See Alan Kreider, "An English Episcopal Draft Article against the Anabaptists," *Mennonite Quarterly Review*, 49 (1975), 38-42.

103. The Ten Articles survive in two versions: one, passed by convocation and signed by the members of the upper and lower houses (B.L. Cotton MSS., Cleopatra E V, ff. 62-72, with the signatures on ff. 72-74v; reprinted in Gilbert Burnet, *The History of the Reformation of the Church of England* [henceforth Burnet], ed. Nicholas Pocock, 7 vols. [Oxford, 1865], IV, 272-285, and in Charles Lloyd, ed., *Formularies of Faith . . . during the Reign of Henry VIII* [henceforth Lloyd], [Oxford, 1825], 3-17); and a slightly different version (perhaps emended by Henry VIII himself) which Berthelet printed in 1536 (*Articles Devised by the Kynges Highness Maiestie; S.T.C.* 10,033; reprinted in Lloyd, xv-xxxii; cf. Burnet, IV, 272n.).

104. Latimer, *Works*, I, 50-51.

105. B.L. Cotton MSS., Cleopatra E V, ff. 140-143 (Latimer, *Works*, II, 245-249; *L.P.*, XII, i, 1312). The *L.P.* editors inserted this undated document at the end of May 1537. By 1537, however, Henry's position on purgatory was close enough to Latimer's to make these irritable jottings improbable for that date. In the latter half of 1537, Henry made grammatical emendations to a draft statement "concerning the souls of them which be departed from this life" which dispensed with the word "purgatory" and utilized Latimer's argument from silence (SP 6/8, ff. 95-98). Furthermore, in 1537 Latimer's convocation sermon of 1536 was printed three times, once in Latin by Nycholson (*S.T.C.* 15,285) and twice in English by the king's printer Berthelet (*S.T.C.* 15,286-15,287). Latimer's brief against purgatory, therefore, probably dates from 1536, after the passage of the act dissolving the lesser monasteries. The period during which convocation was meeting, at which time argument might yet persuade the king to intervene to alter the long-promised statement "Of Purgatory" before convocation officially adopted it, seems to be a likely time for it.

106. Wilkins, III, 804-807.

107. The place where the faithful departed are purified and the pains which they suffer "be to us uncertain *by scripture*" (Lloyd, xxxi; italics mine).

108. Wilkins, III, 803.

109. Mentz, *Wittenberger Artikel*, provides the text in both Latin and German. For an English translation, see Neelak S. Tjernagel, *Henry VIII and the Lutherans: A Study in Anglo-Lutheran Relations from 1521 to 1547* (St. Louis, 1965), 255-286. It

has generally been assumed that Bishop Foxe brought the Wittenberg Articles to England. But in view of the fact that they had been completed by April (Mentz, p. 9), and in view of Foxe's leisurely homeward progress (*L.P.*, X, 847, 954; ibid., XI, 80; John Gough Nichols, ed., *The Chronicle of Calais*, Camden Soc., orig. ser. 35 [1846], 47), this seems improbable. It is more likely that Barnes, who had left Wittenberg in early April and who was certainly back in the realm by May, was the bearer of the articles to England (*L.P.*, X, 644, 665, 880-881).

110. Henry VIII to the bishops, 19 November 1536, SP 1/111, f. 163 (*L.P.*, XI, 1110).

111. SP 6/13, f. 123v.

112. Lloyd, xxvi-xxvii. Cf. the bishop's draft on justification (SP 6/1, ff. 2-2v). The final version of the fifth of the Ten Articles draws much material from the Wittenberg article "de bonis operibus" (Mentz, *Wittenberger Artikel*, 32-35; Tjernagel, *Henry VIII*, 262-263).

113. Charles Hardwick, *A History of the Articles of Religion*, 2nd ed. (Cambridge, 1859), 41. Cf. H. Maynard Smith, *Henry VIII and the Reformation* (London, Macmillan, 1948), 157.

114. It is instructive to compare the two versions of the Ten Articles (most easily in Lloyd, xv, xxxii, 3-17) after having studied Henry's extensive annotations to the Bishop's Book, most of which are printed in Cranmer, *Works*, II, 83-114.

115. See Mentz, *Wittenberger Artikel*, 22-25 ("de baptismo"), 24-33 ("de poenitentia et iustificatione"), 48-49 ("in sacramento corporis et sanguinis domini"), and 32-49 ("de bonis operibus"). The correlative passages in Tjernagel's English translation (*Henry VIII*) are 257-258, 258-262, 262-269.

116. Heath to Melanchthon, 27 August 1536, in E. G. Rupp, *Studies*, 111, citing Luther, *Briefwechsel*, Weimarer Ausgabe, VIII, 222; Henry VIII to the bishops, 12 July 1536, Wilkins, III, 807 (*L.P.*, XI, 65).

117. Lloyd, xxxi-xxxii.

118. Pole to Cardinal Contarini, 31 August 1536, *L.P.*, XI, 376; Cranmer to Sir Thomas Cheyney, 2 October 1537, Cranmer, *Works*, II, 351. The Bishops' Book of 1537, to which Cranmer is referring, incorporated the 1536 article on purgatory almost verbatim. Bishop Barlow also denied that with the Ten Articles "the old popish purgatory is found again" (SP 1/101, f. 233). Cf. Gustave Constant, *The Reformation in England*, 2 vols. (London, Sheed and Ward, 1934-1942), I, 407, and Ernest C. Messenger, *The Reformation, the Mass, and the Priesthood*, 2 vols. (London, 1936-1937), I, 251.

119. Following the publication of Luther's *Ein Widderruff vom Fegefeur* in 1530, the Lutheran theologians turned their heaviest guns to other issues. In Melanchthon's *Apology* and in the Augsburg Confession (both printed in 1536 by Redman in Richard Taverner's translation "at the commandment of his master, the right honorable Master Thomas Cromwell" as *The Confessyon of the Faythe of the Germaynes . . . to which is added the Apologie of Melancthon* [*S.T.C.* 908-909]), the issue of purgatory is treated only obliquely (e.g., sigs. Nii^V, Uv^V-Uvi). The Wittenberg Articles do not mention purgatory. Cf. Rupp, *Studies*, 113.

120. Lloyd, xvi. For a similar statement, see the Royal Injunctions of 1536 (Frere and Kennedy, II, 4-5).

121. Messenger, *Reformation*, I, 251.

Chapter 5: "Extinguishing the Flames of Purgatory" (II)

1. Henry VIII to the bishops, 12 July 1536, Wilkins, III, 807-808. Wilkins indi-

cated that this letter was written to Cranmer, and it was so listed in *L.P.*, XI, 65. But since Wilkins found the letter in the register of Bishop Foxe of Hereford, and since it refers to "all you the bishops," it must have been a general circular to *all* the bishops.

2. Starkey to Cromwell, 24 July 1536, B.L. Cotton MSS., Cleopatra E VI, ff. 384v-385 (*L.P.*, XI, 157).

3. SP 1/105, ff. 102-103 (*L.P.*, XI, 136-137); Wisdom to Cromwell, n.d., SP 1/105, f. 104 (*L.P.*, XI, 138); parishioners of All Hallows, Oxford, to Longland, 31 July 1537, SP 1/123, ff. 145v-146 (*L.P.*, XII, ii, 374); Sherwin Bailey, "Robert Wisdom under Persecution, 1541-1543," *J.E.H.*, 2 (1951), 180-189.

4. Stokesley to Thomas Bedyll, July 1536, SP 1/104, f. 198 (*L.P.*, XI, 186); Marshall to Cromwell, 18 August 1536, SP 1/106, ff. 21-21v (*L.P.*, XI, 325).

5. Dickens, *English Reformation*, 185; and cf. Lacey Baldwin Smith, *Tudor Prelates*, 240.

6. SP 6/8, f. 95; Lloyd, 375-377.

7. B.L. Cotton MSS., Cleopatra E V, f. 142 (*L.P.*, XII, i, 1312).

8. Starkey to Henry VIII, [July 1536 ?], SP 1/105, f. 126 (*L.P.*, XI, 156); SP 1/156, f. 76 (*L.P.*, XIV, ii, 804).

9. John Marshall to Cromwell, 15 February 1539, SP 1/143, ff. 81-82 (*L.P.*, XIV, i, 295).

10. This is based upon a study of all the volumes of the *C.P.R.* between 1279 and 1509, and of the volumes of the *L.P.* between 1509 and 1534. Cf. Rosenthal, *Purchase of Paradise*, 32-33.

11. E.g., the two chantries in Thurgarton (Notts) (A. Hamilton Thompson, ed., "The Chantry Certificate Rolls for the County of Nottingham," *Trans. Thoroton Soc.*, 18 [1914], 86-89; see also E 301/20/59; E 301/56/15; *Valor*, III, 60; ibid., V, 26.

12. Tunstall to Cromwell, 14 November 1537, SP 1/126, f. 158 (*L.P.*, XII, ii, 1082); Leach, *English Schools*, II, 60; *V.C.H., Durham*, I, 374-375.

13. E 301/4/19; E 301/54/7; Maclean, "Chantry Certificates, Gloucestershire," 237.

14. Culstrope [probably Cowthorpe] in Kirk Hammerton (W.R., Yorks) (*Y.C.C.*, II, 270).

15. Sheering (Essex) (E 301/30/3); Patrick Brompton (N.R., Yorks) (*Y.C.C.*, I, 109); Hull (ibid., II, 345-346).

16. E 315/104, ff. 1, 19, 28, 39, 45v-46, 71, 78v, 79, 92, 98, 109v, 142v-143.

17. E 36/119, f. 2 (*L.P.*, XII, i, 70).

18. C. S. L. Davies, "The Pilgrimage of Grace Reconsidered," *Past and Present*, no. 41 (1968), 67. Cf. Margaret Bowker, "Lincolnshire 1536: Heresy, Schism or Religious Discontent?" in Derek Baker, ed., *Studies in Church History*, 9 (Cambridge, Cambridge University Press, 1972), 210-211.

19. B.L. Cotton MSS., Cleopatra E V, f. 413 (*L.P.*, XI, 381).

20. E 36/119, f. 105 (*L.P.*, XII, i, 901 [2]).

21. SP 1/117, ff. 204v-205 (*L.P.*, XII, i, 786); *L.P.*, XI, 1284. See also SP 1/123, f. 202v (*L.P.*, XII, ii, 436).

22. SP 1/113, ff. 53-54 (*L.P.*, XI, 1393 [2]); B.L. Cotton MSS., Cleopatra E V, f. 396v (*L.P.*, XII, i, 818).

23. SP 6/13, f. 125; SP 1/110, f. 102 (*L.P.*, XI, 954); SP 1/111, ff. 163-163v (*L.P.*, XI, 1110); SP 1/115, f. 85 (*L.P.*, XII, i, 256 [2]); B.L. Cotton MSS., Cleopatra E IV, f. 318v (*L.P.*, XII, ii, 830).

24. Alesius to Cranmer, [November ?] 1536, *L.P.*, XI, 987.

25. SP 1/111, f. 163 (*L.P.*, XI, 1110).

26. SP 6/13, f. 126. According to Bishop Foxe of Hereford, the Bishops' Book was

a response to the "tragedies and tumults" of the previous year (Foxe to Martin Bucer, [August ?] 1537, *L.P.*, XII, ii, 410).

27. On 18 February 1537 John Husee wrote to Lord Lisle that "the most part of the bishops are come" (SP 3/5, f. 64v [*L.P.*, XII, i, 457]).

28. SP 1/117, ff. 220, 221v (*L.P.*, XII, i, 789 [2]). Cf. Rupp, *Studies*, 138.

29. SP 6/8, ff. 14-33, 52-66v (especially f. 59v); SP 1/123, ff. 162-163; B.L. Cotton MSS., Cleopatra E V, ff. 48-50.

30. Gardiner to Cranmer, July 1547, J. A. Muller, ed., *The Letters of Stephen Gardiner* (Cambridge, 1933), 351. For a colorful account of one of the stormy sessions at Lambeth, see the excerpts from Alexander Alesius, *Of the Auctorite of the Word of God*, in Ellis, 3rd ser. 3, 196-201 (*L.P.*, XII, i, 790).

31. For Henry's interesting emendations to the third of a succession of six drafts of the statement on confirmation, see SP 6/3, ff. 5-9. Edmund Bonner's letter to Cromwell of 1 June indicates that by that date Henry was no longer in regular communication with the divines (SP 1/121, f. 8 [*L.P.*, XII, ii, 7]).

32. Lloyd, 210-211.

33. Dr. Richard Coren to Layton and Starkey, 24 March 1537, SP 1/117, f. 97 (*L.P.*, XII, i, 708).

34. Sampson to Cromwell, 7 June 1540, B.L. Cotton MSS., Cleopatra E V, ff. 308v-309 (*L.P.*, XV, 758).

35. Cranmer to Cromwell, 21 July 1537, Cranmer, *Works*, II, 337-338; John Husee to Lord Lisle, 25 July 1537, SP 3/5, f. 84a (*L.P.*, XII, ii, 337); Foxe to Cromwell, 20 July 1537, SP 1/123, ff. 24-24v (*L.P.*, XII, ii, 289); Foxe to Cromwell, 25 August 1537, SP 1/124, f. 103 (*L.P.*, XII, ii, 578). See also *L.P.*, XIII, i, 686.

36. Lloyd, 26-27.

37. Both Cranmer and Foxe complained that they had not seen the king for a long time (Cranmer, *Works*, II, 338; SP 1/123, f. 24v; SP 1/124, f. 103); Foxe to Cromwell, 24 July 1537, SP 1/123, f. 82 (*L.P.*, XII, ii, 330).

38. *S.T.C.* 5163-5167; the only modern version is in Lloyd, 23-211. There is no evidence that the draft letter, in which Henry expressed his approval of the bishops' work, was ever sent (SP 6/2, ff. 102-105; SP 6/9, ff. 73-76; Cranmer, *Works*, II, 469-470; *L.P.*, XII, ii, 618).

39. SP 1/124, ff. 66, 148v-149 (*L.P.*, XII, ii, 547, 620); SP 1/125, ff. 114, 133-133v, 251 (*L.P.*, XII, ii, 818, 834, 952); SP 1/126, ff. 164-164v (*L.P.*, XII, ii, 1093); Wriothesley to Sir Thomas Wyatt, 10 October 1537, B.L. Harleian MS. 282, f. 281v (*L.P.*, XII, ii, 871).

40. Bodleian 4° Rawlinson 245; SP 1/126, f. 193v (*L.P.*, XII, ii, 1122 [2]); B.L. Cotton MSS., Titus B I, f. 472 (*L.P.*, XIII, i, 187).

41. I have inferred the existence of this volume by collating folio numbers in B.L. Royal MS. 7 C xvi, ff. 199-207, and C.C.C.C., MS. 104, pp. 241-270, with surviving copies of the Bishops' Book.

42. B.L. Royal MSS., App. 78, ff. 21-23; B.L. Cotton MSS., Titus B I, f. 444 (*L.P.*, XII, ii, 1151). Since the text of B.L. Royal MS. 7 C xvi, ff. 199-207, refers repeatedly to "Hethe &c.," it is probable that several other theologians (possibly Day, Thirlby, and Skip) joined Heath in commenting upon the revision.

43. Cranmer to Cromwell, 14 January 1538, Cranmer, *Works*, II, 358-359; C.C.C.C., MS. 104, pp. 241-270; Cranmer to Cromwell, 25 January 1538, Cranmer, *Works*, II, 359-360.

44. B.L. Royal MS. 7 C xvi, ff. 199-207.

45. Ibid., 17 C xxx.

46. Ibid., ff. 26-27, 43-91, 131-134, 141-149.

47. C.C.C.C., MS. 104, p. 243; B.L. Royal MS. 17 C xxx, f. 4v; Cranmer. *Works*, II, 359.

48. The bishops of reforming tendencies must have found many of Henry's alterations extremely unpalatable. See Cranmer's annotations in C.C.C.C., MS. 104, pp. 241-270 (Cranmer, *Works*, II, 83-114).

49. Frere and Kennedy, II, 44, 61; Sampson to his commissary, 17 June 1538, SP 1/133, f. 51v (*L.P.*, XIII, i, 1199); Sampson to Alexander Welles, 21 August 1538, B.L. Cotton MSS., Cleopatra E V, f. 305 (*L.P.*, XIII, ii, 147).

50. Gardiner to Cranmer, July 1547, Muller, *Letters of Stephen Gardiner*, 323, 351; *L.P.*, XVIII, ii, 68. For a useful analysis of Henry's work of revision, see J. J. Scarisbrick, *Henry VIII* (London, 1968), 405-407.

51. For example, see the concluding sentence of the lengthy article on the sacrament of orders (Lloyd, 123, 289; B.L. Royal MS. 17 C xxx, ff. 90v-91).

52. SP 1/126, f. 193v (*L.P.*, XII, ii, 1122). The divines apparently submitted their "determination" in December, since its existence is recorded in a remembrance in Cromwell's hand on the flyleaf of a letter which had been sent from Venice on 24 November 1537.

53. SP 6/8, ff. 95-98v.

54. B.L. Royal MSS., App. 78, ff. 23-23v.

55. B.L. Royal MS. 17 C xxx, ff. 144v-149, on which the following paragraphs are based.

56. Scarisbrick, *Henry VIII*, 406-407; Lacey Baldwin Smith, *Henry VIII: The Mask of Royalty* (London, 1971), 127-128.

57. B.L. Royal MS. 17 C xxx, sigs. X^V, Aiv, Biii^V.

58. Ibid., f. 47v, sigs. Oii^V, U.

59. For the view that the king "stuck so fervently to transubstantiation, clerical celibacy, and purgatory," see Scarisbrick, *Henry VIII*, 409.

60. B.L. Royal MS. 7 D xi.

61. SP 6/3, f. 82v (*L.P.*, XIV, i, 376).

62. See below, text and nn. 86-87.

63. Wriothesley, *Chronicle*, I, 71, 97-99; SP 3/2, f. 61v (*L.P.*, XIV, i, 1088); SP 1/156, f. 76 (*L.P.*, XIV, ii, 804).

64. Wriothesley, *Chronicle*, I, 181; Thomas Rymer, ed., *Foedera, conventiones, literae, et cujuscunque generis acta publica*, 3rd ed., VI (The Hague, 1745), iii, 142-145.

65. SP 1/111, f. 163 (*L.P.*, XI, 1110).

66. Frere and Kennedy, II, 4-5, 34-43.

67. Wilkins, III, 807-808; SP 1/132, f. 102 (*L.P.*, XIII, i, 981).

68. Frere and Kennedy, II, 56, 17; Cranmer to Cromwell, 26 May 1537, Cranmer, *Works*, II, 336; *Valor*, III, 335.

69. *L.P.*, XI, 300 (2), 649; ibid., XII, i, 5, 757; ibid., XIII, i, 1009; ibid., XIII, ii, 278, 953.

70. SP 1/138, f. 16v (*L.P.*, XIII, i, 695 [2]); Sir Thomas Audley to Cromwell, 24 July 1537, SP 1/123, f. 80 (*L.P.*, XII, ii, 329).

71. SP 1/101, f. 233; B.L. Cotton MSS., Cleopatra E V, f. 383 (*L.P.*, XII, i, 93 [2]).

72. Lee to Cromwell, 15 January 1537, B.L. Cotton MSS., Cleopatra E V, ff. 382-382v (*L.P.*, XII, i, 93 [1]); SP 1/113, ff. 112-113 (*L.P.*, XI, 1427); SP 1/140, f. 175 (*L.P.*, XIII, ii, 1132); SP 1/241, ff. 73-74 (*L.P.*, Addenda, I, 1225).

73. London to Bedyll, 18 July 1536, SP 1/240, ff. 31-32 (*L.P.*, Addenda, I, 1085); London to Cromwell, 16 July 1536, SP 1/105, ff. 70-71 (*L.P.*, XI, 96); Bedyll to

Cromwell, 19 July 1536, SP 1/105, f. 76 (*L.P.*, XI, 118); London to Cromwell, 27 December 1536, SP 1/113, f. 38 (*L.P.*, XI, 1376); *D.N.B.*, s.v. "John London." Cranmer likewise had little patience with those who upheld purgatory and other traditional doctrines and practices (Cranmer, *Works*, II, 351).

74. Wylley to Cromwell, n.d. [1537 ?], SP 1/116, f. 158 (*L.P.*, XII, i, 529).

75. SP 1/124, ff. 110-111 (*L.P.*, XII, ii, 587); E 36/120, ff. 69-70 (*L.P.*, XII, ii, 530).

76. Walsshe and others to Cromwell, 18 August 1537, with the annexed information against Dr. Smyth, SP 1/124, ff. 55-56 (*L.P.*, XII, ii, 534); Wilkins, III, 808.

77. *L.P.*, XII, ii, 621; Brodrick, *Memorials*, 254-255; Foster, *Alumni Oxonienses, 1500-1714*, IV, 1378.

78. Banastre and others to Cromwell, 25 May 1538, SP 1/132, ff. 182-183 (*L.P.*, XIII, i, 1066). The documents give no indication what happened to Yakesley. Freurs had figured prominently in the appeal against the silencing of Robert Wisdom (SP 1/123, ff. 145v-146 [*L.P.*, XII, ii, 374]).

79. Butler to Cranmer, 9 July 1537, SP 1/122, ff. 214-215 (*L.P.*, XII, ii, 231); Cromwell to the Council of Calais, 17 July 1537, B.L. Cotton MSS., Cleopatra E IV, f. 55 (*L.P.*, XII, ii, 267); Cromwell to Lord Lisle, 24 July 1537, SP 3/2, f. 170 (*L.P.*, XII, ii, 328); John Husee to Lord Lisle, 25 July 1537, SP 3/5, f. 115 (*L.P.*, XII, ii, 337); Husee to Lady Lisle, 3 and 7 August 1537, SP 3/11, ff. 132, 64 (*L.P.*, XII, ii, 424, 661); Sir Thomas Palmer to Lord Lisle, 7 September 1537, SP 3/14, ff. 89-90 (*L.P.*, XII, ii, 661); John Bunolt to Cromwell, 15 September 1537, SP 1/124, f. 238 (*L.P.*, XII, ii, 697). Conservative agitation persisted in Calais. On 19 January 1538 Butler complained to Cranmer that the chaplain of the High Marshal of Calais was preaching against purgatory. Without the assistance of preachers such as Dr. Crome or Dr. Barnes it would be hard to counter the influence of "the papistical sort" in the town (SP 1/127, ff. 127-127v [*L.P.*, XIII, i, 108]). For Richardson, see also Cromwell to the Earl of Southampton, [December 1539], SP 1/155, ff. 162-162v (*L.P.*, XIV, ii, 726); Nichols, *Chronicle of Calais*, 47-48.

80. SP 1/82, f. 235 (*L.P.*, VII, 261); SP 1/116, f. 171 (*L.P.*, XII, i, 537); *L.P.*, XII, i, 741; SP 1/130, ff. 141-142 (*L.P.*, XIII, i, 604); Robert Holgate to Cromwell, 20 August 1538, SP 1/135, f. 130 (*L.P.*, XIII, ii, 142).

81. SP 1/132, ff. 98, 101v-102 (*L.P.*, XIII, i, 981); Wriothesley, *Chronicle*, I, 78-79; Knowles, *Religious Orders*, III, 369-371, 373-376.

82. Katherine Bulkeley to Cromwell, 26 November 1538, SP 1/139, f. 191 (*L.P.*, XIII, ii, 911).

83. Robert Ferrar to Cromwell, 21 February 1539, SP 1/143, f. 126 (*L.P.*, XIV, i, 334), and n.d. [1538], SP 1/139, f. 218 (*L.P.*, XIII, ii, 953); Sampson to Cromwell, 4 September 1538, B.L. Cotton MSS., Cleopatra E V, f. 306v (*L.P.*, XIII, ii, 278).

84. SP 1/152, ff. 11-14 (*L.P.*, XIV, i, 1064). Professor Elton, pointing out the discrepancies between this "bill" and actual parliamentary draft bills, has called this document a "disguised pamphlet" (*Reform and Renewal*, 69).

85. B.L. Cotton MSS., Cleopatra E V, ff. 53-54 (*L.P.*, XIV, i, 971).

86. Friedrich Myconius, *Historia Reformationis vom Jahr Christi 1517 bis 1542*, ed. E. S. Cyprian (Leipzig, 1718), 57-58; *L.P.*, XIII, ii, 37. For Anglo-German negotiations of 1538, see Tjernagel, *Henry VIII and the Lutherans*, 180-184.

87. B.L. Cotton MSS., Cleopatra E V, ff. 240v-241 (*L.P.*, XIV, i, 642). See also Strype, I, ii, 386-388, and *L.P.*, XIV, i, 698.

88. SP 1/139, f. 148 (*L.P.*, XIII, ii, 873); B.L. Cotton MSS., Cleopatra E V, f. 138 (*L.P.*, XIV, I, 1040); Jasper Ridley, *Thomas Cranmer* (Oxford, 1962), 180-181.

89. SP 1/136, ff. 28, 33 (*L.P.*, XIII, ii, 248); Cranmer to Cromwell, 23 August

1538, B.L. Cotton MSS., Cleopatra E V, f. 225 (*L.P.*, XIII, ii, 164). On the theological convictions of these bishops, see also Sampson to Cromwell, 7 June 1540, B.L. Cotton MSS., Cleopatra E V, ff. 308-309 (*L.P.*, XV, 758).

90. Irvin B. Horst, *The Radical Brethren: Anabaptism and the English Reformation to 1558* (Nieuwkoop, 1972), 82-85.

91. B.L. Royal MS. 17 C xxx, f. 52.

92. Sir Thomas Palmer to Cromwell, 23 July 1538, SP 1/134, f. 231 (*L.P.*, XIII, i, 1444); Lord Lisle to Cromwell, n.d. [June ? 1538], SP 3/9, ff. 58-58v (*L.P.*, XIII, i, 1291); SP 1/136, ff. 26-33 (*L.P.*, XIII, ii, 248).

93. Lacey Baldwin Smith, *Henry VIII*, 136-138; Horst, *Radical Brethren*, 165-166.

94. Paul L. Hughes and James F. Larkin, eds., *Tudor Royal Proclamations*, I, *The Early Tudors* (New Haven, Yale University Press, 1964), 270-271. See also Henry VIII's emendations to a draft of this (B.L. Cotton MSS., Cleopatra E V, ff. 355-384, and especially f. 368).

95. SP 1/135, ff. 152-155v, 179-190v; Tjernagel, *Henry VIII*, 192-193.

96. SP 1/152, ff. 15-22, of which f. 19 deals with private masses (*L.P.*, XIV, i, 1065); Wilkins, III, 845-846.

97. B.L. Cotton MSS.; Cleopatra E V, ff. 327-335.

98. One of Cromwell's remembrances, which the *L.P.* dates in April 1539, refers to "a device in the parliament for the unity in religion," which may have been the original draft corrected by Henry (E 36/143, f. 67 [*L.P.*, XIV, i, 655]).

99. B.L. Cotton MSS., Cleopatra E V, f. 330; cf. f. 328 for a similar passage.

100. Ibid., f. 138 (*L.P.*, XIV, i, 1040); Husee to Lord Lisle, 13 June 1539, SP 3/9, f. 32 (*L.P.*, XIV, i, 1108); *L.P.*, XIV, i, 1152. The final version of the statute (31 Henry VIII, c.14) is in *S.R.*, III, 739-743.

101. Bucer to Cranmer, 29 October 1539, Robinson, *Original Letters*, II, 530; Melanchthon to Henry VIII, 1 November 1539, Foxe, V, 350-358 (*L.P.*, XIV, ii, 444), and 30 June 1540 printed in *The Epistle of P. Melancton made vnto Kynge Henry the Eyght, for the Reuokinge of the Six Artycles* (1547; *S.T.C.* 17,789); Melanchthon to Myconius, 28 August 1540, *L.P.*, XV, 1015. For the 1540 edition of the second letter, see *L.P.*, XVI, 351, 420, 424.

102. Scarisbrick, *Henry VIII*, 419, 409-410.

103. Sampson to Lord Lisle, 20 July 1539, SP 3/2, f. 151 (*L.P.*, XIV, i, 1290); Husee to Lord Lisle, 22 June 1539, SP 3/5, f. 94v (*L.P.*, XIV, i, 1144).

104. *L.P.*, XIV, i, 1058, 1086, 1088, 1166, 1210, 1264; Stokesley to Cromwell, n.d. [July 1538 ?], SP 1/134, f. 289v (*L.P.*, XIII, i, 1500); Hilsey to Cromwell, 23 and 29 July 1539, SP 1/152, ff. 207, 226 (*L.P.*, XIV, i, 1297, 1328).

105. Barnes to Johannes Aepinus, 21 May 1540, Robinson, *Original Letters*, II, 616-617; R. H. Brodie, "The Case of Dr. Crome," *T.R.H.S.*, n.s. 19 (1905), 299-304; Richard Hilles to Heinrich Bullinger, [1541], Robinson, *Original Letters*, I, 211-215.

106. For examples of these cases, which dealt with the doctrine of praying for souls, see W.R.O., MS. B.A. 2764/802, ff. 137, 139; E 36/120, ff. 86, 126 (*L.P.*, XV, 587, App. 3); SP 1/150, ff. 203-204 (*L.P.*, XIV, i, 863); SP 1/243, f. 78 (*L.P.*, Addenda, II, 1463 [18]); C.C.C.C., MS. 128, p. 42 (*L.P.*, XVIII, ii, 546, p. 304); Foxe, V, 448; Strype, I, ii, 473; *L.P.*, XVIII, ii, 546, p. 301; Dickens, *Lollards and Protestants*, 45-46.

107. Hilles to Bullinger, [1541], Robinson, *Original Letters*, I, 204.

108. See Dickens, *English Reformation*, 192, and *Lollards and Protestants*, 173; and especially Peter Clark, *English Provincial Society from the Reformation to the Revolution: Religion, Politics, and Society in Kent, 1500-1640* (Hassocks, Sussex,

1977), 58 (which the author has generously allowed me to read in typescript). The astonishing depth and quality of Clark's evidence from Kentish wills does much to overcome Dr. Spufford's justifiable reservations about the methods which he has used (Margaret Spufford, "The Scribes of Villagers' Wills in the Sixteenth and Seventeenth Centuries and Their Influence," *Local Population Studies*, no. 7 [1971], 29, 41, 42).

109. C.C.C.C., MS. 128, pp. 11, 41 (*L.P.*, XVIII, ii, 546, pp. 293, 304).

110. SP 1/161, ff. 2-3; L.P.L. MS. 1108, ff. 69-70; B.L. Cotton MSS., Cleopatra E V, ff. 39-43v. The answers of the individual divines were evidently too exhaustive for the preoccupied sovereign to peruse (ibid., ff. 56-59; L.P.L. MS. 1108, ff. 71-141).

111. Marillac to Montmorency, 21 May 1540, *L.P.*, XV, 697.

112. It is not clear when the divines stopped working on the formulary. On 10 June 1540 Marillac reported that "no articles of religion are yet concluded," but that "the bishops are daily assembled to resolve them" (*L.P.*, XV, 766). Their efforts continued later than 7 July (on which date Thomas Thirlby was first referred to as the bishop-elect of the new see of Westminster), for a number of documents refer to Thirlby as "my lorde electe of Westminstre" (*L.P.*, XV, 860; ibid., XVI, p. 951; B.L. Cotton MSS., Cleopatra E V, ff. 43v-44; L.P.L. MS. 1108, ff. 141-143). But most of the bishops probably returned to their dioceses after the dissolution of convocation on 28 July, even though Thirlby was not finally installed in his new see until 18 December (*L.P.*, XV, 921, 942 [90]).

113. Henry VIII to Sir Ralph Sadler, 24 August 1543, B.L. Add. MS. 32,651, f. 257 (*L.P.*, XVIII, ii, 68); Gardiner to Cranmer, July 1547, Muller, *Letters of Stephen Gardiner*, 323; Cooper, *Athenae Cantabrigienses*, I, 157.

114. Cf. B.L. Cotton MSS., Cleopatra E V, ff. 8-38, and SP 1/178, ff. 108-110, with corresponding passages in the final version of the King's Book (Lloyd, 225-250, 289-290).

115. For one example, see n. 51 above. For another, see the King's Book's treatment of the fifth petition of the Lord's prayer ("and forgive us our trespasses, as we forgive them that trespass against us") which, as Professor L. B. Smith has noted, inserts the significant qualification that the people "shall understand that forgiveness, afore spoken of, is not so meant in scripture, that by it justice or laws of princes should be broken, condemned, or not executed" (*Tudor Prelates*, 246). This was not simply a product of "the conservatives' view of religion"; it was a phrase which Henry had almost certainly written himself, probably on one of the interfoliated leaves in the royal revisions to the Bishops' Book which he had submitted to the theologians and legists for criticism (B.L. Royal MS. 7 C xvi, f. 209v; C.C.C.C., MS. 104, p. 267; Cranmer, *Works*, II, 112); it was definitely in the unpublished "king's book" of 1538, which the King's Book of 1543 reproduced verbatim (B.L. Royal MS. 17 C xxx, ff. 132-132v; Lloyd, 349). In a far fuller sense than Professor Smith or anyone else has realized, the doctrinal formulary of 1543 was indeed the king's book.

116. Wilkins, III, 868; *A.P.C.*, I, 127; Lloyd, 216; Gairdner, *Lollardy and the Reformation*, II, 352-354.

117. *S.T.C.* 5168-5174, 5176-5178. J. Mayler also published one edition in 1543 (*S.T.C.* 5175). The colophon of the first edition gives the publication date as 29 May 1543. See also Berthelet's account book (B.L. Add. MS. 28,196, f. 11v). Good modern editions are in Lloyd, 212-377, and T. A. Lacey, ed., *The King's Book* (London, S.P.C.K., 1932).

118. Privy Council to Duke of Suffolk, 13 May 1543, SP 1/178, f. 17v (*L.P.*, XVIII, i, 534); Chapuys to Charles V, 11 June 1543, ibid., 684.

119. Sadler to Privy Council, 17 August 1543, in Arthur Clifford, ed., *The State Papers of Sir Ralph Sadler* (Edinburgh, 1809), I, 264-265 (*L.P.*, XVIII, ii, 50); Henry

VIII to Sadler, 24 August 1543, B.L. Add. MS. 32,651, f. 257 (*L.P.*, XVIII, ii, 68).

120. Hughes, *Reformation in England*, II, 54; Lacey Baldwin Smith, *Henry VIII*, 128n.; Rupp, *Studies*, 149-154.

121. Lloyd, 375, 377. For the tenth article of 1536 and the concluding article of the "king's book" of 1538, see Lloyd, xxxi-xxxii, and B.L. Royal MS. 17 C xxx, ff. 144v-149.

122. C.C.C.C., MS. 128, p. 32 (*L.P.*, XVIII, ii, 546, p. 301); cf. W.R.O., MS. B.A. 2764/802, ff. 143, 147.

Chapter 6: Anticipatory Dissolutions

1. Reg. Warham, ff. 48v, 47v, 51v, 50. See also ff. 45v-46, 52v, 53, 54, 55, 58.

2. Snell, *Chantry Certificates for Devon,* 50; *Y.C.C.*, I, 138-139; E 301/32/5; Maclean, "Chantry Certificates, Gloucestershire," 263.

3. *L.P.*, XI, 972, 973, 975; *L.P.*, XII, i, 70, 456, 901, 1011, 1316; *L.P.*, XII, ii, 357; *L.P.*, XIII, ii, 986 (10, 19); *L.P.*, XIV, i, 87. See also Elton, *Policy and Police,* 70.

4. E 301/13/38, 5; SP 1/130, ff. 10v-11 (*L.P.*, XIII, i, 477).

5. E.g., Sir Charles Brandon, who with Lord Dacre seized the lands of the Trinity Chantry and Almshouse of Northallerton in 1544 (*Y.C.C.*, I, 123), died seven years later leaving a pious Protestant will (Dickens, *Lollards and Protestants*, 216). Brandon and Dacre left no support for the priest or the 13 people; but somehow the hospital—though not the chantry—managed to survive (C. J. D. Ingledew, *The History and Antiquities of North Allerton* [London, 1858], 266-268).

6. 37 Henry VIII, c.4 (*S.R.*, III, 988-993).

7. Wilkins, III, 876 (*L.P.*, XXI, i, 69); E 301/126.

8. E 301/53/85, 3; E 301/57/52; *V.C.H.*, *Warwickshire*, II, 342; ibid., IV, 172.

9. E 301/56/19, 17, 12, 14, 1; E 301/58/55, 131.

10. Hertford to Hungerford, 9 April 1540, H.M.C., *Fifteenth Report*, app. X, 165; E 301/56/22, 23, 27. Hertford's chantries (in Chippenham, Highworth, and Marlborough), unlike the other institutions which were reported to be dissolved prior to 1545, were reported by the Edwardian chantry commissioners still to be functioning and possessing active incumbents (E 301/58/22, 34, 53). From other sources we learn that in November 1545 Hertford presented Clement Ledentum to be the new incumbent of the Chippenham chantry (Reg. Salcot, f. 28), but did not receive the grant of the Marlborough chantry properties until July 1547 (Wordsworth, "Marlborough Chantries," 560). The whole situation remains cloudy.

11. *Y.C.C.*, I, 101, 123, 126-127, 170; ibid., II, 270, 296; H. B. McCall, ed., *Yorkshire Star Chamber Proceedings*, II, Y.A.S.R.S., 45 (1911), 114-116; DL 41/12/1.

12. *Y.C.C.*, I, 168.

13. E 301/18/28; E 301/20/55, 58, 60; John E. Ray, ed., *Sussex Chantry Records*, Sussex Rec. Soc., 36 (1931), 10-12, 56-57; Snell, *Chantry Certificates for Devon*, xxi-xxii; Green, *Survey of Somerset*, 36-37, 43-44, 59, 63, 83, 93-94, 106, 110-111, 124, 129-130, 151-152, 162.

14. DL 38/7; Thompson, "Chantry Certificate Rolls for Nottingham," *Trans. Thoroton Soc.*, 18 (1914), 177; E 301/83, m. 4; Maclean, "Chantry Certificates, Gloucestershire," 252-253.

15. Clark, *English Provincial Society,* 44.

16. DL 42/96, f. 49v.

17. Wenham, "Chantries of Richmond," passim.

18. *Y.C.C.*, I, 140-142; II, 517-518.

19. *L.P.*, XIV, ii, 619 (31); Morant, *History*, I, i, 153-156; J. H. Round, *St. Helen's Chapel* (London, n.d.), 13-18.

20. H.M.C., *Fourteenth Report*, app. VIII, 31, 263-265, 34, 40.

21. Raine, *York Civic Records*, I, 76, 82, 136-137, 167; ibid., II, 15, 36, 81, 102; ibid., III, 109-110. See also the pathetic description of the city in "Àn Act for the uniting of certain churches within the city of York" (1 Edward VI, c.9 [*S.R.*, IV, 14-15]).

22. *V.C.H., City of York*, 121; Bartlett, "Expansion and Decline," 30-32.

23. Information derived from statute 27 Henry VIII, c.32 (*S.R.*, III, 582-584). See A. G. Dickens' argument that the city was exaggerating its complaints of chantry-induced impoverishment ("A Municipal Dissolution of Chantries at York, 1536," *Y.A.J.*, 36 [1944-1947], 164-173).

24. Raine, *York Civic Records*, III, 110, 129-130.

25. E 36/139, f. 11v (*L.P.*, VII, 923, vii); Raine, *York Civic Records*, III, 138-139.

26. Mayor and aldermen of York to Cromwell, 29 October 1535 and 1 June 1536, SP 1/98, f. 106 (*L.P.*, IX, 705) and SP 1/93, f. 1 (*L.P.*, VIII, 804; incorrectly dated in 1535); "An Act containing a concord and agreement between the earl of Rutland and the city of York and others" (27 Henry VIII, c.32 [*S.R.*, III, 582-584]).

27. Wood-Legh, 111-119.

28. 31 Henry VIII, c.13 (*S.R.*, III, 733).

29. For the total number of colleges and hospitals, see B.L. Cotton MSS., Cleopatra E IV, f. 471v.

30. R. W. Dixon, *History of the Church of England from the Abolition of the Roman Jurisdiction*, 6 vols. (Oxford, 1878-1902), II, 381n., 382n.; F. G. Emmison, *Tudor Secretary: Sir William Petre at Court and Home* (Cambridge, Mass., Harvard University Press, 1961), 46-47.

31. Maltravers to Henry VIII, 28 September 1542, SP 1/173, f. 68 (*L.P.*, XVII, 861); Parker to the Queen's Council, 1545, in Matthew Parker, *Correspondence*, ed. John Bruce and T. T. Perrowne (Parker Soc., Cambridge, 1853), 31. Sir Anthony Denny, who apparently interceded in Parker's behalf, impressed the king with his report of Parker's "honest and virtuous using of that college [Stoke]," and Henry was persuaded "to permit the same to remain undissolved" (Denny to 1548 chantry commissioners for Norfolk and Suffolk, 29 February 1548, C.C.C.C., MS. 108, p. 99).

32. E 301/81; E 301/92; E 315/400, pp. 62-86 (in Francis A. Hibbert, *The Dissolution of the Monasteries as Illustrated by the Suppression of the Religious Houses of Staffordshire* [London, 1910], 268-278), on which the following paragraph is based.

33. *L.P.*, XIV, ii, 430, 521; *L.P.*, XVI, 1135 (9); *V.C.H.*, *Staffordshire*, III, 297-298; Knowles, *Religious Orders*, III, 358, 389, 391.

34. W. C. Richardson, *History of the Court of Augmentations,, 1536-1554* (Baton Rouge, Louisiana State University Press, 1961), 47n., 81-82, 141n., 155, 238n., 240; *L.P.*, XXI, i, 302 (30); *C.P.R., Edward VI*, II, 135-137.

35. The pottle was "a measure of capacity for liquids . . . equal to two quarts" (*O.E.D.*, s.v. "pottle").

36. For example, at Crediton the commissioners provided pensions for the master, the treasurer, the schoolmaster, and the prebendaries, but only "rewards" and wages for the vicars' stipendiaries and the choristers (E 301/81, m. 6v). Similarly, the same commissioners pensioned the warden of Ottery St. Mary (who got £33 6s. 8d. per annum), the prebendaries, the stipendiaries, and the schoolmaster, but gave only "rewards" and wages to the vicars' stipendiaries, the secondaries, the choristers, and the college clerks (E 301/92, mm. 9v-10). I have found reference to "rewards" and "payments" in only three other instances (E 315/253, f. 67; E 315/254, f. 116; E 315/400, ff. 72-75).

37. Preamble to statute 33 Henry VIII, c.27 (*S.R.*, III, 867).

38. Thompson, *English Clergy*, 122, 122n; *L.P.*, XX, i, 534, 1335 (46).

39. 33 Henry VIII c.27 (*S.R.*, III, 867). On this statute, see Burnet, I, 497.

40. E.g., E 315/252, ff. 1, 18; E 315/253, f. 14; E 315/254, f. 28; E 315/255, ff. 30, 46. Six years later Edward's Privy Council gave explicit expression of this means of obtaining "voluntary" surrenders in Ireland: "by granting to them [priests of Irish colleges and chantries] pensions reasonable with respect to their former livings and also to the merit and worthiness of the conditions and learnings of the parties." Failing that, "we think best you caused the same [surrenders] to [be] obtained by an act of Parliament" (Council to Sir James Croft, November 1551, SP 61/3, ff. 209v-210).

41. E 315/253, ff. 19v-20; E 315/254, ff. 29v-30v; E 322/272, m. 2.

42. Of the master and two fellows of the hospital of Newport (Essex), only Philip Fawdon received a pension (*Valor*, I, 440; E 315/254, f. 31v). Of the master, five prebendaries, and ten vicars choral of the college of Warwick, only William Wall was granted a pension (*Valor*, III, 83-84; E 315/254, f. 33). Neither of these men seems to have been master of his institution. Why they were pensioned, and not their colleagues, remains a mystery, as does the whole subject of the pensioning of those who "voluntarily" surrendered their foundations prior to 1546. Additional research may someday clarify the matter.

43. It thus appears that the intercessory priests who surrendered their institutions at an early date were almost as likely to be unpensioned as were the ex-religious who had left religion before 1538. Cf. G. A. J. Hodgett, "The Unpensioned Ex-Religious in Tudor England," *J.E.H.*, 13 (1962), 195-202.

44. Parker, *Correspondence*, 31.

45. E.g., Slapton College (Devon), surrendered to the crown in November 1545, and granted the following January to Sir Thomas Arundel, chancellor of the Queen's Household; Mettingham College (Suffolk), granted by Henry VIII to his boon companion Sir Anthony Denny within a week of its dissolution in 1542; Lady Chantry of Brundish (Suffolk), granted in August 1544 to its patron, Richard Fulmerston, who the previous month had procured its surrender (*L.P.*, XX, ii, 744; ibid., XXI, i, 149 [19]; ibid., XVII, 243, 283 [43]; Robert Dacres to Denny, 13 May 1542, ibid., XVII, 322; ibid., XIX, i, 983; ibid., ii, 166 [36]).

46. Henry Brinklow, *Complaynt of Roderyck Mors*, ed. J. Meadows Cowper, E.E.T.S., extra ser. 22 (1874), 47-48.

Chapter 7: The Henrician Chantries Act, 1545

1. SP 1/118, f. 254 (*L.P.*, XII, i, 1011).

2. SP 1/130, ff. 10v-11 (*L.P.*, XIII, i, 477).

3. SP 6/7, ff. 30-30v (cf. Elton, *Reform and Renewal*, 71-76); B.L. Cotton MSS., Cleopatra E IV, f. 208 (reprinted in Lawrence Stone, "The Political Program of Thomas Cromwell," *B.I.H.R.*, 24 [1951], 9-11); SP 1/152, ff. 11-14.

4. Thomas Dorset to mayor of Plymouth and others, 13 March 1536, Wright, 38 (*L.P.*, X, 462); Hume, *Chronicle of Henry VIII*, 87-88; Chapuys to Charles V, 10 February 1536, *L.P.*, X, 282.

5. *L.P.*, X, 612, 640; Singleton, *A Sermon Preached at Poules Crosse*, sig. Bv.

6. *L.P.*, XVI, 1135(9), 1391(2); *L.P.*, XVII, 71(8, 18); Hibbert, *Dissolution*, 177; *V.C.H., Staffordshire*, III, 297-298; Foster and Thompson, "Chantry Certificates for Lincolnshire," *A.A.S.R.P.*, 37 (1923-1925), 251-253; *V.C.H., Lincolnshire*, II, 237.

7. E 301/117, mm. 1-2; *L.P.*, XXI, i, 302 (30); Kitching, "Studies," I, 87. The

chapel of St. Lawrence, Kilham, was the only one surveyed by the commissioners of 1546 and 1548 (*Y.C.C.*, I, 139; E 301/119, m. 8).

8. Vaughan to Paget, 10 May 1545, SP 1/200, f. 231 (*L.P.*, XX, i, 700); Chapuys to Charles V, 18 June 1545, ibid., 984; *L.J.*, I, 274-275.

9. Van der Delft to Charles V, 30 November 1545, *C.S.P.Span.*, VIII, 279.

10. Charles Sturge, *Cuthbert Tunstall: Churchman, Scholar, Statesman, Administrator* (London, 1938), 230-231, 248-249.

11. *L.J.*, I, 275-276.

12. Ibid., 269-271; Kenneth Pickthorn, *Early Tudor Government: Henry VIII* (Cambridge, Cambridge University Press, 1934), 496-497; Sir William Petre to Paget, 24 December 1545, SP 1/212, f. 112v (*L.P.*, XX, ii, 1030 [2]).

13. Petre to Paget, as in n. 12 above. The original document of the statute (37 Henry VIII, c.4) in the H.L.R.O. is a clean copy, with few crossings out, erasures, or interlineations.

14. Hall, *Chronicle*, 865.

15. SP 1/212, f. 111 (*L.P.*, XX, ii, 1030 [2]).

16. *S.R.*, III, 988-993.

17. Chapuys to Charles V, 18 June 1545, *L.P.*, XX, i, 984.

18. See Richard Ehrenberg, *Capital and Finance in the Age of the Renaissance* (London, 1928), 97-117; H. R. Trevor-Roper, "The General Crisis of the Seventeenth Century," in Trevor Aston, ed., *Crisis in Europe, 1560-1660* (London, 1965), 73-80.

19. Ehrenberg, *Capital and Finance*, 25-32.

20. Hatfield House, Cecil Papers, MS. 230, no. 7.

21. Frederick C. Dietz, *English Government Finance, 1485-1558* (Urbana, Illinois, 1921), 159, 164-165. On benevolences, see Jacob, *Fifteenth Century*, 632.

22. Hall, *Chronicle*, 865; *A.P.C.*, II, 185.

23. Dietz, *English Government Finance, 1485-1558*, 167, 174; W. C. Richardson, *Stephen Vaughan: Financial Agent of Henry VIII* (Louisiana State University Studies, Social Science Series, III) (Baton Rouge, 1953), chaps. 5-6; J. D. Gould, *The Great Debasement: Currency and Economy in Mid-Tudor England* (Oxford, Clarendon Press, 1970), 9-12, 43-51.

24. Dietz, *English Government Finance, 1485-1558*, 148-149; Joyce Youings, *The Dissolution of the Monasteries* (Historical Problems, Studies and Documents, XIV) (London, George Allen & Unwin, 1971), 117-118.

25. Richardson, *Stephen Vaughan*, 63.

26. 33 Henry VIII, c.27 (*S.R.*, III, 867).

27. *S.R.*, III, 988.

28. Knowles, *Religious Orders*, III, 353; Geraint Dyfnallt Owen, "Agrarian Conditions and Changes in West Wales during the Sixteenth Century with Special Reference to Monastic and Chantry Lands" (Ph.D. diss., University of Wales, 1935), 275.

29. Kitching, "Studies," I, 26.

30. For another indication of the government's fears on this point, see the instructions of May 1545 to the commissioners for the dissolution of the colleges of Crediton and Ottery St. Mary (E 301/81, m. 3).

31. *S.R.*, III, 990.

32. Hall, *Chronicle*, 865.

33. For the commission of 28 July 1545, see Rymer, *Foedera*, VI, iii, 129-130; Burnet, I, 533-534; *L.P.*, XX, i, 1335 (52).

34. For the commissions for the survey of the chantries, see C 66/777, m. lv (*L.P.*, XXI, i, 302 [30]). For the visitation injunctions which faithfully reflect the terms of the

commission, see SP 1/213, f. 80 (Wilkins, III, 875-876; *L.P.*, XXI, i, 69); E 301/126. Cf. Craib, "Surrey Chantries," 12-14.

35. It is barely possible that Van der Delft's enigmatic comment—that the Council "are very busy with the affairs of last Parliament, which put all chantries in the king's hands, and the coming Parliament, which will deal with the employment of the proceeds"—may indicate that Henry VIII was preparing to reform the chantries for charitable purposes (Van der Delft to Charles V, 14 December 1546, *L.P.*, XXI, ii, 546). It is my own strong feeling that the sentence had a fiscal rather than a philanthropic significance.

36. Cox to Paget, 12 October 1546, SP 1/225, f. 183 (*L.P.*, XXI, ii, 260); William Harrison, *Description of England in Shakspere's Youth*, ed. F. J. Furnivall (London, 1877), 88; Brinklow, *Complaynt*, 47-48; Ralph Morice, "Anecdotes and Character of Archbishop Cranmer," in Nichols, *Narratives*, 247; Ridley, *Thomas Cranmer*, 273.

37. Vaughan to Paget, 22 December 1545 and 10 February 1546, *L.P.*, XX, ii, 1025, and XXI, i, 189; Chamberlain to Paget, 7 and 22 January 1546, ibid., 27, and SP 1/213, f. 143 (*L.P.*, XXI, i, 107); Parker, *Correspondence*, 34.

38. W. K. Jordan, *Edward VI, The Young King* (henceforth Jordan, *Edward VI*, I) (Cambridge, Mass., 1968), 102-103.

39. Cf. Scarisbrick, *Henry VIII*, 475-478. Professor Scarisbrick carefully presents the weaknesses and uncertainties in this case.

40. Foxe, V, 562, 563-564.

41. Lacey Baldwin Smith, "Henry VIII and the Protestant Triumph," *American Historical Review*, 71 (1966), 1252, 1254. On the importance of the doctrine of private masses in the interrogation of Anne Askew, see Foxe, V, 538, 541.

42. B.L. Cotton MSS., Cleopatra E V, ff. 140-143 (*L.P.*, XII, i, 1312), and f. 330.

43. B.L. Harleian MS. 425, ff. 65-66; *A.P.C.*, I, 414, 417, 418-419, 420, 423, 440, 466-467; SP 1/221, f. 6 (*L.P.*, XXI, i, 1138); Burnet, IV, 531-532. See also the July 1546 pardon of George Blagge (*L.P.*, XXI, i, 1383 [72]).

44. Lacey Baldwin Smith, "Henry VIII and the Protestant Triumph," 1264; Rymer, *Foedera*, VI, iii, 150-157; *A.P.C.*, II, 38-43; Wriothesley, *Chronicle*, I, 181.

45. *S.R.*, III, 988; 1 Edward VI, c.14 (*S.R.*, IV, 24-33).

46. If profit had been its primary motive, the Edwardian government should not —evidently on humanitarian grounds—have exempted the hospitals from dissolution (ibid., IV, 24-33).

47. Ibid., III, 990-991.

48. 33 Henry VIII, c.27 (*S.R.*, III, 867). See above, chap. 6, text and n. 39.

49. SP 1/211, ff. 29-30 (*L.P.*, XX, ii, 852). The document has two endorsements in sixteenth-century hands: "Touching chantries and soul priests to be the king's except &c, *quaere*"; and "An Article to be put into the act of Parliament." It is not dated, and there is no internal evidence that enables a precise dating. But in view of its general tone, and in view of the fact that it makes no reference to previous chantry legislation, it probably was written sometime in 1545.

50. Cf. G. R. Elton, "Parliamentary Drafts, 1529-1540," *B.I.H.R.*, 25 (1952), 119.

51. C 66/777, m. 1v (*L.P.*, XXI, i, 302 [30]); E 117/12/9-10; E 315/67, ii, f. 453; E 301/120, 123, 128-129; Henry B. Walters, *London Churches at the Reformation* (London, S.P.C.K., 1939), 631-632.

52. Leach, *English Schools*, I, 63.

53. E 301/13/5; E 301/18/46; E 301/25/46; E 301/31/82; E 301/32; *Y.C.C.*, I, 113.

54. *S.R.*, III, 990.

55. 27 Henry VIII, c.42 (*S.R.*, III, 599-601).

56. "The repair up of M. Parker and W. Maye after survey to the king's Majesty," Parker, *Correspondence,* 33-34; Catherine Parr to the chancellor and vice-chancellor of Cambridge, 26 February 1546, ibid., 36-37; J. B. Mullinger, *The University of Cambridge,* 3 vols. (Cambridge, 1873-1911), II, 78; Mary Dewar, *Sir Thomas Smith: A Tudor Intellectual in Office* (London, 1964), 24-25.

57. Parker, *Correspondence,* 34-35. All copies of Henry's letter of the same date to the vice-chancellor of Oxford and others, commissioning them to survey the Oxford colleges, have been lost. We know of this letter only because it was mentioned in a list of "documents signed by stamp" (*L.P.*, XXI, i, 148 [77]).

58. Richard Taverner to Parker, 21 January 1546, B.L. Add. MS. 19,400, f. 23 (*L.P.*, XXI, i, 101).

59. This paragraph relies heavily upon Matthew Parker's description of the situation at court (n. 56, above).

60. Goodrich to Parker, Redman, and May, 1 February 1546, B.L. Add. MS. 19,400, f. 24 (*L.P.*, XXI, i, 152); Parker, *Correspondence,* 35; *L.P.*, XXI, i, 244, 299 (2); E 315/440, 441 (*L.P.*, XXI, i, 299 [1, 2]). For the draft returns of the Cambridge colleges, see C.C.C.C., MS. 108, pp. 449-456, 489-558.

61. University of Oxford to Henry VIII, 10 February 1546, *L.P.*, XXI, i, 244; vice-chancellor and university of Cambridge to Henry VIII, 13 February 1546, *L.P.*, XXI, i, 203, and to Paget, 13 February 1546, ibid., 204; Catherine Parr to the chancellor and vice-chancellor of Cambridge, 26 February 1546, Parker, *Correspondence,* 36-37.

62. This paragraph is based upon Matthew Parker's "repair up" (n. 56, above). Parker's phrase may perhaps best be translated, "formerly slavering wolves."

63. Mullinger, *University of Cambridge,* II, 80-81; *L.P.*, XXI, ii, 648 (43); G. M. Trevelyan, *Trinity College: An Historical Sketch* (Cambridge, Cambridge University Press, 1943), 9-10.

64. *L.P.*, XXI, i, 791.

65. See Appendix 2.

66. *A.P.C.*, II, 107-108; *L.P.*, XXI, ii, 200 (16); C 47/7/3, mm. 3-4.

67. *L.P.*, XIX, i, 278 (50); *V.C.H., Wiltshire,* III, 388; Hugh Shortt, ed., *City of Salisbury* (London, Phoenix House, 1957), 54.

68. *L.P.*, XXI, i, 1166 (16); ibid., ii, 332 (87); C 47/7/3, m. 2; Rymer, *Foedera,* VI, iii, 138.

69. *C.P.R., Edward VI,* I, 238; *L.P.*, XXI, ii, 648 (61); ibid., i, 1166 (15); ibid., ii, 648 (52).

70. Cf. J. D. Mackie, *The Earlier Tudors, 1485-1558,* Oxford History of England, VII (Oxford, 1952), 399; G. R. Elton, ed., *The Tudor Constitution: Documents and Commentary* (Cambridge, 1960), 369n.

71. E.g., Otwell Johnson to John Johnson, n.d. (1546), SP 46/5, f. 177; Clay, *Testamenta Eboracensia,* VI, 235; Van der Delft to Charles V, 14 December 1546, *L.P.*, XXI, ii, 546; Selve to the French ambassador in Flanders, 27 December 1546, ibid., 621.

72. Cf. Scarisbrick, *Henry VIII,* 477n.

Chapter 8: The Edwardian Chantries Act, 1547

1. *Certayne Sermons, or Homilies, appoynted by the Kynges Maiestie, to bee declared and redde, by all persones, vicars, or curates, euery Sondaye in their churches, where thei haue cure* (London, Grafton, 1547; *S.T.C.* 13,639); reprinted in their en-

tirety in John Griffiths, *The Two Books of Homilies Appointed to be Read in Churches* (Oxford, 1859), and in part in Cranmer, *Works*, II, 128-149.

2. *Certayne Sermons, or Homilies*, sig. Aii^V.

3. Van der Delft to the Queen Dowager, 6 September 1547, *C.S.P.Span.*, IX, 148. Despite the hostility with which the government now viewed masses for the dead, the practice of praying for the departed proved more durable. Prayers for the dead were included in the canon of the Eucharist by the first Edwardian Prayer Book and were not wholly excised from the liturgy of the English Church until the 1552 Prayer Book (F. Procter and W. H. Frere, *A New History of the Book of Common Prayer* [London, Macmillan, 1955], 82, 472; Dom Gregory Dix, *The Shape of the Liturgy* [London, Dacre Press, 1945], 660).

4. Frere and Kennedy, II, 130.

5. Ibid., 116. For the Henrician background to this order, see ibid., 38, 59, 67-68; E 315/118, ff. 198-200; Wilkins, III, 857-858.

6. Frere and Kennedy, II, 127, 187; Wilkins, IV, 29; Shield, "Reformation in the Diocese of Salisbury," 182-183.

7. Frere and Kennedy, II, 127-128; E 301/25/1; Maclean, "Chantry Certificates, Gloucestershire," 304; Graham, *Chantry Certificates*, 42.

8. Frere and Kennedy, II, 122-123, 129, 113. Bishops Latimer, Shaxton, Voysey, and Bonner had each previously ordered the chantry priests in their dioceses to teach school (ibid., 17, 56, 63, 85), thus providing precedents for the injunctions of 1547.

9. *L.J.*, I, 304.

10. J. E. Neale, "The Commons Journals of the Tudor Period," *T.R.H.S.*, 4th ser. 3 (1920), 140-142.

11. *A.P.C.*, II, 193-195 (reprinted in shortened form in J. R. Tanner, ed., *Tudor Constitutional Documents*, 2nd ed. [Cambridge, 1930], 535-536, and in Elton, *Tudor Constitution*, 297-298).

12. 1 Edward VI, c.14 (*S.R.*, IV, 24-33) (reprinted in full in Henry Gee and W. J. Hardy, eds., *Documents Illustrative of English Church History* [London, 1896], 328-357; in abridged form in Tanner, *Tudor Constitutional Documents*, 103-107, and in Elton, *Tudor Constitution*, 382-385).

13. *C.J.*, I, 2; *L.J.*, I, 304, 306-308.

14. It is not clear that Cranmer actually spoke against the bill at this time. Jasper Ridley (*Thomas Cranmer*, 273) was probably correct in dating in 1552 the archbishop's attempt to halt the sale of chantry properties until Edward VI had come of age. Cf. Nichols, *Narratives*, 247, and Burnet, II, 101.

15. *C.J.*, I, 3-4; *L.J.*, I, 312-313. Of the eight bishops who had voted against the bill on 15 December, only five opposed the final chantries bill on 24 December. On that occasion Cranmer and Heath were both absent, while Rugg, despite his conservative bent, voted for the measure.

16. These words appear on the original act, which is in the H.L.R.O.

17. *S.R.*, III, 988.

18. The concept of the "superstitious use," which was to have a profound effect upon the English law of charity, had its origin in this passage. See Gareth Jones, *History of the Law of Charity, 1532-1827* (Cambridge, Cambridge University Press, 1969), 10-11.

19. For this and other passages quoted from the 1547 Chantries Act, see *S.R.*, IV, 24-33.

20. Cf. Leach, *English Schools*, I, 68.

21. Cf. the corresponding clause in the 1545 act, which had specified a time limit of almost ten years (*S.R.*, III, 988).

22. Cf. Thompson, "Chantry Certificates for Northamptonshire," 91.

23. The royally endowed obits continued to be said in St. George's Chapel, but with a reformed liturgy which studiously avoided prayers for the present felicity of the dead (Frere and Kennedy, II, 220-221). The chantries in the chapel were likewise not dissolved by the 1547 act. The chapter acts record a steady stream of presentations to the livings of the cantarists up to 1607 (Shelagh Bond, ed., *The Chapter Acts of the Deans and Canons of Windsor* [Windsor, Oxley and Sons, 1966], 26, 34, 39, 49, 61). Cobham College, Kent, which had been dissolved in 1539 and granted to Lord Cobham, was also exempted by a proviso in the Lords' bill which was then included in the 1547 act (*S.R.*, III, 738; *V.C.H., Kent*, II, 231: *S.R.*, IV, 31).

24. *A.P.C.*, II, 193-195.

25. The burgesses for Coventry were Christopher Warene and Henry Porter (T. W. Whitley, *The Parliamentary Representation of the City of Coventry* [Coventry, 1894], 41). William Overend, a merchant who was mayor of his borough in 1548, and Thomas Gawdy, esq., represented King's Lynn (H. J. Hillen, *The History of the Borough of King's Lynn* [Norwich, 1907], I, 265). On the poverty of Coventry, see Mayor and aldermen of Coventry to Cromwell, 20 October 1537, SP 1/137, f. 238 (*L.P.*, XIII, ii, 650); Rowland Lee to Cromwell, 12 January 1539, B.L. Cotton MSS., Cleopatra E IV, f. 311 (*L.P.*, XIV, i, 57); *V.C.H., Warwickshire*, VIII, 162-163; Mary Dormer Harris, *The Story of Coventry* (London, 1911), 162-163. For the guild lands, see E 301/53/1; E 301/57/1-7.

26. The grant to Lynn is dated 21 May 1548 (*C.P.R., Edward VI*, II, 11-13), that to Coventry not until 13 December 1548 (ibid., 81). The reason for the delay appears to have been that in July 1548 the government was considering selling a substantial part of the Coventry guild lands to "foreign persons." The mayor and aldermen, fearing that the only lands which would be left for them would be "in such ruin and decay that to maintain the reparations thereof will amount to half the value of the said tenements," were threatening to call off the deal (E 315/67, ii, ff. 351v-352). As it turned out, both of the grants returned only a portion of the total guild lands of the two boroughs (*C.P.R., Edward VI*, II, 231; ibid., III, 383; Hillen, *History*, II, 265).

27. According to Sir Thomas Smith, who wrote in 1565, "At the afternoon they keep no parliament" (*De Republica Anglorum*, ed. L. Alston [Cambridge, 1906], 55). J. E. Neale, however, identified a few afternoon sessions in Edward VI's reign (*The Elizabethan House of Commons* [London, 1949], 379).

28. *C.J.*, I, 3-4.

29. Elton, *Reform and Renewal*, 82. Procedural efficiency was essential, for the time of prorogation was close at hand. Furthermore, since this was in effect a second draft of the chantries bill which had been revised in response to the Commons' criticisms of the Lords' bill, the government may have felt safe in having the bill engrossed prior to its first reading on 21 December.

30. Neale, *Elizabethan House of Commons*, 370-372. The original act in the H.L.R.O. consists of three sizable pieces of parchment, glued together. Since each of these is in a different handwriting, it is likely that the government assigned three scriveners to the task in order to have the bill engrossed as quickly as possible.

31. *A.P.C.*, II, 194.

32. These "appended provisos" (see Stanford E. Lehmberg, "Early Tudor Parliamentary Procedure: Provisos in the Legislation of the Reformation Parliament," *E.H.R.*, 85 [1970], 3) were sewn together on top of each other at the bottom left corner of the engrossed bill. They vary considerably in penmanship, and only two of them were probably written by professional scriveners.

33. Lehmberg, *Reformation Parliament*, 252; Elton, *Reform and Renewal*, 161.

34. Petre to Paget, 24 December 1545, SP 1/212, f. 112 (*L.P.*, XX, ii, 1030[2]).

35. *C.J.*, I, 2-3.

36. The Lords' bill refers only to the "maintenance of bridges and highways."

37. *S.R.*, IV, vi. It was Professor S.T. Bindoff who informed me of the existence of this document. The endorsements on it ("Soit baillez aux commons avecquez lez provisions annexez") indicate that it originated in the Lords. This, then, must be the engrossed draft bill which the Lords passed on 15 December 1547 and which the Commons threw out on 17 December. As such, despite its numerous internal provisos, some of which may conceivably not have been in the government's earliest drafts, this document brings us as close as possible to the original intentions of the Edwardian government. The following paragraphs are based upon it, as compared with the statute (*S.R.*, IV, 24-33); cf. also Lehmberg, "Early Tudor Parliamentary Procedure," 4.

38. A proviso specifically protects the general corporations of towns and repeatedly expands the draft's references to a "parish" to "town or parish" (*S.R.*, IV, 31, 27).

39. The Lords' draft orders that chantry lands used for "the keeping of a grammar school" should continue to be devoted to this purpose; the act orders the continuance of every such grammar school "or preaching" (*S.R.*, IV, 27).

40. Harris, *Story of Coventry*, 73-83; Charles Gross, *The Gild Merchant* (Oxford, 1890), I, 161; *C.P.R., Edward VI*, II, 11-13.

41. B.L. Hargrave MS. 4, f. 299v, a contemporary law report dealing with the 1547 Chantries Act, indicates that Hales was "the chief drawer and penner of this Act." The *L.J.* corroborates this by reporting that on 20 December 1547 "the bill for chantries is committed to Mr. Hales, Serjeant at the Law" (I, 311).

42. The prebends of St. Andrew and St. Michael in Beverley Minster; the Killingwoldgraves Hospital in Bishop Burton; the hospitals of St. Mary Magdalen and St. Sepulchre in the parish of Hedon; and the college of Sutton-in-Holderness (*C.P.R., Edward VI*, I, 170, 250).

43. Thompson, "Chantry Certificates for Northamptonshire," 168.

44. Van der Delft to the Emperor's Council of State, 5 December 1547, *C.S.P. Span.*, IX, 221-222; James Clarke to the earl of Shrewsbury, 27 March 1548, in Edmund Lodge, *Illustrations of British History, Biography, and Manners*, 2nd ed., 3 vols. (London, 1838), I, 149-150; Otwell Johnson to John Johnson, 18 April 1548, SP 46/5, ff. 252-252v (Barbara Winchester, *Tudor Family Portrait* [London, Jonathan Cape, 1955], 193-194). Despite this initial flurry of selling, many scattered plots of ex-chantry land remained unsold years after the dissolution (Kitching, "Studies," 341).

45. Jordan, *Edward VI*, I, 102-103.

46. Dietz, *English Government Finance, 1485-1558*, 178; Jordan, *Edward VI*, I, 391-393.

47. *A.P.C.*, II, 185.

48. Ibid., 184.

49. Gairdner, *Lollardy and the Reformation*, III, 55; Dixon, *History*, II, 460; Graham, *Chantry Certificates*, vii; Snell, *Chantry Certificates for Devon*, xi.

50. For this view, cf. Dixon, *History*, II, 461-462; Dickens, *English Reformation*, 206. For an earlier statement of a similar position, see Sir Henry Hobart, *The English Reports*, LXXX, 123. This was also a favorite argument of the informers who during the reigns of Elizabeth I and of James I attempted to provide a rationale for their presentation of the properties of the London livery companies as "concealed lands" (George Unwin, *The Gilds and Companies of London*, 4th ed. [London, 1963], 211-212). The MS. law report which I have mentioned earlier (B.L. Hargrave MS. 4, ff. 298-305) argues clearly — and correctly — against such an interpretation.

51. E 301/34, mm. 36-40.

52. For the view that Maitland's thesis concerning the alleged threat posed by the civil law to the predominance of common law in early sixteenth-century England is grossly exaggerated (F. W. Maitland, *English Law and the Renaissance* [Cambridge, Cambridge University Press, 1901]), see S. E. Thorne, "English Law and the Renaissance," *La Storia del Diritto nel Quadro delle Scienze Storiche* (Florence, Leo S. Olschki, 1966), 437-440; E. W. Ives, "The Common Lawyers in Pre-Reformation England," *T.R.H.S.*, 5th ser. 18 (1968), 169-170; Holdsworth, *History*, IV, 217-219, 283-286; and G. R. Elton, "The Political Creed of Thomas Cromwell," *T.R.H.S.*, 5th ser. 6 (1956), 78.

53. Jordan, *Edward VI*, I, 84; Ives, "Common Lawyers," 155-156; *L.J.*, I, 308, 313; Sturge, *Cuthbert Tunstall*, 13; *D.N.B.*, s.v. "Edmund Bonner," "Cuthbert Tunstall."

54. Dewar, *Sir Thomas Smith*, 20-22, 24, 26-39; F. W. Maitland, intro. to Smith, *De Republica Anglorum*, ed. Alston, ix.

55. See n. 49 above.

56. Cranmer, "On the Oblation and Sacrifice of the Mass," in *Works*, I, 349-350.

57. This apt phrase, used by Professor Dickens (*English Reformation*, 141) with reference to the monastic houses, is equally applicable to the chantry foundations.

58. Frere and Kennedy, II, 113, 129.

59. See above, Table 1.7.

60. Green, *Survey of Somerset*, 101; Maclean, "Chantry Certificates, Gloucestershire," 300.

61. E 301/19/169, 161, 148, 144.

62. *S.R.*, IV, 24.

63. Jordan, *Edward VI*, I, 83-84; Simon, *Education and Society*, 310n. E.g., Sir Walter Mildmay, one of the two commissioners responsible for deciding which of the useful services of the dissolved institutions should be continued, was instrumental in securing the refoundation of the Chelmsford Grammar School in 1551 (*C.P.R., Edward VI*, IV, 116-117; Stanford E. Lehmberg, *Sir Walter Mildmay and Tudor Government* [Austin, Texas, University of Texas Press, 1964], 22-24).

64. The warrants ordering the payment of pensions to schoolmasters and curates have survived for numerous counties, and are generally located in the category E 319 (but cf. also E 315/30, f. 44 and DL 42/135).

65. As Dr. Kitching has pointed out ("Studies," I, 159): "Every item . . . was rated on its own merits, and it is very improbable that the commissioners had an overall twenty-year figure in view even if it was on this basis that estimates of profits were made." From the outset, urban properties tended to be sold at rather less than twenty years' purchase, and many rural properties fetched substantially more than that. Twenty years' purchase, however, is a reasonable average of the value of the early sales of chantry properties.

66. Lawton, *Collectio*, 459; *V.C.H., Yorkshire*, I, 476-477; Robert Somerville, *History of the Duchy of Lancaster*, I, *1265-1603* (London, Duchy of Lancaster, 1953), 302.

67. The government's refoundation of the ex-chantry schools, which by 1560 had apparently increased considerably the capital value of the educational endowments in the realm, seems to have begun in earnest only in 1550 (Jordan, *Edward VI*, II, 198; Simon, *Education and Society*, 230-231).

68. Jordan, *Philanthropy*, 286-293; Simon, *Education and Society*, chap. 13; Lawrence Stone, "The Educational Revolution in England, 1560-1640," *Past and Present*, no. 28 (1964), 46-47; Trevor-Roper, "General Crisis," 85.

Bibliography

Manuscript Sources

1. London
   Public Record Office
C 47	Chancery, Miscellanea
C 66	———, Patent Rolls
C 82	———, Warrants for the Great Seal
DL 1	Duchy of Lancaster, Court of Duchy Chamber, Proceedings
DL 3	———, Depositions and Examinations
DL 5	———, Entry Books of Decrees and Orders
DL 14	———, Drafts and Particulars for Leases
DL 28	———, Accounts Various
DL 29	———, Ministers' Accounts
DL 38	———, Certificates, etc., of Colleges and Chantries
DL 41	———, Miscellanea
DL 42	———, Miscellaneous Books
E 36	Exchequer, Treasury of Receipt, Miscellaneous Books
E 101	———, King's Remembrancer, Miscellaneous Books
E 117	———, Church Goods
E 159	———, King's Remembrancer, Memoranda Rolls
E 178	———, Special Commissions of Inquiry
E 301	Exchequer, Augmentations Office, Certificates of Colleges and Chantries
E 315	———, Miscellaneous Books
E 319	———, Particulars for Grants, etc., for Schools, etc.
E 321	———, Proceedings of the Court of Augmentations
E 322	———, Deeds of Surrender
LR 2	Exchequer, Land Revenue, Miscellaneous Books
LR 6	———, Receivers' Accounts
Req 2	Court of Requests, Proceedings
SC 6	Special Collections: Ministers' and Receivers' Accounts
SP 1	State Papers, Henry VIII
SP 2	———, Folio
SP 3	———, Lisle Papers
SP 6	———, Theological Tracts
SP 10	State Papers, Edward VI
SP 12	State Papers, Elizabeth I
SP 46	State Papers, Various
SP 61	State Papers, Ireland
St Ch 2	Star Chamber Proceedings, Henry VIII

   British Library
   Additional Manuscripts
   Burney Manuscripts
   Cotton Manuscripts: Cleopatra, Titus, Vespasian, Vitellius
   Hargrave Manuscripts

Harleian Manuscripts
Lansdowne Manuscripts
Royal Manuscripts
Stowe Charters
Guildhall Library
    MS. 9531: Bishops' Registers
House of Lords Record Office
    Draft Bill of 1 Edward VI, c. 13
    Original Acts
Lambeth Palace Library
    MS. 1108
2. Cambridge, Corpus Christi College Library
    MSS. 104, 106, 108, 128
3. Canterbury Cathedral Library
    MS. CCL, X/10/2
4. Chelmsford, Essex Record Office
    DP   Churchwardens' Accounts
    MSS. D/ACV 1, D/AEV 2 Visitations Records
5. Hatfield, Hatfield House
    Cecil Papers (microfilm in B.L.)
6. Lichfield, Joint Record Office
    MSS. B/A/1 Bishops' Registers
7. Oxford, Bodleian Library
    Rawlinson Manuscripts
    4° Rawlinson 245 (MS. annotations by Henry VIII)
8. Salisbury, Diocesan Record Office, Wren Hall
    Bishops' Act Book, 1550-1558
    Bishops' Registers
9. Worcester, Worcestershire Record Office, St. Helen's Church
    B.A. 2764/802: Act Book of Bishop John Bell
    Bishops' Registers
10. York
    Borthwick Institute of Historical Research, St. Anthony's Hall
        MSS. R.VI.A.1, R.VI.A.5, R.VI.A.6
        R.I.: Archbishops' Registers
        "Tudor Crockford"
    Minster Library
        L 1(7-10): Torre Manuscripts
        MS. M.2(4)a

Printed Primary Sources

1. Chantry Certificates

Brown, J. E., ed. *Chantry Certificates for Hertfordshire.* Hertford, Stephen Austin & Sons, n.d.
———, and Page-Turner, F. A., eds., *Chantry Certificates for Bedfordshire with Institutions of Chantry Priests in Bedfordshire.* Bedford, Bedford Arts Club, 1908.
Cotton, Charles, ed. *The Canterbury Chantries and Hospitals in 1546.* Kent Records, 12, Supplement, 1934.
Cozens-Hardy, Basil, ed. "Chantries in the Duchy of Lancaster in Norfolk, 1548." *Norfolk Archaeology,* 29 (1946), 201-210.

Craib, Theodore, ed. "Surrey Chantries." *Surrey Archaeological Collections,* 25 (1912), 3-32.

Foster, C. W., and Thompson, A. Hamilton, eds. "The Chantry Certificates for Lincoln and Lincolnshire." *A.A.S.R.P.,* 36 (1921-1922), 183-294; ibid., 37 (1923-1925), 18-106, 247-275.

Fry, E. A., ed. "Dorset Chantries." *Dorset Natural History and Antiquarian Field Club,* 27 (1906), 214-233; 28 (1907), 12-29; 29 (1908), 30-79; 30 (1909), 13-57; 31 (1910), 85-114.

Graham, Rose, ed. *The Chantry Certificates and the Edwardian Inventories of Church Goods.* Oxfordshire Record Society, vol. 1, 1919; also published as Alcuin Club, vol. 23, 1920.

Green, Emanuel, ed. *The Survey and Rental of the Chantries, Colleges, and Free Chapels, Guilds, Fraternities, Lamps, Lights, and Obits in the County of Somerset.* Somerset Record Society, vol. 2, 1888.

Hussey, Arthur, ed. *Kent Chantries.* Kent Records, vol. 12, 1934-1936.

———— *Kent Obit and Lamp Rents.* Kent Records, vol. 14, 1936.

Jones, Evan D., ed. "Survey of the South Wales Chantries, 1546." *Archaeologia Cambrensis,* 89 (1934), 135-155.

Maclean, Sir John, ed. "Chantry Certificates, Gloucestershire." *Transactions of the Bristol and Gloucestershire Archaeological Society,* 8 (1883-1884), 229-308.

Page, William, ed. *The Certificates of the Commissioners Appointed to Survey the Chantries, Guilds, Hospitals, etc., in the County of York.* Surtees Society, vols. 91-92, 1892-1893.

Raine, J., ed. "The Certificate of . . . all Colleges, Deanries, Chauntries . . . within the Countie of Northumberland, the Towne of Newecastell uppon Tyne, and the Bisshopprycke of Duresme," in *The Injunctions and Other Ecclesiastical Proceedings of Richard Barnes.* Surtees Society, 22 (1850), lix-lxxvi.

———— "The Certificates of all the Chauntryes, &c., within the Countye of Northumberland," in *The Injunctions and Other Ecclesiastical Proceedings of Richard Barnes.* Surtees Society, 22 (1850), lxxvii-xc.

Raines, F. R., ed. *A History of the Chantries within the County Palatine of Lancaster.* Chetham Society, original ser., vols. 59-60, 1862.

Ray, John E., ed. *Sussex Chantry Records.* Sussex Record Society, vol. 36, 1931.

Redstone, L. J., ed. *Chantry Survey of the Upper Part of Teesdale . . . 37 Henry VIII.* Teesdale Record Society, vol. 3, 1937.

Redstone, V. B., ed. "Chapels, Chantries, and Gilds in Suffolk." *Proceedings of the Suffolk Institute of Archaeology and Natural History,* 12 (1906), 1-87.

Snell, Lawrence S., ed. *Documents towards a History of the Reformation in Cornwall, I, The Chantry Certificates for Cornwall.* Exeter, James Townsend & Son, 1953.

———— *Documents towards a History of the Reformation in Devon: The Chantry Certificates for Devon and the City of Exeter.* Exeter, James Townsend & Son, 1961.

Storey, R. L., ed. "The Chantries of Cumberland and Westmorland." *Transactions of the Cumberland and Westmorland Antiquarian and Archaeological Society,* new ser. 60 (1960), 66-96, and 62 (1962), 145-170.

Thompson, A. Hamilton, ed. "The Certificates of the Chantry Commissioners for the College of Southwell in 1546 and 1548." *Transactions of the Thoroton Society,* 15 (1911), 63-158.

———— "Certificates of the Shropshire Chantries." *Transactions of the Shropshire Archaeological and Natural History Society,* 3rd ser. 10 (1910), 269-392.

———— "Certificates of the Shropshire Chantries, Notes and Appendices." *Transactions of the Shropshire Archaeological and Natural History Society,* 4th ser. 1

(1911), 115-190.

———· "The Chantry Certificate Rolls for the County of Nottingham," *Transactions of the Thoroton Society*, 16 (1912), 91-133; 17 (1913), 59-119; 18 (1914), 83-184.

———· "The Chantry Certificates for Leicestershire returned under the Act of 37 Henry VIII, Cap. IV." *A.A.S.R.P.*, 30 (1909-1910), 463-570.

———· "The Chantry Certificates for Northamptonshire." *A.A.S.R.P.*, 31, i (1911), 87-178.

Walcott, Mackenzie E. C., ed. "Inventories of the Church Goods, and Chantries of Wilts." *W.A.N.H.M.*, 12 (1870), 354-383.

2. Other Printed Primary Sources (Selected)

Benton, G. Montagu, ed. "Essex Wills at Canterbury." *Transactions of the Essex Archaeological Society*, new ser. 21 (1937), 234-269.

Brinklow, Henry. *Complaynt of Roderyck Mors*. Edited by J. Meadows Cowper. E.E.T.S., extra ser., vol. 22. London, 1874.

———· *The Lamentacyon of a Christen agaynst the Cytye of London*. Edited by J. Meadows Cowper. E.E.T.S., extra ser., vol. 22. London, 1874.

Calendar of the Patent Rolls Preserved in the Public Record Office. 48 vols. London, H.M.S.O., 1901-1973.

Calendar of State Papers, Spanish. 13 vols. London, H.M.S.O., 1862-1954.

Caley, John, and Hunter, Jos., eds. *Valor Ecclesiasticus temp. Henr. VIII auctoritate regia institutus*. 6 vols. London, 1810-1834.

Certayne Sermons, or Homilies, appoynted by the Kynges Maiestie, to bee declared and redde, by all persons, vicars, or curates, euery Sondaye in their churches . . . . London, Richard Grafton, 1547; *S.T.C.* 13,639.

Chambers, D. S., ed. *Faculty Office Registers, 1534-1549*. Oxford, Clarendon Press, 1966.

Clay, J. W., ed. *Testamenta Eboracensia: A Selection of Wills from the Registry at York*, VI. Surtees Society, vol. 106, 1902.

Cranmer, Thomas. *Works*. Edited by J. E. Cox. 2 vols. Parker Society, Cambridge, 1844-1846.

Dasent, J. R., ed. *Acts of the Privy Council of England*. 32 vols. London, H.M.S.O., 1890-1907.

Ellis, Henry, ed. *Original Letters Illustrative of English History*. 3 series, 11 vols. London, 1824-1846.

Elton, G. R., ed. *The Tudor Constitution: Documents and Commentary*. Cambridge, Cambridge University Press, 1960.

Eshelby, H. D., ed. "The Episcopal Visitations of the Yorkshire Deaneries of the Archdeaconry of Richmond in 1548 and 1554." *Y.A.J.*, 14 (1898), 390-421.

Fish, Simon. *A Supplicacyon for the Beggers*. Edited by F. J. Furnivall. E.E.T.S., extra ser., vol. 13. London, 1871.

Fisher, John, Saint. *Hereafter Ensueth Two Fruytfull Sermons*. London, W. Rastell, 1532; *S.T.C.* 10,909.

Foster, C. W., ed. *Lincoln Wills*. 2 vols. Lincoln Record Society, vols. 5 (1914) and 10 (1918).

Fowler, J. T., ed. *Memorials of the Church of SS. Peter and Wilfrid, Ripon*. 2 vols. Surtees Society, vols. 74 (1881) and 78 (1884).

Foxe, John. *Actes and Monuments*. Edited by Josiah Pratt. 8 vols. London, 1870.

———· ed. *The Whole Works of W. Tyndall, J. Frith, and Doct. Barnes*. London, John Daye, 1573; *S.T.C.* 24,436.

Frere, W. H., and Kennedy, W. M., eds. *Visitation Articles and Injunctions of the Period of the Reformation.* 3 vols. Alcuin Club, vols. 14-16, 1910.

Hall, Edward. *Chronicle; Containing the History of England during the Reign of Henry the Fourth, and the Succeeding Monarchs to the End of the Reign of Henry the Eighth.* London, 1809.

Here Begynneth a Lytell Boke, that Speketh of Purgatorye. London, Robert Wyer, [1534?]; *S.T.C.* 3,360.

Historical Manuscripts Commission, *Reports.*

Jessopp, Augustus, ed. *Visitations of the Diocese of Norwich, 1492-1532.* Camden Soc., new ser. 43, 1888.

Journals of the House of Commons.

Journals of the House of Lords.

Latimer, Hugh. *Works.* Edited by George Elwes Corrie. 2 vols. Parker Society, Cambridge, 1844-1845.

Leach, A. F., ed. *Early Yorkshire Schools.* 2 vols. Y.A.S.R.S., vols. 27 (1899) and 33 (1903).

Leland, John. *Itinerary.* Edited by Lucy Toulmin Smith. 5 vols. London, George Bell & Sons, 1906-1910.

Letters and Papers, Foreign and Domestic, of the Reign of Henry VIII. Edited by J. S. Brewer, J. H. Gairdner, and R. H. Brodie. 21 vols. London, H.M.S.O., 1860-1920.

Lloyd, Charles, ed. *Formularies of Faith . . . during the Reign of Henry VIII.* Oxford, 1825.

Lumb, George Denison, ed. *Testamenta Leodiensia: Wills of Leeds, Pontefract, Wakefield, Otley, and District, 1539-1553.* Thoresby Society, vol. 19, 1913.

Mentz, Georg, ed. *Die Wittenberger Artikel von 1536.* Quellenschriften zur Geschichte des Protestantismus, Heft 2. Leipzig, A. Deichert, 1905.

More, Thomas, Saint. *The Workes of Sir Thomas More Knyght, Sometyme Lorde Chauncellour of England, Wrytten by Him in the Englysh Tonge.* Edited by William Rastell. London, J. Cawood, J. Waly, and R. Tottell, 1557; *S.T.C.* 18,076.

Muller, James Arthur, ed. *The Letters of Stephen Gardiner.* Cambridge, Cambridge University Press, 1933.

Nichols, John Gough, ed. *The Chronicle of Calais.* Camden Soc., original ser., vol. 35, 1846.

————· *Narratives of the Days of the Reformation.* Camden Soc., original ser., vol. 77, 1859.

Nicolas, Nicholas Harris, ed. *Testamenta Vetusta.* 2 vols. London, 1826.

Parker, Matthew. *Correspondence.* Edited by John Bruce and Thomas T. Perrowne. Parker Society, Cambridge, 1853.

Phillipps, Sir Thomas. "Institutiones Clericorum in Comitatu Wiltoniae." 2 vols. B. L. MS. list, 1825.

Raine, Angelo, ed. *York Civic Records,* I-VI. Y.A.S.R.S., vols. 98 (1939), 103 (1941), 106 (1942), 108 (1945), 110 (1946), 112 (1948).

Raine, James, Jr., ed. *Testamenta Eboracensia: A Selection of Wills from the Registry at York,* V. Surtees Society, vol. 79, 1884.

Robinson, Hastings, ed. *Original Letters Relative to the English Reformation.* 2 vols. Parker Society, Cambridge, 1846-1847.

Rymer, Thomas, ed. *Foedera, Conventiones, Literae et cujuscunque Generis Acta Publica.* 3rd ed. Vol. VI. The Hague, 1745.

Saint German, Christopher. *A Treatise Concernynge the Diuision betwene the Spirytualtie and Temporaltie.* London, R. Redman, 1532; *S.T.C.* 21,586.

Singleton, Robert. *A Sermon Preached at Poules Crosse the Fourth Sonday in Lent,
the Yere of Our Lorde God 1535.* London, T. Godfraye, [1536]; *S.T.C.* 22,575.
Smith, Sir Thomas. *De Republica Anglorum.* Edited by L. Alston. Cambridge, Cam-
bridge University Press, 1906.
Statutes of the Realm. 11 vols. London, Record Commission, 1810-1828.
Tanner, Joseph R., ed. *Tudor Constitutional Documents.* 2nd ed. Cambridge, Cam-
bridge University Press, 1930.
Thompson, A. Hamilton, ed. *Visitations in the Diocese of Lincoln, 1517-1531,* I. Lin-
coln Record Society, vol. 33, 1940.
Thorne, S. E., ed. *Prerogativa Regis.* New Haven, Yale University Press, 1949.
Tyndale, William. *Doctrinal Treatises.* Edited by Henry Walter. Parker Society, Cam-
bridge, 1848.
Weaver, F. W., ed. *Somerset Medieval Wills, 1383-1500.* Somerset Record Society,
vol. 16, 1901.
———— *Somerset Medieval Wills, 1501-1530.* Somerset Record Society, vol. 19, 1903.
———— *Somerset Medieval Wills, 1531-1558.* Somerset Record Society, vol. 21, 1905.
Wilkins, David, ed. *Concilia Magnae Britanniae et Hiberniae.* 4 vols. London, 1737.
Wood-Legh, K. L., ed. *A Small Household in the Fifteenth Century, Being the Ac-
count Book of Munden's Chantry, Bridport.* Manchester, Manchester University
Press, 1956.
Wright, Thomas, ed. *Three Chapters of Letters Relating to the Suppression of the
Monasteries.* Camden Soc., original ser., vol. 26, 1843.
Wriothesley, Charles. *A Chronicle of England during the Reigns of the Tudors.* Edited
by William D. Hamilton. Camden Soc., vols. 11 (1875) and 20 (1877).
Wyclif, John. *The English Works . . . Hitherto Unprinted.* Edited by F. D. Matthew.
E.E.T.S., vol. 74, 1880.

Selected Secondary Sources

Bartlett, J. N. "The Expansion and Decline of York in the Later Middle Ages."
Ec.H.R., 2nd ser. 12 (1959-1960), 17-33.
Bean, J. M. W. *The Decline of English Feudalism, 1215-1540.* Manchester, Man-
chester University Press, 1968.
Beresford, Maurice W. "The Deserted Villages of Warwickshire." *Transactions of the
Birmingham Archaeological Society,* 56 (1950), 49-106.
Bowker, Margaret. *The Secular Clergy in the Diocese of Lincoln, 1495-1520.* Cam-
bridge Studies in Medieval Life and Thought, new ser., vol. 13. Cambridge, Cam-
bridge University Press, 1968.
Brodrick, George C. *Memorials of Merton College.* Oxford Historical Society, vol. 4,
1885.
Burnet, Gilbert. *The History of the Reformation of the Church of England.* Edited by
Nicholas Pocock. 7 vols. Oxford, 1865.
Chester, Allan G. *Hugh Latimer: Apostle to the English.* Philadelphia, University of
Pennsylvania Press, 1954.
Clark, Peter. *English Provincial Society from the Reformation to the Revolution: Religion, Politics and Society in Kent, 1500-1640.* Hassocks, Sussex, Harvester Press,
1977.
————, and Slack, Paul, eds. *Crisis and Order in English Towns, 1500-1700.* Lon-
don, Routledge & Kegan Paul, 1972.
Clay, Rotha Mary. *The Mediaeval Hospitals of England.* London, Methuen & Co.,
1909.

Clebsch, William A. *England's Earliest Protestants, 1520-1535.* Yale Publications in Religion, vol. 11. New Haven, Yale University Press, 1964.

Cook, G. H. *Mediaeval Chantries and Chantry Chapels.* Rev. ed. London, Phoenix House, 1963.

Cooper, Charles H., and Cooper, Thompson, eds. *Athenae Cantabrigienses,* I, *1500-1585.* Cambridge, 1858.

Dewar, Mary. *Sir Thomas Smith: A Tudor Intellectual in Office.* London, University of London Press, 1964.

Dickens, A. G. *The English Reformation.* London, Batsford, 1964.

———. *Lollards and Protestants in the Diocese of York, 1509-1558.* London, Oxford University Press for the University of Hull, 1959.

———. "A Municipal Dissolution of Chantries at York, 1536." *Y.A.J.,* 36 (1944-1947), 164-173.

———. "Sedition and Conspiracy in Yorkshire during the Later Years of Henry VIII," *Y.A.J.,* 34 (1939), 379-398.

Dietz, Frederick C. *English Government Finance, 1485-1558.* University of Illinois Studies in the Social Sciences, vol. 9, no. 3. Urbana, University of Illinois Press, 1921.

Dixon, Richard W. *History of the Church of England from the Abolition of the Roman Jurisdiction.* 6 vols. Oxford, 1878-1902.

Dobson, R. B. "The Foundation of Perpetual Chantries by the Citizens of Medieval York." In G. J. Cuming, ed. *Studies in Church History,* IV, *The Province of York,* 22-38. Leiden, Brill, 1967.

Edwards, Kathleen. *The English Secular Cathedrals in the Middle Ages.* 2nd ed. Manchester, Manchester University Press, 1967.

Ehrenberg, Richard. *Capital and Finance in the Age of the Renaissance: A Study of the Fuggers and Their Connections.* Translated by H. M. Lucas. London, Jonathan Cape, 1928.

Elton, G. R. *Policy and Police: The Enforcement of the Reformation in the Age of Thomas Cromwell.* Cambridge, Cambridge University Press, 1972.

———. *Reform and Renewal: Thomas Cromwell and the Common Weal.* Cambridge, Cambridge University Press, 1973.

Foster, Joseph. *Alumni Oxonienses, 1500-1714.* 4 vols. Oxford, 1891-1892.

Gairdner, James. *Lollardy and the Reformation in England.* 4 vols. London, Macmillan & Co., 1908-1913.

Gasquet, Francis Aidan. *Parish Life in Medieval England.* London, Methuen & Co., 1906.

Hanham, H. J. "The Suppression of the Chantries in Ashburton." *Transactions of the Devonshire Association,* 99 (1967), 111-137.

Harris, Mary Dormer. *The Story of Coventry.* London, J. M. Dent & Sons, 1911.

Heath, Peter. *The English Parish Clergy on the Eve of the Reformation.* London, Routledge & Kegan Paul, 1969.

Hibbert, Francis Aidan. *The Dissolution of the Monasteries as Illustrated by the Suppression of the Religious Houses of Staffordshire.* London, Pitman & Sons, 1910.

Hill, Rosalind. " 'A Chaunterie for Soules': London Chantries in the Reign of Richard II." In F. R. H. Du Boulay and C. M. Barron, eds., *The Reign of Richard II: Essays in Honour of May McKisack,* 242-255. London, University of London Press, 1971.

Hillen, H. J. *The History of the Borough of King's Lynn.* 2 vols. Norwich, East of England Newspaper Co., 1907.

Holdsworth, Sir William. *A History of English Law,* IV. London, Methuen & Co., 1924.

Horst, Irvin B. *The Radical Brethren: Anabaptism and the English Reformation to 1558.* Bibliotheca Humanistica & Reformatorica, vol. 2. Niewkoop, B. de Graaf, 1972.

Hughes, Philip. *The Reformation in England.* 5th ed. 3 vols. London, Burns & Oats, 1963.

Hunter, Joseph. *Hallamshire: The History and Topography of the Parish of Sheffield.* Edited by Alfred Gatty. London, 1869.

————· *South Yorkshire: The History and Topography of the Deanery of Doncaster.* 2 vols. London, 1828-1831.

Ives, E. W. "The Common Lawyers in Pre-Reformation England." *T.R.H.S.*, 5th ser. 18 (1968), 145-173.

Jacob, E. F. *The Fifteenth Century, 1399-1485.* Oxford History of England, VI. Oxford, Clarendon Press, 1961.

Jordan, W. K. *The Charities of Rural England, 1480-1660.* London, George Allen & Unwin, 1961.

————· *Edward VI:* I, *The Young King*; II, *The Threshold of Power.* Cambridge, Mass., Harvard University Press, 1968-1970.

————· *Philanthropy in England, 1480-1660.* London, George Allen & Unwin, 1959.

————· *The Social Institutions of Lancashire.* Chetham Society, 3rd ser., vol. 11, 1962.

Kitching, C. J. "The Chantries of the East Riding of Yorkshire at the Dissolution in 1548." *Y.A.J.*, 44 (1972), 178-194.

————· "Studies in the Redistribution of Collegiate and Chantry Property in the Diocese and County of York at the Dissolution." Ph.D. diss., University of Durham, 1970.

Knowles, Dom David. *The Religious Orders in England,* III, *The Tudor Age.* Cambridge, Cambridge University Press, 1959.

————, and Hadcock, R. Neville. *Medieval Religious Houses: England and Wales.* 2nd ed. London, Longman, 1971.

Leach, A. F. *English Schools at the Reformation.* 2 vols. Westminster, 1896.

————· *History of Warwick School.* London, Archibald Constable, 1906.

Lehmberg, Stanford E. "Early Tudor Parliamentary Procedure: Provisos in the Legislation of the Reformation Parliament." *E.H.R.*, 85 (1970), 1-11.

————· *The Reformation Parliament, 1529-1536.* Cambridge, Cambridge University Press, 1970.

Loades, D. M. "The Collegiate Churches of County Durham at the Time of the Dissolution." In G. J. Cuming, ed., *Studies in Church History,* IV, *The Province of York,* 65-75. Leiden, Brill, 1967.

Maclean, Sir John. "Notes on Greyndour Chapel and the Chantry in the Church of Newland." *Transactions of the Bristol and Gloucestershire Archaeological Society,* 7 (1882-1883), 117-125.

Maclure, Millar. *The Paul's Cross Sermons, 1534-1642.* University of Toronto Department of English Studies and Texts, VI. Toronto, University of Toronto Press, 1958.

Maxwell-Lyte, Sir H. C. *Historical Notes on the Use of the Great Seal of England.* London, H.M.S.O., 1926.

Messenger, Ernest C. *The Reformation, the Mass, and the Priesthood.* 2 vols. London, Longmans, Green & Co., 1936-1937.

Morant, Philip. *The History and Antiquities of the County of Essex.* 2 vols. London, 1768.

Mullinger, J. B. *The University of Cambridge.* 3 vols. Cambridge, Cambridge University Press, 1875-1911.

Neale, Sir John. *The Elizabethan House of Commons.* London, Jonathan Cape, 1949.

Newcourt, Richard. *Repertorium Ecclesiasticum Parochiale Londonense. An Ecclesiastical Parochial of the Diocese of London.* 2 vols. London, 1708-1710.

Owen, Dorothy M. *Church and Society in Medieval Lincolnshire.* History of Lincolnshire, ed. Joan Thirsk, V. Lincoln, Lincolnshire Local History Society, 1971.

Oxley, James E. *The Reformation in Essex to the Death of Mary.* Manchester, Manchester University Press, 1965.

Richardson, W. C. *Stephen Vaughan: Financial Agent of Henry VIII.* Louisiana State University Studies, Social Science Series, III. Baton Rouge, Louisiana State University Press, 1953.

Ridley, Jasper. *Thomas Cranmer.* Oxford, Clarendon Press, 1962.

Rock, Daniel. *The Church of Our Fathers as Seen in St. Osmund's Rite for the Cathedral of Salisbury.* Edited by G. W. Hart and W. H. Frere. 4 vols. London, John Hodges, 1903.

Rosenthal, Joel T. *The Purchase of Paradise: Gift Giving and the Aristocracy, 1307-1485.* London, Routledge & Kegan Paul, 1972.

Rowse, A. L. *Tudor Cornwall: Portrait of a Society.* London, Jonathan Cape, 1941.

Rupp, E. G. *Studies in the Making of the Protestant Tradition.* Cambridge, Cambridge University Press, 1947.

Scarisbrick, J. J. *Henry VIII.* London, Eyre & Spottiswoode, 1968.

Seymour, Margaret A. "The Organisation, Personnel, and Functions of the Medieval Hospital in the Later Middle Ages." M.A. diss., University of London, 1946.

Shield, I. T. "The Reformation in the Diocese of Salisbury, 1547-1562." B.Litt. diss., Oxford University, 1960.

Simon, Joan. *Education and Society in Tudor England.* Cambridge, Cambridge University Press, 1966.

Smith, H. Maynard. *Pre-Reformation England.* London, Macmillan & Co., 1938.

Smith, Lacey Baldwin. "Henry VIII and the Protestant Triumph." *American Historical Review,* 71 (1965-1966), 1237-1264.

———· *Henry VIII: The Mask of Royalty.* London, Jonathan Cape, 1971.

———· *Tudor Prelates and Politics, 1536-1558.* Princeton Studies in History, VIII. Princeton, Princeton University Press, 1953.

Smith, Lucius. *The Story of Ripon Minster.* Leeds, Richard Jackson, 1914.

Stone, Lawrence. "The Educational Revolution in England, 1560-1640." *Past and Present,* no. 28 (1964), 41-80.

Strype, John. *Ecclesiastical Memorials.* 3 vols. Oxford, 1822.

Sturge, Charles. *Cuthbert Tunstal: Churchman, Scholar, Statesman, Administrator.* London, Longmans, Green & Co., 1938.

Thirsk, Joan, ed. *The Agrarian History of England and Wales,* IV, *1500-1640.* Cambridge, Cambridge University Press, 1967.

Thompson, A. Hamilton. *The English Clergy and Their Organization in the Later Middle Ages.* Oxford, Clarendon Press, 1947.

Thomson, John A. F. *The Later Lollards, 1414-1520.* London, Oxford University Press, 1965.

———· "Piety and Charity in Late Medieval London." *J.E.H.,* 16 (1965), 178-195.

Tjernagel, Neelak S. *Henry VIII and the Lutherans: A Study in Anglo-Lutheran Relations from 1521 to 1547.* St. Louis, Concordia Publishing House, 1965.

Trevor-Roper, Sir Hugh. "The General Crisis of the Seventeenth Century." In Trevor Aston, ed., *Crisis in Europe, 1560-1660,* 59-95. London, Routledge & Kegan Paul, 1965.

Tyler, Philip. "The Status of the Elizabethan Parochial Clergy." In G. J. Cuming, ed.,

Studies in Church History, IV, *The Province of York*, 76-97. Leiden, Brill, 1967.
Victoria County Histories.
Walker, John W. *Wakefield, Its History and People.* 2nd ed. 2 vols. Wakefield, West Yorkshire Printing Co., 1939.
Weever, John. *Ancient Funerall Monuments.* London, 1631.
Wenham, L. P. "The Chantries, Guilds, Obits, and Lights of Richmond, Yorkshire," *Y.A.J.*, 38 (1952-1955), 96-111, 185-214, 310-332.
Whitaker, Thomas Dunham. *The History and Antiquities of the Deanery of Craven.* 3rd ed. Leeds and London, 1878.
Wood-Legh, K. L. *Perpetual Chantries in Britain.* Cambridge, Cambridge University Press, 1965.
———· *Studies in the Church Life under Edward III.* Cambridge, Cambridge University Press, 1934.
Wordsworth, Christopher. "Marlborough Chantries and the Supply of Clergy in Olden Days." *W.A.N.H.M.*, 36 (1909-1910), 525-584.

Index

Harvard Historical Studies

84. *Marvin Arthur Breslow*. A Mirror of England: English Puritan Views of Foreign Nations, 1618-1640. 1970.

85. *Patrice L. R. Higonnet*. Pont-de-Montvert: Social Structure and Politics in a French Village, 1700-1914. 1971.

86. *Paul G. Halpern*. The Mediterranean Naval Situation, 1908-1914. 1971.

87. *Robert E. Ruigh*. The Parliament of 1624: Politics and Foreign Policy. 1971.

88. *Angeliki E. Laiou*. Constantinople and the Latins: The Foreign Policy of Andronicus, 1282-1328. 1972.

89. *Donald Nugent*. Ecumenism in the Age of the Reformation: The Colloquy of Poissy. 1974.

90. *Robert A. McCaughey*. Josiah Quincy, 1772-1864: The Last Federalist. 1974.

91. *Sherman Kent*. The Election of 1827 in France. 1975.

92. *A. N. Galpern*. The Religions of the People in Sixteenth-Century Champagne. 1976.

93. *Robert G. Keith*. Conquest and Agrarian Change: The Emergence of the Hacienda System on the Peruvian Coast. 1976.

94. *Keith Hitchins,* Orthodoxy and Nationality: Andreiu Şaguna and the Rumanians of Transylvania, 1846-1873. 1977.

95. *A. R. Disney*. Twilight of the Pepper Empire: Portuguese Trade in Southwest India in the Early Seventeenth Century. 1978.

96. *Gregory D. Phillips*. The Diehards: Aristocratic Society and Politics in Edwardian England. 1979.

97. *Alan Kreider*. English Chantries: The Road to Dissolution. 1979.